D1168470

WITHDRAWN

COMMERCE DES LUMIÈRES

COMMERCE DES LUMIÈRES
John Oswald and the British in Paris, 1790–1793

David V. Erdman

University of Missouri Press
Columbia, 1986

Library of Congress Cataloging-in-Publication Data
Erdman, David V.
Commerce des lumières.
Bibliography: p.
Includes index.
1. Oswald, John, d. 1793. 2. France—History—
Revolution, 1789–1799. 3. Revolutionists—France—
Biography. 4. Soldiers—Great Britain—Biography.
5. Journalists—Great Britain—Biography. I. Title.
DC146.078E73   1986   944.04'092'4   [B]   86–4306
ISBN 0-8262-0607-7

∞™ This paper meets the minimum requirements of
the American National Standard for Permanence of Paper
for Printed Library Materials, Z39.48, 1984.

To the Universal Patriots
of the
United Nations
of a
Surviving World

PREFACE

John Oswald of Edinburgh, poet, soldier, satiric and political journalist, author of *Constitution for the Universal Commonwealth*, active member of the Paris Jacobin Club, tactician and self-styled "Anglo-Jacobin," died in battle in the Vendee in September 1793 yet lived vividly in the memories of his contemporaries. He must have looked something like Napoleon Buonaparte—at least as represented in contemporary prints—for one of his Edinburgh and London associates in the 1780s leapt to the conclusion that the commanding genius who stepped onto the French revolutionary stage late in 1793 to become its military champion was none other than his old companion John Oswald, so accustomed to writing under pseudonyms that when he chose to take upon himself a "good part" in the action in France he coined the name "Buonaparte" to obscure his Grub-Street origins, while letting a rumor reach London that "Oswald" had died in battle.

The associate who made this mistake was William Thomson, himself a dealer in pseudonyms. By 1809 he had written a biography of Oswald as Buonaparte, but he put it aside when undeceived by the Corsican general Paoli. Several brief but substantial biographical notices of John Oswald did appear, however, during and after his lifetime, and a century later the French socialist historian and novelist André Lichtenberger assembled much of the reported information about this "curious person" who had been "drawn to Paris by an irresistible and disinterested enthusiasm for the French Revolution." He both promised himself "to devote a monograph of some detail to this singular mediator between the Jacobinism of Paris and that of England" and, not succeeding to his own satisfaction, wished that his essay would "lead some scholar to verify and fill out what his biographies and his works tell us of him."

If the present work properly fulfills Lichtenberger's wish for a more thorough study of John Oswald—who was indeed not Napoleon, not even *a* Napoleon but a dedicated kindler and observer of the fire in the minds of men and women living in Paris in the shadow of the fallen Bastille—it will be because of the many helping scholars and librarians who have participated in making it more thorough and more accurate than any lone scholar could have managed. My gratitude cannot be adequately expressed by a mere listing; yet to tell the kinds and specifics of all their assistance would require another book.

I must, however, single out Terry Harpold and Patrice Higonnet and Robert Maniquis, who searched Paris archives in successive years; Jack Lipkind and Janet Steins and Hélène Volat-Shapiro, of the SUNY, Stony Brook, Library, for much data-gathering; and Betty Rizzo, James Dybikowski, Ralph Anthony Manogue, and David Worrall, who kept on the alert for Oswaldiana with some marvelous results. Also I must thank, for acute and valuable criticism of various drafts of the manuscript, Don Bialostosky, Richard Elman, Kenneth R. Johnston, Charles Rosen, Bernard Semmel, and David Sheehan.

Others who searched, or read, or advised on particular problems include: Robert J. Barth; Alan Bell; Myra Berman; Martin Butlin; James K. Chandler; Jerome C. Christensen; William Leo Coakley; Michael Crump; Stuart Curran; Martha England; Tom Flanagan; Robert F. Gleckner; Douglas Grant; Draper Hill; Peter Houle; Bishop C. Hunt; M. J. Jubb; Gary Kate; Molly Lefebure; Marilan Lund; Thomas McFarland; Victoria Mitchell; Karen Mulhallen; Zygmunt Piotrowski; Burton Pollin; Phillip Pulsiano; Donald H. Reiman; Nicholas Roe; Sue Schopf; Nina Shapiro; Arthur Sherbo; Robert N. Smart; Stephen Spector; Madeleine Stern; Edward P. Thompson; Gerhard Vasco; Genevieve Vieth; Carl Woodring; Marilyn Zucker.

And, the most valuable helper of all, Virginia B. Erdman, who advised, read, criticized, at every stage of the work.

For illustrations in this volume, I am grateful for the assistance of the British Library (BL); the National Portrait Gallery, London; The New York Public Library (NYPL); The Frank Melville, Jr., Memorial Library, State University of New York at Stony Brook (SB); and the University of South Carolina Library (USC); and for the photographic help of Charles Webber of the Educational Communications Center of SUNY, Stony Brook.

The books from which pictures have been gathered, and the libraries permitting their use, are noted in the picture captions. (For full titles of books, see listing in the Bibliography.)

D. V. E.
Stony Brook, New York
July 1986

Contents

ILLUSTRATIONS

Commerce des lumières: a complex Enlightenment image, allowing a blend of meanings: the meeting of luminaries; exchanges of bright ideas, insight, wisdom; with a suggestion of aural—even mesmeric—contact.

1.
INTRODUCTION

Universal Patriotism and Freedom's Dawn

> The most unfailing herald, companion, and follower of the awakening of a great
> people to work a beneficial change in opinion or institution is poetry. At such periods
> there is an accumulation of the power of communicating and receiving intense and
> impassioned conceptions respecting man and nature.
> —Shelley, *A Defence of Poetry*

My subject is the involvement of British intellectuals in revolutionary thought
and action between the end of the American Revolution and the fourth year of
the French Revolution. John Oswald, briefly famous as a herald and warrior
and Pythagorean, then accidentally famous as a poet, was in fact an actively
involved and highly articulate British member of the Jacobin Club of Paris, and
to pursue his career is to move into the center of British-French revolutionary
organization at the blissful, if anxious, dawn of the era of militant democracy—
and English romantic poetry.

As a member of the British army in India, at the close of the American War,
and a commander in the volunteer army of the French Revolution until his
death in September 1793; as a friend of Tom Paine and Brissot, of Horne Tooke
and Danton; as a close watcher of political debates in the British Parliament
and the French Assembly or Convention, serving for some years as reporter for
the *London Gazetteer* and, for a few months, for the *Universal Patriot* (hoping
to cover debates on both sides of the Channel in 1790); as an analyst and com-
mentator on the interactions of adjacent and distant nations, of tyrants and
slaves—from Madras to Peru—and a "political herald" of future revolutions in
the unquiet years between the American and the French ones—John Oswald
has long deserved a full biography as well as a collection of his sharp-witted
and often intellectually powerful works.

In 1787 he was, properly but briefly, included among the *Five Hundred Celebrated Authors of Great Britain Now Living* (can anyone have been left out?).
In 1821 he was presented as one of the memorable *Scottish Poets*; ultimately he

I

was given space (but not an accurate account) in the *Dictionary of National Biography*. And in fact John Oswald was active and articulate and highly memorable, and since he kept close to the centers of thought and action in London and Paris just before and during the early years of the French Revolution, a thorough investigation of his military and intellectual career should considerably advance *our* comprehension of the ideas and efforts of British and French intellectuals during those exciting years of celebrative and combative Liberty, Equality, Fraternity—when the printing presses and the debating societies were abuzz with liberation, and the Channel was a two-way thoroughfare for "citizens of the world."

A full historical account of British participation in the Revolution has yet to be assembled, but the present undertaking should help prepare the way, its virtue being the focus and intimacy obtained from the effort to reconstruct the pattern and detail of an articulate revolutionary's life, whose sensational features were widely known but whose actual presence and personality were kept very private. When he was responsible for much of the thinking and some of the writing in the *Political Herald and Review*, a London monthly of 1785–1786, his Grub-Street manager William Thomson, whom he called "brain-sucker" in the jargon of the day, buried his contributions and collaborations by signing them "IGNOTUS" (the Unknown). Yet both his energy and his grasp of the military and political conflicts of nations and classes had so impressed Thomson that in the 1790s when a similar political and military genius arose in France, calling himself "Buonaparte," Thomson gradually became certain that, despite rumors of Oswald's death, this was only a new pseudonym for his familiar Ignotus. Not until 1809, by which time Thomson had written a biography of Oswald as "Napoleon," was a witness from Corsica able to convince him that Buonaparte was truly not his fellow Scot.[1]

We have long known a good deal about some of the participants in cross-Channel Enlightenment. Brissot, in the 1780s, had the idea, at least, of a conference center in London to project change in Paris. Wordsworth went to France two or three times in the first years of the Revolution and wrote of his personal involvement in making love and revolution—but disguised the love story in cryptic analogy ("Vaudracour and Julia") and so overlaid his account of involvement in "philosophic war" with the value judgments of a later decade as to prevent *The Prelude* from affording accurate recovery of his youthful deeds and intentions.

John Goldworth Alger's five books and articles of a century later (see Bibliography, section G) are invaluable collections of names and bits of action and comment garnered from "English Eyewitnesses of the French Revolution" or *Farewell Letters of Victims of the Guillotine* (to cite two of them). Alger and several other historians have told us a good deal about serious as well as casual

---

1. "But they both loved Ossian!" was his final protest.

visitors to France, including some of the British citizens who gathered in Paris as a "British Club" of sympathizers, some of whom were dedicated revolutionaries. The advantage, however, of our investigating the entire career of a British military intellectual (odd-sounding term, but precise) who was often in the center of significant activity in London and Paris during the critical years, and who wrote and published from the center of the action, is not merely the advantage of narrative continuity (not always complete) but also of immediacy. Reading the Oswaldian analyses of the interactions of nations in "The Present Times" or investigating his French comrades' verbal and organizational efforts to knit the processes of history into universal harmony, we become familiar with the intentions and views of those among the British visitors in France who were more than idle watchers or passing tourists—or were attempting to become more.

Accumulating the records and evidence of the career of John Oswald may seem, of course, to raise more questions than it resolves, not only about his own deeds and ideas but also about those of his associates—friends or foes. Oswald was actually very well known in his post-Ignotus years, however. When his pamphlets were published, reviewers often wrote more about his life than about his writing, the most sensational biographical oddity being his combining a military career with a Pythagorean diet. The first biographical essay of some length (in 1821) and the next (in 1859) dealt with him primarily as a poet; yet Oswald himself was well aware that poetry was *not* his forte: his grimmest chores in Grub-Street he defined as having to write odes (instead of editorials). Not until 1897 did the extensive essay by André Lichtenberger appear, fitting him into the early history of socialism as a precursor to Babeuf.

My initial investigation of Oswald's career was inspired by an interest in Wordsworth's obscure account in *The Prelude* of his "Residence in France" in 1791–1792. Finding in an index to the proceedings of the Jacobin Club of Paris the name "Oswald," which Wordsworth had used for a sympathetic character in *The Excursion* (in about 1806)—a leader of military volunteers who was, like the real Oswald, opposed to the shooting of animals—and later for an unsympathetic revolutionary in *The Borderers* (though not used there, we now know, until 1841), I have in pursuing the career of the Jacobin Oswald discovered a great deal, if not about Wordsworth, about the thinking and the contemplated actions of the British who were in Paris out of sympathy and curiosity during those years: thus also, indirectly, about Wordsworth.

I find that when, in late 1792, a number of well-known and unknown British men and women met in White's Hotel in Paris to celebrate the successes of the French army and the National Assembly, and defined themselves as a "British Club," John Oswald was one of the main organizers of that meeting and secretary of the continuing, less public but actively revolutionary, organization. Its activities, indeed, were kept so secret that even the surface evidence has been ignored by most historians: that their aims were, not only to encourage and assist the French people against their own and invading tyrants, but also to enlist the French people and government in assisting British revolutionaries in Dublin and London.

Moreover Oswald, we learn by digging beneath faulty traditional accounts of the Jacobin Club, was active not only in traveling back and forth between London and Paris but also in efforts to keep the Jacobin Club from overlooking its international revolutionary responsibilities—active as author and publisher and collaborating editor, serving in the latter capacity as one of the magic "Fourteen" (*le Quatorze*) who had saved and were dedicated to sustaining the vision and goals of the Revolution, as "Friends of Truth" (and despisers of propaganda).

My argument, then, is that a faithful biography of John Oswald ought to improve our comprehension of the spirit of democratic revolution that was alive in London and Paris after the American Revolution—and should open doors, left ajar by Oswald, into the times of bliss and terror which blended intellectual war and "philosophic war" in projects that required or assumed such liberating invasions as King William's in 1688, which had led to the Glorious Revolution that the British felt they had kept constitutionally alive for the whole century—and were ready to share or enlarge in new times of burgeoning freedom.

Oswald's political pamphlets are also important contributions to the history of ideas, though by a freak of misprision it was his poetry that first drew the attention of nineteenth-century biographers, as we shall see. The poems offer an occasional biographical clue but are of little literary interest. As one biographical essayist remarked in 1848, "happily for mankind, one may be a friend of progress without also being a great poet."

His prose, especially his constitutional pamphlets, did have a moment of glory, being recommended in 1792 to Edmund Burke along with the works of Paine, Siéyès, Barlow, and Mirabeau, as both more profound and more popular (or relevant?) than the pamphlets of Milton, Harrington, and Sidney. Today it is the vitality of Oswald's writings, their combination of vigor and wit-crossed idiosyncracy, that can give both interest and significance to an endeavor such as the present one. When Burke did take the advice, he found Oswald's definition of the sovereignty of the people and his advocacy of freedom from "the yoke of property" most alarming, and when war between France and Britain had been declared, Burke in Parliament singled out John Oswald as the central source in Paris of the spreading contagion of democracy. (Whereupon another Scot almost lost to history, the Black Watch colonel Norman Macleod, with whom Oswald had fought a duel in 1781 and formed a lasting friendship, rose to his feet to protest Burke's exclusion "of people from government.")

Pursuing Oswald, and his friends, I encounter the mysterious arbitrariness of narrative history. If only Thomas Carlyle had come upon this information we should have had an Irish-Scottish confrontation in the House of Commons.

And why have no scholars of Burke—of whom there are many—publicly alluded to Oswald or his ideas?

And where was William Wordsworth on the day of that debate? We know he was in London, having just written his pamphlet defending the execution of Louis and expressing his outrage at counterrevolutionary war. He might easily have wandered into the visitors' gallery at Westminster—or entered in fascination to hear the politicians debating whether there was real "sedition" in London—Sheridan ridiculing the idea; Burke and the Lord Mayor and others citing the report of sans-culotte daggers in Britain with alarm. But I cannot have him there without entering the realm of fiction—and quite spoiling the finesse of the present undertaking, which requires constant sensitivity to the difference between fact and conjecture.

What John Oswald was doing and saying in Paris in these first weeks of open war I do know, though the writers of histories do not. A speech he delivered at the Jacobin Club on 4 February was so well appreciated by the revolutionaries that it was voted to be sent to a printer—and never got back into the archives. Did Wordsworth's reputedly extensive collection of pamphlets include this *Discours d'Oswald*, Anglo-Franc? Alas, the collection was scattered before anyone made an inventory. But a printed copy of the *Discours* survives in that Wordsworthian enclave, the Cornell University Library. We shall come to its revelation of what conspiracies were afoot during Wordsworth's days in Paris—all in due course.

John Oswald: Enigmatic Portrayals

In the "Advertisement" (preface) of his vegetarian pamphlet *The Cry of Nature* (London: J. Johnson, 1791), John Oswald revealed some of the complexity of his impatient, defiant, benevolent personality:

> Fatigued with answering the enquiries, and replying to the objections of his friends, with respect to the singularity of his mode of life, the Author of this performance conceived that he might consult his ease by making, once for all, a public apology for his opinions. Those who despise the weakness of his arguments will nevertheless learn to admit the innocence of his tenets, and suffer him to pursue, without molestation, a system of life that is more the result of sentiment than of reason, in a man who imagines that the human race were not made to live scientifically, but according to nature.[2]

William Wordsworth, in the preface of his psychological/political drama *The Borderers* (1795–1797, published 1842), wrote of the villain of the piece,

2. See Figure 1 for the full title of *The Cry of Nature*; the frontispiece is unsigned but clearly by James Gillray (I am assured by Martin Butlin and Draper Hill). It is inscribed at the top: "Pub. June 22ᵈ 1791 by J. Johnson Sᵗ Pauls Church Yard."

Fig. 1. Frontispiece by James
Gillray (unsigned) of Oswald's
The Cry of Nature, 1791. (BL)

whom in final draft he named "Oswald": "He has rebelled against the world &
the laws of the world & he regards them as tyrannical masters; convinced that
he is right in some of his conclusions, he nourishes a contempt for mankind the
more dangerous because he has been led to it by reflection" (*B*, 439).

Neither of these descriptions, the confessional self-portrayal by Oswald himself, nor Wordsworth's definition of the revolutionary brigand in his play, can
be quite trusted as accurate character analysis. Many people, retrospectively,
regarded Oswald as a bloody villain; Wordsworth's comment may reflect hearsay, not personal acquaintance, and even the Oswaldian details of his fictive
revolutionary's career may derive from hearsay only, since "everybody" had
heard sensational tales of the military vegetarian.

It is of course of interest to discover the currency of gossip which Wordsworth when in Blois or Paris *may* have heard "about this English protégé of Brissot, in whose circles he [Wordsworth] *may* have moved."[3] (Where Wordsworth may have been or what he may have heard remains conjectural.) But as the details accumulate and authentic information even imperfectly separates out from legend, I find the historical John Oswald crying out to be recognized in his own right.

For other witnesses, let me begin with the nearest thing we have to a direct camera shot of Oswald (undeveloped, however, for about nine years), a recollection by Henry Redhead Yorke, Esq., a man who had often argued with him in Paris in 1792–1793 in the British Club, who revisited a decade later the scenes of that revolutionary time, and who published in London in 1804 (having recanted some time ago) two volumes of his *Letters from France in 1802*:

> I remember the last interview I had in the garden [of the Palais-Royal] with the mad Colonel Oswald, who had written several insane publications in behalf of what he called his fellow creatures, the brutes; also "A Review of the British Constitution," &c. I have, in my possession, a little pamphlet, which he circulated under the title of "The Government of the People," in which he asserts, that a representation of the people is as great a despotism as absolute monarchy. He insists that the voice of the people cannot be represented; and by way of illustration he roundly asserts, "that as a man cannot p--- by proxy, neither can he *think* by proxy."[4] On the full conviction of this principle, he proposes to new model the governments of all nations of the world; men and women are to assemble in an open plain, and there make, or repeal their own laws.[5] I have often endeavoured to persuade him, that his plan was not sufficiently extensive, as he had excluded from this grand assembly of the animated world the most populous portion of his fellow-creatures, namely, cats, dogs, horses, chickens, &c.
>
> Oswald was originally a captain of a Highland regiment in the British service, and had travelled by land from India, during which he lived a considerable time with some Brahmins, who turned his head. From that period he never tasted flesh meat, from what he called a principle of humanity. He did not, however, enter into the whole theology of the Brahmins, for he was a professed atheist and denied the Metempsychosis; but he believed in the immortality of the body, and drank plentifully of wine. From what has been said above, it is of no consequence what his opinions were, but such a man living in a fermented capital was capable of doing much mischief. (160–63)

3. Pollin, "Names in *The Borderers*," 34. On Wordsworth's Oswald, see Erdman, "Citizen Stanhope and the French Revolution."

4. Oswald's *The Government of the People* was published in English and French, some time during "The First Year of the French Republic" that began in September 1792—and perhaps not long before Burke quoted it in Parliament in March 1793.

5. In scorning Oswald's rejection of representative government in favor of participatory democracy, Yorke seems to have forgotten that in some respects that was what the "sovereignty of the People" implied. His contempt for Oswald's earthy language amounts to an accusation that he was a sans-culotte—with perhaps a shiver at Oswald's Priapism. For excerpts from Oswald's *The Government of the People*, see our final chapter.

We may observe that Yorke in 1802, like Wordsworth writing *The Prelude* in the same era, employs a narrator's voice that distances the author from his youthful self of 1792.[6] To his retrospective satisfaction, Yorke has dismissed Oswald's opinions by burying the revolutionary democracy under absurdities of atheism and vegetarianism. As Yorke continues, he manages to place Oswald on one side and the rest of mankind, including narrator and reader (and the *Dictionary of National Biography*, which would inherit Yorke's views), on the other. That is, we are to agree that Yorke was shocked at the time, not merely in retrospect; perhaps even Danton may have been shocked, though he would have agreed on the pragmatics:

> He [Oswald] dined on his roots one day at a party of some members of the Convention, at which I was present, and in the course of the conversation, very coolly proposed, as the most effectual method of averting civil war, to put to death every suspected man in France. I was shocked at such a sentiment coming from the mouth of an Englishman; but Oswald had been for some time the commandant of the pikemen of Paris, and in this capacity had forgotten his national character. The expression was not suffered to pass unnoticed; and from the famous Thomas Paine he received a short but cutting reprimand; "Oswald," said he, "you have lived so long without tasting flesh, that you now have a most voracious appetite for blood."[7]
>
> In consequence of a strong and successful opposition which I had made against some proposals respecting Ireland, that Oswald had offered to the government, I met him by his own appointment, in the garden of the Palais Royal [probably in February or March 1793, as we shall see]. As soon as he perceived me approaching towards him, he darted forwards, and drawing his sword, exclaimed, "You are unfit to live in a civilized society." Having uttered these words, he returned his sword into the scabbard, and turning from me, disappeared in a moment. We never saw each other more. His regiment [departing from Paris, 26 March] was ordered to La Vendée, where, while bravely leading on his men at the battle of Pont-de-Cé, he was killed [14 September, at Thouars] by a cannon ball, and at the same instant, a discharge of grape shot laid both his sons, who served as drummers in the corps of which he was colonel, breathless on their father's corpse.[8]

6. Wordsworth, however, subtly minimizes the distance, still celebrating his youthful enthusiasm. Yorke's very name was changed between his 1792 existence as an English republican in Paris and his observer status during the Peace of Amiens, when he revisited his haunts of a decade earlier.

7. Yorke himself, nevertheless, safe at home in Derby by July 1793, had been undaunted by the prospect of "necessary" bloodshed. At the approach of the fourth anniversary of Bastille Day, he sent a pamphlet letter to Ridgway addressed to John Frost, who would be celebrating his "First Year of Imprisonment in Newgate" on 14 July: *These Are the Times to Try Men's Souls: A Letter to John Frost, A Prisoner in Newgate*. In it his idea of cheering a fellow member of the British Club is to assure him that no one will think a revolution that brings happiness "is dearly earned, altho' a whole generation perish in the contest." Whether Frost is to receive the happiness of freedom or perish in jail is not made clear. Yorke responded to his own imprisonment in 1795 for two years in Dorchester gaol with less revolutionary panache: "In the event Yorke married the governor's daughter, and turned his political coat inside out" (Brown, *The French Revolution in English History*, 146; see also 65, 104; also Alger, *Paris*, 360).

8. At the end of his tale of Oswald, Yorke remarks: "The history of one maniac brings to my recollection a curious rencontre . . . with another . . . I mean *Anacharsis Cloots*, who called him-

His wives (for he had two) still reside in Paris. They were extremely handsome, and he had brought his domestic economy to such a perfect state of discipline, that they lived together in the greatest friendship and harmony. A singular fact! which has, I believe, no parallel in the history of the fair sex.

Redhead Yorke may well have captured the style of the man, and the exclamation about the two wives, perhaps emphasizing the extremes of mad Brahminism, need not imply Yorke's lying. The "still reside in Paris" implies that he was assured of their existence during his visit of 1802 and that it could be verified. On the other hand we cannot trust his report, inevitably based on hearsay, of Oswald's dying with his two sons, à la Laocoön. It is true (according to the register of his battalion, the First Battalion of Pikemen [Piquiers]), that he was killed after a day of fierce fighting at or near the bridge of boats called Ponts-de-Cé, on the river Loire.[9] And it is true that two sons were in his battalion. But the register shows that they survived, as we shall see in Chapter 9.

A witness closer by nine years than Yorke, and much closer in sympathy, is Captain Sampson Perry, whose "Anecdote of Lieutenant Colonel John Oswald, who commanded a Regiment in the French Service" was published while London Jacobinism was still alive, in Perry's weekly *Argus or General Observer* for 26 December 1795:

> Mr John Oswald is well known as a man of letters; he has written two or three small tracts which shew him to have possessed an enlarged understanding, and his conversation evinced a depth of reasoning not often met with. The science of politics most engaged his attention of late years, especially since he had become an assistant in the conducting of a newspaper. He took the house of commons debates for the Gazetteer a few years ago, and spent much of his leisure time in discussing political questions at the public societies, where he has been heard with great attention. He treated the abuses of government with so much freedom, that it was impossible he could live in England, except in a prison.[10]
>
> After the breaking out of the revolution in France, he went over to that country, and formed a strong intimacy with many of the first characters there, with CAMILLE DESMOULINS and DANTON in particular, and was not unfrequently at the levees of ROLAND. As he had served in the India wars, and was a perfect *tactician*, he was soon

---

self the *Orator of the Human Race.*" Cloots has survived in history, partly because of his droll name, partly his grandstanding; and we remember Byron's idea about Don Juan that he would make his hero "finish as Anacharsis Cloots in the French Revolution." Robespierre sent him to the guillotine in March 1794—and might have done the same for Oswald if he had lived so long.

9. A rapid march by Wordsworth's friend Michel Beaupuy saved the boats a month later, 18–19 October.

10. Here Perry spoke from experience, having been jailed in July 1791 for seditious or libelous publication, he wasn't sure which. In the autumn of 1792 he had fled to Paris; staying there into the period of Thermidor, he had been jailed as an enemy alien. Returning to London in 1795, he had been jailed once more. (See Werkmeister, *Daily Press*, 363–76, for the complicated story of Perry's prosecutions and persecution for radical utterance in 1791–1792.) Oswald seems to have moved back and forth between London and Paris during the early years of the Revolution. He escaped jail by dying before the years of repression.

offered a batallion, which at first carried pikes, not fusees. He writ a treatise on the exercise to be performed with the first of these weapons, and laid down some new evolutions, which were highly esteemed by the French general officers, as they saved time in the movements, and occupied less space in the performance. As he was an English subject, it was not thought proper to send him to the frontiers after the war broke out with this country. The regiment addressed the convention to allow them to change their pikes for firelocks, and march against the rebels in the Vendee. The request was complied with, and colonel Oswald, with his corps, filed through the convention with a knapsack on his back, the same as a private soldier.[11]

We know from the battalion records that Oswald's battalion (not regiment) left Paris on Wednesday, 26 March 1793, armed with guns, not pikes. With Perry's help we can recapture something of the news behind the meager statement in that day's *Moniteur* that "The battalion barracked in Paris in the rue de Babylone march against the insurgents, obtain permission to file before the Assembly, and swear allegiance to liberty and equality."[12] To resume Perry's account:

> This conformance to the principle of equality by the commander of a regiment, who was besides an accomplished scholar, produced an uncommon sensation, and excited a burst of acclamation in the members of that senate. He was exceedingly admired for the plainness of his dress and manners, and above all for the simplicity of his life. He had eaten no meat for the last twelve years, and scarce ever drank more than half a dozen glasses of wine. About five weeks[13] after his march from Paris, his battalion went into action in the plain of Saumur, on the day when the bloody battle terminated in the loss of twelve thousand men of both armies, whose bodies infected the whole country, for there was no time allowed on either side to bury the dead. Colonel Oswald, and two hundred and ten of his battalion fell in that action, as well as two of his sons, who were drummers in the same regiment of which he was colonel. An account [not located] was given to the convention of the gallant and exemplary conduct and courage of this officer, even when the name of an Englishman was in no repute in Paris. He left an infant son and daughter,[14] whom, it is to be expected, the nation will take care of, as the father had not a shilling to leave behind him; and indeed, though he had been before, and was now a soldier, he was the meekest man living, and had not resolution to keep a sixpence in his pocket if a distressed object presented itself to his view.

I find no record of the surviving infants, nor of the two wives whose harmonious economy must have included them. As for the heaps of slain, they seem to belong to earlier or later battles. In the battalion history we find only Oswald and three others slain on 14 September. And General Rossignol's report of that

---

11. Close readers of Wordsworth's drama will recall that in it a soldier's knapsack ("scrip," line 1642) is a fateful stage property.

12. *Moniteur* 15 (1793): 796. See details in Chapter 10 below.

13. Months, actually; a slip in Perry's text, or memory.

14. No record has been found in the archives.

date, read to the Assembly on the 16th and printed in the next day's *Moniteur*, gives only six slain, naming some of them but not Oswald. The battalion history does say, however, that the fighting on the 13th at Ponts-de-Cé (20 miles from Thouars) was fierce, Parisian commander Bourgeois having hurled back a formidable assault on the 12th. And we read that on the 19th "the debris of the levée en masse" (conscripts hurriedly brought into the regiment unready for battle), "horribly beaten in the battle for Pont-Barre," took refuge at Ponts-de-Cé. This gets us closer to Perry's account. The neatness of Yorke's cannonball for the father and grapeshot for his two boys sounds quite unreal for the fighting described in various reports. Of the particular battle or skirmish in question no firsthand reports survive; the erroneous legend about the two drummerboys exposes all published reports as gossip-based. But most *reports* of battles seem to be of that sort; only writers of history, or of novels, manage to shape them by selection and conflation into coherent stories.

2.
FROM SCOTLAND TO THE MALABAR COAST

John's Coffeehouse, Edinburgh

Thomson's biography of Oswald as Napoleon might have given us a full account of his childhood and prerevolutionary years. Very little can be constructed from the brief biographical sketches that survive, though the anonymous account in *Lives of the Scottish Poets* (1821) draws upon "a gentleman who knew Oswald well" and is sometimes circumstantial.[1] All accounts agree that he was born in Edinburgh, where "either his father or mother" kept John's Coffeehouse, "well known of old as a place for public business" (*Lives*, 173). We can imagine the precocious boy listening at the edge of talk about the war with France, then with the American colonies; about the mental "Scottish border." Anderson's *Scottish Nation* has it that his father was a goldsmith; all agree that the son was brought up in that trade; one adds that he also worked as a veterinarian.[2]

An account in the *European Magazine*[3] for March 1790, which seems to represent what Oswald was willing to tell inquirers when he was "about 30 years of age," describes his father as a "man of great learning and extreme modesty . . . who imagined that all his misfortunes had proceeded from his devotion to the Muses" and hence "endeavoured as much as possible to discourage in his son the same *unhappy passion*, as he termed it, for the Belles Lettres. The opposition of his father, however, only tended to stimulate the youth in the career of learning." John learned Latin in a few months, by "intense application . . . without a master"; then Greek; and then "in the course of his peregrinations," his voyage to India and the return journey, "made himself familiar with

---

1. *Lives*, vol. 1, part 2. The title page gives "The Society of Ancient Scots" as author. The catalogue of the University of St. Andrews Library gives the publisher as Joseph Clinton Robertson but has no author indicator. (Information supplied by Robert N. Smart, Keeper of the Muniments.)

2. William Anderson, *The Scottish Nation* (1863), 3:268–69.

3. A monthly begun by James Perry in January 1782. Thomson, Oswald's biographer, was a contributor.

the Arabic language, together with the French, Italian, Spanish, and Portuguese dialects."[4]

An Edinburgh goldsmith might have been burdened with a zeal for literature that interfered with his business; or the learned father may not have been in business at all, leaving that to the mother—though his name may have been given to the coffeehouse (if it *was* John). His son John was obviously the sort who would have responded with keen interest to the stir of talk, pamphlets, and even lecture series that filled Edinburgh intellectual conversation with ideas circulated by Adam Smith and his close associates, including Thomas Reid, leader of the "common sense" school of philosophy—Oswald in his writings uses that term in Reid's sense—and James Oswald, author of *Common Sense in Religion*, who organized lectures in Edinburgh and whose name would have attracted John's attention, whether or not they were relatives.

If born in 1760, he would have been out of his jewelry apprenticeship in 1774, but he "followed that occupation for some years" (*Lives*), probably with increasing interest in the discussions of public business in the family coffeehouse. His first recorded act of a public nature was to join the British army, in 1776 or 1777. The summary of this matter in the *European Magazine* proves to be accurate; it probably represents Oswald's way of putting things in 1790; but it leaves out a good deal: "He was late a Lieutenant in the 42nd regiment of foot, and served in the last war under Colonels Humberstone and McLeod in the East Indies. In the year 1783 he left India, and returned by land to England."

The "last war" began as the war with the American colonies, but by the time Oswald joined the 42nd Regiment—the Second Battalion, organized in late 1779—the enemy included France, Spain, and Holland, vulnerable in far-flung posts and colonies. (The East Indies meant India and its neighbors.) And by the time his battalion was ready to sail from Britain in early 1781, threats to British supremacy in India implied the need of the East India Company for royal army support.

During the Seven Years' War (1756–1763) the French and British had fought on three continents for colonial control and Britain had regained supremacy in India, the French being allowed to have trading posts but not to maintain troops or build forts. By the end of the American War, the Treaties of Paris and Versailles (early 1783) would give France control of Tobago in the West Indies and of Bengal in India. By the time the 42nd Regiment actually reached India, in March 1782, the Company's forces were under great pressure from the French—at sea and in Bengal—and the troops of Hyder Ali and his son Tippo in the Carnatic, though the Company held Madras. Company headquarters at Bombay had to be the first port of call, but marching orders had to be revised as

4. Graham, *Scottish Men of Letters*, 253. Reading in the fo'c's'le and talk with mates and crew in ports of call doubtless preceded the acquisition of Arabic, which must have begun during those idle months in the Island of Joanna. (See below, pp. 21ff.)

the months went by and the troops and their officers improvised plans in response to surprise and rumor—and expected or unexpected opportunities for "prizes" (plunder). The situation during Oswald's surprise visit to Bombay and Madras and the Maharrata Confederacy was to be characterized succinctly in a resolution in the House of Commons in 1784:

> The result of the Parliamentary inquiries has been that the East India Company was found totally corrupted and totally perverted from the purposes of its institution, whether political or commercial; that the powers of war and peace given by the Charter had been abused by kindling hostilities in every quarter for the purposes of rapine; that almost all the treaties of peace they have made have only given cause to so many breaches of public faith; that countries once the most flourishing are reduced to a state of impotence, decay and depopulation.[5]

How well prepared for sailing to support the defense of the Company was the proud regiment Oswald had joined as a young lieutenant? The 42nd or Royal Highland Regiment was already famous as the Black Watch—so named from the darkness of the tartans of the various clans that first joined: the soldiers of other regiments were "red coats," who wore clothing uniformly colored. The 42nd was also permitted to wear sporrans (purses) of opposum rather than badger. Organized originally in 1725 as a force of Highland police to prevent cattle stealing, it had become a regiment of the line in 1739; what was now to be called the First Battalion was fighting under General Howe in America. Expansion of the war had produced what army historian John Fortescue calls "feverish activity in raising levies for defence," including legislation enabling individuals to raise "loyal corps" of volunteers.[6]

In the summer of 1779 Lord John Murray added a second battalion to the 42nd Highlanders. It was authorized on 30 July and was embodied at Perth on 21 March 1780, of the "very best materials for forming good soldiers" over a thousand strong: one lieutenant-colonel (Norman Macleod of Macleod) (and captain), one major (and captain), eight captains, twelve lieutenants (including John Oswald), eight ensigns, a chaplain (John Stewart, who died on 24 October 1781, on the voyage to Bombay), an adjutant (a post given to Oswald for a while, in India), a quarter-master, a surgeon (Thomas Farquharson, who lost his left hand at the battle of Paniane), one mate, thirty sergeants, forty corporals,

---

5. R. Palme Dutt, *The Problem of India* (1943), 48–49, quotes in explanation a letter of 1765 from Robert Clive, main founder of British rule in India, calculating for the directors the purposes and rewards of empire, and makes this comment and paraphrase: "Of the total revenue extracted from the population one-quarter is considered sufficient for the purposes of government; one-quarter is still needed to square the claims of the local potentates (Nabob and Mogul); the remainder, or half the revenue, estimated at £1 1/2 million is 'clear gain.' Bottomley's old dream of the 'Business Man's Government' is here realized with a completeness never equalled before or since. Enormous fortunes were made by individual officers of the Company . . . ten times as much was taken out of the country as was sent into it under the ruling care of this new type of merchant company governing a country."

6. *History of the British Army*, 4:290.

twenty drummers, two pipers, and seven hundred private men. The battalion was quartered in Fort George and Dundee, then was removed to Queens-ferry, whence, in December 1780, it embarked for Chatham, thence to Portsmouth to form part of an expedition of three regiments under Major-General William Meadows, to attack the French at the Cape of Good Hope.

But we are not ready to embark with Oswald until we try to find out how he got into the Black Watch, and whether he was immediately a lieutenant. John Stewart's regimental history lists him as "originally a private in the 18th Foot; son of an Edinburgh merchant."[7] David Stewart (who knew of William Thomson's biography and seems to have drawn upon it) is more helpful here:

> The history of this officer is rather singular. He was the son of a goldsmith in Edinburgh, and had received a good education [n.b.], but from some frolic, enlisted with a recruiting party of the 18th, or Royal Irish, in which regiment he was appointed sergeant, and when quartered at Deal, married a young woman possessed of some money. Soon afterwards, he obtained his discharge from the Royal Irish, and purchased an ensigncy in the 1st battalion of the Royal Highlanders, from which he was immediately promoted to a lieutenancy in the 2d battalion in 1780.[8]

The rapid promotions are easy to account for. A new recruit enlisting as a private would receive a bounty of five or six guineas (Coleridge in 1793 would be tempted by 6½ guineas to enlist in the royal dragoons). Oswald must always have had a lively approach that made him "highly esteemed" by general officers, as Sampson Perry observed. A sergeant is only a glorified private, but purchasing a commission required a vacancy—and money. Oswald apparently purchased his ensigncy from someone in the old Black Watch battalion (an ensign, technically flag-bearer, was the lowest commissioned rank) and was at once upgraded to lieutenant in the new (2nd) battalion. The anonymous author of the Oswald chapter in the 1821 *Lives of the Scottish Poets*, also apparently informed by an acquaintance, tells a different story, however; that Oswald worked at jewelry "till, by the death of a relation, he succeeded to a considerable legacy, which he employed in purchasing a commission in a Highland regiment."[9] If both accounts are right and he received both an inheritance and a dowry, neither need have been very large.

Although we find no mention of the wife at Deal, the future drummer boys must have been born there, conceived between the summer of 1776 and the autumn of 1779, making them between 14 and 17 years of age when they marched to the Vendee with their father in 1793.[10] Their mother may have died while Oswald was in India, perhaps earlier. In his "Louisa: A Funereal

---

7. *Chronicle of the Royal Highland Regiment*, 50.
8. *Sketches*, 2:215.
9. *Lives*, 173.
10. There was no strict rule about the age of drummers in the volunteers, however; I find *tambours* who had enlisted at ten and at twelve.

Wreathe," a group of four elegiac "Sonnets" dated 1787 but describing a loss not recent, he laments that the grave has taken "my Consort"—more intimately called "Louise" in an earlier version.[11]

When he returned from India, he settled in the Deal-Dover neighborhood, using "Ramsgate" as his address in letters to the printer of the *London Chronicle*, and according to the parish register of Folkestone (close to Dover) he there married Bathsheba Fagge Owen, a widow, on 1 June 1784. Their daughter Jane was born within the year and baptized at Folkestone on 1 June 1785.[12] Perhaps Louise had died early, or perhaps Oswald's poem "The Dawn" (dated 1779) records an extramarital passion for "Phoebe" (Bathsheba?), who is urged to quit the "frigid couch" of her aged and "languid" spouse in order to "crown with bliss a lover swain" who describes himself as a "bold Mars" for her Venus (*Poems*, 33–35). Even, possibly, the two sons were *her* dowry.

Life among the Bloodybacks

When Oswald joined the Royal Irish Regiment stationed in Deal (and Dover, nine miles away) he was joining the exhausted survivors of three companies that had been sent to America in 1767 and dispersed on the Ohio and in Philadelphia, New York, and Boston. They had marched in April 1775 from Boston via Lexington to Concord, getting involved in the initial shooting that precipitated the American Revolution. Reduced by desertion and illness, they had been sent home by royal order and reassembled. Sent at first to Nova Scotia, the remains of the Royal Irish had been sent on to Dover Castle in July 1776, where they rested for a year and a half. By 1778 the regiment, strengthened by recruitment, was included in a large encampment in Coxheath and moved to a slightly smaller one in the summer of 1779 at Warley in Essex, at which time Oswald must have departed for Scotland and the Black Watch.[13]

Presumably he left his sons in good hands—whether of Louise or Bathsheba the poems do not disclose; nor can we deduce whether he was fleeing from a painful domestic situation or responding sympathetically to the rhetoric and alluring bravado of an advertisement such as this in the *Scots Magazine* of August 1779:

11. See the "Preface" and note the general autobiographical theme of the *Poems* of 1789.
12. We shall return to the "Ramsgate" letters. Discovery of the marriage and birth entries in the Folkestone Paris Register was the work of Prof. Betty Rizzo and the archivist, A. M. Oakley. Bathsheba, daughter of Thomas and Jane Fagge, had been baptized at Folkestone on 23 March 1759. (According to the computerized record, Jane was baptized on 18 October 1785; perhaps 1 June was the day of her birth.)
13. Davies, *Documents of the American Revolution*, 2:63; also Cannon, *Historical Record of the Royal Irish*, 49–50. Oswald never served "in America" (as the *DNB* has it) nor was he ever "quartered in Dublin" (as Anderson deduced). These were plausible guesses: part of the Black Watch did serve in America—the First, not the Second, Battalion—and the Royal Irish had served in Ireland, but not in Oswald's day.

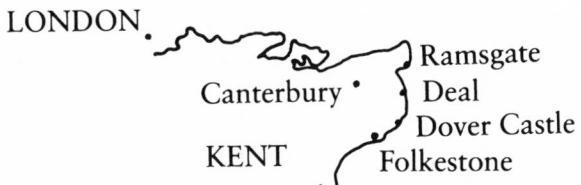

Fig. 2. Oswald's neighborhood
1776–1779, 1784+.

Forty-Second or Royal Highland Regiment,—
To all North Britons in general, but chiefly to you, O ye Highlanders! is this advertisement addressed. You who, uncorrupted by the universal depravity of your southern countrymen, have withstood, immoveable as a rock, all assaults of surrounding luxury and dissipation; you who, while others, effeminated by voluptuous refinements and irrevocably lost to honour, lolling in the arms of Pleasure, can see the danger of their country with criminal indifference; or, slaves of a traitorous and rebellious faction can behold Britannia insulted by her inveterate foes, the French and Spaniards, and yet dare even to dispute whether she ought to be assisted! You, O ye hardy race! Ye Highlanders! who have yet arms unenervated by luxury capable to defend your King and Country! to you Britannia addresses herself! She invokes your aid! She calls upon you to exert that well-known military ardour which has long distinguished you from all the nations of the earth, and has rendered you the admiration and terror of your enemies! She points to the field of Honour!... And though she scorns to allure the brave by any other motives than the love of glory and their country, every gentleman-volunteer who is willing and able to serve His Majesty in this honourable and uncontaminated corps shall receive five guineas reward and one guinea extraordinary if he enlists before the 24th September, by repairing to the drum head, or applying, etc.
    N.B.—The officer will not part with a good recruit, notwithstanding the terms offered, for the difference of a few guineas, as it is only young fellows of spirit he wishes to enlist.[14]

If Oswald was about thirty in 1790, he would have been about nineteen in 1779: a fellow of spirit he certainly was. His knowledge of war and his political education, begun by his classical reading, must have been kept up by newspaper accounts of the war in America, read in the coffeehouse, to be rapidly and richly increased when he entered the barracks of the survivors of the 18th Regiment, the "bloodybacks" who had trudged in 1775 from Boston to Lexington and Concord and back "for a few trifling stores" and whose conversation over several months would proceed in a context of drunken orgies, anxious expectation of being sent to America—and then a long wait after assignment to "the Indies."[15]

14. Quoted in the *Chronicle of the Black Watch*, 47–48.
15. Barker, *The British in Boston*, 37–40. Foot soldiers used the term *bloodybacks* as a self-definition that kept them sane. See Hargreaves, *The Bloodybacks*.

A rare document of the foot soldier's view of the American War exists in a sarcastic journal kept by one John Barker of "the King's Own Regiment," which shared the adventures of the 18th in America. Such conversations as echo in Barker's notes of his Bunker Hill experience must have been Oswald's daily texts since his recruitment. Here are samples:

> 19th April [1775] . . . [Only] Officers knew what expedition we were going upon. After getting over the Marsh where we were wet up to the knees, we were halted in a dirty road and stood there till two oclock in the morning waiting for provisions to be brought from the boats and to be divided, and which most of the Men threw away, having carried some with 'em. . . . about 5 miles on this side of a Town called Lexington which lay in our road, we heard there were some hundreds of People collected together intending to oppose us . . . we still continued advancing, keeping prepared against an attack tho' without intending to attack them, but on our coming near them they fired one or two shots, upon which our Men without any orders rushed in upon them, fired and put 'em to flight; several of them were killed, we cou'd not tell how many because they were got behind Walls and into the Woods . . . . We then formed on the Common but with some difficulty, the Men were so wild they cou'd hear no orders . . . at length proceeded on our way to Concord, which we then learnt was our destination. . . . [Much later] Captn. Lawrie . . . sent to Coll. Smith begging he would send more Troops to his Assistance and informing him of his situation; the Coll. order'd 2 or 3 Compys. but put himself at their head by which means stopt 'em from being time enough, for being a very fat heavy Man he wou'd not have reached the Bridge in half an hour tho' it was not half a mile to it; in the mean time . . . .
>
> May 1st . . . Here is a report that the Mob at New York has disarmed that part of the 18th Rgt. which is there and taken 'em Prisoners . . . . The Rebels have erected the Standard at Cambridge; they call themselves the King's Troops and us the Parliaments. Pretty Burlesque! . . . we want to get out of this coop'd up situation. We cou'd now do that I suppose but the G[eneral] does not seem to want it; there's no guessing what he is at. . . .

A man of Oswald's wit would have enjoyed the burlesque reversal of the Civil War of the seventeenth century. But what was the climate of opinion in Edinburgh and Perth when he transferred into the Black Watch? The military historian Sir John Fortescue can give us the superior officers' point of view.[16] In Britain in the autumn of 1779, "amid the general harmony of patriot feeling there were not wanting discordant notes. Fox was still unable to look at any military operation . . . except with an oblique eye to its effect on the Government.[17] . . . The Duke of Richmond, who was the Fox of the Lords, behaved even worse." When the government issued a proclamation for removal of cattle and supplies in case of French or Spanish invasion, the duke "summoned a public meeting,

---

16. *History of the British Army*, 5:292–95, quoted in the next two paragraphs.
17. Charles James Fox, leading Opposition spokesman in the House of Commons during this crisis in the war with America, would declare in November that since his majesty's "empire was [being] dismembered, . . . the people were beginning to murmur; and . . . there certainly would be insurrections . . ." ("British and Foreign History," *New Annual Register* for 1780, 1:13).

wherein he declared his disapproval of the proclamation and his intention not to execute it. A private soldier who uttered such sentiments would have been rightly tried for mutiny and shot without mercy." (When we first find Oswald writing about Fox and Richmond, seven years later, he will take a position strongly similar to theirs expressed here; he will criticize Richmond then, however, for focusing too narrowly on fortification.) In Scotland there was a rebellious spirit among the bloodybacks. In April 1779 a draft of sixty men for a Highland regiment had "mutinied and refused to embark for America." They were quelled by a Fencible Regiment, but not before "thirty of the mutineers had been killed and wounded, and an officer of the Fencibles killed," also "several men." Next there was "a mutiny of the Fencible Regiment itself in Edinburgh, which was checked in the nick of time by the firmness of General Oughton, who contrived to surround and disarm five companies, and vowed 'no mercy unless they surrendered.'" (Fencibles enlisted only for home service.)

The general reported to the secretary of state that the Highlanders, "though splendid troops on active service, were . . . capricious, obstinate, and mutinous" at home, not out of "mere caprice" but because of the prevailing spirit of insubordination throughout Scotland "just at that time." Indeed, "great numbers of the clergy of all denominations were avowed Americans and Republicans." And Ireland, not surprisingly, was even worse. In April an assembly which had given itself "the name of the Citizens of Dublin, passed resolutions after the American model against the importation of British goods. . . . Seizing hold of the concessions proffered by England to America, and arguing not unreasonably that they should be extended also to Ireland, the Irish patriots claimed that English Acts of Parliament were no longer binding in Ireland, and that in consequence the English Mutiny Act, among others, was of no force."

We can understand why the Royal Irish Regiment was sent home for recuperation to Dover, not Dublin. As for the troops sent on active duty to India in 1780, though not mentioned in the Black Watch chronicles, the mutinous behavior among the bloodybacks when they were turned loose upon and then denied the spoils of Bedinore and Mangalore in Mysore, India, would reach proportions frightening to army historians. As for Lieutenant Oswald, who shunned the officers' mess and preferred to eat with the common ranks, we must not suppose that he was innocent of and silent about republicanism until he suddenly heard of the fall of the Bastille nine years later.

Duel on Board Ship

Even the routine drunken duelling could move close to the edge of mutiny when between ranks. Barker records a typical duel (Boston, March 1774) thus:

> Three Officers of the 5th put in arrest for a Riot . . . the same evening another duel stop'd . . . some words passing between them, the Lt. Cl. struck Mr. P---k in the face

upon which they both immediately drew their Swords . . . agreed to fight with Pistols
. . . an Officer . . . took the Pistols and fired 'em in the air, which alarmed the Guard
which turned out and took him Prisoner . . . .[18]

We lack any such account of the duel engaged in by John Oswald while
the Royal Highlanders were on their thirteen-month voyage to India, having
boarded ships at Portsmouth, 21 January 1781, but it seems to have been of a
different quality. "He accompanied the regiment to India," said David Stewart,
"and fought a duel with the officer [Col. Norman Macleod] commanding on
board his transport, while the squadron lay in Porto Prya Bay." Two rounds
were fired, but no one was injured. Oswald had not been the aggressor, and the
incident seems not to have harmed his reputation.[19] The anonymous author of
the 1821 *Lives of the Scottish Poets* was "told by a gentleman who knew
Oswald well," perhaps Thomson, "that he once saw him saluted in London as
an old acquaintance, by a Highland colonel of distinguished gallantry," presumably Macleod (who was in the House of Commons in 1789–1793), "with
a degree of hearty warmth which forbids the suspicion of any thing disgraceful
attaching to his character. It was at the theatre they met, and the two friends
were so rejoiced at recognizing each other, that they leapt across several inter-
vening boxes to shake hands."[20] By that time both Oswald and Macleod were
ardent democrats; perhaps indeed they had shared radical sentiments during
their original acquaintance, when the British frustrations in America had sent
them to the rescue of British commerce in India.

Nevertheless, the instability of Oswald's temper must have created strained
relations with his commander. Says Stewart, "From this circumstance [the
duelling] and his finances being low, he did not associate, or dine with the officers in the cabin, but employed his whole time in acquiring a knowledge of the
Greek, Hebrew, and Gaelic languages, and was particularly fond of Ossian's
poems."[21]

Wordsworth's variant of the duel, in *The Borderers*, is interesting, but impure
("maculate," Oswald would have called it). His Oswald, having embarked for

18. *The British in Boston*, 9, 27.
19. *Sketches*, 215; Stewart does not give the officer's name, but the account in Haslewood, *The
Secret History of the Green-Room*, supplies it, and various narratives of the voyage confirm it.
Macleod was "Lord Macleod, son of Lord Cromartie, and late of the Swedish service," who "came
forward (1777 about November) first to create the corps which now bears the famous title of the
71st Highland Light Infantry" (Fortescue, *History of the British Army*, 3:289).
20. *Lives*, 2:172–73: the duel was fought "certainly not from any cause injurious to his
honor. . . . To the price of [his] commission he would, of course, be entitled when he quitted the
army, and it was probably on the reversion of this fund that he subsisted after his return from
India."
21. There may have been an egalitarian motive in Oswald's dining away from the officers' mess;
he seems, however, to have been on terms of intellectual comradeship with Humberston and Macleod—to judge from the similarity of his and Macleod's political ideas (which we discover later)
and from the emphasis on Humberstone's geniality and intellectual cultivation in what seems to be
Oswald's obituary essay on him (see note 24 below).

Syria (suggested by John Oswald's voyaging?), develops a raging hostility to his "Captain" which at last explodes. This Oswald, too, is not technically the aggressor: "He struck me; and that instant had I killed him . . . but my Comrades / Rushed in between us"—and no one was injured. Wordsworth, however, completely departs from John Oswald's story by drawing (as has been recognized) on his familiarity with the story of Fletcher Christian of the mutiny on the *Bounty*, for he adds, after the duel, a tale of mutiny in which his Oswald shares the crew's guilt in marooning the commander.[22]

No mutiny occurred in the expeditionary force which had sailed from Portsmouth on 12 March 1781, after "various delays," and consisted of the 96th and 100th as well as the 42nd or Black Watch Regiment (under Col. Humberstone) with four other companies from different regiments and a detachment of Royal Artillery. It had reached the Cape Verde Islands in April, "touching at St Jago," and there had been attacked by a French squadron under Admiral Suffrein, which was repulsed "with little loss on either side."[23] It was there, before or after the battle, that the duel seems to have taken place, Porto Praya (Praia in Portuguese) being a bay in the Isle of Santiago.

The Customs of Joanna

After the skirmish at St. Jago, the British sailed on for the Cape, "but Suffrein having arrived there before them, the attempt was abandoned, and the troops ordered to proceed to India. However, a valuable convoy of Dutch East Indiamen, who had taken shelter in Suldanha Bay," about 60 miles north of the Cape, "was captured there." The troops expected to share the prize money—a strong reason for signing on for overseas duty—but their "right to share was . . . disputed by Commodore Johnstone, on the plea that the troops had not landed." Here, indeed, was strong cause for mutiny; there must have been some strong grumbling, but they sailed on. (The claim was not dropped; "after a lapse of many years" it was "determined in their favour"—long after such men as Oswald were beyond reach.)[24]

After rounding the Cape they took many months to reach only as far as the Comorro Islands, northwest of Madagascar, where they halted because of scurvy among the troops. The commodore "put into the Island of Joanna,

---

22. See Moorman, *William Wordsworth*, 299–300; Schneider, *Wordsworth's Cambridge Education*, 232.

23. D. Stewart, *Sketches*, 216. Humberstone happened to be on shore at the moment of the attack, "but such was his ardor to share the danger of the day, that he swam off to one of the ships that were engaged with the enemy" (Humberstone obituary; see note 24 below). Suffrein or Soufrein with his French fleet would continue to harass British fleets near India—for instance when "anchored in the Madras Road" in February 1782 (see *Annual Register* for 1782, 25:268–79)—helping maintain the successful pressure which gave Bengal back to France in the Treaty of 1783.

24. Humberstone obituary (by Oswald?) in the *London Chronicle*, 10–12 November 1785.

where fresh provisions were abundant. But, in attempting to cure one evil, they unfortunately encountered another; for, after the troops had landed, and were encamped, for the benefit of air and exercise, they caught the fever of the country, and, carrying the contagion on board, a great many of the men fell a sacrifice to it."

Oswald evidently escaped any debilitating illness, for the months spent on the Island of Joanna found him as busy reading the peoples of the Comorro Islands as he had been on shipboard reading the classics. In London six years later he published in his *British Mercury* two chapters "Extracted from the Materials of a Voyage to the East Indies in 1781, with some Account of the Manners, Customs, History, Religion, Philosophy, &c. of Hindostan; a Work intended for the Press"—now extant only in this sample, an "Account of the Natives of Joanna, an Island in the African Sea." [25]

His ambitious title suggests he intended to emulate Thomas Shaw's *Travels* or *Observations Relating to Several Parts of Barbary and the Levant* (1738), which he quotes elsewhere [26]—but with saucy language and "odd" anecdotes to spice the account, and perhaps some satiric improvisations. Did the Joannamen, for instance, really worship "duck deities"—or if they did (and the worship of certain rare birds was indeed practised in Madagascar) can it have been as casual and coincidental in origin as Oswald suggests? And did he really have the facility to communicate with the two kinds of "natives" he pretends to have conversed with? "The first . . . are the Aborigines, who are blacks of the same species of man with the Abyssinians. The other are the descendants of Arabian settlers, a white people, but exceedingly tanned by the sun, and somewhat maculated, by intermixture with the original Joannamen."

Such a polyglot as Oswald would, of course, have picked up a good deal of Arabic and of "aboriginal" language: and the natives could meet him with pidgin English. The islands were independent—and he would be glad to know that they are so today, attempting "government by the people"—but had long been on a main navigation route. One of the Arabians, "who still called himself Captain of the Prince of Wales's Guard," explained his abhorrence of Christians in these words: "You eata de pork, and you drinka de rum!" And the aboriginal priest, who escorted those "gentlemen" of the British "fleet" who "had the curiosity to pay a visit to the sacred seat" of the divine ducks, delivered "a long oration" in his own tongue yet had enough English to inform the gentlemen simply what he had said, "that the persons who came to consult their sacred oracle, were Englishmen; that Englishman, Joannaman, were all one brother." In short, Oswald's account and anecdotes have an air of authenticity—somewhat maculated by ingenuity.

The striking thing about them is the double-edged quality of his compari-

25. *British Mercury*, 82–87, 107–13.
26. Oswald quotes it in his *Review*, 44.

sons of the natural Aborigines and the civilized Arabians. If the settlers are maculated by intermarriage with the originals, it is the latter who are the purer. Indeed his description of the civilized customs of the Arabians is ambiguous if not sardonic. The Arabians are clothed and "inhabit convenient houses" built of a stucco "not much inferior to marble." However—but he does not say "however."

> Their habitations are surrounded by high walls, to guard their women, of whom they are extremely jealous, from the wanderings of desire, and from the wanton eye of curiosity. They have servants and slaves, and property in abundance; they apply to letters . . . have some knowledge . . . of commerce . . . and in short, are mancipated [a think-twice word] to those anxious and operose[27] modes of life, which constitute a people civilized. The Aborigines, on the contrary, are naked savages . . . ignorant of arts, of jealousy, of ambition; happy, careless, content with the bounty of Nature, beyond whose simple wants, their wishes have not as yet been taught to expatiate.

But then he makes fun of them, as in his anecdote of "Purser Jack," one of the king of Joanna's customs officers, victim of a practical joke by a ship captain and prostitute who represent civilization—or is Purser Jack already maculated and mancipated by his office and contact with the civilized?

Perhaps, at least by the time he was writing this account, Oswald saw a similar maculation and burlesque of ignorant innocence in the duck priest's accepting as "all one brother" these Englishmen who were on their way to "fight the French, the Dutch, and Hyder Ali" and his deities' blessing of their enterprise. Actually, Oswald anticipates the sentiments of the romantic poets in his downright approval (or is it such?) of "the facility of savages who abhor the fatigue of reasoning and slow conjecture, no less than they delight in bold flight of imagination . . . ." His most characteristic remarks swing both ways: "A nation, urged to action by the demons of science and superstition, are as much superior to the savage, and for the same reason, as a maniac is more powerful than a man in his sober senses."[28]

Bombay to Madras

Toward the end of September, the squadron finally set sail for India—unaware that just at that season the monsoon would turn against them—and did not arrive at Bombay until 5 March (1782). Four officers and 116 noncommissioned officers and soldiers had died on the thirteen-month voyage from England. On 30 April they sailed for Madras.

---

27. Note that *mancipated* is the opposite of *emancipated*; *operose* means labor-intensive. Oswald's latinate wit tangles the realities; he makes hard, slavish life sound elegant—and he intends to do so.
28. *B Merc*, 109–10, 83, 197.

Fig. 3. Bombay Harbor, official port of call for the British troops in India. From *The Political Magazine*, 1 February 1796.

It may be to the latter part of the seven-week stay in Bombay or, more probably, to the summertime in Madras, that Stewart refers when he reports that Oswald "for a short time acted adjutant to the battalion, and soon afterwards sold his commission." [29] Resolving the question (on which the biographers differ) whether Oswald's resignation from the army was voluntary or compulsory, Stewart concludes that he was removed—but without dishonor. And the explanation Stewart proposes proves close to the truth—but topsy-turvy. "For the short time he acted as adjutant in India he was so severe and tyrannical, that the spirit of the soldiers revolted, and had he not been removed, he would have occasioned a mutiny." The truth is that he found himself in a mutinous situation in India—as we shall see—but not of the sort any severity on his part would have caused.

The flotilla would have been a month or two making the voyage from Bombay to Madras, and the adjutant would have had the task of making sure that all able bodies were ready for active duty by 2 September. He himself continued on active duty, evidently, until after the storming of Bednore.

There seem to have been no military demands upon him during the spring, for the off-duty weeks in Bombay were full of pleasure until the order came to depart. In a poem dated "Bombay, 1782," Oswald laments having to leave a loving woman to go off to war, and the poem must belong to this March-April period, since his regiment did not return to Bombay.

29. *Sketches*, 216–17.

Commanded by "Relentless Destiny," the poet must be a soldier once more: "To ruthless deeds and rude alarms." Quoting Virgil in a footnote, he compares himself to Aeneas leaving his Dido. In the poem she is "Eliza," from whose "rose-budding lip" he may no longer sip "Love's ambrosial bliss,"

Nor livelier type of deeper joy,
The melting, moist, impassion'd kiss
On thy mellow mouth impress . . . .[30]

He will not forget her, but as a soldier, even an Aeneas, he must be forever "to sordid life and little cares consign'd"—appointed adjutant to drill the troops! The Madras period, through the winter of 1782–1783, is that during which Oswald "served under Humberstone" (as the biographies say). David Stewart gives the clearest account:

General Meadows remaining on board [of the transports in Bombay] and Colonel Macleod in the Myrtle not having arrived [he reached Bombay a week too late], the command of the troops intended for actual service devolved on Lieutenant-Colonel Mackenzie Humberstone of the 100th regiment, under whom an expedition was undertaken for the purpose of attacking Palacatcherry, situated in a country considered of importance to Hyder Ali. The troops, consisting of seven companies of the Highlanders, a detachment of the 100th regiment, and some native corps, took the field on the 2d of September 1782; and, after taking several small forts on the march, reached their destination on the 19th of October, when, on a full examination, the fort was found everywhere much stronger than had been represented; at the same time that intelligence was received of Hyder's having sent his son Tippoo Saib, with a large force for its relief. In such circumstances, a regular siege could not be attempted; and, as it could not be taken by assault, Colonel Humberstone determined to withdraw to Mangaracotah, one of the small forts he had taken. The intelligence of Tippoo's advance being well founded, Colonel Humberstone continued his retreat, and, blowing up the forts of Mangaracotah and Ramguree, arrived at Paniané, closely pressed on the march by the enemy, who had pushed forward with considerable rapidity, and in great force. (218–19)

Paniane was important because there Humberstone had "a strong post" and his reserve supplies. In the Oswaldian account we are told that Tippoo caught up with the British "when they were yet thirty-six miles from their post, and had three large rivers to cross."[31] "Our little army," the account continues, the personal pronoun implying the voice of a participant (Oswald), "was now surrounded with multitudes of cavalry on every side; and which ever way they turned their eyes they saw their numerous enemies." But they "left them behind by a rapid march" and "regained the fort of Paniane." To return to Stewart's account:

30. "The Farewell. An Irregular Ode," in *Poems*, 38–40.
31. Humberstone obituary.

Lieutenant-Colonel Macleod, who had arrived, now assumed the command, and found himself surrounded by an enemy of 10,000 cavalry and 14,000 infantry, including two corps of Europeans under the French General Lally. The British force was reduced by sickness to 380 Europeans, and 2200 English and Travancore Seapoys, fit for duty. The post was strong by nature, and some attempts were made to strengthen it still more by field-works; but, before these were completed, the French General Lally attacked the post on the morning of the 29th November. He [Lally] advanced with great spirit at the head of his European troops; but, after a smart contest, well supported on both sides, the enemy were repulsed, and entirely defeated.

The weight of Lally's attack was directed against the post occupied by the Highlanders, whose repeated charges with the bayonet were principally instrumental in promoting the success of the day. "This little army, attacked, on ground not nearly fortified, by very superior numbers, skilfully disposed, and regularly led on: they had nothing to depend on but their native valour, their discipline [some of it supplied by Oswald, one would think], and the conduct of the officers. These were nobly exerted, and the event has been answerable. The intrepidity with which Major Campbell and the Highlanders repeatedly charged the enemy was most honourable to their character." (General Orders.) The loss of the British and Native troops was 8 officers and 88 soldiers killed and wounded. That of the 42d regiment was 3 sergeants, and 19 rank and file, killed; and Major John Campbell, Captains Colin Campbell and Thomas Dalyell, Lieutenant Charles Sutherland, 2 sergeants, and 31 rank and file, wounded.

After this defeat, Tippoo retreated towards Seringapatam, the movement being hastened by accounts received of the death of his father, Hyder Ali.

The *Chronicle* of the regiment adds that "Two hundred Mysoreans were bayoneted by the Regiment and afterwards buried."[32] For the chronicler this is a mere body count, but if it represents an action *after*, not during, the battle it anticipates the slaughtering of prisoners deplored in the Oswaldian review in the *London Chronicle*. In the next action, in which Colonel Macleod led the Black Watch and a corps of Sepoys (native Indian troops) in the storming of a succession of seven "field works erected on the face of mountains," the killing *seems* (in the Black Watch account) to have been part of the battle. Attacking with the bayonet and "pursuing like Highlanders"—the natives learn quickly—they "were in the breast-work before the enemy were aware of it. Four hundred were bayonetted, and the rest pursued to the walls of the fort." The fortress, Beddinore (or Bednore or Bednure) was richly stocked with arms, powder, and shot, and the soldiers' expectation of "great sums of prize money" was "considerably excited."

Reasons for Quitting the Army

A very different account is to be found in Dodsley's *Annual Register* for 1783—detailed in the "History of Europe" section (26:76−101) and docu-

32. *Chronicle of the Black Watch*, 52−53; for the rest of this chapter, D. Stewart, *Sketches*, 217, 221−22.

mented in the "Appendix" (286–94) by a "Letter" of 25 November 1783, from the Bombay Committee to the London Directors of the East India Company. The letter includes documents supplied by Colonels Macleod and Humberstone formally complaining about the "extraordinary" and "mysterious" and "in many instances totally unintelligible" conduct (26:91) of a General Matthews, whom the directors had put in command of the forces of Humberstone and Macleod in October 1782—and who had made a bloody farce of the storming of Bednore in February 1783! The outraged Macleod and Humberstone had rushed to Bombay on 27 February, learned from the committee that General Matthews had never bothered to report any information, and declared that "they were under a necessity of quitting the army" (26:94).[33] Major Shaw was also with them and joined in their declaration. And since this happens to be about the time Lieutenant Oswald must have resigned from the army, it seems almost certainly the occasion. Colonels Macleod and Humberstone were soon persuaded by the Bombay Committee, convinced that it must remove General Matthews, to remain in the army and take command at Bednore. The Company recognized them as "the principal officers of his majesty's troops" (26:287). Oswald would not have qualified in that category, but his request to resign without dishonor would have been supported by Macleod.

Once this complaint had been made, Matthews helped by blowing his top. In a letter to the committee dated 4 March, "he taxe[d] the whole army in terms the most severe, but altogether general and indiscriminate, with offences of the highest criminality." There is much more of the same. But the Bednore experience is most to our purpose here.

The general's argument against the committee's paying attention to Macleod's complaints, which might lead to "dangerous proceedings," was:

> that the troops in Bednore were almost in a state of mutiny; the enemy collecting a force within thirty miles; the prospect of resettling the city every moment more distant, owing to the dejection of the Jemautdar Hyat Saib [governor of the city], who, from the illiberal and indecent expressions of officers, was filled with apprehensions that made him utterly despond, and rendered him incapable of any exertion. (26:287)

The city of Bednore, of some thirty thousand inhabitants including many wealthy nobles, was an ancient capital, one of the "largest and finest cities in India" (26:92).[34] Hyat Saib, "who seems to have most worthily discharged the trust reposed in him; and to have acted with a very extraordinary degree of judgment and policy" to resist "impending ruin," aware at once that he could not defeat the military power approaching, had dispatched agents to the English camp,

33. "These gentlemen on their arrival each gave in memorials, stating their reasons for quitting the army." Macleod declared it "impossible for him to continue to serve under the command of Brigadier General Matthews" (26:287–88).

34. Is it typical of military history that the Black Watch chronicler treats Bednore as simply a fortress, with no mention of city and inhabitants?

who entered into a private negociation with the general [Matthews], and some sort of a strange treaty was concluded . . . that the capital, the country, the fortress at Bednore, with the public treasures and property, were to be delivered up to the English; that the persons and property of the inhabitants were to be fully secured from all molestation and injury; and that Hyat Saib was to continue in the government, under the authority of the English, holding much the same powers that he had done under Hyder. (93)

What then happened was that General Matthews ignored this treaty (though the government of Bombay was informed) and, "immediately upon getting possession of Bednore, broke [the agreement] by suddenly seizing and confining Hyat, to a close imprisonment." He found "great treasures" amounting to "fourteen lacks" (fourteen hundred thousand pagodas [£560,000]), showed them publicly to the officers as now "the property of the army," with "much other treasure, and jewels," but then later told the army that they were all "claimed by Hyat Saib as his private property" and so "actually restored to him by the general."

> The effect of this conduct on the army need not be described; but it was increased . . . by a recollection of some former management tending to the same object, which had been practiced at the sack of Onore, and by which they considered themselves as having been wronged of the greater part of the booty found at that place. Nor did the general's measure, of carrying some of the principal officers to Hyat Saib, and prevailing upon him to make a present of half a lack of pagoda's, amounting to about 20,000*l.* to the army, serve in any degree to allay the discontents, or to remove the suspicions which so generally prevailed. (26:94)

Here is the nearly mutinous spirit which Stewart's Black Watch account suggests attributing to John Oswald! But (as the account proceeds) it was at this point that Macleod and Humberstone and Shaw and Oswald had hurried to Bombay to turn in their resignations; Oswald successfully.[35]

Enough said, if we were merely concerned with the context of Oswald's leaving the army. But further details will give us the sociopolitical context for Oswald's sentimental education (in the eighteenth-century sense) and his turning to Hindu vegetarianism.

The *Annual Register* "History" (26:91−92) before it gets to the Bednore operation gives the report of an unnamed officer (whose sympathies seem like Oswald's) making the point that Bombay's ideas of "conciliating the good-will of the natives" were "either not at all understood, or, at least, were by no means adopted by the army."

> The officer, indeed, who gives an account of the massacre at the fortress of Annampore, which was taken by storm, under some preceding circumstances of aggravation

---

35. In the Humberstone obituary which I take to be by Oswald, the matter is reported thus: "General Matthews . . . had given such proofs of misconduct, of rapacity, and injustice, that col. Macleod and col. Humberstone carried complaints to the council at Bombay, and backed them with such convincing evidence, that he was superseded in his command."

on the side of the governor, and from whence only one horseman, desperately wounded, had the fortune to escape the general slaughter, seems to feel no small compunction and horror, in describing the spectacle which was there exhibited, of four hundred beautiful women, all bleeding with wounds of the bayonet, and either already dead, or expiring in each others arms; while the common soldiers, casting off all obedience to their officers, were stripping off their jewels, and committing every outrage on their bodies. He says that others of the women, (without taking notice whether their lives were offered or not) rather than to be torn from their relations, threw themselves into large tanks, and were drowned. He, however, observes, that the troops were afterwards severely reprimanded for this action. (26:91−92)[36]

General Matthews, in his letter of 4 March accusing the whole army and especially the officers of having been ignited into flaming discontent by the breath of "a few zealots for plunder and booty," seems to have felt that their disrespect for himself as general, including any such reprimands of the troops as just cited—for it was he who had done the dealing and double-dealing—had only inspired "the soldiery" to become "loose and unfeeling as the most licentious freebooters" (*AR*, 26:287).

That word stirs an echo in Wordsworth's *Borderers*, in the complaint of the heroine's father, the King-Lear-like Herbert, that she has "given her love to a base freebooter" (1.1.175) and the wild vision of Mortimer (later Marmaduke) that all their band of warriors are but buzzing flies, i.e., "black and winged freebooters" (5.2.1992). Is it possible that Wordsworth, curious about the early career of John Oswald, as I am now, read through these *Annual Register* reports of the war in India and came upon this outpouring of the mad General Matthews?

Reading through once more, I realize that of all the warriors we have been watching the only survivors were Oswald, who sold his commission, and Macleod, whose good fortune went with him. A consequence of the fiasco of Bed-

---

36. In 1786, while Oswald was writing for the *Political Herald and Review*, variants of this scene of "confusion, cruelty, anarchy, and plunder" were forced strongly, though apologetically, upon the *Herald*'s readers—first in a serialized treatise (unsigned, but written by William Godwin, perhaps with help from Oswald) called "Memoirs of the Government of Madras during the Presidency of Lord Macartney" (*Herald*, 3:414−15) and then in a review of a pamphlet on the "gallant Defence made at Mangalore," which occasioned a vivid paraphrase of this *Annual Register* account and the comment that these "intrepid and gallant spirits" of the army in India "shall be handed down to posterity among the Pizarros and Almagros, the robbers of provinces and the murderers of nations . . ." (*Herald*, 3:474). Oswald had resigned from that army but could never forget—nor let his countrymen forget.

It is a curious symptom of Grub-Street ethics, however, that the paraphrase in the *Herald* was not concocted by anyone on the *Herald* staff; it is attributed, accurately, to "a publication remarkable for its impartiality," the *New Annual Register* "for 1784" (i.e., of 1783, for 1784). (A sample: "Four hundred beautiful women, pierced with the bayonet, and expiring in one another's arms, were, in this situation, treated by the British with every kind of outrage.") As we shall see, by this time Godwin was compiler of the historical section of the *New Annual Register*, hence responsible for the paraphrase. Did he also supply the *Herald* review? Any one of the three, Godwin, Thomson, or Oswald, could have done so. For evidence of Godwin's contributions to the *Herald*, and for the business of the Macartney "Memoirs," see Marken, "William Godwin and the *Political Herald and Review*."

nore was that when a Mahratta peace was "duly proclaimed at Bombay" (after its signing at Poonah in February), Colonels Macleod and Humberstone and Major Shaw and others sailed off on the *Ranger* on 5 April to rejoin the army—apprized of the peace and under orders "not to commit hostilities against the Mahrattas"—only to be attacked on the 8th, three days after leaving Bombay, by the Mahratta fleet, unaware of the peace treaty. "Major Shaw was shot dead: Colonel Humberstone was shot through the lungs: Lieutenant Stuart of the 100th regiment, was almost cut to pieces. . . . In the beginning of the action Colonel Macleod received two wounds in his left hand and shoulder; and, a little before it was over, a musket ball passed through his body, which pierced his lungs and spleen" (26:290).

As for General Matthews, he meets his match after marching out "to fight the prodigious army under Tippoo Sultan" (I quote the *Register* contents page). Matthews is

> instantly defeated . . . and besieged [whereupon his garrison panic and] set fire to the magazines, and abandon the place. [Whereupon] General Matthews capitulates upon honourable conditions. [Then the tables are turned:] Capitulation violated by Tippoo Sultan. General, and principal officers, seized and imprisoned. [Matthews slain;] army plundered and inhumanly treated. [British attempt rescue; French join Tippoo; and then:] Account of the peace being received, an immediate cessation of hostilities takes place. (26:76)

In 1784 peace was concluded with Tippoo, on the basis of a mutual restitution of all conquests.[37]

Macleod had been promoted to brigadier-general and had recovered from his wounds, "but too late to save the unfortunate army at Beddinore." Oswald, leaving the army early in 1783, must have taken at least a year in his roundabout traveling home to Kent.

Lichtenberger, without investigating the political ambience of Oswald's Grub-Street years with its severe judgment of British cruelties in India, was sound in his assumption that Oswald's "ideas, philosophical, political, and social became bitter . . . from the philanthropic indignation which he felt at the miserable condition of the Indians" as well as "from the series of humiliations which his low fortune brought upon him"—and that these things "determined him to turn his activity elsewhere"—away from the sordid life of ship and camp.[38]

37. On 20 January 1783, a Treaty of Versailles had given Bengal back to France—a reason for Tippoo's trying to add Madras and Mysore.

38. A historian friend has suggested that a truly impartial account of the war in India should be sought in the three-volume *History of British India* by James Mill. I find that Mill does cite the old *Annual Register* (not the *New*) and that he does touch upon the careers of the officers we are interested in, Colonel Macleod, Colonel Humberstone, and Major Shaw, and their dislike of General Matthews (2:747–49). But he never gets close to the action or interaction. Mill dismisses "suspicions of rapacity" as "easily raised" and will accept no charges against Matthews's reputation, since "he lived not to vindicate" it (749). As for the blood shed at Annampour and Mangalore, he

gives no details but simply summarizes: "the English army have been accused of a barbarity unusual at the hands of a civilized foe. It appears not, however, that quarter, when asked, was refused; but orders were given to shed the blood of every man who was taken under arms, and some of the officers were reprimanded for not seeing those orders rigidly executed" (748). No women mentioned, beautiful or otherwise. Indeed, Mill dwells almost exclusively on the command and staffing levels of the action, and almost never gives facts and figures. "It appears" to Mill that some officials were less competent than others. But, from Mill's argument that Utility had been achieved by the Indian shift from Hinduism to Mohammedanism, it is implied that still greater social Utility was promoted by British—i.e., Christian—transcendence.

3.
AMONG THE TURKOMANS AND CURDEES

━━◁━━━

In India he imitated the Gentoos, abstained from animal food, and regularly performed the usual ablutions.[1]

*   *   *

In the year 1783 he left India, and returned by land to England. His predominant passion for travel, and burning avidity to survey mankind under various points of view, determined him to trace out for himself a new route. He directed his course to the more northern and mountainous parts of Turkey, and pitched his tent for some time among the barbarous hords of Turkomans and Curdees, whom for many years no traveller has visited except himself and the celebrated *walking Stuart.*[2]

John ("Walking") Stewart (1749–1822), memorialized by De Quincey in "London Reminiscences" and more recently and more informatively by Bertrand Bronson in *Facets of the Enlightenment* (1968), went to India at fourteen and became a general under Hyder Ali and prime minister to the Nabob of Arcot. By 1783 he had walked through Asia Minor and northern Africa and through France and Spain. The next year he walked to Vienna and through some of the United States. Inevitably Stewart and Oswald, when both in London, and both guests of John Rickman at a party for Tom Paine, were introduced to each other and talked (probably for hours), perhaps comparing impressions of Turkomans and Joannamen.[3] Unfortunately their conversation was not recorded.

In the 1788 *Catalogue of Celebrated Authors*, Oswald is defined as a gentleman who "served in the late war on the Malabar coast, and is at present engaged in writing a History of the East Indies." We shall find only one chapter of that history—on the Comorro Islanders—and we have nothing from which to construct an itinerary; yet Oswald's political writings frequently glance at customs in Turkey or India or among Arab tribes, and for the *Political Herald* of 1785–1786 he could write with much knowledge and wisdom about the processes of past and present history in most nations of the world.

1. D. Stewart, *Sketches*, 216.
2. *European Magazine*, March 1790, 198–99.
3. Stewart, in his *Travels*, 231, defines the "Turcomans" as "a nation of Tartars inhabiting the uncultivated parts of Turkey."

We do have, also, a literary reconstruction of the Oriental Oswald in Wordsworth's *Borderers*, and in an imaginative way it tells us more about the "Syrian" period of his life than can be garnered from the thumbnail sketches in English magazines.[4]

If we were staging Wordsworth's drama, we should, from what we know of the actual Oswald, have our hero (ours, for the time, if not Wordsworth's) dress without cravat or wig, wearing his hair à la Titus or à la Brutus, short behind to defy the guillotine.[5] Exemplifying the "certain curious beliefs" he imbibed from the Brahmins in the East, Wordsworth's Oswald gives the honest English freebooters some concern about the religion he exhibited when "a voyager / Upon the midland Sea" and when "in Palestine" (the play is set in the time of the Crusades) "where he despised alike / Mohammedan and Christian"—both maculate? Once, when asked to swear fealty to a king, he gave a "strange answer . . . 'I hold of Spirits, and the Sun in heaven.'" The troops come to suspect that Oswald is in league with "imagined Beings" or "infernal fiends." Compare the "devilish pleas" and "blasts from hell" which Wordsworth himself, retrospectively, sensed in Paris revolutionaries such as Oswald, Robespierre, Danton—he names no names—after Britain went to war with France (*Prelude* 10.311, 315).

Even if we suppose for a moment that Wordsworth's knowledge of John Oswald came only from anecdotes such as surface in the paragraphs of Redhead Yorke and Sampson Perry, we may compare such lines as Yorke's "He dined on his roots one day" with the sinister twist Wordsworth gives to Oswald's vegetarianism on his first entrance, in act 1:

Enter Oswald (*a bunch of plants in his hand*).
Osw. This wood is rich in plants and curious simples.
Marmaduke. (*looking at them*). The wild rose, and the poppy,
And the nightshade:
Which is your favourite, Oswald? (1.44–46)

His answer: that which is "strong to destroy" yet also "strong to heal," i.e., the nightshade; the words are repeated by "Oswald" "(*to himself*)" in his last entrance, in act 5. They do in a way acknowledge the Oswaldian goal of social healing; yet in the ironies of the dramatic plot they chiefly stress the contradictions of benevolent warfare, the focus of Wordsworth's thought when he wrote the play.

---

4. See especially *The Borderers*, lines 16–19, 1145–47, 1154–88.

5. *Lives*, 178. The English Jacobin Joseph Gerrald is described as epitomizing the French costume when, on trial in Edinburgh for his participation there in a British Convention (frightening concept), he refused "to powder his hair in the 'loyalist' fashion, and appearing at the bar 'with unpowdered hair hanging loosely down behind—his neck nearly bare, and his shirt with a large collar, doubled over'" (Lord Cockburn, *Memorials of his Time*, 2:41–43, quoted in E. P. Thompson, *The Making of the English Working Class*, 128). Romney's portrait, in 1792, of Pamela (Lady Edward Fitzgerald to be) shows hair "bobbed . . . à la Titus" (Lucy Ellis and Joseph Turquan, *La Belle Pamela*, facing p. 228).

4.
LONDON

Political Herald in Grub-Street

How directly Oswald returned to London, and exactly when, we can only surmise. The year given in most accounts is 1784, but in his *British Mercury* for June 1787 he says that he had arrived "almost four years ago," which suggests the latter part of 1783. His first independent publications appear in 1786 but his tracks are unmistakable in the contributors' columns of the daily *London Chronicle* by 1785[1] and in the leading editorials of the monthly *Political Herald and Review*, from its launching in the autumn of 1785 to its demise at the end of 1786. When he then had a journal of his own, the *Mercury*, he was able to express his frustrations in a tale of "the Miseries of Authorship" as a Grub-Street slave under the tyrannous command of a "Brain-Sucker" (common

---

1. The extent of Oswald's contributions to the *London Chronicle* is hard to judge. The frequent military items within the range of his competence and views may tempt us to assume his presence; yet doubtless the *Chronicle* and also the *Herald*, and certainly Thomson, had many helpers in Grub-Street. Any of these could have compiled, for instance, the "Chronology of Standing Armies" from 1440 to 1784 in the *Chronicle* of 2 April (319) out of Twitchell's book on the subject. And on the political topics dealt with, Oswald and Thomson may have had similar views.

The obituary notice of Humberstone, which I quote as probably Oswald's, is exceptional in its air of expressing the insider's knowledge of "transactions" which "were never duly and fairly communicated to the public." Style, on the other hand, or at least a wit one becomes familiar with, sometimes breathes from the "Bagatelles," particularly those in the 1785 *Chronicle*. In this vein are the definitions in the *Chronicle*'s "DICTIONARY for 1785" (58:67), e.g., "Buffoonery—such of the deliberations of our Senate as end in laughter." It is tempting, also, to imagine that some of the brief parliamentary reports in the *Chronicle* are Oswald's, especially since they are clear and full in 1785 but dwindle sharply in the next year: a sign perhaps of his moving on to the *Gazetteer*?

In November there is a column of "Curious Particulars observed among the Bramins" by "our correspondent," who has been among them. Some letters to the printer signed "Z." have the curiosity and learning of Oswald. He quotes a book on the Montenegrins; reviews one on the state of Persia in 1770, 1780, and 1784; scathingly reviews some Latin verses on Pitt (22–25 October; 22–24 November; 20–22 December). And since we come to know the operatic Maria Crouch as a public object of Oswald's admiration, it is plausible to suppose he wrote some of the *Chronicle*'s reviews, e.g., of the "new Comic Opera, The Stranger at Home," that opened 10 December and is appraised with emphasis on Mrs. Crouch's performance as Viola.

Designed & Etched for the British Mercury.

THE BRAIN-SUCKER,
or the Miseries of Authorship?

Published May 9 1787.

Fig. 4. Designed and etched for *The British Mercury* by Thomas Rowlandson (unsigned). Published 9 May 1787. (BL)

parlance for bookseller, i.e., publisher)[2] who compelled him to write "Odes" (see Figure 4).

The monster who sucked Oswald's brain turns out, in fact, to have been none other than his Scottish friend and future biographer William Thomson, already well established in London as writer, compiler, and publisher. That Thomson could later imagine he recognized in Napoleon his one-time "ghost" suggests something about the dynamism of their relationship in Grub-Street; indeed the grim-faced slave in the Rowlandson print of the Brain-Sucker does somewhat resemble the profile of Buonaparte in caricature prints of his years of fame.

A shrewd but jolly fellow, the "gaiety" of whose disposition had "put an end to his ecclesiastical prospects" soon after he left the University of St. Andrews, Thomson had managed to obtain an annual pension from the earl of Kinnoul. Settling in London, he "was engaged to revise and complete Dr. Watson's History of Philip the Third," and "performed his part so well, as to gain great

2. *British Mercury*, 14ff. The term *brain-sucker* is not in the *OED*, but I find it being used by a London debater in 1780: "those brain-suckers, the Booksellers" (*Westminster Forum*, 2:71).

credit, the friendship of many men of literary eminence, and a degree from the University of Glasgow." One of his first employments as "an Author by profession" was to complete a commentary on the Bible, "published under the name of Harrison." He was "editor" (whatever that meant in any given case) "of many books which have passed under different names": among them Stedman's *History of the American War*; *Man in the Moon* (1783); *Travels in Europe, Asia, and Africa* (1782); *Memoirs of the War in Asia, from 1780 to 1784* (1788, 2 vols.); Buchanan's *Travels in the Hebrides* (1793); and many in later years. During Oswald's London period Thomson established control of a number of periodicals, including the *English Review*, the *European Magazine*, the *Political Herald*, and the *Whitehall Evening Post.*[3]

The professionalism of such a writer involved ghost-writing other people's memoirs but also farming out such writing to his own ghosts. Bibliographers differ as to which works Thomson wrote. *The Memoirs of the Late War in Asia* (Murray, 1788) or *The War in Asia from 1780 to 1784* (J. Lewell, 1789), though attributed in the title to "an officer of colonel Baillie's detachment," has been ascribed to Thomson;[4] yet it was Oswald, not Thomson, who had drilled and fought and walked away from that war, and it seems likely that when his detailed and critical acquaintance with armies and travels became available to Thomson, the latter's publications in those categories improved and flourished. For example, "Some Account of the Life and Character of the late Colonel Humberstone," which I take to be largely Oswald's, appeared as "An original Communication" in the *New Annual Register* for 1784 (published late in 1785) and was reprinted in Thomson's *London Chronicle* for 10–12 November 1785.[5] It concerns the military world of Oswald's experience. And surely Oswald had some part in Thomson's *Memoirs of the Life and gallant exploits of the old Highlander Serjeant Donald Macleod* (1791), kin to Oswald's friend Norman Macleod.[6]

---

3. *Gentlemans Magazine*, 87: 1: 647–48, collated with entries in the Bibliothèque Nationale and *DNB*.

4. The *Memoirs* were perhaps shaped into *The War*, but I have not located either. A Thomson project of 1786, a translation into French (later said to be by Brissot) of *Travels in Europe, Asia, and Africa . . . begun in the year 1777 and finished in 1781* (Murray, 1782) first attributed to William Mackintosh, later to Thomson, may have benefited from some editorial help from Oswald. Oswald's own "Voyage to the East Indies in 1781, with some Account of the Manners, Customs, History, Religion, Philosophy, &c. of Hindostan," announced in his *British Mercury* of 1787 (197) as "a Work intended for the Press," apparently never got into it.

5. William Godwin had begun writing the historical section of *The New Annual Register* in 1784, his first assignment being to finish the 1783 section, "roundly" condemning British policy in India (see Marshall, *William Godwin*, 67–68); so it seems possible that he drew upon Oswald's experience, with or without Thomson's intermediation, long before their association in Thomson's *Political Herald* (to which we come shortly).

6. In his 1804 edition of *Military Memoirs, relating to the Campaigns, Battles, and Stratagems of War, Antient and Modern*, Thomson in effect, though without naming names, thanks General Miranda and Oswald as "private authorities, from which he drew not a little of his information" and whose names "would have done credit to the book, had he been at liberty to state them" (preface, p. xv, quoted in Robertson, *The Life of Miranda*, 2:222, who quotes a letter from Thomson

By the summer of 1785, while continuing his involvement in several other projects, Thomson had organized a team of writers of editorial essays ("speculations") and book reviews—and had evidently obtained sufficient financial support from the Foxite Whigs—to launch a new monthly "Pamphlet" (of eighty pages, half speculations, half reviews) to be "confined entirely to Politics and History," to be addressed to "the People," and to be called *The Political Herald, and Review.*[7] Though overlooked by historians of magazines, the *Herald*, published by G. G. J. and J. Robinson, Pater-Noster-Row, in eighteen numbers (three six-month volumes) from August 1785 through January 1787, maintained an impressive level of political journalism. But its history is shrouded in mystery—and mystification. Not only were the contributors' names omitted or disguised by pseudonyms, as was the general custom; apparently the major contributors were also kept unacquainted with each other. There must have been the occasional editorial huddle over a particular "speculation" or review, but apparently Thomson preferred to conduct such sessions individually. We are led to suppose that conferences between Thomson and Oswald took place in the latter's garret rather than any editorial office.

We may suppose that Oswald knew from the beginning that another slave of Thomson's was Gilbert Stuart, a more intimate Scottish friend since he and Thomson were both St. Andrews University men; also that Stuart had to be handled with great care since he had a reputation for intemperate charges and language that had sunk other Reviews.[8] And probably Oswald came to know that the thirty-year-old William Godwin was the "Mucius" who supplied several essays—two in the third and fourth issues (October and November 1785), three in the following April, May, and July, and something in each of the final six issues (August 1786 to January 1787). But we discover that Godwin was apparently kept unaware of the help supplied by Oswald behind the skirts of Thomson.[9]

Everyone in Grub-Street, however, must have assumed, whether or not they knew of Godwin's involvement, that the title for the new magazine had been suggested by a Godwinian hoax of late 1783 entitled *The Herald of Literature,* a single "pamphlet" published by John Murray, purporting to review "The

---

to Miranda saying that Miranda had "gently dissuaded" him from mentioning *his* name, but declaring he *will* mention it in a second edition; Oswald, of course, was still at this time believed by Thomson to be alive, as Napoleon, but unreachable).

7. Subtitle: *A Survey of Domestic and Foreign Politics; and a Critical Account of Political and Historical Publications.*

8. Details about Stuart, summarized in an account of *The English Review* by Wilbur T. Albrecht in Alvin Sullivan, ed., *British Literary Magazines: The Augustan Age, 1689–1788* (1983), 102–6. (Sullivan has no entry for the *Political Herald and Review* but hopes to have a supplement.)

9. For a well-documented account see Marken, "William Godwin and the *Political Herald and Review.*" For the political context see Marshall, *William Godwin,* 66–72. Marken (531–32) misconstrues, I believe, the letter from Thomson to Godwin after Godwin had taken over the editorship in the autumn of 1786, in which Thomson suggests using the pseudonym "Ignotus" (the Unknown) for the essays he has turned over to Godwin or to the printer, but not for things written by Thomson himself "in the form of Letters." See the discussion that follows.

Most Considerable Publications" of the time, and producing a minor sensation among *its* reviewers. For Godwin had invented both the titles and the extracts of the imaginary works reviewed.[10]

For those of us who know Oswald from his own *British Mercury* of 1787, which was, in effect, a successor to the *Political Herald* freed of the incubus of Thomson, his presence flashes out in the very first editorial "speculation" upon "The Present Times" (beginning a series which would serve as the intellectual backbone of the whole project) in a first-hand report about the politics of Mayotta and Joanna a few years back (see below).

It was probably a commitment from Oswald—or a shrewd conjecture of Thomson's—that initially made the *Herald* seem feasible. For Thomson must have judged not only that Oswald had the abilities required, but also that his personal ambition could be kept chained to the publishing enterprises of Thomson himself. For all his geniality, the latter was a most devious operator; associates found out sooner or later that his "obdurate and irascible temperament made him unsuited for complete trust."[11] And clearly the strength and reliability of a John Oswald would be required in this new venture.[12]

Gilbert Stuart's career was such that it would earn him a chapter ("Literary Hatred") in Isaac Disraeli's *The Calamities and Quarrels of Authors*. In 1773, after five years as a contributor to Ralph Griffith's *Monthly Review*, Stuart had founded with William Smellie an *Edinburgh Magazine and Review*, which had collapsed after three years because the vituperative violence of Stuart's reviews of the works of more successful historians had been too much for Smellie to control. Seven years later, in 1783, he had managed to persuade the London publisher of the *Edinburgh*, John Murray, to launch an *English Review*, with help from Thomson. That help had not been enough, however, and Murray had been "no better able to curb Stuart's attacks on his enemies . . . than Smellie had been." Murray fired Stuart after "only a few numbers," and the *Review* survived.[13]

Taking Stuart with him into the new project, Thomson did apparently succeed in keeping him under control—one reason possibly being Stuart's weakening physical condition, another Thomson's being able to count on Oswald for the steadiest work.[14] And, indeed, the *Political Herald and Review* did live up

10. Marshall, *William Godwin*, 59–60.

11. Marken, "William Godwin," 522.

12. Thomson, with many irons in the fire, plainly did not intend to carry the main burden of the editorial section—though he would ambiguously claim to be doing so when he complained to Godwin, after the latter had taken over the editorship, "I certainly did understand that I was to have a just & fair proportion of the Review part which is the only *bonus* . . . in the Herald" (ibid., 532, n. 18). He claimed, during "the last three months," to "have 82 pages of Essay & only 28½ of Reviews." In other words, "Ignotus" was supplying a heavy share of the essay section but few reviews. Was Thomson selling the books after reviewing them, or was reviewing simply "the beauty part"?

13. Albrecht, "The English Review."

14. Thomson's own vigor had evidently been brought to the venturing point by *A Tour in En-*

Fig. 5. Charles James Fox (1749–1806), a constant opponent of Pitt on India policy, on the commercial treaties, and on the French Revolution. Portrait by Sir Joshua Reynolds. (Thiers, *History of the French Revolution*, 1:506; SB)

Fig. 6. William Pitt (1759–1806), prime minister from 1783 to 1801. Portrait by Gainsborough. (Thiers, *History of the French Revolution*, 1:237; SB)

to the promises of its initial "Advertisement," to devote itself to politics and history in the "Spirit of the Constitution," with a "view to instruct, to please, and to reform" and a hope that it would not be without "its use as a literary composition."[15] I take Stuart to be the author of the opening essay, a "Critique of the Administration of Mr. Pitt," ultimately running to six installments, but in its first paragraph introducing the importance of viewing "present events" in the light of history—introducing, in effect, a series of Oswaldian essays on "The Present Times." Starting directly after the "Critique," these ran ultimately to eleven installments, summarized after the ninth in a broad survey of "The Present State of Civil Liberty in the World, offered to the particular Consideration of the Subjects of Great Britain" (again immediately following a chapter of the "Critique of the Administration").

Stuart's identifiable contributions over the pseudonym "Lucius"—and some of the reviews that seem to be his—do at times attack rival historians fiercely or attack his bête noire of the cabinet, Dundas, but no more intensely than God-

---

gland and Scotland, in 1785, "By an English Gentleman," which he had recently completed (and which he turned into an illustrated volume in 1788, "printed for" the Robinsons). (He seems to have had no companion on the trip.)

15. *Herald*, 1:3–4. I shan't give page numbers for all items cited, since each of the three volumes of the *Herald* is thoroughly indexed.

win (as "Mucius") attacks Grenville, the joint paymaster, as "the poorest tool of tyranny" who can expect, like a poisoner or an assassin, to be "hung upon a gallows" (1:175–82). And Stuart's grievance against historians such as Robertson, who were given royal honors while he was not, is aired rather quietly in the leading book review in number 3 (1:175–82; 213).[16] In short, Stuart was kept on a firm leash, and the *Herald* did not suffer—but before the end of volume 2 (i.e., in the summer of 1786), he grew so ill of jaundice and the dropsy that Thomson, turning editorial responsibility over to Godwin, accompanied his friend home to Dundee, where Stuart died in early August.

Stuart's last "Lucius" contribution appeared in April; Godwin began to work for the *Herald* in a caretaker capacity in July; and Thomson seems to have let him and Oswald continue through volume 3 (August 1786 to January 1787)—but not to have let them work together. Though Thomson returned to London, he seems to have been ill himself, only advising Godwin how to manage. And during this stage the ghost of Stuart haunted the *Herald* as Stuart during his lifetime had not. In the November issue (number 16) the editors (whoever they were) deplored a public attempt by the earl of Buchan to malign Stuart as "a person that has 'miscarried.'" They should have liked to "have his memory embalmed in the Political Herald," but it was to be understood that he was a great historian who had, happily, "condescended to write in the Political Herald" and that the editors would never, without this provocation, have broken their silence (3:281).

A curious side effect of this public disclosure was an effort by the silent partner Oswald to salvage his own potential reputation from the attribution of any Stuartian essays to himself. On the last page of the October issue, which may have been in the press before Buchan's speech (reported in the papers of 9 October) but not before gossip about Stuart (who died 13 August) had begun to spread, the printer of the *Herald* (George Robinson) announced that "Certain essays in this pamphlet having been erroneously ascribed to the author of *The Present Times*, at the desire of that gentleman, we give the following list of the papers for which we have been indebted to his pen"—a list running from numbers 2 to 14—with a concluding observation that this author would now assume "the title of IGNOTUS" (3:240).

Oddly, the opening essay of number 16, for November, had a variant title implying perhaps a new series: "Of the *Character* of the Present Age"—and

---

16. In no. 6 a review of Erskine on Scottish law is hostile but not nasty; yet in the same number Stuart's Pitt series concludes with a blast at historians for damaging the reputation of one Thomas Powys, whose service in the cause of truth only earned him the label of "a spy!" This defamation is called the "quintessence and the sublimate" of all examples of ill humour and malignity, but the historians guilty are not named (2:414). A footnote in no. 4 sounds like Stuart praising his fellow historian Oswald—or perhaps Thomson; it is attached to the Ignotus essay on the "Character and Reign of William III. King of England" and gives bad marks to the competition: "The intelligent reader will perceive, that in this paper there are several particulars which have not yet found the[ir] way into the histories of England" (1:241).

lacked the *Ignotus* signature. This oversight disturbed the "gentleman" (or gentlemen) concerned. Either Oswald or Thomson complained to the printer, and Thomson wrote to the acting editor, Godwin, asking him to "assign to the signature of *Ignotus* the Character of the present Age & one or two more Essays from w^h the printer told me you had expunged it."[17] The two subsequent Ignotus essays, "On Public OEconomy" in November and "Observations [on] the commercial treaty between France and England" in December, were both already in the printer's hands, and *were* given the Ignotus signature. In a further note Thomson, realizing that every piece that went from his hands to the printer should not be attributed to that mysterious editorial entity, the Unknown, added: "What I write in the form of Letters [i.e., 'to the Printer'], I think, would not be right to mention as belonging to *Ignotus*."

Jack Marken deduces that Thomson is hereby confessing his own identity as Ignotus. My own first reaction to the printer's letter was to deduce that "Ignotus," the Unknown, hereby assigns all the listed essays to one person, John Oswald. But neither deduction will stand. Both Oswald and the Brain-Sucker are concerned to disguise their editorial collaboration as the writings of, one might suppose, another "Junius." And the more familiar I have become with both of these gentlemen and the unquestionably authentic writings of the later Oswald, the more confident I am that these essays, which were the mainstay of the speculations of the *Herald* and had been handed unsigned by Thomson to the printer, must represent a ghostly collaboration the ingredients of which defy sorting out. When "Ignotus" is reporting the sentiments of the Comorro Islanders, the voice is Oswald's. But when "Ignotus" writes with contempt of those Pythagoreans who insist on a vegetable diet, the voice is clearly not his. Most of the time, presumably, the two halves of this gentleman were in harmonious agreement. In the rest of the present discussion it will be advisable to speak of all these *Herald* essays as the "Ignotus" essays. As for the reviews, never signed, and seldom our concern, the question need not arise.

With the accession of Godwin as editor, however, the end was in sight. His own contributions were impressive, and especially to that printer, George Robinson. Four years after the demise of the *Herald*, Robinson was so confident of Godwin's abilities and his standing in the professional world that he funded Godwin's living expenses when he was ready to begin writing his great *Enquiry Concerning Political Justice*.[18] And despite Robinson's Whiggish sympathies, it may be that he was also impressed by Godwin's determined independence of party, a posture which Robinson had become well acquainted with in the last months of the *Herald*. For late in 1786, when attempts had been made to revive the journal under Godwin's own editorship, with "funds set apart for political purposes" by the Foxite Whigs, Fox's ally Sheridan had had "repeated

17. Marken, "William Godwin," 531. (Here Marken mistakenly deduces that "Ignotus" was simply William Thomson.)
18. Ibid., 533.

interviews with Godwin on the subject," but the latter had declined to receive a personal stipend and insisted upon his independence.[19] "Shy and aggressive by turns," Godwin in his later *Herald* days had begun to expand his circle of acquaintances, becoming "a regular member of the literary parties of the publisher George Robinson, where he saw Thomas Warton, the poet, James Heath, the engraver, and James Perry and William Woodfall, the newspaper editors," and others. And we must suppose that Oswald at this time was developing some acquaintances in publishing circles; possibly he and Godwin had met early on. One curious coincidence of dates occurs in the report that in 1790, when Godwin discontinued his writing of the historical section of George Robinson's Whiggish *New Annual Register*, which he had been doing since 1784, a very similar job, that of preparing the historical section of Dodsley's old *Annual Register*, was taken on by William Thomson (with somebody perhaps as ghost)—if we can trust Chambers' *Biographical Dictionary* of 1870 (p. 458). But may it have been that Thomson had trained up in that capacity years earlier, before the burgeoning of his publishing successes? It is curious that the historical sections—on the distant empire, at least—have a similar tone in both the Tory *Annual Register* (Dodsley's) and the Whig *New Annual Register* (Robinson's).

In the final number of the *Political Herald* (published in January 1787) there were no "Ignotus" contributions, but in the penultimate (December) issue there had been a strong "Ignotus" editorial against Pitt's commercial treaty between France and England, which drew a rather foolish response, a "Reply to Ignotus" signed "Marcus." Godwin published this in the final number with the editor's unsigned "Strictures on the Reply of Marcus" (3 : 421–23; 423–31), calling the observations of Marcus "much too frivolous and futile to deserve a very serious answer," yet trying to treat "our kind correspondent with all possible civility and deference." (Did he recognize some notable behind that pseudonym?) For a serious discussion of the merits of the treaty, he proposed to leave Marcus "to the cool and impartial strictures of Ignotus" (425), presumably in the next issue.[20]

Godwin must have known that there would be no fourth volume of the *Herald* in which Ignotus might reply. Yet it is also probable that he knew of Oswald's preparations to publish a separate pamphlet on the commercial treaty, captioned *The Alarming Progress of French Politics* (London, 1787, no copy

19. Another force that brought the *Herald* down was the refusal of Lord Macartney to turn over his papers to Godwin, who had written four long installments of the "Memoirs of the administration of the government of Madras, during the presidency of lord Macartney," the third and fourth filling forty pages in the last two numbers (3 : 321–45; 401–15). See Marken, "William Godwin," 532–35; Marshall, *William Godwin*, 29, 71–72.

20. Marken ("William Godwin," 532, n. 17) guesses curiously when he assigns *both* the "Marcus" letter and the "Strictures" on it to Thomson. According to Marken's earlier identification of "Ignotus" as Thomson, this would mean that Thomson first wrote the "Marcus" letter and then wrote the reply which advises him to wait for a cooler reply from "Ignotus"!

located: possibly a reprint or extension of the Ignotus essay). Whether or not Godwin knew by this time that the persisting voice in "Ignotus" was John Oswald, it is pleasant to find him expressing such confidence in his cool strictures even in the last issue of the magazine.

Can Godwin or Thomson have been in some way involved in the phoenix rebirth of the *Political Herald* as the fortnightly *British Mercury*, a herald, with wings, financed by another Whiggish publisher, James Ridgway, with John Oswald as sole contributor and editor? Preparations must have begun well before the actual demise of the *Herald*, since the new political and literary magazine was actually published in May 1787. And I suspect that Oswald's active campaigning for a new podium, as the *Herald* was collapsing, involved careful calculation combined with rapid movement, and that years later, when Thomson was watching Napoleon move from defeat in Egypt to triumph in Paris, he was reminded of the ambition and swift marches of his Unknown soldier of Grub-Street.

Although the *British Mercury* survived for less than two months, its four fortnightly issues constitute a great liberation of the spirit for Oswald and, actually, a lasting monument to his wit, breadth of vision, and satiric range. It was a brief but successful attempt to keep, in the Byronic sense, "nine muses on the push," one being the Muse of Caricature, which Ridgway subsidized by engaging both Gillray and Rowlandson to engrave grandly sensational illuminations—an investment that paid off through sales of a second edition of these four issues of the *Mercury* a year later.[21]

It was also a step forward in Oswald's march into the center of what would become revolutionary politics. One feature which had been announced for the *Herald* was actually realized in the *Mercury*: the reporting of parliamentary debates. It was probably at about this time—though I have found no certain evidence before 1789—that Oswald became a regular parliamentary reporter for the daily London *Gazetteer*. No doubt even in the *Herald* years he had engaged in some informal gallery listening. Ignotus, commenting on Pitt's style of delivery for instance, writes as one who has seen and heard Pitt and others on their feet in the House of Commons. And several of these reports sound quite firsthand: "Lord Sydney rose up, but instantly sat down again. Lord Carmarthen stuck fast to his bench" (*Herald*, 1:194n).

But before leaving those early London years, we must investigate the political-intellectual milieu by retracing the ground "surveyed" by Ignotus in 1786: "the extended scene of human transactions and events, . . . the variations which he has been able to remark, that are of any considerable importance in that scene, accompanied with such reflections as these variations naturally excite in the breast of a man, and a subject and native of Great Britain" (2:270).

---

21. It is reasonable to conjecture that Ridgway invested in Oswald's project in the expectation or hope of support from Sheridan and Fox, which in the event was not forthcoming.

"Hopes of an Approaching Revolution"

As the years went by after the Americans' war of liberation and the news reaching London confirmed the hope that a free constitutional republic was being formed, it was not uncommon for thoughtful as well as idle speculators to wonder when and where the next resistance to tyranny would spring forth. A frequently explicit theme in the "Ignotus" essays on "The Present Times," as well as an implicit one in the "Considerations on the Rise, the Progress and Decline of Civil Liberty, applied to the present Situation of Great Britain," [22] is the need to understand the social and political and cultural *processes* which could produce, in the many different nations that needed them, revolutions resulting in true popular liberty. The discussion anticipates the ideas about international democratic cooperation which Oswald and Bonneville and Brissot express to listening nations of the world who have heard the fall of the Bastille. Things *could* get more desperate, but we must not stand idly waiting.

> The terraqueous globe [Oswald loves the term] appears to the attentive eye of the political arithmetician, as one mighty prison, in which millions and millions of human souls are confined by their fellow-men . . . from the coasts of China and Japan to where the inmost recesses of the Arabian and Persian gulphs seem to threaten a junction with the Mediterranean sea—all this vast space, half the surface of the known world, is buried under the chilling torpor of despotism. The wandering tribes of Arabs and Tartars [Oswald has lived among them] enjoy, in anarchy, a turbulent semblance of freedom. But . . . the boisterous and precarious independence of a few Arabian and Tartarian chiefs [does not] secure to themselves, or confer on their followers, the blessings of regular freedom. . . . True liberty, though of an undaunted mien, wears a mild and gracious aspect.

That whole area is a "mansion of slavery," even on its western boundary: Persia, Greece, the Mediterranean. "Italy itself, abandoned by the republican vigour of Rome, is now enslaved by priests, and . . . foreign powers. Spain with Portugal . . . ; and France . . . has not only banished freedom from her own coasts, but seeks still, and with too much success, to extend her sway . . . . Liberty has been banished from Denmark and Poland, as well as from Sweden; and the Russians are not yet in a capacity to receive it." Africa has no "African freedom" though there is "European" freedom in the Cape.

"What then are the abodes of liberty in the old world? There are a few free states . . . Venice, Genoa, Lucca . . . a few free towns in Germany . . . in Holland. . . . But it is chiefly in the British isles that the genius of liberty still lingers"; yet "despotism and slavery have traveled from east to west" and seem likely to reach Great Britain and Ireland. What might the future hold?

22. *Herald*, 2:395–402, 3:166–77, with varying title.

Were a war to arise in Europe, in which the subjects of free governments were to be arranged on the one side, and those of arbitrary power on the other, how unequal, in respect of numbers, were the contest! What commotions, and insurrections and revolts, the standard of liberty erected in the British isles, or the mountains of Switzerland, or the shores of the Baltic, or the marshes of Holland, would create . . . in the event of such a war between freedom and slavery . . . it is difficult to conjecture . . . . (2:396–401)

The "Present Times" essays concentrate on the ten most important nations to consider, focusing sometimes on the geopolitical conditions, sometimes on the spirit and acts of tyrants, sometimes on the auspicious spread of science and the arts, sometimes on enlightened rulers, such as the Russian Czarina, "the Argonaut of modern times," improving trade and inviting freedom—or such as the "Spanish American of great consequence" who is visiting London and must not be named but who possesses "the confidence of his fellow-citizens" and "aspires to the glory of being the deliverer of his country" (1:29). Again and again Ignotus stresses the importance of the printing press, of deeply humane literary culture, citing Milton, Tasso, the classics—which Rome preserved, along with republican forms. The Jews, he considers, denied themselves the culture of Rome by resisting the empire and remaining slaves of religion: in his travels among the Arabs, Oswald had formed the belief that the Jews were "a little tribe of Arabs" whose "direful superstition" had been adopted by the Christians as a "SUN-DAY" of fear-inspired worship of a divine demon of tyranny.[23]

That anonymous Spanish-American deliverer is described as having the right intellectual qualifications, being "a man of sublime views and penetrating understanding, skilled in the antient and modern languages, conversant in books, and acquainted with the world." [24] It is striking how exactly this charac-

---

23. *British Mercury*, 131–32. George III, in proclaiming a Sunday of total abstinence from happiness (see below), was trying to perpetuate a superstition that had originated "amidst the barren rocks of Arabia." Ignotus in the *Herald* (1:201) had expressed the same Enlightenment view of superstition (the Jews "are not in a state of improvement") while reminding readers that the world, that civilization, owed the Jews much: The "sacred historical records . . . the just and merciful tenour of the Mosaic laws; the pure and benevolent spirit of christianity, which has . . . contributed greatly to the abolition of slavery . . . and . . . to soften and humanize the world." Nevertheless, at the present day, Oswald would observe in his *Review of the Constitution* (30), both Jews and Christians serve as mere commercial "sponges" for the cruel pashas of Turkey.

24. There is a good probability that this man, actually famous for his efforts to free South-American and Central-American nations from the Spanish crown, became acquainted with Oswald during his London visits. He was Francisco de Miranda, a pioneer of feminism and conspirator of liberation, who managed to become acquainted with, and frequently captivate, "more distinguished figures of his age in both the Old World and the New than any other contemporary. General Washington, the dashing Marquis Lafayette, Haydn the Composer, the enigmatical autocrat Catherine II, William Pitt, Alexander Hamilton, the Domineering General Dumouriez, Napoleon," and, topping the list, "Simon Bolivar, who was destined to become the Liberator of Colombia" (Robertson, *Life of Miranda*, 1:ix). In his personal archives (13:39) Miranda kept a copy of the "Ignotus" paragraph about himself,

Fig. 7. Francisco del Miranda
(1750–1816) of Venezuela,
champion of independence,
precursor of Bolivar, pioneer
feminist. Portrait engraved by
F. Bonneville. (Robertson, *The
Life of Miranda*, 1 : 216; SB.)

terizes John Oswald himself—even to the requisite anonymity (Ignotus). It will
be recalled that what William Thomson took as clinching evidence that his former colleague had emerged as Napoleon was their common literary interest—
in Ossian.

That Britain itself needs to be liberated is more or less the obvious message of
essays in the *Herald* that dwell upon the failures of policy and of action, the
incompetence and infantile behavior of Pitt and of his henchman, that bane of
the Scottish, Henry Dundas, and of their whole cabinet. Ignotus can, in desperation, even toy with the possible emergence of some political intelligence in the

and during the time of Oswald's involvement in the British Club in Paris one of Miranda's busiest
correspondents would be Thomas Christie, a man in search of *lumières* who would refer to Oswald
as a mutual acquaintance. Always the object of Miranda's travels was "rather to converse with Men
[and Women] than to see Countries," as Dr. Andrew Turnbull observed in a letter introducing him
to Dr. Priestley. Visiting Zurich in 1788, Miranda looked up Lavater, the physiognomist, who had
just published his *Aphorisms on Man*. Then visiting in France until June 1789—too busy talking
to sense the approach of revolution—he moved to settle in London, in the house of Joel Barlow, not
transferring himself and his attention to Paris until March 1792 (Robertson, *Life of Miranda*,
1 : 36, 86–88, 120). Important reformers whom Miranda called upon or intended to seek out in
the summer of 1785 in London included Brand Hollis, John Jebb, James Adair, Dr. Priestley, Benjamin Vaughan, and W. S. Smith (*Archivo*, 5 : 280–83).

profligate Prince. An essay on "The Difficulty of judging of Characters: An Idea of the Prince of Wales" is followed immediately by "Thoughts on political Profligacy" (i.e., let's *pretend* that Dundas has some potential for honesty) and an unrelievedly gloomy "Censure . . . of the Present Administration," the moral of which is that the need for competent, constitutional rule is as desperate as the likelihood is dim.[25]

Thinking along these lines, the next prospect to consider was the possibility that Britain might be liberated from abroad. This led Ignotus to present a long "Historical Sketch of the Reign of William III of England" (3 : 241–53), which stresses that what made Britain's revolution of 1688–1689 "Glorious" was William's "invading" with a minimum of military support and depending essentially on the strength of his welcome. (When, in 1792, Oswald as commander of a battalion of Paris Volunteers tried to persuade the Jacobins to descend upon London with military power *in aid of* a rising of the British sansculottes, he seems to have had a similar scenario in mind. Several of the British in Paris in that season would express the hope that they would soon be inviting their French brethren to assist in an English Revolution, or an Irish.)

The *Herald* of 1785–1786, however, conscientiously introduced into the discussion the darker possibilities. Nuclear war had not yet been invented, but natural convulsions—had Oswald already met his later Dilettanti acquaintance, the vulcanologist Lord Hamilton?—were known to have subverted "the arrangements of matter on the surface of this globe, and buried in everlasting oblivion the labours and arts of toiling mortals." And we know of "subterraneous fires" which bespeak "some latent source of devastation" that might "overthrow the monuments of human improvement, and set bounds to the conquests of man over nature." Also, *man* is not always man's best friend. Barbarous force, dominant in many nations, may again prevail over art. The "fury of religious zeal" may defeat "the mild and leisurely influence of persuasion." In his monthly reports, Ignotus examines with impressive insight the "process" of political and economic forces within and between nations, particularly the counterbalances of power, including the positive effects of negative epochs. "If the darkness of the middle ages had not intervened, we should neither have had a Newton, a Galileo, nor a Copernicus. The Turkish empire is now in a state of repose, which precedes the activity and energy of a new day" (1 : 260). "The modern Italians are obedient to one or other of the great northern powers, but have extended literature and refinement over the world" (1 : 264–65). The "bigotry of superstition, armed with the powers of the inquisition . . . prescribed

25. Thomson, to keep the support of the Whig Opposition, doubtless encouraged—perhaps even at times forced—his writers to proceed on the clear assumption that the Pitt administration could do no good and the Prince of Wales (forlorn hope of the Whigs) no evil. At times the *Herald* rose to heights of absurdity in praise of the Prince, probably despite the suppressed grumbling of Oswald if not also of Thomson himself. Godwin's refusal to make any partisan commitment to Sheridan was what tipped over the apple cart.

bounds to natural philosophy" in Spain. "But . . . the ardent and subtle and inventive genius of Spain appears in their moral, political, theological, and poetical writings. There is no nation more capable of profound thinking" (1 : 335). The *Herald*'s favorite is "the famous dramatic poet Lopez de Vega" (336).

As for Britain, "The national debt is a millstone hanging about the neck of Great Britain, which . . . will one day plunge her in the ocean. . . . The first war in which we are involved, will, therefore . . . occasion some change or convulsion that will produce a new face of affairs in this country" (1 : 428). At present, however, "poor John Bull" has "been so often duped" by the administration that he is in "a fit of moping and melancholy: he seems to have lost all his spirit. He is castrated, it would seem, and has become an ox . . . muzzled and led by the nose . . . by the very BOYS"—young Pitt and company (2 : 308).

Yet "unthought of good often accompanies or flows from what are regarded as great misfortunes." The North Americans are having great losses at sea from the Barbary pirates, and warlike attacks from the American Indians. Yet these difficulties are "a common bond of union, without which" the separate provinces, "differing in religion, manners, and customs, would be in danger of crumbling into pieces, and of falling back, each of them separately, under some foreign yoke" (3 : 100–102). And the American inspiration continues to spread. "Already we every where discern the influence of the great revolution across the Atlantic on commerce, on the balance of power [about which Ignotus has a great deal to say], and the genius of nations" (1 : 29).

"This spirit of liberty, this elevation of conception, this enthusiastic exertion of the human faculties, with all the happy fruits with which it is pregnant, springs from the wide diffusion of science, an early and expeditious correspondence among men and nations, by means of navigation, the institution of posts, and, above all, from the art of printing." So, the Herald will not put down his pen. And he sustains the air of the personal, citing the visiting liberator and the "elevation of thought" conveyed by Americans "in their private letters . . . and their private conversation" (1 : 28).

Occasionally he bases his remarks about a distant nation on the observations of "a recent traveller" or "travellers"—did Oswald, perhaps, on his way home from Turkestan, visit the Crimea, and then parts of Italy? Immediately after his first notes on "AMERICA" and "SPANISH AMERICA," Ignotus moves into familiar Oswald territory, his favorite island of Joanna:

AFRICA

The resolutions that have passed in some of the American States against slavery, extend the influence of the late great revolution, in some degree, to the swarthy sons of Africa. . . . Of the Comorra islands which are situated in the channel of Mozambic between Zanguebar and the island of Madagascar, the chief in extent, population, and power, is Joanna, which of course claims a pre-eminence and authority over the rest. The natives of Mayotta, one of these islands, about two years ago refused to pay to their neighbours on the large island, the customary tribute. On being asked the reason of this, they replied, "Mayotta like America."

After eleven installments of essays on "The Present Times," concluding in the September 1786 issue, Ignotus offers a summarizing essay on "The Progress and Decline of Civil Liberty, applied to the Present Situation of Great Britain"—a situation characterized by "The Puerility of Pitt . . . The Mock-Minister" (*Herald* 3 : 118–22, also signed Ignotus). Pitt's ministry misses or subverts every opportunity for lasting harmony among free nations, always letting "his left hand know what his right hand did" (3 : 119).

Here Ignotus could not resist a private jest on a hidden name. A Mr. Richard Oswald had been the British representative at Versailles in the negotiation of the Treaty of 1783 shaping the peace between France and Britain at the end of the American War. With such a representative, Pitt had been able to make the *least* of the opportunities of the occasion—a stance of puerility aptly represented by a blind Oswald:

> The genius of Great Britain was then very fitly and emphatically represented by Mr. Richard Oswald, the commissioner for peace, an old man, with a faded visage, decrepid [*sic*], purblind, and leaning on a staff.[26] This was the real character in which Britannia appeared. She no longer sat, proudly pre-eminent, on a terraqueous globe, waving her sceptre and trident over the subject seas. (3 : 119)

Pitt's infant competence had been characterized more wittily in *Herald* 1 : 432–33 (again by Ignotus):

> It is not a long period of years since the minister, in the state of an embryon, experienced all those quick movements which the microscopic eye discovers in the source and substance of animal life: it is still a shorter period since he lay tossing his legs and arms in his nurse's lap . . . .
>
> Since providence . . . has placed the administration of our public affairs in the hands of this youth . . . it would appear to be of no small service to our country, if we could give his motion a proper direction, and, keeping him in play, as it were, by useful, or at least innocent exercise, prevent those mischiefs which usually accompany or flow from a course of action undirected either by reflection or experience.

Unsatisfied to be making merely negative or ironic suggestions, Ignotus turns to serious (and half-serious) positive advice, hastening "to mention some of those objects which lie within the sphere of the abilities of administration, and to which if they would direct their serious attention, they might do no unimportant services to their country."

They seem to have had some success in a campaign against smuggling. Why not turn now to robberies? "Mr. Dundas would be an excellent thief-catcher!" And the duke of Richmond, whose plans for military fortification the *Herald*

26. On "poor Richard Oswald," see also 3 : 193.

has been viewing with alarm, might go to work improving the public prisons. Then Ignotus proposes quite seriously a project "for improving the metropolis, not only in respect of police, but with regard to convenience, beauty, and salubrity." Much could be done to "the buildings, wharfs, and quays, on either side of the Thames," and something could be done about the narrow, filthy streets "and the air that is engendered by such labyrinths of uncleanness." And why not clean and open to "the sojourner" the "great ornaments of . . . St. Paul's, the Monument, the Bank, the Mansion-house, Westminster-abbey, &c."? The ministers know "how easy a thing it is to create marquisses, earls," etc. Why not "beautify the metropolis" and attract visitors (if we British can possibly adopt "a courtesy of demeanour") the way Rome and Paris do (1:438–41)?

What share of the book-review section of the *Herald* may have been Oswald's seems impossible to deduce, since apparently Stuart and Thomson and Godwin and he generally thought along the same historical and political lines, and there are no signatures, even pseudonymous. Yet occasionally one seems to hear his voice, as in a long review of a *History of Ayder Ali Khan*, which concludes with the pronouncement that British governmental indifference to the fate of the inhabitants of India will soon cause the Ganges to "re-echo the cry of the Thames and the Tweed; and the native of Indostan will join with the descendant of Britain in the common cause of liberty and virtue. The revolt of America is a lesson to kings, and example to the world" (2:139).[27]

Political Bagatelles

The replacement of the *Herald* by *The British Mercury* within a few months —its first issue is dated 12 May 1787—manifestly gave Oswald a tremendous boost of self-confidence, and of hope for the successful exertion of his literary talents. He would begin as usual with "The Present State of the World: or, a Philosophical Inquiry into the Origin and Progress of Commerce, Literature, and Politics, and Their Connection and Influence on Each Other." And he would now be able to serialize his book of travels (starting with "The Natives of Joanna"). But he could also release his merriest impulses (quite restrained in the *Herald*, we realize) with a mock tale of "The Brain Sucker" (Thomson): "Humorous Strictures" on a music festival; a "Humorous Account" of the night life of "Charlemagne and his Twelve Peers"; as well as "many Original Bon Mots, Jeux d'Esprit, &c": vive "La Bagatelle"! (I quote from the contents page of number 1.)[28]

27. Note the implicit axiom that insurrections begin in London (e.g., the riots of 1780) and on the Scottish border. On his return from India, Oswald as an ex-soldier would have been very much aware of the flight from the British army "of almost every man who was intitled to his discharge" (Fortescue, *History of the British Army*, 3:521).

28. He could also, while still unnamed, speak as a unified plural, "the Editors." He was now the whole show.

For some time Oswald had been releasing his "bagatelles" in Thomson's *London Chronicle* as ostensibly unsolicited offerings. His first identifiable contribution is a "Letter to the Printer" signed "H.K." and dated "Ramsgate, April 6,"[29] in the *Chronicle* for 20–22 April 1786, followed by a reply signed "Vindex" and dated 23 May in the paper for 27–30 May, just conceivably written by Oswald also: the first was written with tongue in cheek, the second perhaps with finger beside nose; yet perhaps not. (The discussion concerns the new Sunday School movement, which H. K. sees as threatening to impose "the joyless listlessness of Sunday" even upon children.)[30]

Attention is called to this April "Letter" in a forty-eight-page pamphlet well known as Oswald's, which is introduced by what purports to have been another letter to the printer of the *Chronicle* signed "H.K. Ramsgate, 30th June." The full title of the pamphlet is *Ranae Comicae Evangelizantes: or, The Comic Frogs turned Methodist*, and it cannot have been written before August, the earlier date being part of its hoaxing plot. The publisher is a London bookseller, E. Macklew, No. 9, Haymarket.[31] The "Advertisement" quoting H. K.'s foreword claims that the manuscript was picked up by chance "in the Park of St. James" in London and offers it to the *Chronicle*, which has published his previous "trifles." The connection is tightly made by a correction satirically offered of a Latin misprint in the April letter. In this foreword, H. K. thanks "the Editor of the *London Chronicle*" for his "ready insertion of my last Trifle; which was very correct, except that an error of the press had substituted for '*Divus Pater subigus*[']', an unknown God of the name of [']*Lubigus.*'" He now requests "a corner in your Paper" for the "inclosed *Bagatelle*."

"Lubigus" it is, in the letter dated 6 April. And even the pretended misprint is vintage Oswald: to replace *subigus* (god of the wedding night) with *Lubigus* was to invent a new deity—of sensual desire.

The theme of that April letter "To the Printer" is the sad descent from the "beautiful mythology of the Ancients," whose religious spectacles were presided over by "the Paphian Goddess, with Comus, Priapus, and Divus Pater Lubigus" and served "the cause of festivity and cheerfulness, mother of benevolence and of every social virtue"—to a joyless Sunday that has become "a foe to festivity and gladness, to merriment and song" and whose "sackcloth and ashes" are now, by the "novel institution of Sunday Schools," threatening even

---

29. The false initials suggest that "Ramsgate" may be a false address, too. It often appeared in datelines indicating fresh news from across the Channel. Having married in Folkestone, he and Bathsheba and the three children may have settled there, but trips to Grub-Street would be easier from Ramsgate. There are, however, no clear allusions in Oswald's writings, poetry or prose, to his residential or domestic arrangements.

30. For still more on these recurrent themes, see *British Mercury*, 129–33.

31. A scurrilous political pamphlet of 1801, *A Letter to the Rt. Hon. Spencer Perceval*, chortles at the jailing of Gilbert Wakefield for his *Reply to the Bishop of Llandaff*, and asserts that Wakefield is also the author of what it calls *Ranae Canorae*, a thing so contemptible that it "did not pay McClough the printer's bill" (giving Macklew's name a Scottish spelling to imply motives of greed). See *Notes & Queries*, 2d ser., 12 (21 December 1861): 503.

our children. The whole essay clearly summarizes the Oswaldian philosophy—a credo of romanticism whose social principle is the direction of "even the most fantastic flights of genius . . . toward the public good."

Organs of Generation

How truly fantastic, as well as wise and witty, were the flights of Oswald's genius under the inspiration of Lubigus (or Priapus, indeed) will appear as we examine both *The Comic Frogs* and some of the contents of the new *British Mercury*—published not by the Robinsons but by another Whig printer, James Ridgway.[32] Oswald's spare-time scholarly pursuits, we shall find, have not only sharpened the detail in his observation of the "Manners, Religion, Philosophy, &c" of the lands he had visited but have also pollinated his wit, so to speak, with the strange researches of two British investigators into the ancient *and contemporary* worship of Priapus, ripening it into the sort of intellectual satire that can remind us of Rabelais, Swift, Samuel Butler—or Oswald's contemporary, the William Blake who wrote of England as "An Island in the Moon" (in 1784 or 1785).

By these comparisons I mean to suggest a certain spirit of critical laughter at one's own "imaginations," like that of Blake's three philosophers: wry visions that burst from minds potentially prophetic and revolutionary but under-nourished in a period of social disillusionment and pragmatism. The researches I refer to were those of Sir William Hamilton and Richard Payne Knight, two members of a serious philosophical group calling themselves the Society of Dilettanti, who set Grub-Street agog long before the actual printing of their book, *An Account of the Remains of the Worship of Priapus, lately existing at Isernia, in the Kingdom of Naples* (in letters from and to Sir William) to which is added, *A Discourse on the Worship of Priapus, and its Connexion with the mystic Theology of the Ancients*, by R. P. Knight, Esq. (London, Printed by T. Spilsbury, Snowhill, 1786).[33]

It is a plausible conjecture that these two names suggested the initials "H.K." which Oswald signed to his somewhat Priapic parodies of the same year. *The Worship of Priapus* was not ready for its distribution (and then only to members of the Society of Dilettanti and about eighty friends) until March 1787,[34]

32. George Robinson had been willing to continue the *Herald* at his own expense, but not to pay the editorial salary which Godwin had refused to accept from the Whigs.

33. Until the publication in 1982 of *The Arrogant Connoisseur: Richard Payne Knight 1751–1824*, ed. Michael Clarke and Nicholas Penny, the state of Knight biography and bibliography has been meager and flawed, despite his considerable writings on taste, on the Greek alphabet, and on the symbolical language of ancient art; his poetry; and his valuable collection bequeathed to the British Museum (but consigned to a dark room, according to H. W. Ashbee, *Index Librorum prohibitorum* [1962], 1 : 8—a seriously inaccurate work itself). I draw thankfully, and heavily, on Clarke and Penny for their information about Knight and his circle.

34. The book (contrary to a legend of its suppression) was never offered for sale to the public,

but its printing had been authorized by vote of the society in 1784, and rumors of Hamilton's sensational discoveries had reached England as early as 1781, when Sir William wrote from Naples to confirm the report that he had "actually discovered the cult of Priapus in full vigour" in Isernia. An engineer working on a new road near the village church had told Sir William of a feast in honor of Saints Cosmus and Damianus during which waxen ex-voti representing "the male organs of generation, of various dimensions, some even the length of a palm" were "publickly offered for sale" and then taken to the church "chiefly by the female sex," who kissed them as they placed them in a bowl in the vestibule, offering such dedications as "St Cosimo, I thank you," "Blessed St Cosimo let it be like this." Visiting Isernia, Hamilton had been able to salvage some of the "Great Toes," as the local inhabitants called them, and it was on his return to London in 1784 to deposit them in the British Museum that he quickly obtained the society's imprimatur.[35] A shocking feature of the book was Hamilton's argument that still alive within the Catholic Church was the practice of pagan worship of phallic and vaginal fetishes. As well as the ex-voti representing the male parts, there were others representing the "shell, or concha veneris . . . the female part"; together they constituted "a fresh proof of the similitude of the Popish and Pagan Religion."

As a psychological historian, Knight argued that a central component of ancient and modern religions was sexual "play"; the illustrations included "Phallic Figures Found in England," an "Indian Temple Showing the Lingam," and numerous other sexual fetishes. The parodistic phallic signposts in Gillray's print for Oswald's *British Mercury* were perhaps designed only after the Hamilton-Knight volume appeared, though the "Big Toes" on deposit in the British Museum, while apparently not on public display—Hamilton's instructions to staff had not been to keep them out of sight, however, only to "keep hands off"—must have been as accessible to Oswald as the unique Charlemagne manuscript he also parodies in the *Mercury*.

During his travels in India and Asia Minor, Oswald's interest in the curious rituals and religions of pagan lands evidently went well beyond the duck wor-

---

but Oswald must have had easy access to it (Thomson was a fellow of the Antiquarians) and, earlier, to the collections in the town houses of Knight and the collector Charles Townley, in whose London home D'Hancarville (P. F. Hugues) assembled the material for *Récherches sur l'Origine des Arts de la Grèce* (1785). Oswald had access to rare manuscripts in the British Museum, such as the unique *Pèlèrinage de Charlemagne* (shelf-mark: Royal 16.E.viii; missing for the last one hundred years), from which he spun a bagatelle for his *Mercury*, a "Humourous account of the Reception" of the emperor.

35. The first published account of these matters was the "Baron" d'Hancarville's *Récherches*, with a theme that sounds like Blake's "All Religions are One": "In this extraordinary book d'Hancarville attempted to describe an ancient and universal theological system from which all subsequent religions had derived, and which was revealed by the symbols . . . in ancient remains . . . and also in the remains of eastern nations" (Peter Funnell, in *The Arrogant Connoisseur*, ed. Clarke and Penny, 52). Knight, in his *Discourse*, reiterated this account of the ancient theology, discovering the same symbols. The evidence of cultic practices as well as fetishes seemed to establish that the ancient theology was of an intensely sexual character, expressive of ideas of generation and creation.

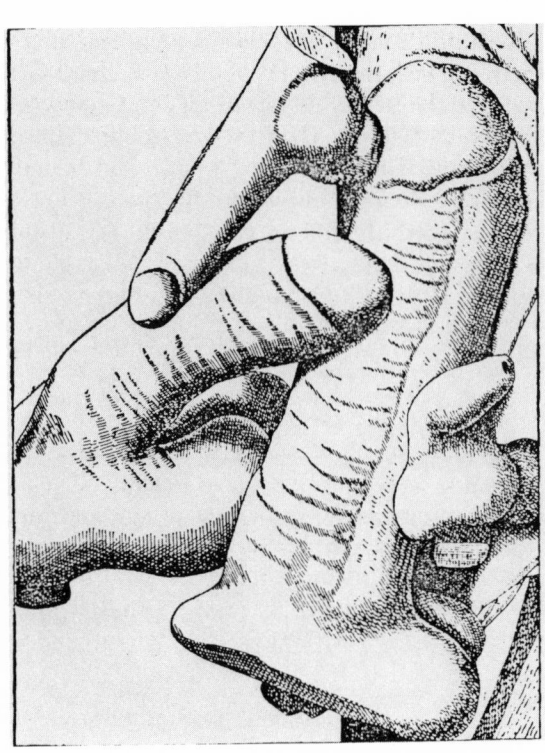

Fig. 8. Ex voti of wax, from
Isernia, the fetishes known as
"Great Toes." Plate i in the
Knight-Hamilton *Worship of
Priapus*, 1787. (SB)

ship of Joanna.[36] In his *Ranae Comicae* he goes beyond Hamilton and Knight
by demonstrating, in verbal parody, that the enthusiasm of Methodism in Great
Britain is still that old worship of the penis. If Bonneville could drive the Jesuits
out of Masonry (see below), Oswald might advance the cause of the religion of
humanity by persuading the Sunday scholars that all deities reside in the human appetite.

The *Ranae* begins with a Hudibrastic imitation of a chorus from Aristopha-
nes' *Frogs*—clumsy enough to be almost mock-Hudibrastic: Byron would have
enjoyed it—and proceeds as an insane and topical exercise in Methodist ser-
monizing. This satire is offered as "an innovation in *English* prose-writing,
which will, no doubt, mightily offend," says H. K.—and then he adds: "those
who have no ears."[37]

36. A propos, a later attack on Knight's *Discourse*, in the *British Critic* in October 1794, was
inspired by the published *Narrative* of another British army officer returned from India, Lt. Edward
Moor, who told of the "monstrous delineations" and "heating exhibitions" he had seen on the
walls of Hindu temples, and who included a fairly undistorted paraphrase of Knight.

37. For a more explicit account of these mysteries, see Oswald's essay "Of the Serpent that
Tempted Eve" (*British Mercury* for 23 June 1787). The serpent was the devil who tempted Eve—
but which devil was he? Not Vanity or Lucre, who tempt women in "this degenerate age," but Baal

Oswald's ranting preacher is identified as a cobbler, a literary allusion to Jerry Tugwell, the village cobbler of Richard Graves's novel *The Spiritual Quixote, or, the Summer's Ramble of Mr. Geoffry Wildgoose* (1772). Tugwell is the Sancho to Graves's Quixote Wildgoose, who preaches satiric Methodist sermons à la Whitefield. But Oswald calls his cobbler Dr. Strap, a name from Smollett's *Roderick Random* (1748).

The Pagan-Christian sexual "enthusiasm" of both the damned and the elect is presented in a series of crescendo tours de force—essays in what has been called the caricatural sublime[38]—but here a small sample must suffice:

> And O! my Brethren, the terrible Day of Judgment! How shall I with becoming *bathos*, describe the terrible Day of Judgment? Even now, methinks I see, with swoln cheeks and starting eyes, the seventh Angel incircle, with mouth immense, a mighty trumpet. And hark! the thundering clang I hear, which calls from yawning graves the drowsy dead. Roused by the dreadful din they start upon their breech. Their hollow sightless sockets they rub with knuckles bare. Bones rattle, mort heads clash, clattering skeletons jostle and jar; and for their members, every where half-formed figures fumble.[39] Here and there a litigated limb sets muttering mummies by the ears. But ready Angels rush the ghastly grinning combatants between, and restoring unerringly to the rightful owner every *bone of contention*, settle, celestial Mediators! the mortal fray. And see! in pristine bloom and vigour, by the help of those adjusting Angels, appear the reanimated dead, perfect in all their precious limbs and organs, and, without the least misprision of sex or individual, properly fitted and hung; whatever of their bodies the various *transmogrifications* might have been, devoured by the devil-fish, swallowed by the shark, or assimilated in shape of turtle, by gormandizing Alderman; whether they had fed the ravens of the field, fattened the parish parson's churchyard pigs, or cramm'd into a *sausage*, tickled the sickly maw of man-eating Patagonian. The reviving dead scarce credit th'amazing change. . . .

When Oswald published the *Ranae Comicae* as a forty-two-page booklet in the autumn of 1786 he was being bold, but not too bold. Any illustrations he may have thought of were put off a year, phallic engravings by Rowlandson and Gillray published in the safer context of the *British Mercury*. And the shock of his subject matter was pushed aside by the sensational claim that the manuscript of this "abominable rhapsody" had been picked up "some time ago in the Park of St. James," i.e., some time before 30 June, the date of the foreword, and that it consisted of papers left near the King's Palace by the insane Margaret Nicholson, who tried to stab the King on 2 August. Oswald was also launching his pamphlet on the tide of public sensation in offering a clue to the sort of crypto-sexual enthusiasm that inspired the mad woman's approach to

---

Peor, i.e., Lord Peor = Penis = Priapus. When "lady Betty" objects that nobody could be tempted by a "feeble, nerveless, and flaccid . . . serpent," it is explained that Priapus was "rigid and erect." (The Bible is a bit vague about this, but no doubt Oswald knew his Milton: when tempting Eve the serpent was "not . . . Prone on the ground, as since," but "erect" [*Paradise Lost* 9.496–501].)

38. *The Arrogant Connoisseur*, ed. Clarke and Penny, 62.
39. A footnote here quotes Dryden's *Don Sebastian*.

King George, a benign expectation of joyous consequences whether she wound up in heaven or in hell. Does it also reveal in the actual author of these papers a potentially regicidal interest in the royal vulnerability? We should say, rather, that he was enjoying an occasion to participate in the George-baiting that was a pastime of the period and finding an ingenious way to give it benevolent direction.[40]

The episode is recorded by Fanny Burney as told to her by the King himself. The attempt to stab him was made as he was alighting from his horse at St. James's Palace for his levee or public reception:

> While the guards and his own people now surrounded the King, the assassin was seized by the populace . . . when the King, the only calm and moderate person then present, called aloud to the mob, "The poor creature is mad! Do not hurt her! She has not hurt me!"
>
> Then he came forward, and showed himself to all the people, declaring he was perfectly safe and unhurt; and then gave positive orders that the woman should be taken care of, and went into the palace, and had his levee.[41]

On the 9th she was taken to Bethlehem Hospital for the insane (Bedlam) "where she was chained to the floor of her cell, and there she remained until she died" (in 1828).[42] Naturally, for weeks afterward, people of all ranks flocked to pay their respects to the King. It was a typical Oswaldian gesture to attribute his saucy burlesque to the mad Margaret.

The "Commerce" of John Bull

Oswald's next known publication, *The Alarming Progress of French Politics: A Pamphlet on the Commercial Treaty* (London, 1787), which has not been located, was probably a reprint or a rewriting of the "Observations" of Ignotus in the *Political Herald*, perhaps including his scornful "Hints to Mr. Eden and to his Superiors" (*Herald*, 3 : 321 – 29 and 188 – 94). The drift of his arguments against a "peaceful" treaty with a hostile French court, whose aim was to make Britain ignore France's military adventures in India and the Netherlands, underlies the extravagant sarcasm of his comic opera of the same year, *The Humours of John Bull: an Operatical Farce, in Two Acts*,[43] a politically focused

40. In the *Political Herald*, 3 : 196–98 (Autumn 1786), the "attempt against his majesty" by "Mad Margaret Nicholson . . . if indeed she made any attempt" was treated by Ignotus as an insipid media event "in these dead times" when the gazettes "contain nothing but the creation of peers and the lists of preferment to civil and ecclesiastical offices." At least "the madness of Magg. Nicholson has made a knight of alderman Hammet."

41. Frances Burney's Diary, quoted in Brooke, 1 : 314.

42. A. Aspinall, ed., *The Later Correspondence of George III*, 1 : 240n.

43. The *Pamphlet* is mentioned in later Oswald title pages; it is listed *after* the *British Mercury* in Marshall's *Catalogue* of 1788. *The Humours* was apparently published separately, by John

satire the butt of which is the treaty negotiated by Pitt and William Eden at Versailles in September 1786 and defended by them in Parliament in the spring of 1787. The ridiculed and almost fatal "humour" (leading propensity) of John Bull impels him to contract marriage (commercial intercourse) with a French wife whose gourmandise could be as fatal for him as Eve's was for Adam. (The perspective is that of the present degenerate era.) But this now-rather-forgotten season of French-British relations, when the young Pitt was rushing into what even Ignotus conceded to be "a fair and reasonable" treaty, *except* for its international implications, needs a bit of exploration before we buy tickets to Oswald's "Farce."

The *Herald*'s commercial argument (in 1786) is that "England will be a better customer to France, than France will be to England," since the wealth of France "centers in a few hands" while "that of Great Britain is dispersed among many" (3 : 322–23). A more crucial consideration is that cross-Channel commerce, while it "increases our manufactures, diminishes our navigation." The British are doing nothing to sustain their navy, and nothing in the treaty is to prevent the French from becoming "the carriers of English goods to all the nations with which they are in alliance" (325). "The military spirit may die away. We may become, in process of time, a mere race of manufacturers and shopkeepers." (Getting and spending, as Wordsworth would say when he saw the need for a revival of British military spirit to resist Napoleon.) It is the power balance that "Ignotus" sees drastically upset. Month by month he has been analyzing the policy movement of the courts of Versailles and Madrid, the "prosperous house of Bourbon," neighbors who "regard peace as the means, and war as the end" (326–27). "The military genius is kept alive in France by the very spirit and constitution of their government." Opportunities continually arise for armed adventure. "It is extremely probable . . . that the arms of France will be employed in settling a new order of affairs in the United Provinces" of Holland (328). And the power of France in India, with a fleet "equal to ours," can easily take over "the southern parts of Indostan" (329). They are now "busily employed in fortifying Pondicherry" as a grand military depot, and "It will be their object to foment jealousies and heart-burnings among the native princes of India against the English," especially after the atrocious rule of our East India Company, which Burke is now exposing. "The military and high spirit of Great Britain once exchanged for that of a mere love of gain, what would the most favourable treaty of commerce avail?" (193). A related theme in the *Herald* has been the folly of Pitt's men in neglecting shipping while scheming to build great fortifications to protect the British coast. The *Herald*'s views are firmly on the side of the parliamentary opposition, led by Charles Fox.

Murray, before being combined with the *Poems* of 1789, as the makeup of that volume indicates; but no separate copy has been located.

Lord John Russell, of a later Whig generation, summarizing the situation in his edition of Fox's papers, ignores the power relations and fails to see a connection between commercial rivalry and war:

> While the financial measure of Mr. Pitt created for him a just popularity with the mercantile classes, a treaty with France, based on sound commercial principles, made him odious to the manufacturers. Mr. Fox unwisely and inconsiderately joined in the ignorant, but popular, clamour, and even countenanced the barbarous and hateful doctrine that the French were our natural enemies.
>
> The treaty took effect; its provisions were very beneficial to both countries; the French improved their hardwares and their pottery; the English their silks and ribbons; but the war soon put an end to this beneficial intercourse.[44]

To the *Herald*, war had seemed a predictable sequel.

John Ehrman, who has made exhaustive studies of the commercial negotiations, also ignores the power struggles among European nations and dismisses the Foxite opposition as chiefly political, the point being that only economic arguments were valid, and Pitt had the support of leading merchants and most manufacturers. "The original objectors were mainly smaller men . . . rather slow to organise." At first "Pitt and Eden were flooded with congratulations, manufacturers passed laudatory resolutions, Consols [the government stocks] rose, Opposition newspapers found little to say." By the end of 1786, however, pamphlets siding with the smaller men were appearing, and in February 1787 they defeated the larger northern and midland industrialists in the General Chamber of Manufacturers, which fell apart and "virtually ceased to exist for the next seven to eight years."[45] Oswald's, clearly, were among those powerful pamphlets.[46]

Indeed, Oswald's *Alarming Progress of French Politics* did belong to this stage of the campaign. And the timing of his new *British Mercury*, begun in May and employing this new line of attack, suggests that with Ridgway as the publisher there may have been some financial support from the Foxite Whig organization. At least Oswald and/or his backers had thought up a fresh basis for resistance to French "customs" (the pun is frequent).

44. *Memorials and Correspondence of Fox*, 2:259–70 (in 1839).
45. Ehrman, *The Younger Pitt*, 1:491ff.
46. Ehrman does not entertain the thought—what a pity he did not read the *Political Herald*, or Oswald's work—that pamphlets might contain wise, statesmanlike arguments; he describes Fox and his colleagues, as the debate wore on, as simply "falling back on" such arguments as "the general danger of a closer connexion with France." In short, Ehrman holds to the view of Lord Russell, cited above. The "Ignotus" essay, going into past and recent history, makes a strong case for suspecting the ambitions of the neighboring monarchy. "In the midst of the profoundest peace, France still foresees and prepares for some conjuncture, in which she may avail herself of her military skill and valour. In peace she sows the seeds of division; in war she seeks to reap the horrid harvest." The "idea of uniting the two greatest, and most cultivated and humane nations on earth, in the bonds of peace" is "liberal, pleasing and gracious," but it behoves the British "to be greatly on our guard" (*Herald*, 3:328). In a few years, when the neighboring monarchy was turning into a republic, this pleasing idea would seem feasible, at one turn or another, to both Fox and Oswald, in rather different scenarios.

The comic *Humours of John Bull*, apparently a few months earlier, is closer to the original question. British farming, Fox had said in the debate of 1785, would be ruined by a treaty based on the mistaken presumption that "the French character would not admit of equal industry as the English." French farmers would match the English if the markets were open. The British Lion would lose its naval power if trade could be carried on simply across the Channel. France "was the inveterate and unalterable enemy of Great Britain." (When the Bastille was toppled, a few years later, both Charles Fox and John Oswald would insist that the enemy had been the Grand Monarque, not the French people.)

Such "intercourse" (there was the word!) "must be extremely hurtful to the superior national character of England. . . . The nearer the two nations were drawn into contact . . . in the same proportion the remaining morals, principles, and vigour of the English national mind, would be enervated and corrupted."

Oswald, reversing these arguments in 1789, would remember the English smaller men's hostility to the Monarch of France and interpret it as evidence of their fraternal sympathy with the monarch's subjects, now that they were free. When his *Operatic Farce* of 1787 was reprinted on the eve of the French Revolution, he warned the reader in a preface that John Bull's *Humours* (including the author's?) "could not possibly furnish matter for any thing but a Farce." Its never having been put on stage is explained with the typical Oswaldian gesture (compare his preface to *The Cry of Nature*) toward "disgusts" that are beneath his contempt: "Several political allusions to events of the period at which it was written, would have effectually prevented the appearance of this Performance on our *chaste* Stage, even if the Author's stomach had not been too squeamish to digest the various disgusts of theatric solicitation."

Grub-Street he could barely tolerate; show business would have been just too much. But is he not, also, admitting that the piece was written for service in a pamphlet war now out of date?

It is nevertheless a witty piece, by a playwright less "ingenuous" than his hero,[47] plotted to expose on all levels the absurdity of "commerce" with France, including its threat to the animal diet of the British—an allusion, by the vegetarian Oswald, which makes the whole thing a tongue-in-cheek performance. The first scene concludes with this definition of the "Love" problem by the frustrated suitor of Lucy Pimpleface, daughter of a London landlord who has acted upon the principle of Pitt's treaty: "The father doats upon his daughter, but is entirely under the guidance of his new wife, a French termagant, whom,

47. *The Humours of John Bull* could have been staged, of course. The reviewer in the *European Magazine* calls attention to an amusing aspect I have not mentioned, that it "is not so much a regular drama as a severe and witty dramatic satire on the *sing-song* and *raree-show* insignificance of our wretched modern operas." As editor of the *British Mercury*, Oswald reveals as much genuine as sarcastic interest in the performing arts.

since the Treaty of Commerce, he imported from Calais, with a cargo of brandy, and other combustibles, which the ingenuity of that nation manufactures against the vitals of this; and she is a deadly enemy to my suit."

The English landlord's comprehension of the world—this "testacious globe," literally hard-shelled, a salacious malapropism for *terraqueous* (a favorite Ignotus word)—includes hostility toward vegetarians, "those savage cannibals the Gintoos, who eat nothing but herbs, and entertain a most treasonable antipathy to roast beef, the glory of Old England." Yet he has been gulled into making "an alliance with the Grand Monarque!" Indeed he has taken a French wife, with her *"pechés de bouche,"* whose priest has warned her "dat Adam and Eve vas be turned out of de Paradise for de gourmandise." (Is the lack of accent on the first *e* to lead the mind from *péché* to *pêche*? Oswald will later give Eve a peach rather than an apple, for the pun's sake.)

Their daughter Lucy is distressed:

> Since my father took to his bosom this foreign mischief, his temper has undergone a total alteration. Formerly my conduct was left entirely to the unsuspected guidance of those principles of honour which I had early imbibed from the most virtuous of mothers. But now I find myself surrounded by informers, spies, guards, and the rest of those vile implements of French policy, that leave no room for the exercise of virtue.

Act 1 concludes with a chorus of watermen:

> The Frenchman vends us caprioles,
> The Italian sells us squall,
> Windy, flighty gifts, while we
> With roast beef pay for all.

So much for reciprocal commerce.

The coffee-room scene in act 2 is, again, so doubly ironic that it puts Fox's argument itself in a farcical view: peace of any kind, not simply peaceful trade with France, would destroy the whole (drunken) effectiveness of the Navy and the Army (whose united force is needed to "hold in derision the whole House of Bourbon, with all their bugbear menaces of invasion"). If the landlady is "an Ambassadress from the Grand Monarque, to sue for Peace," "by the God of War, he sues in vain." A poor Constable is saved from destruction by army and navy officers by pleading that "a poor Night Constable" is "as much an enemy to Peace as yourselves." The Grub-Street poet (our author?) is also an enemy to peace: "O, Sir!" complains the impressario, "me coulda not make una concord vid de dam Poet."

But the final lines come clear. The French wife has dissolved "the matrimonial treaty of commerce," and "The Manchester weavers Sir, hearing that you are going to be divorced from your French wife, are come to express their joy at the event—for she was a bitter enemy to their business." Only the master weavers would have been in Ehrman's category of the treaty's supporters.

Clearly Oswald's own thinking could dance on either side of a political question, mocking an argument while he expressed it, and perhaps only seem to be moralizing when he wrote on the dangers and joys of intercourse. Throughout the *British Mercury*, however, he presents a forthright political policy, spelled out in an editorial announcement (28) that it will concentrate on reporting debates "of national importance" and on exhibiting "the successive movements by which the Constitution of this Country verges towards Despotism, or reverts to Independence"—a promise consistently sustained, even—or especially—in the "bagatelles."

And when the editor looks across the Channel, what he sees are "Commotions in Holland" (115–16), "civil rage" sweeping across the land. The Prince of Orange, having thrown off "the masque of moderation" and assumed "the sovereign style of William *by the Grace of God, &c*," is hoping with the assistance of the Emperor and the King of Prussia to destroy Holland as a Republic.[48] Should Britain join such a league "in the cause of usurpation and tyranny," the Court of France would support the Republic—in a war which the British ministers seem tempted to "plunge" into; yet they "would not dare, against the voice of the people": "We have a great deal to lose, and possibly gain nothing. Our tottering dominion in India is detested by the country powers, whom we have taught the art of war, and who will seize with avidity, the first occasion to accelerate its ruin. The little that remains to us in the new world will soon be swallowed up by the Americans, who cannot refuse, and who, in fact, are bound in gratitude to assist France." On the other hand, if the Republic of Holland recovers "her former independence" and resumes "her antient alliance with Great Britain, . . . the cause of liberty" will be "strengthened in Europe, and the balance of power be established on a firmer foundation" (115–16). Perhaps it was already becoming evident to such nation-watchers as Oswald that for the full triumph of liberty in Europe urged by the republics of America and Holland, there should be matching republics in Britain—and France.[49]

48. Prussia, alas, since the death of Frederick the Great, in 1786, has lacked the wisdom of his policy of peace among neighbors, highly praised in a long "Ignotus" essay in the *Political Herald*, 3:177–88. (It pleased Oswald that Frederick had women in his army: "Every regiment has a number of women and children belonging to it, not less than of men" [3:183]. We know that Oswald managed to take his own children into the army.)

49. One consequence of the Commercial Treaty, seldom mentioned by historians of the French Revolution, was that the industrial recession and unemployment which produced the unrest in France that prepared the people for insurrection was "widely attributed to the malign influence of England operating by means of the Commercial Treaty" (Jarrett, *The Begetters of Revolution*, 177). While the Parisians were storming the Bastille, in Rouen the French weavers were using Luddite tactics against English manufacturers, burning their looms (*Gentleman's Magazine* for July 1789, cited by Jarrett). In 1790, Lord Lansdowne "made an impressive speech in the Lords tracing England's unwarranted hostility to France back to 1786 and suggesting that it was a cause, rather than an effect, of the excesses of the French revolution" (Jarrett, 283). Oswald would have assumed that the anglophobia of the French workers was directed against the rulers and not the people of Britain.

In 1787 Ignotus had observed (*Herald*, 3:429) that, despite a strong and ardent military spirit

What Oswald's father and mother would have thought of their runaway son's entrapment in London in the toils of the employers of wits and poets—perhaps what they did think, for he may have renewed contact with them—is intimated in the two-part essay that accompanies the illustration titled "The Brain-Sucker, or the Miseries of Authorship," dated May 1787 and made in advance for the first number (see Fig. 4).[50] The title over the essay replaces "Miseries" with "Distress" and adds "A Serio-Comic Caricature. In a Letter from Farmer Homely to an absent Friend." The letter is addressed by the father to a friend; so the mother can be described in the third person as "Susan rubbing her eyes and yawning early on a winter morning," who would not have recognized her son, his beard so matted with filth, his hands crusted "like an allegator's scales," his face lined like "a map of the terraqueous globe."

I think Father Homely's tale of his disobedient son tells us a good deal about the John Oswald whose father (here presented as he had wished to be, as uncorrupted by learning) had disapproved of his getting trapped in the humanities: "I spent several days in London in fruitless enquiries after my son. I learned at length the place of his residence. I posted immediately to Grub-street.—I hurried up seven pair of stairs, while a hundred various sensations agitated my breast; indignation at his imprudence, pity for his misfortune, and joy at the idea of pressing once more in my arms my darling boy."

Too late! They embrace and their mingled tears water the floor. But the son has lived on water-gruel so long that when he breaks down and devours the turtle soup, roast beef, and mutton which his father supplies, he consumes "about twenty pounds of butcher's meat" without halt. (How Oswald loves to mock his own vegetable diet!) And he is no longer an innocent lad. His father finds that he has "contracted" the disease of

> telling with pleasure the most egregious falsehoods, or *transmogrifications*, as he called them: as for example, how that Midas, a great king . . . and pretended patron of music, was discovered by his shaver, to have ass's ears; that the north wind had committed with a young Trojan, the reproach of Sodom and Gomorrah; and that Endymion, the man of the moon, sometimes descended in the night, and inhumanly filled with moonshine Dian, the miller's maid, as she slept, unguarded girl, on the grass.

He engages in midnight orgies with Bacchic satyrs and nymphs, dancing and drinking. The message his father is to take to the sweet adoring Nancy he left behind is that he has "turned Saracen" and now lives "in a state of incest with

---

among Britons, government policy was so weak that any outbreak of war, such as the "threatened invasion from France" during the American War, would probably "destroy that artificial capital which stimulates our trade," and so "break those ideal bands which connect us in *a splendid commerce* with one another, and with the whole world" (my italics).

50. Unsigned, but probably by Thomas Rowlandson. See Figure 4.

nine Sisters!," all devoted to Phoebus. The Muses, of course: so much for Yorke's tale of Oswald's having only *two* wives in Paris!

The second illustration, declaredly "Designed for The British Mercury by T. Rowlandson," returns to the political horrors summoned up by Charles Fox (another Farmer Homely, in some respects) at the thought of intercourse with France. It shows the British Lion, roaring and lying wounded on the shield of Brittania, having been pierced by an arrow of "French Policy" shot through a dripping, phallic gun extended from a fortress labeled "Bastile." Beside the lion a human Fox—appropriately fat and bewigged—displays a remnant of the severed Magna Charta. Spurning the lion with her hooves is a donkey whose human face identifies her as La Belle France. Caption: "The Insults of the Brave I have born with some degree of patience, but thus to expire spurned by an Ass, said the agonizing Lion, is more than I can bear. AEsop's Fables."

A goat-legged man facing her on his knees is probably Fox's erstwhile collaborator William Eden, who negotiated the commercial treaty. The spurning must refer to the fact (almost dropped out of history books) that in the spring of 1787, after the treaty had been ratified by both sides, Pitt proposed a mutual reduction of naval power—which the French promptly rejected.[51] This was news as the *Mercury* went to press.

The building beside the "Bastile" is labeled "The Inquisition," in allusion to the related treaty with Spain, still under negotiation. The corpse being robbed of "rupees" is of course India being plundered by Hastings—under protection of a muscular, axe-bearing, naked man who suggests the British army as executioner—an interesting comment on Oswald's perception of the naked truth about his own Indian service.

The arrow of "French Policy" as it pierces the lion attaches a piece of legislation to him labeled "Farmer's General Bill," something unrelated to the commercial treaty but a fresh topic for Opposition rhetoric against French influence on Pitt. In Parliament on 26 April a tax farming bill was proposed by Pitt and opposed vehemently by Fox. Tax "farmers general" had been a notorious abuse by the ancien régime in France, which Jacques Necker had made efforts to correct about six years past. The French government practice was to "farm" (i.e., lease) the right of tax collection to farmers general, who kept the difference between what they gathered and the annual figure they had agreed upon. Necker had been forced to resign before making reforms in this area, but the British government, closely watching France's financial administration during the American War, had been impressed.

Pitt might more tactfully have used the term *lease* instead of *farm*, but he had little difficulty getting Parliament to agree to establish "farmers" for the collection of one tax, that on post horses. "The powers to be given to the farmer were no greater than those at present intrusted to collectors," the argument ran;

51. Ehrman, *The Younger Pitt*, 494.

The Insults of the Brave I have born with some degree of patience, but thus to expire spurned by an Afs said the agonizing Lion is more than I can bear. Esop's Fables.

Fig. 9. "The Insults of the Brave I have born [*sic*] with some degree of patience, but thus to expire spurned by an Ass, said the agonizing Lion, is more than I can bear. AEsop's Fables." "Designed and Etched for the British Mercury, by T. Rowlandson." (BL)

"after considerable discussion, the bill passed both houses without a division."[52] Fox, however, had conducted a spirited attack at the time of the bill's first reading and again on 2 May, at its second. It is not surprising to find the "Post Horse Farming Tax" featured in the department of "Parliamentary Proceedings" in the first issue of Oswald's *Mercury*:

> Mr. Fox . . . and his party contended that no measure could militate stronger against the constitution of a free country, than the tax proposed. It was impossible to collect the revenues through the medium of farmers-general, without exposing the people to the most atrocious oppression. The French themselves, from whom this tyrannic system was borrowed, had found it highly odious in its principle, and oppressive in its execution. By what madness then were the ministers of this country impelled, when they endeavoured to impose on a free people, a system of oppression intolerable even to slaves?
>
> The second reading of the bill was carried however, by a majority of 67.[53]

52. Bisset, *A History of the Reign of George III*, 2:83.
53. On the bill's third reading, 11 May, "To this most pernicious unconstitutional Bill a vigorous opposition was made by the Country Gentlemen." Ayes, 116; Noes, 56 (*British Mercury*, 32). One

No doubt the peculiarities of the topic intrigued Oswald—and Rowlandson—but this kind of emphasis on a topical but slight matter (only two sentences are given to a motion for Parliamentary Reform, made not by Fox but by "Mr. Sawbridge") lends credence to the conjecture that *The British Mercury* was begun with support (or the expectation of it) from Fox and his party—which at the time included Sheridan and Burke as its major speakers. The toad that had to be swallowed was their unsavory attachment to the Prince of Wales, who would become king, or regent, whenever George the Third should drop dead, or go to Bedlam.

The subject of the Prince's debts is handled delicately in this first issue, Fox and Sheridan are given prominence, and critics of imperial policy in India are given the strongest words, on the subject of the "East India Budget" (30) and on the approaching impeachment of Warren Hastings, who is condemned both by the arguments made in his defense and by Oswald's resounding summary of the charges of his accusers (30–32). The tale (47) of a Grub-Street writer who goes mad and confesses having had to write a defense of Warren Hastings is plainly a worst-case nightmare. Having walked away from the wars that were "laying waste the provinces of India," and lived and learned to converse with the native inhabitants, aboriginal or civilized, Oswald was clearly happy to assist in the movement, championed by Sir Philip Francis and Edmund Burke, of exposure and revulsion against the whole greedy project. In Hastings a guilty instigator was targeted. As governor general of India he had provoked the war with Hyder Ali in which the Black Watch had become mired. These wars, it was now charged, Hastings "had wilfully provoked, to gratify a rage of avarice, which not all the wealth of Hindostan could glut" (31).[54]

The "Wisdom" of George the Third

The session proved uneventful, however; and once Hastings was impeached (to stand trial half a year later) and the Prince's debts were paid, there was little other business; so Parliament was prorogued earlier than usual, on 30 May. The King's speech of thanks on 14 May, closing the session, is reported with apparent accuracy, but this ended the *Mercury's* reportorial function for the season and may have been one reason for its ceasing publication.[55]

---

could feel that the publicity had had *some* effect. A grim non sequitur to the revolutionary condemnation of farmers general would be, in May 1794, a mass trial of farmers general for "a conspiracy against the people of France." Sent to the guillotine as one of them, his reputation as a scientist notwithstanding, would be Citizen Lavoisier.

54. On this matter Oswald and Macleod were not in accord. In comment on the impeachment, in 1791 and 1792, Macleod would argue that Hastings had been an efficient organizer of Company policy and did not deserve to be singled out for punishment. (See below.)

55. The "Catalogue of New Publications" (32–36) is attractively broad in coverage. Introduced by a newsworthy volume, *Philosophical and Miscellaneous Papers* by Benjamin Franklin, it man-

Topical and satiric attention to King George, however, fills several pages and was evidently much to the popular taste, as may be inferred from caricature prints of his reign. In a direct "Address to the King" (9 June) the editor-author expresses a fond wish that George himself would supply his own "oral wit and wisdom," his "wise maxims and witty retorts," for the edification of his subjects—and goes on to suggest what history herself will record, for example, "the magnanimity with which you threw away thirteen provinces" and (the tone changes) "the heroic unconcern with which you sent Britons to murder Britons in another world."

With a passing sneer at "Farming General," Oswald's Mercury concludes in a raven voice of warning (comparable, thematically, to that of Coleridge in his "Ode on the Departing Year" of 1796):

> Let us pray . . . that, if the liberty of this country hastens to an end, at least the facility with which it was oppressed, may not encourage future tyrants. . . . No! rather if this fair fabric of liberty must fall at length to the ground, in the midst of tempests and thunder and lightning, let it fall [amid] fearful commotions of the elements; . . . let a torrent of blood, running for ever red and perturbid in the historic page, chill in the bosom of terrified tyrants the projects of despotism, and teach a late posterity how liberty should be prized.

And then the Oswaldian modulation: better that blood should run down palace walls than that "the British lion . . . should expire with tenfold agony, under the vilifying spurnings of an ass."

In a saucy piece on the illustrious 4th of June (the "King's Birthday") the éclat of the occasion is said to have been threatened, "not by the dangerous, and then supposed mortal illness of the Prince, for that's a matter of small moment" (could this slip have cost Oswald the support of the Whigs?) but by a strike of tailors. Could it be that "our gracious sovereign was not a great prince . . . but some contemptible button-maker"? (George, it was known, had indeed learned to make buttons!) The "writer of this article," having "served his time at Tipperary to a man-milliner"—can this have been true of Oswald in some sense?—and being "a very good hand at *fur-below stitching*" (a lewd pun he repeats later), offers to come to the rescue.

More plausibly autobiographical is the concluding essay, which in a title as weighty as Goldsmith's "Citizen of the World" purports to be a "Letter of a Chinese Philosopher, Sojourning in England . . . on the meaning and tendency of a late Proclamation" (129–33). The author would like to leave England and go back to the more philosophical land he came from.[56]

---

ages to come up next with a Ridgway pamphlet on a heavily Whiggish topic: a defense of the embarrassing debts of "His Royal Highness the Prince of Wales." But then, in a long list, there are dissertations on the Goths and on Arctic zoology; John Adams on the Constitution of the United States; an undergraduate letter to Priestley; Music; New Prints; Foreign Books and Pamphlets.

56. His "arrival here . . . almost four years ago" would fit the summer of 1783—or, more

I have travelled in pursuit of knowledge over the greater part of Europe, but my hopes have been miserably disappointed. The Europeans, my friend, are excellent jugglers: they can walk upon their heads; they can fly in the air; they can teach an ass to dance, and give intelligence to pigs; in short they can turn nature upside down, but they are totally unacquainted with the science of government; they have no philosophy, no certain principle of morals. . . . [T]here is not, from one end of Europe to the other, a single example of a government, modelled on _family oeconomy_;[57] and as to their principles of morality, you may easily guess . . . what an absurd system of ethicks that must be, which is founded on a fantastic tale . . . of an old woman who ate, in the garden of Eden, an apple that God had forbidden her to touch! (133)

The most curious thing in this letter is its ostensible topic, a recent "very solemn proclamation" by the king, against the profanation of the sabbath, directed against "certain profane wretches, who have the impiety to frequent caravanserahs of a Sunday; to play a game at chess, or perhaps to pass an idle day with their mistresses, in dancing on the green."

At times Oswald's recurrent emphasis on freedom of mental and bodily "play" is almost Blakean. Here its prohibition binds a whole culture: "The edict has also another important object in view; to check, and perhaps entirely overturn, under the specious pretence of suppressing licentious publications, the liberty of the press." And since "Caricature (a burlesque species of engraving . . .)" is the most effective "mode of communicating an idea of personal or political ridicule or information," we are warned that "several prosecutions have been already commenced on the part of ministry, against certain venders of prints."

This sounds more like 1792 or 1794 than 1787; yet King George _did_ issue a Proclamation on 1 June 1787, and Oswald's language of irony and sarcastic alarm, far from exaggerating the language of the proclamation, scarcely does it justice. Official historians—and even professional ones—do not mention this royal "ban" of vice; in biographies of William Wilberforce, however, it is discussed and its origins made clear.

During the spring of 1787, in his twenty-eighth year, Wilberforce was busy in two moral campaigns, to abolish the slave trade and to reform the morals of the people of Britain. Having successfully participated in forming an anti–slave trade committee on 22 May, he soon learned that his efforts to persuade Pitt and King George to give a send-off to the organization of a committee for the suppression of vice (which did formally assemble in November) had been suc-

---

probably, the winter ("almost").

57. This is a matter of greatest importance, according to an Ignotus essay "On Public OEconomy" in the _Herald_ (3:256–62): "The term oeconomy, when applied to the affairs of an individual, implies nothing more than a due attention to expence, and the usual maxims and expedients of a necessary and prudent frugality. But in trade and business it means something more"; and when applied to the affairs of nations, it "is sometimes taken in so comprehensive a sense, as to embrace the whole conduct and management of public affairs." Ignotus goes into considerable detail, ranging from the management of the national budget to "the principles of jurisprudence," and is critical of Pitt on all these matters.

cessful. King George had agreed to issue a new version of the Proclamation against Vice that had been a feature of his coronation in 1768, based on a version drafted in 1692.[58] The introductory expressions of alarm may have been written by Wilberforce—or by George himself:

> George R. Whereas we cannot but observe with inexpressible concern, the rapid progress of impiety and licentiousness, and that deluge of profaneness, immorality, and every kind of vice, which, to the scandal of our holy religion, and to the evil example of our loving subjects, have broken in upon this nation: We, therefore . . . have thought fit, by the advice of our Privy Council, to issue this our Royal Proclamation, and do hereby declare our Royal purpose and resolution to discountenance and punish all manner of vice, profaneness and immorality, in all persons, of whatsoever degree or quality, within this our Realm, and particularly in such as are employed near our Royal Person.

Rumors were soon abroad that the King was going out of his mind; he was indeed in a great stew about the gambling and whoring debts of his royal sons. The eight customary paragraphs that followed would indeed, as Pollock remarks, "if taken literally . . . make Georgian England and its 8 million inhabitants very different from top to bottom." The King charged and commanded all his officers, ecclesiastical and civil, "to be very vigilant and strict in the Discovery and effectual prosecution and Punishment" of any of "Our loving Subjects" who were "guilty of excessive Drinking, Blasphemy, Profane Swearing and Cursing, Lewdness, Profanation of the Lord's Day, or other dissolute, immoral, or disorderly practices" or *any* games. Said officers were also commanded "effectively to suppress all publick Gaming Houses and other loose and disorderly Houses; and also all unlicensed Public Shews . . . and Places of Entertainment. . . . Also to suppress all loose and licentious Prints, Books and Publications, dispensing Poison to the minds of the young and unwary and to punish the Publishers and Venders thereof. . . ." The statutes preventing "commerce" on Sunday were also to be enforced. The clergy were to read the Proclamation quarterly after divine service; copies were sent to the high sheriff of every county.

The *British Mercury*'s Chinese philosopher had indeed found something alarming—and newsworthy. But there is almost nothing in the surviving newspapers or journals. The volunteer society of enforcers established in November, informally known as the "Proclamation Society," forerunner of the "Vice Society" (The Society for the Suppression of Vice) of Peterloo days, solemnly in-

58. Pollock, *Wilberforce*, 61. Except in lives of Wilberforce, I have not found this proclamation mentioned. After extensive searching, Ralph Anthony Manogue located a copy for me, in the Society of Antiquities, London. Pollock (317) finds it located under "Virtue and Vice" in *Handlist of Proclamations 1714–1810*, Bibliotheca Lindesiana, 1913. Recent studies sometimes refer to "the Proclamation Society, i.e., the Society for the Suppression of Vice and Encouragement of Religion," but without mention of its origin.

cluded six dukes, eleven lesser peers, nineteen archbishops and bishops,[59] and a dozen commoners. The London *Times* reported nine months later (11 August 1788) that "St. George's Fields is now a scene of open gambling in the fields and hedge alehouses; the amusements which for centuries the people were at liberty to enjoy being now interdicted. The proclamation no doubt was well intended, but instead of serving the cause of morality it has benefited the practices of vice. The people must have some relaxation, and the most harmless they could enjoy was that of trap-ball, skittles, and nine pins." Three months later the *Times* further reported (27 November): "The Debating Societies will shortly undergo the same interdiction as the Sunday sacred music six-penny meetings—to the great grief of idle apprentices and industrious pick-pockets—a new room is opened, contrary to an express act of Parliament, near Soho Square, for disputing on religion, and inculcating atheistical principles . . . ."

We may sympathize with the objective behind Wilberforce's campaign against immoral behavior, which was that only by putting a complete stop to potential criminal activities could capital punishment be rendered unnecessary: all these prohibitions were to prevent people being hanged. But Oswald's reaction to the Proclamation will help us understand his strong objection to the Sunday School movement of this decade. By the time he was writing his editorial for the *Mercury*, seven or eight days after the Royal Proclamation, he may perhaps have heard of prosecutions begun against certain vendors of prints. "And the vengeance of government will soon, in all probability," he wrote, "begin to operate on the other branches of the typographic art." Rumors may have circulated in Grub-Street of measures being considered to suppress the Priapic etchings "Designed for The British Mercury," and he may have feared for the *Mercury* itself.

It could conceivably have been Bow Street pressure that caused this 23 June issue to be its last. These prophetic concluding remarks are uncannily similar to the words of defiance in the final issues of the Parisian *Chronique du mois* with which Oswald would be associated in 1791–1793. In any case this last *Mercury* was boldly defiant in both text and illustration. The finale consisted of a saucy, salacious drinking song by "The Priests of Apollo" accompanied by a large cartoon (by Gillray, though unsigned) of "Moses, erecting" a huge phallic serpent between his legs, near a Priapic signpost right out of Payne Knight.[60] Indeed this large foldout print, the most flamboyantly Priapic of the lot, may have been inspired by the extra illustration (also issued separately) which was the most realistically phallic of those in *The Worship of Priapus*.

In the inscription, Oswald manages to turn even the Ten Commandments to

---

59. One of these, Richard Watson, bishop of Llandaff, we shall meet again.

60. "Published June 23d 1787 by J. Ridgway." Draper Hill confirms the attribution to Gillray. The Oswald-Gillray print is reproduced in Fuchs (*Die Juden in der Karikatur*, 43; fig. 63) as a witty symbolic caricature without any direct anti-Jewish feeling, "Rabalais translated into English."

Fig. 10. By James Gillray (probably, although unsigned), for *The British Mercury*. Published 23 June 1787. (BL)

his erotic purposes. The only legible words are "Thou shalt not make any Graven Image or any likeness of any thing . . ." with the word *thing* on a separate line.

In the event, Ridgway was able to republish the whole four numbers of *The British Mercury* a year later, with the etchings (probably also sold separately): an act of triumph over whatever threats or fears there may have been.

That James Gillray was not merely attached to the *Mercury* as its anonymous illustrator, but that he shared Oswald's feelings about the royal proclamation of 1787, may be deduced from the artist's response, again anonymously, to the very famous and effective Royal Proclamation of 21 May 1792—against "divers wicked and seditious writings" as well as meetings. For the earlier Proclamation seems to have suggested Gillray's theme in 1792, which focuses not on the matters now forbidden but on "Vices overlooked in the new proclamation." In his etching of 24 May 1792, Gillray depicts the vices of the royal family proclaimed against in 1787, in four panels: (1) Avarice (the King and Queen hugging hoarded millions: paying off the Princes' debts had been one problem); (2) Drunkenness (portrait of the Prince of Wales, exemplifying it); (3) Gambling (Duke of York); (4) Debauchery (Duke of Clarence with Mrs. Jordan).[61]

A good joke—but powerless against the truly political new Proclamation, which was fired like grapeshot with dreadful effects: splintering the Whigs to consolidate Pitt's control; splintering British radical and liberal "friends of the

61. See my notes in *Factotum*, nos. 12 and 15.

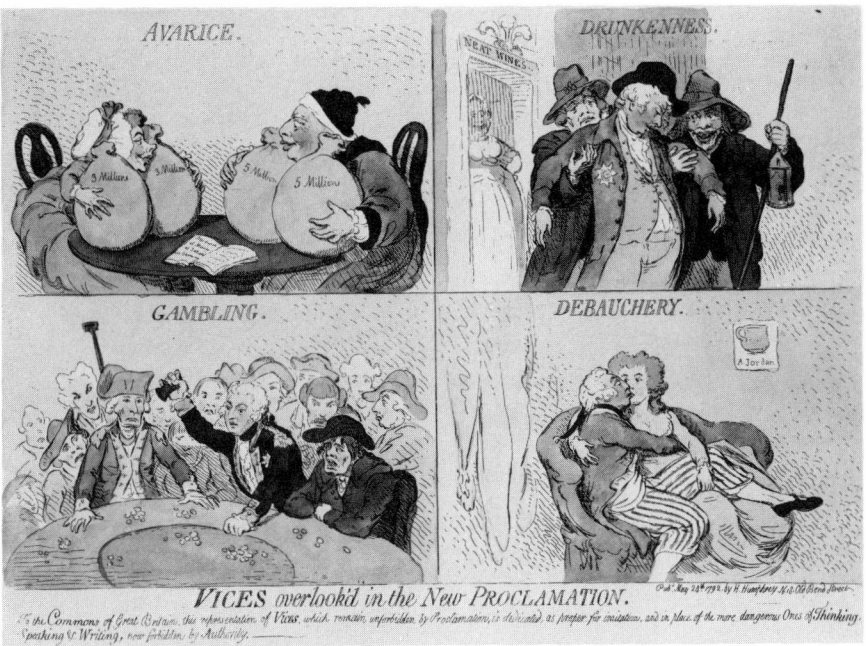

Fig. 11. By James Gillray. Published 24 May 1792. (Prints Division, NYPL)

Constitution" (British or French); silencing the debating societies; stifling the radical press; and preparing for all-out war against the French Revolution—all within the year.

Frequent and Free Discourse

David Stewart was on firm ground when he described Oswald as "a warm Republican" before the "breaking out of the Revolution." [62] He was the kind of idealist who assumed that the people of France, once freed of their monarch, would want a constitution at least as democratic as the one that the Americans were drafting in 1787–1788. He assumed, also, that the British popular scorn of Louis—which he of course encouraged—implied the readiness of the people of Britain to embrace as liberated brethren the people of France, the sans-culottes, as soon as Louis was dethroned.

Historians since Tocqueville have attended to the groundswell of enlightened thought in Paris that preceded the French Revolution; much less attention has

62. *Sketches*, 50.

been given to the London variety of such thought, since nothing like a British Revolution occurred *except* in thought—and in rumors inspired by the government and its enemies. When Oswald arrived from his travels, however, treaties of peace had been signed (in September 1783) with France, Spain, and the United States; peace with Tippoo in India was negotiated in 1784. As a military man he was well aware of the universal disaffection of the bloodybacks, rhetorically the bastions of Empire; he was impressed by the flourishing of bayonets by which the Irish volunteers had obtained at least a semblance of independence. As for India, the legislation proposed by Fox in November 1783 to "cleanse the Augean stable of Company rule in India," and Pitt's bill that replaced it, were the universal topic of conversation in London—and of editorials in many issues of the *Political Herald*.

As we have seen, Oswald early on was interested in the official debates in Parliament; his writing frequently appears to be responding to coffeehouse discussions (a habit perhaps begun in Edinburgh). He at least once refers to the more organized debating in "The Robin Hood club."[63] And in 1790 he would lead a critical debate in the Society for Free Debate at Coachmakers' Hall. Several such societies were flourishing in London when Oswald first came on the scene: City Debates on Mondays (and Saturdays); Westminster Forum on Wednesdays; Coachmakers' Hall on Thursdays. Almost none of the actual discussions were published, with the rare exception of two volumes of Westminster Forum debates in 1780–1781.[64] But topics announced in the newspapers ranged from "The State of the Nation" (at some particular crisis) to "Suicide?" or "Which makes the worse husband, a spendthrift or a miser?" In 1780 the Forum "almost unanimously" decided "That it would be more consistent with the interests of the people of Great Britain, to immediately acknowledge the American Independence" (10 April). Oswald doubtless frequented one or more of these intellectual "circles" with other serious Grub-Street thinkers.

A different sort of gathering place, where Grub-Street necessity, as well as curiosity, may have compelled Oswald to dine "with his roots," was the Intrepid Fox Tavern in Wardour Street, named after Charles Fox by the admiring landlord, and frequented by the buyers of votes and dispensers of venison during Westminster elections: it took "enormous" expense of that kind to win, for example, the by-election of 1788 for Lord Townshend. Here one met the trenchermen of the Prince of Wales and received orders (or hints and sugges-

---

63. In the *Political Herald*'s final issue (no. 18, December 1786) a correspondent who advocates the silencing of people who would "investigate the measures of Government" is answered thus: "He is not contented by one bold decision to silence the coffee-house discussion and the grave debates of the Robinhood, to annihilate political pamphlets and to set aside the liberty of the press, but he aims a final and a master blow even at parliament itself" (3 : 425, answer to "Marcus").

64. A *History of the Robinhood Society* was published in 1764, and the club continued for many years, but the *History* is largely parody and invention, seldom if ever reporting actual debates.

tions) for writing libels or counterlibels, perhaps even odes, in the Foxite cause.[65]

Oswald and many others would have agreed with the Englishman in the Westminster Forum who "hoped to see the thirteen Stripes wave in every English harbour, from a foederal union" with Britain,[66] and would have added the hope for a union of *all* free peoples. The wide currency of such sentiments in London in the 1780s delighted many American and French visitors, two important ones for Oswald's future Jacobin career being Jacques Pierre Brissot, whom he would learn not to trust, and Nicolas de Bonneville, whose greatest skill has been said to be that of making friends—even among political theorists with combative tendencies. Both of these Oswald met in London, early in his Grub-Street days.

Brissot, a few years older than Oswald, had been in London for some time (he left for Paris in July 1784) with large plans for an organization he called a Lycée, which was to spread illumination by three means: correspondence, a special publication on the arts and sciences, and meetings in a conference center in London, from which Europe was to be "inundated" with writings against despotism—including Oswald's, of course.[67] Brissot developed connections with Joseph Priestley and David Williams and Oswald's Thomson. He particularly listened to and admired Williams, whose friendship with Oswald must have begun in this period. And he arranged with Thomson for the publication of several books and pamphlets he was writing, or translating, or editing—including the "Mackintosh" *Travels* published by Thomson in 1786. Brissot returned to London in 1787, having kept in touch but never quite managing to finance his Lycée—an idea whose day would come with the Cercle Social in revolutionary Paris.

A more fully sympathetic bond was that formed with Bonneville, Oswald's collaborator in 1791 to 1793 on the monthly magazine of the Cercle, the *Chronique du mois* (in which Brissot also was involved). Visiting London in 1786, Bonneville worked at a translation into French of a *History of Modern Europe* by William Russell, in four volumes. Fluent in English and French, he could have attended the debating clubs with Oswald, and both might have found interesting potentialities in the Foxite group at the Intrepid Fox Tavern. For by 1790 that group of practical politicians on the side of Reform would publicly announce themselves Freemasons, constituting "The Constitutional Whigs, Grand Lodge of England, founded upon pure Revolution Principles," and meeting—in rivalry to the London Revolution Society—on the 4 November anniversary of the Glorious Revolution, "in order to celebrate the Anniver-

65. On the Intrepid Fox Whigs, see my "Citizen Stanhope and the French Revolution," *The Wordsworth Circle* 15 (1984): 8–17; esp. 15–16, n. 10.

66. *Westminster Forum*, 2:181; see below, Chap. 8, note 14.

67. Ellery, *Brissot de Warville*, 20; see also 29. See Kates's book for Bonneville's role.

Fig. 12. Jacques-Pierre Brissot (1754–1793). Founder of the Amis des Noirs; editor of the *Patriote français*; "at the center of the Cercle Social's intense network of friendships" (Kates, *The Cercle Social*, 76). Portrait by Raffet, in Lamartine, *Histoire des Girondins*, 5:71. (SB)

sary of the Landing of our great Deliverer, King William the Third, of glorious and immortal memory." [68]

Quite possibly there were earlier announcements I have missed. This may have been an ancient lodge going public, but more probably it was newly formed under the influence of such future revolutionaries as Bonneville, who was already deeply involved in "driving the Jesuits out of the Masonry" (to paraphrase the title of a two-volume work he published in 1788 with Robinson,[69] in London: perhaps where the Westminster Committee got the idea). Bonneville's reputation as a disciple of philosophes, especially d'Alembert, and a proponent of Freemasonry gave him a ready introduction to such theorists as David Williams and Horne Tooke. And since Oswald later emerges as a communicant of Tooke and a reporter of Williams's observations, we may suppose Oswald was in some degree involved in the strong friendship of these men with Bonneville.

When in London, both Bonneville and Brissot made a point of visiting various Masonic lodges, evidently encouraging them to move on from the mesmeric principle of a "Society of Harmony" to that of *extending* social harmonics.[70] Brissot in fact had joined such a group in Paris in 1785. Quoting one of the organizers, he noted: "Bergasse did not hide from me the fact that in raising an altar to mesmerism, he intended only to raise one to liberty. 'The time has now come,' he used to say to me, 'for the revolution that France needs. But to attempt to produce one openly is to doom it to failure.'"[71]

By 1787 this French group included Etienne Clavière and Antoine-Joseph Gorsas, future Girondist leaders, and probably Lafayette. Said Brissot: "I used to preach republicanism there; but, with the exception of Clavière, no one appreciated it. D'Epremesnil only wanted to 'de-Bourbonize' France." Gorsas (one of Wordsworth's favorite journalists)[72] was, according to Brissot, "then trying out the satirical pen with which he has so often slashed apart monarchism, autocracy, feuillantism and anarchy."[73] Bonneville in France shortly after the Revolution reported that "a printing press and formal branch of the Social Circle" had been founded under "'one of our English franc-brothers'— John Oswald." One of "the first foreigners to hail the French Revolution," says Billington, Oswald "became, in effect, Bonneville's London correspondent. He

---

68. There was a similar announcement in 1790. For details on the "Constitutional Whigs," see my "Stanhope" article.

69. Full title: *Les Jesuites chassées de la Maçonnerie et leur poignard brisé par les Maçons.* Robinson had been printer of the *Political Herald.*

70. On mesmerism, see Darnton, *Mesmerism and the End of the Enlightenment in France,* passim; and especially for Bonneville's involvement, Billington, *Fire in the Minds of Men: Origins of the Revolutionary Faith.*

71. Ellery, *Brissot de Warville,* 28.

72. His *Courrier des 83 départements* was one of the two newspapers subscribed to by the Jacobin Club of Blois (Kennedy, *The Jacobin Clubs,* 365), where Wordsworth lived in 1792. Beside the name "Gorsas" in Wordsworth's set of the *Works* of Burke (now in Dove Cottage Library) is penciled: "I knew this man. W. W."

73. Brissot, *Á ses commettans,* 2:53–56.

translated from and contributed to Bonneville's publications, and transmitted them to 'franc-Scottish' and 'franc-Irish' as well as to 'Anglo-franc' brothers."[74] By May 1790, they would be ready to launch a twice-weekly English-language newspaper, printed in Paris but distributed in both London and Paris and covering the political news of both capitals, until suppressed by the British government (see Chapter 6).

This is taking us ahead of our story a bit, to emphasize the prophetic dynamics of radical political thinking in both London and Paris (and many other centers) while the public wrangling focused on treaties and election contests. A fuller definition of the "Social Circle" idea will also help. David Williams, a Welsh priest whose center was in a Druid sanctum, it seems, supplied the blackboard diagrams, a system of graphic circles which Bonneville used to distinguish degrees of freedom and slavery in ancient and modern "constitutions."[75] Bonneville's Cercle Social combined the Masonic idea of a purified inner circle with the Rousseauian idea of a social, and not merely a political, contract. Its organized form would evolve out of the editorial meetings of Bonneville's *Tribun du peuple*—and participation in the radicalization of the Paris sections. Then in late 1791 the editors of the *Chronique du mois*—with Oswald and Bonneville doing most of the editing, Condorcet and Lanthenas most of the writing—would announce themselves as a magic group of fourteen, "le quatorze," the inner ring of an ever-widening circle of the Friends of Truth.[76]

During the first years of the Revolution, what evolved from the Whig and Masonic circles of London in collaboration with the more public Friends of the People and Revolution Society—and various provincial "corresponding" and "revolution" societies—was a wide network of correspondence with Jacobin clubs ("Friends of the Constitution") in Paris and hundreds of French towns. The circling was often tangled, broken, or incomplete. But near the center, in the Cercle Social and the Paris Jacobin Club, we find John Oswald struggling mightily to keep unbroken the momentum toward an ideal community of all free peoples.

74. *Fire in the Minds of Men*, 50, citing Ioannisian, *Idei*, where information from Bonneville's *Bouche de fer* and other works does, as laid out, support these inferences.

75. David Williams's *Lessons to a Young Prince, by an Old Statesman, on the present disposition in Europe to a General Revolution* (London, H. D. Symonds, 1790) had four diagrams showing the relative powers and linkage of class hierarchies in the "Political Constitution of England by Alfred," "English Government at the Revolution," "English Government in 1790," and "French Revolutionary State." The English People, in the third diagram, constitute an outer ring having no more "election, choice, or share" than did the "Peasants in slavery" in the time of Alfred; in the fourth, the French have only one remaining class distinction: the outer ring of propertyless are still not citizens. These four diagrams were reproduced in a French translation of the *Lessons* published in *La Bouche de fer* and then used in Bonneville's *De l'Esprit des réligions* (Paris, à l'imprimerie du Cercle Social, 1791). James Dybikowski makes the plausible suggestion that Oswald may have done the translating, since the original was the work of the London affiliate of the Cercle Social. In French the ring diagrams are titled "Cercles Constitutionels." (Bonneville was apparently unaware of a fifth circle, added in Williams's second and subsequent editions, depicting the constitutional shape of the new American Republic.)

76. Here I paraphrase Billington, *Fire in the Minds of Men*, 39.

The Arts of Peace

Although the *British Mercury* was not continued beyond its two full months, evidently its intellectual and social value for Oswald had been to transport him from the galleys of booksellers' London to a respectable place on the ramparts.

Ridgway had evidently allowed Oswald a free editorial hand in the *Mercury*, and he had engaged the best caricaturists in London to illustrate it. He proceeded to publish a "New Edition" in 1788[77] (with another bookseller, L. Macdonald), and in 1789 he put his name down for copies of Oswald's book of *Poems* (by "Sylvester Otway"), printed by Macrae for a bookseller who stood high in the trade, J. Murray, No. 32, Fleet-street. And happily the booksellers were not frightened by Oswald's connections with the revolutionaries of Paris in the next few years. The title page of *The Cry of Nature*, 1791, facing the frontispiece by Gillray (unsigned), bravely declares the author to be (in the printer's spelling) "John Oswald, Member of the Club des Jacobines," with an apt quotation from Juvenal, and the publisher: Joseph Johnson, No. 72, St. Paul's Church-yard. Also in 1791 Ridgway let his name stand as "Ridgway BOOKSELLER London" above "The Printing Office of the Social Circle, Paris," on Oswald's English translation of *The Almanach of Goodman Gérard*, a Jacobin Club tract we shall hear more of.

Apparently Ridgway, like Sampson Perry, early recognized in Oswald a writer of wit, "enlarged understanding," and "a depth of reasoning not often met with."[78] Ridgway's private views are not on record, and whether he was merely a shrewd opportunist who "earned a living in sundry ways—including radical activity (when it was profitable)"—as Bruce Gronbeck opines[79]—or whether

77. In this year, by the way, Oswald attained at least bibliographical fame of the "Who's Who" sort by being included in an alphabetical *Catalogue of Five Hundred Celebrated Authors of Great Britain, Now Living*, published by a Mr. Marshall; the section on Oswald is brief enough to be given here in full. Note that he is not yet identified as using the "Sylvester Otway" pseudonym:

Oswald, John: a native of Scotland, and late a lieutenant in the forty-second regiment of foot. He is the author of *Ranae Comicae Evangelizantes*, or the Comic Frogs turned Methodist, published in 1786; a number of essays and articles in the British Mercury, a periodical publication which appeared in 1787; the Alarming Progress of French Politics, a pamphlet on the subject of the commercial treaty; and Euphrosyné, or an Ode to Beauty, addressed to Mrs. Crouch, of Drury-lane theatre. This gentleman served in the late war on the Malabar coast, and is at present engaged in writing a History of the East Indies.

78. The wide political and philosophical range of the "Catalogue of New Publications" in the *Mercury* suggests that it was the hope of Oswald and Ridgway to establish a reviewing pattern similar to that of the defunct *Herald*.

79. In an article in the *Biographical Dictionary of Modern British Radicals* (1979), Gronbeck garbles the information in Werkmeister, *Newspaper History*, 152ff., making it seem as though Ridgway published a pamphlet by the anti-Jacobin John Reeves just before publishing Paine's part 2, and was arrested for both! We see from Werkmeister, however, that Reeves (who formed an "Association" but did *not* write a work with that title) was cited by Lord Grey in Parliament as publishing riot-inciting handbills *against* the radicals, bills more properly to be condemned as "mischievous libel" than the works of Paine; but of course it was Paine and Ridgway who were indicted, and tried, not Pitt's friend Reeves.

he was a genuine radical sometimes forced to cover his flank, cannot be certainly deduced from his career. When Oswald arrived in London, Ridgway had been printer of Almon's *London Courant* (begun in 1779) and had stayed with it when it supported Wilkes and Tooke and the reform radicalism of Cartwright. Perhaps the championing of Fox's campaign against the Commercial Treaty was for both Ridgway and Oswald partly a matter of Grub-Street morality. Gronbeck supposes that Ridgway was without government or party subsidy, but his turning against the Foxite Whigs (and the prince of Wales) during the Regency crisis of 1789 and later—publishing a spate of libels upon their sexual irregularities—may mean he had expected party subsidy and been disappointed. Perhaps he was bought off when, in 1792, he became "an outlet for Grey and Sheridan's 'Friends of the People,'" or perhaps he found their new politics congenial. He moved along, however, on a course in London about as radical as Oswald's in Paris, to publish Paine's *Rights of Man*, part 2,[80] and even Paine's *Letter Addressed to the Addressers,* with its call for revolution in Britain. He received a series of indictments, followed by fines and prison, yet continued from Newgate a further radical series—including Redhead Yorke's *These Are the Times to Try Men's Souls.* All this was good for sales, true, but hardly denotes mere opportunism.

Independent as it proved to be, Oswald's *British Mercury* was autobiographically retrospective, looking back to the spirit of the American Revolution and the early part of his traveling. And by defining himself as a visitor from China, rather than from India or Kurdistan or Turkey or Arabia, he was fitting himself comfortably into British philosophical and satiric convention,[81] not drawing upon his actual experience—with the striking exception of vivid allusions to Joanna and its neighbor Madagascar.

Clearly his first long stay on shore, among the Joannamen, had produced a cultural shock of memorable strength. When he sat in his Grub-Street garret and reached out for the sensational, he could find it in his recollections of those islanders. In the second number of his *Mercury* he ridicules the French commercial treaty with a pseudo-report from Paris that a plan to import slaves from Madagascar has now been laid aside, since it will soon be possible to import slaves from Great Britain "much cheaper than they could have them from Madagascar, whose black and brawny inhabitants have ever manifested the most rooted antipathy to slavery and the *Grande Monarque.*" And, in one of his only two "Extracts from Foreign Books," he supplies an English transla-

---

80. Shortly after publication, in mid-February 1792, General Miranda made a memorandum recording "the singular fact that while on a visit to the House of Commons he saw placed on sale there with sandwiches the second part of Tom Paine's *Rights of Man*" (Robertson, *Life of Miranda,* 1 : 119). It was sold in stalls in St. James's Park, one owned by Ridgway himself.

81. Lucyle Werkmeister (*London Daily Press,* 155) calls attention to a "Chinese Philosopher" writing in the London *World* of 18 November 1787—who just possibly could be Oswald (but that day's *World* seems to have vanished).

tion of a French version of *Chansons Madecasses* from "the isle of Bourbon, Madagascar." [82]

Implicit perhaps in his *Herald* speculations, but clearly presented in his "State of the World" essay in the *Mercury*, are Oswald's philosophical ponderings about the military side of international relations. Establishing the point that "the great modes in which nations . . . address and correspond with one another are war and commerce," and the hopeful point that "the rulers of the present times are chiefly attentive to the arts of peace, because these, not the most heroic efforts of war, constitute the real strength or resources of a nation," he examines the dynamics of "the military art."

The fact that it has become "more complex and mixed with machinery" in modern times means that the military art "admits of more certain calculation" and is thus less blindly resorted to than when "the enginery of war was more simple, and battles were decided by the wavering tides of courage, and fear, and other passions" (38). Oswald nevertheless puts much more faith in the civilizing effects of literature and art: "the propagation of literature tends to humanize the mind, to restrain the fury and the frequency of war, and to promote peace, and good will, and friendly intercourse among men: it softens and humanizes the manners."

He expands Terence's "nihil humani" into "I myself am a man, and I cannot remain untouched by the joys or the sorrows of human nature" (40). Yet he sees a certain desperate hope in recognizing that kings now "estimate the commercial and political consequence of what they contend for" and that "just calculation tends to prevent the effusion of blood, by shewing the inutility, as well [as] the inhumanity of such sacrifices" (39). It was just such humane calculation that Ignotus faulted Pitt for ignoring—and praised the Czarina and Frederick the Great for employing wisely.

To reduce the desperation of such meditations, he turns "a steady eye" on the "good cause" which is of most importance, "that of freedom" and "the virtue and vigilance of the people"—whose united efforts against tyranny must be based on "frequent and free discourse," the commerce of free minds (43).

One of the consequences of Oswald's increasing intellectual recognition in the world of publishing was his obtaining—I don't know exactly when—a position as parliamentary reporter for the daily *Gazetteer*, on terms which left him a considerable amount of free time for other activities—such as addressing the London Society for Free Debate and the Paris Jacobin Friends of the Constitution. His moving from the *London Chronicle*, where such reporting was minimal, to the *Gazetteer*, while not leaving Ridgway as publisher, was a con-

---

82. These *Songs of Madagascar* clearly inspired William Blake's pivoting the apocalyptic turning point of *The Four Zoas* on a song "Composed by an African Black from the little Earth of Sotha": island seen as globe (*FZ* 9: pp. 134–35). Another image of the small circle transforming the large.

siderable advancement into the combat area of verbal "calculations" about war and peace.

Fortunately a good deal is known about the London *Gazetteer*, since most of its records have survived.[83] We can see that its parliamentary reporting was principled and prominent, and spot-checking indicates that it was a principal source for the permanent volumes of the *Parliamentary Debates* of this period published in 1817 by a congeries of booksellers headed by Hansard.[84] The *Gazetteer* had, in fact, been among the first newspapers to carry even brief accounts of the proceedings in the House of Commons (in 1770) and "the first daily paper in London to publish speeches and accounts of the debates with any approach to regularity," a daring innovation at the time. By 1775 this had become a chief element in newspaper competition. Reports of the debates had "replaced the animadversions of political essayists as the most important single item of content in the daily papers, and a corresponding importance was naturally attached to the abilities of the various Parliamentary reporters."[85]

Oswald's return from India had coincided with the takeover of the *Gazetteer* by James Perry, a fellow Scot from Aberdeen about four years older than Oswald, who had been an actor and then a debater before becoming a publisher. He edited the *Gazetteer* from 1783 to 1790 as the "paper of the people" and the organ of Horne Tooke's Society for Constitutional Information. And he introduced "a new and more efficient system of debate-reporting,"[86] which consisted of having reliefs and relays of reporters and also busy spies in the debating societies—whose announcements were printed in the *Gazetteer* with some regularity.

Oswald and Perry quite possibly got acquainted in these private debating groups; Oswald was obviously well equipped for a reporter's job on the people's paper, and I suspect he found himself in it soon—perhaps (a tidy hypothesis) when his *British Mercury* was discontinued in June 1787, but perhaps much. earlier. The possibility that he worked in some or several capacities for the *Gazetteer* quite early, assisting for instance in the fourth-page "Literary Intelligence" column begun in January 1786, is only a plausible conjecture.[87]

83. Haig, *The Gazetteer 1735–97*, 215, 217; also 165–66, 90.

84. For my method of checking the quality of debate reports, see my "Coleridge in Lilliput."

85. Oswald's full attention to the debates (as implied in his conflict with the new editor in 1791: see below) may have been an innovating step. Another quality of Perry's editing that must have encouraged Oswald was his "tendency to popularize the content of the *Gazetteer* in an effort to appeal to a wider reading public. A forthright expression of political allegiance was one aspect of this process, but it is more readily observable in his practice of abstracting and attempting to simplify the most important political issues of the day" and in "the greater variety of subject matter" with "increased emphasis upon 'literary' and 'fashionable' intelligence" (Haig, *The Gazetteer 1735–97*, 265).

86. Andrews, *The History of British Journalism*, 1:231–23.

87. On 7 January a theatrical report on "the continued popularity of *Arthur and Emmeline*," with "the exquisite writing of Dryden and the beautiful airs and chorusses of Percel," and "an assemblage of principal performers" who supply "all the operatical strength of the Theater," including Mrs. Crouch, Oswald's favorite, sounds con amore.

The first firm evidence of his connection with this newspaper is his report of the debate on a bill "for the Cultivation and Preservation of Trees, &c." (20 and 28 May 1789; reported in the *Gazetteer* of 21 and 29 May). He alludes to this clearly in his speech before the London Society for Free Debate on 23 December 1790 as one of "two late instances that came under my own observation" of outrageous arguments presented in the House of Commons. He saw the bill whisked into law "with the most ruffian-like unanimity" (with the honorable exception of Sir James Johnstone), making "the horrid crime of cutting a cabbage" punishable by "being hanged, like a dog, by the neck." The language in the *Gazetteer* is more moderate—at least more careful about the terms used and the numbers in opposition—but not different in its gist.[88]

There is also clear evidence that he was still working as a parliamentary reporter for the *Gazetteer* in February 1791—but also that he had an address in Paris as early as May 1790 and was publishing or planning to publish parliamentary reports in "an English Newspaper printed in Paris," as we shall see, and soon became a Channel-hopping member of the Paris Jacobin Club (Society of Friends of the Constitution), an honor he proudly cited when presenting a poem celebrating "The Triumph of Freedom" to the National Assembly at the opening of its session of 4 September 1790.[89]

> M. Jean Oswald, Citoyen Anglois, Lieutenant au Régiment d'Infantérie Highland, Membre de la Société des Amis de la Constitution, a offert à l'Assemblée Nationale une Ode en langue Angloise de sa composition intitulée: *le Triomphe de la Liberté*, et destinée a célébrer le Révolution Françoise. L'Assemblée a agrée cet hommage, et un exemplaire de l'Ouvrage a été remis dans les Archives.[90]

The information as to his Royal Highland lieutenancy and his membership in the Jacobin Club is repeated from the title page, which adds his authorship of "*Poems*, by Sylvester Otway, &c." The imprint reads simply: "PARIS. Printed for the Author."

The preface—which Oswald doubtless would have recited, in French, if given a chance—breathes scorn of the "*august Grimace*, and Mockery of Greatness" which, in contrast to the Assembly, characterize "the Senate of a neighbouring Nation," i.e., the Parliament of Great Britain. Its debates he was still reporting for the *Gazetteer*, however, as we know from the minutes of a business meeting in February 1791 of the paper's management committee.

---

88. Others besides Johnstone spoke against the bill, including Sheridan, Windham, and Burke—given equal space in the *Gazetteer* report—and there were 11 Noes the first day, if only 4 the second. But this is clearly the debate Oswald reported. To "bark or destroy plants, and shrubs, in an inclosure, in the night," had already been a capital crime. The new bill extended that to the daytime. Most Whigs and Tories approved—or stayed away. The other report Oswald alludes to is from a debate on an enclosure bill, too frequent an item to be pinned down.

89. The Ode was printed "to commemorate the anniversary of The French Revolution" and was probably ready by 14 July but had to await a quiet day on the agenda. The notes report that it was in English—presumably not read aloud but received and filed.

90. *Procès-Verbal*, no. 401.

By this date, James Perry had left that paper and bought the *Morning Chronicle*, continuing his radical Whig orientation through the troubled decades that ensued. The *Gazetteer*'s incoming editor in January was William Radcliffe, husband of the novelist Ann Ward Radcliffe. The February meeting was called because Radcliffe had encountered "some difficulty in the assertion of his authority" and lodged "a complaint against a subordinate"—the parliamentary reporter John Oswald. The committee authorized him "to inform Mr. Oswald that his duty as a Reporter is not to exclude his assistance in other matters & that he is to apply to such other business as Mr. Radcliffe shall point out."[91]

Under Perry, Oswald had obviously been free to travel when Parliament was not in session—and even when it was, if he found substitutes. The biographies agree that "On the breaking out of the revolution in France, Mr. Oswald's principles naturally led him to view that struggle with more than ordinary interest. He was not content with waiting the result at a distance, but hastened over to Paris, to witness, and, if occasion offered, to assist in the work of French regeneration" (*Lives*, 175). They agree that he published a version of his "Remarks on the Constitution of Great Britain" in Paris in May 1790, which "served at once as his passport to admission into the Jacobin Club." Oswald himself, in his 1792 *Review of the Constitution*, says that "outlines" of his thought appeared in May 1790 in "the *Universal Patriot*, an English Paper printed at Paris, which the British Ministry were at some pains to suppress"— successfully, it appears, since no copies are known to exist.[92]

Radcliffe was now about to call a halt, not merely to Oswald's frequent absences (with or without substitute reporters), but also to what was apparently a habit of total absence from London when Parliament was not in session. From the parliamentary calendar we can see what these "vacation" periods would have been. In 1788 he would have had four free months, between July and 19 November, the end of one session and the beginning of the next. He would have had over five months free between 12 August 1789—Parliament had never "sitten so long"[93]—and 20 January 1790, when it tardily resumed. Then he would have had over five months between 11 June and 26 November 1790. But this year he must have spent a good deal of time in France, even during the sitting of Parliament, since by April he must have been busy organizing that "English Newspaper printed at Paris"—including plans to make its parliamentary reporting better than that of the *Gazetteer*, free of British censorship and free also to report the debates of the French Assembly.[94]

I suspect that by the time Oswald was confronted with orders from the new editor of the *Gazetteer* he was ready to resign and settle in France anyway. The

91. Haig, *The Gazetteer 1735–97*, 221.

92. A Prospectus survives, however, and is given below as Appendix B. In it Oswald's name is given as manager or editor of the paper, promised for initial delivery 3 May 1790.

93. Bisset, *A History of the Reign of George III*, 196, 275.

94. See discussion of *The Universal Patriot* below, Chapter 5.

Universal Patriot, soon suppressed, would not supply a career solution, but by the autumn of 1791 the Bonneville circle's plans for a fully revolutionary monthly, the *Chronique du mois*, with Oswald's name among the *fourteen* editors, would be ready to be announced. As late as May 1792, nevertheless, Oswald was maintaining residence in both capitals, for him probably the ideal arrangement. In London he was negotiating, with the help of David Williams (announced as a contributor, via Oswald, to the *Chronique*), to obtain a grant from the Literary Fund—which Williams had been instrumental in founding in 1788.[95] In Paris—again, according to the Scottish *Lives*—he "soon rose above all his countrymen in importance, and was acknowledged as the first of Anglo-Jacobins . . ." (175).

The Labors of Sylvester Otway

According to the Grub-Street caricature in the *British Mercury*, the most onerous task to which the Brain-Sucker compelled poor Oswald was the writing of "Odes." But we know that Oswald was employed on one periodical or another during most of his Grub-Street career. Perhaps we should take the sarcasm of this caricature of Thomson as based on some such remark to Oswald, when the *Herald* had ceased and the *Mercury* was only a dream, as that if this undertaking did not succeed one could always scrape together some kind of a living by writing newspaper verses. I find, indeed, an "Ode to Philosophy" (perhaps too limp for Oswald) in Thomson's *London Chronicle* for 23 June 1785, and "Philanthropy, an Ode," in the *Chronicle* of 24 March 1786, the latter signed "Z. A." (perhaps suggesting a reversed alphabet—everything upside down). (A decade later Coleridge could earn a guinea a week by supplying verses *and* paragraphs to the *Morning Post*.) But the thrust of Oswald's vision of himself starving in a garret at the mercy of a slavemaster demanding "Odes" is that no undertaking more desperate could be imagined.

By a curious freak of fortune, nevertheless, it was his occasional writing of amatory and elegiac poems sold to newspapers or commissioned by families, gathered into an edition of collected *Poems* in 1789, that brought Oswald moments of recorded fame—in Scotland in 1821 and in Paris in 1859. When he chose the nom de plume "Sylvester Otway" for some of his newspaper verse, and for his title page, he was identifying himself with a Grub-Street precursor, Thomas Otway, who had died famous but poor, protesting that his Muse had become a whore.[96]

95. For the origin of the Literary Fund, see the forthcoming biography of David Williams by James Dybikowski.

96. Thomas Otway gained lasting fame, as a dramatist, but his "Complaint to his Muse," an Ode that seems to have inspired the opening laments of Coleridge's "The Mad Monk" and Wordsworth's "Intimations" Ode, classed Otway with Chatterton and Smart as warning examples of the

Oswald must have earned some bread and perhaps some gratitude for his poems-on-command; yet the frontispiece of his *POEMS: to which is added, THE HUMOURS of JOHN BULL*, engraved by Grignion, exhibits the charms not of Eros but of Eris, the goddess of discord, whose apple of contention is still bitter in our bellies—with a motto warning youth against the sting in her tail.[97] And indeed it is the satiric ingredients of the collection that, paid for or not, retain some vitality today.

It is true, however, that one amatory poem had gained Oswald some fame when published by itself. *Euphrosyne, an Ode to Beauty: Addressed to Mrs. Crouch*, dated February 1788, was reviewed in the *Monthly Review* that October and proudly reprinted in the *Poems*.

Sylvester Otway's verses are not and can never have been to everyone's taste, but considering their emphatic phallic motif, Lichtenberger's remark that "Nearly all his verses celebrate a sentimental and platonic love" is odd.[98] His Ode to Beauty *as* Mrs. Crouch (singer and comic actress of great acclaim) appears to have been construed as far from platonic in spirit. Anna Maria Phillips Crouch, a performer from 1780 to 1801 at Drury Lane and at the King's Theatre and frequently in Ireland, is given a chapter in Joseph Haslewood's *Secret History of the Green-Room*, which assures us that she was "universally allowed to be the most beautiful [lady] that ever graced the English Stage."[99] Daughter

---

sad fate of English poets. (See my report on "The Otway Connection," pp. 143–60 in *Coleridge's Imagination: Essays in Memory of Pete Laver*, ed. Richard Gravil et al., 1986.)

97. The tempting goddess looks like Venus, bare to the waist, but the motto warns "Inspice cautus Eris" ("Look out for Discord's tail") and directs us to Aesop, who tells of the serpent with a sting at each end. John D. C. Buck notes that the genre of this frontispiece is standard—in children's books—and calls my attention to a similar frontispiece in *An Account of the Constitution and Present State of Great Britain* (London: John Newbery, ca. 1795), a very Oswaldian topic—a book he would have picked up. It is captioned: "The Genius of History introducing two young Persons to Britannia, who is seated on her Throne, pointing to two Terms, the one representing *Nature*, the other *Art*, before her is the Altar of Liberty, on which lies Magna Charta, denoting the British Constitution." Clearly the sort of work to draw Oswald's attention. "The central drama is common," says Buck, "the *cognoscente* introducing his followers to the mysteries of the subject at hand—in the Oswald case instructing them to be sensitive to the hidden sting. In children's books the followers are children, as they are in the *Account*, quite reasonably, and in Oswald/Otway's *Poems*, perhaps absurdly."

98. "John Oswald Ecossais, Jacobin et Socialiste," 487; perhaps Lichtenberger had in mind the remark in the *Lives* that Oswald's "effusions were all of love" with no intermixture of "politics or strange philosophy" and added his own platonism to the mixture. For the sentiment expressed is often an invitation to copulation, even beyond the grave; or a lament that absence, or death, is preventing the sipping of ambrosial bliss from "rose-budding" lips which, starting with a "melting, moist impassion'd kiss," would lead to a "livelier type of deeper joy"—which scarcely implies philosophy. In his note on "*No Rose that Blows*, sung by Mrs. Crouch, in Zelima and Azor" (she performed in the ballet of *Zemira and Azor* in February and May 1787) "Sylvester Otway" sounds almost as embarrassed as a later poet, John Keats. She is not only "the fairest Rose," but an "extremely odoriferous . . . Rose" whose magic voice is said to transform the "wild warbler" Otway into "some stray kidling"!

99. It is reasonable to conjecture that Oswald's use of the name of Otway—whose "Orpheus and Eurydice" he quotes on his title page—was inspired by Mrs. Crouch's performance in ballets and oratorios derived from Thomas Otway's works; yet the only production of "Orpheus and Eury-

Fig. 13. Maria Crouch, "the Most Beautiful Actress on the London Stage." At left: portrait by Alexander Pope, engraved by W. Ridley, for the *European Magazine*, 1805. (NYPL) At right: portrait by J. Hutchisson, engraved by Ridley for the *Monthly Mirror*, April 1801. (SB)

of a South Wales attorney named Phillips who was a close friend of Benjamin Franklin and a lover of liberty, she closely escaped marriage to a nabob, made her debut at Drury-Lane as Mandane in Thomas Arne's *Artaxerxes* in 1780, and in 1784 married a young lieutenant in the navy, R. Edward Crouch.

In 1791, she "sent Crouch packing with a sizable allowance after a legal separation occasioned, according to rumor, by an intimacy which had sprung up between Mrs. Crouch and the Prince of Wales." When Oswald reprinted his ode in *Poems*, he took pains in a preface to declare that "The allusions in the Poem are made chiefly to Mrs. Crouch in the Character of *First Bacchante*, presenting the enchanted Cup; and to the celebrated Duet now introduced in Comus, and sung by her and the *First Baccanal* [*sic*]"—*Comus* was first performed with the duet in 1787–1788—and to explain that "Since the first Publication of this hasty production, the Author has endeavoured, by several alterations, to render it more acceptable to the Public."

The actual changes were few and minor. But Oswald now added, for the benefit of any who might wonder how Anna Maria herself responded: "To

dice" listed in *The London Stage* was that performed at the King's Theatre, 1 March 1791 (in "private" with a company of 4,000!) and repeated publicly without Mrs. Crouch, 26 March (total, 9 performances). Most of the details of Mrs. Crouch's career are from Haslewood; a few are added from *BDAA*. Neither of these accounts, however, gives any space to the Prince of Wales (see below).

those who are inclined, from prudery, malevolence, or a boorish antipathy to the Muses" (not an easy choice), "to fasten on the innocent play of imagination an improper meaning, the Author shall only say, Honi soit qui mal y pense." Here, in ironic vein but for good reason, Oswald was borrowing the famous motto of the Prince of Wales, whose interest in actresses was of considerable interest to the boorish and the malevolent. I suspect that, in fact, the rumors were already abroad that would cause the Crouch marriage to collapse.[100]

In a new edition of the *Secret History of the Green-Room* in 1795, "with improvements," one of the improvements is a great emphasis on John Oswald, one of Mrs. Crouch's admirers "under the assumed name of Silvester Otway," whose "effusion," the *Euphrosyne* ode, is reprinted in full, both "for its singularity" and for "that of its Author," along with Oswald's prefatory remarks about his allusions to Mrs. Crouch.[101] Haslewood also finds room—a unique feature in this chapter of his book—for a long biographical note on Mrs. Crouch's singular admirer. This proves to be impressively accurate in its account of Oswald's career and implies some mutual admiration between Sylvester and Euphrosyne. Perhaps Oswald *had* managed to be in Ireland during one of Maria Crouch's tours and was not altogether joking when he said he had served in Tipperary once as apprentice to a "man-milliner."[102]

Since, on the eve of the French Revolution, he was able to function as a distributor of Bonneville's tracts to circles in Wales, Scotland, and Ireland, it may well be that—man of travels that he was—he had already visited these places:

100. *BDAA*, 4:84, no source indicated. But the grounds for this rumor were recorded in Joseph Farington's diary, for 3 January 1800:
   The Prince of Wales wished to form a connexion many years ago with her, and settlements were made. Mrs. Crouch had money or bonds to the amount of £12,000 [and] her husband something equivalent to £400 a year to prevent his bringing an action against the Prince. After all this, the Prince was only with her once. When the [Prince's] debts were settled, Mrs. Crouch presented her bonds, on which the Commissioners demanded *what was the consideration* had for them. They persisting in this demand, she quitted them with some abusive expressions. She is now about 36 years of age, much altered in manner and soured in temper.
Nevertheless, in the Prince's town, Brighton, a memorial erected in the Church of St. Nicholas describes how she could "gladden life by the charms of her conversation and refine it by her manners" (Aspinall, *Correspondence of George Prince of Wales*, 3:1075). Michael Kelly, who first appeared at Drury Lane in the summer of 1787 and quickly became its leading tenor, discloses in his *Reminiscences* (1826) that he also became Maria Crouch's lover—and that he had met Walking Stewart in Vienna. I can imagine a Kelly-Oswald conference which begins with discussing Maria Crouch and ends recalling Walking Stewart.
   101. Of the engraved portraits of Mrs. Crouch shown in Figure 13, I rather prefer the one by Alexander Pope, which Oswald would have liked for its Ossianic quality; the hair resembles that of the maid Sulmalla, "bright in her locks," in Thomas Stothard's illustration for book 8 of *The Poems of Ossian*. The Hutchisson picture gives her an incredibly heavy look and staid expression.
   In the list of twenty-three portraits of Mrs. Crouch in *BDAA* 4:87–88, these two are conflated (sight unseen, presumably) and Pope identified as only engraver of the first. This Alexander Pope, not to be confused with the great poet, was a Dublin-trained portraitist who took to the stage in 1785 and played principal tragic parts at Covent Garden, Drury Lane, and the Haymarket, yet continued as a miniature painter, exhibiting at the Royal Academy between 1787 and 1821.
   102. I would not rule out the possibility that Oswald found himself in need of employment in Tipperary at some point. Is the "man-milliner" a glance at "stay-maker" Tom Paine?

his home in Edinburgh, friends of Franklin and liberty in Cornwall, and David Williams in Wales.

One of his *Poems*, an "Elegy on the Death of the Right Honourable Lady Matilda Birmingham, Youngest Daughter of the Earl of Louth," who died in May 1788, suggests the poet's presence at the funeral in Ireland. He addresses his complaint to the black-pennanted ships filling the bay of Galway:

> O why so sad, ye sons of traffic say?
> And why, thou troubled bay,
> Thus swells thy bosom broad?

Why does "Sorrow's sable banner stream?"

Lady Matilda died 31 May at Barège, in France; her remains were sent to the family vault at Athenay; the funeral was probably held in midsummer. Mrs. Crouch would have been through her Drury Lane season that year after 30 May; Oswald might have been able to slip away, though Parliament did not break up until the second week of July. The family of the deceased, which supplied mayors to the town of Galway, could well afford a hired elegist. Yet his imagination could have traveled without his body; none of the nobility named in his poem or advertisement are in the list of subscribers to the *Poems*. "Grub-Street" may well be the proper category for this Elegy.[103]

The names that *are* on the *Poems* subscription list, however, are fairly impressive, even though Oswald could not resist padding it here and there with ribald inventions. Such sequences as "Mr. Fentum, Mr. Fumble, Mr. Fielding" and "Mr. Gotobed, Mr. Gould . . . Mr. Gobble, Mr. Garrow, Mr. Gun" tempt one to suspect the whole list of fabrication.[104] But "Lieut. J. Oswald" is real, and so perhaps are "Mr. Quick, Mr. Quid, Mrs. Quaver." Mr. Quick was an actor of some fame, given a chapter in *The History of the Green-Room*. And Mrs. Quaver may as well be Mrs. Crouch.

Presumably the booksellers listed for multiple copies are (mostly) genuine distributors who will expect delivery and a proper bill: Mr. Becket, 7 copies, Mr. Campbell, 7 copies, Mr. Earle, 3 copies, Mr. Lane, 12 copies, Mr. Ridgway, 6 copies, Mr. Stalker, 12 copies (padding?), and Mr. Trumbull, 4 copies. The largest consignment, 50 copies to Mr. Forbes, points to a quite possible Oswald constituency, for James Forbes, whose *Oriental Memoirs . . . written during seventeen years residence in India* would be published in 1813, was likely a kindred soul.

Mr. Gilvray, 3 copies, is probably Gillray. Mr. Knight is more probably Charles Knight, bookseller, than R. Payne Knight, author of *The Worship of*

---

103. Oswald's note explains that Matilda was the "youngest daughter of the Earl of Louth by Margaretta his wife, youngest daughter and coheiress to Peter Daly, Esq. of Queensbury." And the poem tidily digests remarkable details of her ancestry.

104. There *was*, however, a bookseller named W. Gotobed, in Hosier Lane, a witness at Hardy's trial (as Ralph Manogue has discovered).

Priapus. Other names that fit booksellers are Mr. Anson (of London?), Mr. Johnson (Joseph?), Mr. Robertson (George?).

Other Grub-Street names—of people in the publishing world, often booksellers on the side—are Mr. Carey (David, editor of *The Statesman*), J. Donaldson (James, proprietor of the *Edinburgh Advertiser*), Mr. Edgeworth (father of Maria), Mr. Jolly (Francis Jollie, editor of the *Carlisle Journal*), Mr. Jackson (Professor Jackson, editor of the *Dunfries Journal*), Mr. Jenkins (a reporter of some eminence, in 1808), Mr. Lane (George, drudge of Stuart at the *Morning Post*, later editor of the *British Press*), Mr. Lambert (printer of the *Morning Chronicle*). Mr. Macdonald may be Andrew Macdonald, poet, contributor-editor of Peter Stuart's *Star* (which published the poems of Sylvester Otway); Mr. Noble, Thomas Noble, songwriter and translator, editor of the *Derby Report*; Mr. Price, the patentee of the *Dublin Gazette*; J. Scott, Esq., John Scott, editor of the *Day*; J. Taylor (6 copies), John Taylor, editor of the *Morning Post* and proprietor of the *True Briton* and *Sun*; Mr. Wilson, Peter Wilson, founder of the *Ayr Advertiser* (in 1802). In the list for amusement, of course, are Arbuthnot and Fielding, but Mr. Farington may be Joseph Farington, the painter and diarist. Mr. Hayley has to be the poet, William Hayley, on his way to Paris.

There are also, as we would expect for a military poet, some captains and colonels. The eight lords include several Pittites as well as some leading Whigs. (The earl of Moira and Lord Rawdon are father and son.) John Wilkes is there, but not Horne Tooke. And not William Thomson, unless by proxy: there is "Mrs. Thomson."

Oswald/Otway had also further occasion for self-confidence in this year. By early 1789 he had become a highly praised contributor to the daily London *Star*, as we have just noted. Few issues of that year's *Star* are extant, but a rival paper, dubbed by its historian "the spurious *Star*," is reported to have "said little about its [own] 'entertainment,' possibly because it had no one to compete with 'Sylvester Otway, and the other favourites of the Muses,' the 'lustre of [whose] genius' was now evidently 'illuminating' that newspaper." [105] The legend found in several clearly secondary sources that Oswald's poetry was admired by Robert Burns is traceable to the following letter printed in the London 1821 edition of *Lives of the Scottish Poets* as culled from an issue of the genuine *Star* not now extant:

[With *Delia, an Ode*]
Mr. Printer,
    If the productions of a simple ploughman can merit a place in the same paper with Sylvester Otway, and the other favourites of the Muses who illuminate *The Star* with

---

105. Werkmeister, *London Daily Press*, 246. "Sylvester" seems to have been the spelling in the *Star*, and the one preferred by Oswald, since he uses it on the proud title page of his *Government of the People*; but the printer of *The Poems* spelled it "Silvester."

the lustre of genius, your insertion of the inclosed trifle will be succeeded by future communications from

Yours, &c.,
R. BURNS

Elisland, near Dumfries
May 18, 1789

There is no indication that Burns knew the man behind the pseudonym or even recognized a fellow countryman. It will be noticed that "Otway" is not praised above the "other favourites"; indeed, the import of Burns's remark seems to be that if the *Star* can publish the trifles of Sylvester Otway, it can hardly reject his.[106]

It was only this letter, misconstrued, that got Oswald into the 1821 *Lives of Eminent Scotsmen* (to use the running head of the volume called *Lives of Scottish Poets*) against the better judgment of the anonymous editor.[107] In the "Burns" chapter, where the letter is quoted, a footnote on the name Sylvester Otway reads: "A name now lost to the lists of fame. Among the Memoirs of Ancient Scots, however, there is one of Sylvester Otway, which will be given in Part II of this work. A. S." I take it that "A. S." is editing some manuscript memoirs already written and feels committed to this one. Hence pages 172–80 of part 2 are given to "John Oswald—Sylvester Otway," with this derogatory opening paragraph:

> Among the literary idlers who, about the years 1786 and 1789, occasionally illuminated the columns of the London newspapers with their poetical effusions, the name of *Sylvester Otway* holds a conspicuous place. He evinced merit enough to be admired by Burns (See Life of Burns); and of one whom so great a poet esteemed as of a kindred spirit, it cannot be uninteresting to know some particulars.

The memoir, prepared by a moderately sympathetic "gentleman who knew Oswald well," describes him after he left the army as "living loosely about town," tells of the "absurd principles and dangerous speculation" in his well-written booklets, but cautions people not to think too ill of him as a revolutionary since, after the French declaration of war against Britain, he was one of the Jacobins who "warned his countrymen . . . of the danger they incurred by remaining in the country."

This last detail seems to be a fiction, for Oswald was in the Vendée or dead

---

106. Varé, 14, who noticed the weakness of this evidence, paraphrases Burns's letter thus: "Sir, if the productions of a simple laborer merit a place in your journal, in which the genius of Sylvester Otway shines, &c." A very odd thing is that the poem printed with Burns's letter in the *Star*, "Delia," did not get into early editions of Burns and is even placed among the "dubia" by the modern Burns editor, James Kinsley, implying that perhaps the letter itself was not by Burns! What kind of hoax might that have been?

107. All later editions of the *Lives* omit the "Oswald" chapter. For the tangled context of Burns's letter to the *Star*, see Werkmeister, "Some Account of Robert Burns and the London Newspapers."

before this kind of advice to the British in France would have seemed called for. Yet most later biographers repeat it, by way of giving the devil his due.

At this point it will be convenient to turn to the much more—but not altogether—reliable account in Haslewood's *Green-Room*[108] for a highlighted sketch of Oswald's fortunes as he removed to Paris while keeping a writing desk and even at last mounting a public platform in London, where we shall observe him in the next chapter.

In 1790, being a warm admirer of the French Revolution, he went to Paris, and there associated with the leaders of the Jacobin Club. He was, however, a long time there without being distinguished by any thing but his violent speeches. He lived in a small hut, a short distance from Paris, and during his obscurity he was driven to such distress, that it is said, being truly reduced to *Sans-Culottes* in their clothing, he turned out both his sons to feed on what they could pick up in the neighbouring gardens and forests,[109] for they possessed an equal antipathy with the Father to animal food.

Soon after this, Fortune smiled on him. He proposed to the Convention to introduce the use of the pike not only in the Army, but among the Mob. This proposal being accepted, he had under tuition an immense concourse of both sexes, to instruct in the use of that instrument. He was appointed Colonel Commandant; and thus he was suddenly advanced from the greatest poverty to a state of affluence.

He is also said to have suggested that capering, singing, and fury exhibited by the French army when going into action, which has so much tended to confound and intimidate their opponents.

Here is to be remarked the contrariety of the human character. He whose mildness of disposition could not behold a drop of blood without shuddering with horror—he who could call a Soldier by no milder epithet than that of *Butcher!*—even he instantaneously fled from one extreme to the other. He is said to have commanded at those unspeakably horrid massacres at Paris in July, August, and September, 1791.[110] He also at the head of his infernal pikemen formed the guard which closely surrounded the scaffold on which the late King of France was guillotined. Immediately after the head of the unfortunate monarch fell into the basket, he and his whole troop struck

108. This biography, unknown to Lichtenberger or any of his sources, turned up when I was looking for vegetarian tracts that might have been influenced by Oswald's 1791 *The Cry of Nature*. The *Green-Room* biography is quoted in a Shelley source, Joseph Ritson's *An Essay on the Abstinence from Animal Food* (London, 1802), omitting the third and fourth of the paragraphs quoted here. Ritson as vegetarian felt required to suppress the awkward information that one of his exemplary vegetarians had been known to display martial fury and to dance at the guillotine. But Ritson knew only about Oswald's life; he was unaware of *The Cry*, for it had not been mentioned by Haslewood—a shame. Ritson also, in quoting the second paragraph, changed the word *Mob* to *people*; Oswald would have approved.

109. This sounds right, his living in a hut on the outskirts of Paris and sending his sons to forage for cabbages (shall we say), a safe thing to do in revolutionary Paris though a capital crime in London. Quite probably the address Oswald gave in his May 1790 Prospectus, l'Hotel d'Angleterre, was only a mailing address (see Appendix B).

110. The year of the September massacres was, of course, 1792; I find no other rumor of Oswald's involvement.

up a hymn he had composed for the occasion, and danced and sung, like so many Savages, round and round the scaffold![111]

In 1793 he is said to have met his fate, for he was killed, together with both his sons, in an action with the advocates of Royalty in La Vendee.[112]

Blunt Words for Edmund Burke

In 1790 Burke's publishing his instantly sensational *Reflections on the French Revolution* early in November hurled an ideological petard calculated to divide the Whigs and scatter the forming ranks of British friends of revolutionary France. At the 4 November anniversary banquet of the Revolution Society it was hurled back by the feisty veteran radical Horne Tooke, who called Burke's pamphlet (which, among its charges, deplored the French "confiscation of the revenues of bishops, and deans, and chapters, and parochial clergy") "the tears of the Priesthood for the loss of their pudding" and proposed a toast which caused such an uproar in the Society that he had to withdraw it.[113] Its words, however, had been uttered: "If Mr. Burke be ever prosecuted for such a libel on the Constitution, may his impeachment last as long as that of Mr. Hastings!"[114]

Tooke, undiscouraged, presented a petition to Parliament charging that, in the recent Westminster election which he had contested unsuccessfully, "armed violence" and constitutional irregularities had occurred that pointed to the need for electoral reform. It was presented and discussed, with a pro forma tabling, in the House of Commons on 9 December. The report in the next day's *Gazetteer* was presumably supplied by Oswald, who had returned from Paris in time to report the opening session of 26 November. It seems fairly evenhanded in allotting colorful language to both parties. But the editorial paragraph beside it is manifestly *not* his:

> The Petition or rather the *Manifesto*, presented yesterday to the House of Commons, in the name of the notorious *John Horne Tooke*, is one of the greatest outrages on public decency that the annals of Parliament can furnish.—However lightly it may be treated by the blind and ignorant partisans of Mr. Tooke, the rational part of the citizens of Westminster, if there are any of that description who voted for him, must

111. Confirmation of this singing and dancing will be found in the Fourth Interchapter, below.

112. Ritson adds a note that shows he knew of Oswald's career from other sources as well: "The name of 'colonel Oswald' occurring in the campaign of 1796, this fact [his death in the Vendée] has been disputed but the officer intended may be colonel Ebenezer Oswald [*sic*] of America." But no, it was one of John Oswald's sons, who died at Cremone in 1796.

113. For the circumstances and furor of the early reception of the *Reflections*, see Cobban and Smith, eds., *The Correspondence of Edmund Burke*, 5 : 150ff., esp. 160n.

114. Burke's impeachment of Warren Hastings for "corruption and cruelty" in his India administration had begun in 1788 and would continue until 1795.

revolt with indignation when they see a man, under pretence of asserting their rights, openly daring to insult the House of Commons in the character of a Petition.[115]

Public interest was intense, and the society called City Debates, in Cornhill, announced in the *Gazetteer* a debate on "Mr. Horne Tooke's Petition" on Monday the 20th, inviting Tooke himself to attend. Whereupon "the Managers of Coachmaker's Hall" announced on the 23rd that "THIS EVENING" the Society for Free Debate would address the following "very interesting Question": "Ought the Petition of Mr. Horne Tooke to be reprobated as an impudent Libel on the most important Branch of the British Legislature, or supported by the People as containing bold Truths, and Founded on Constitutional Principles."[116] And they requested Oswald, parliamentary reporter for the *Gazetteer*, to deliver the opening address. (By the usual rules subsequent speakers would be limited to ten or fifteen minutes each round.)

"I am no orator, Mr. Chairman," he begins, meekly but earnestly: "nor ever, except upon this question, have I risen in public to deliver my sentiments on any subject whatever." This can mean that he has been a silent participant in debating societies for years—or that he has spoken only on constitutional subjects. Perhaps he *did* speak up on Monday at the City Debates, on this specific topic. Nevertheless, he would like the audience to bear with him *as though* this were his maiden speech, and he speaks from the heart on "the cause of freedom," trusting "plain common sense," which he takes to be "the true touchstone of all political institutions" (2–3). As he warms to his subject, however, Oswald's style in debate consists in insolent coat-trailing to provoke the audience's fire, followed by witty reversal of the argument, in effect inviting both sides to march in the same direction.[117]

115. The writer of this paragraph was compelled to change his tune the next day. Someone—Oswald?—pointed out to him that even Fox himself, though a competitor with Tooke in the Westminster contest, had taken the petition seriously. On 11 December, the editorial writer opined that "The conduct of Mr. Fox upon Horne Tooke's Petition affords a very noble proof of disinterestedness, of an unconquerable adherence to the constitution, and gentlemanly disdain of a low adversary" (and so on). The *Gazetteer* still identified itself as an Opposition paper; still scoffed at English politicians who cried out against "expected tumult in Paris" (e.g., 10 December, 3). Oswald may have supplied the paragraph which condemns editors who "borrow" reports from French journalists instead of borrowing "a little knowledge from *experience*" (such as Oswald's *in* Paris). No one seems to have remembered (or to have seen fit to recall) that all nine of the *treasury* papers had supported Tooke against Fox in the Westminster election of 1790 (Werkmeister, *London Daily Press*, 14).
116. The City Debates notice had included a firm defense of Tooke as "a Gentleman whose political sentiments have been the constant theme of misrepresentation and abuse both from Opposition and Administration," and a friend of Tooke apparently inspired the question, put thus: "Ought Mr. Horne Tooke's Petition to be considered as a libelous Attack on the House of Commons, or a just Statement of the Defects in the British Constitution, arising from the unequal Representation of the People?" (*Gazetteer*, 18 December 1790).
117. For the text of Oswald's speech we must depend on the only extant edition of his *Review of the Constitution of Great-Britain*, i.e., the "Third Edition, with considerable additions," Paris, 1792. For his speech, he says, he had been drawing upon "outlines" published in May 1790 in *The Universal Patriot*, an English newspaper printed in Paris (which survives only in the Prospectus: see

He approaches the question with provocative irony, seeming at first to take the Tory side: "I come . . . bluntly to the question; and I declare, that after perusing with attention the petition of Mr. Horne Tooke, I cannot but consider it as the most direct and daring libel on the House of Commons that ever ventured within the walls of St. Stephen's Chapel. . . ." In the House debate this was indeed what Pitt and others said, that the petition was "libellous to the constitution of the House"; none had said it was not. Here was Oswald chiming in: "I repeat it, the most direct and daring libel on the House of Commons—for it is the truth itself; and according to the doctrine of our Lawyers, and to the present practice of our Courts, the truer the assertion, the greater is the libel." By this time it is evident to the debaters that Oswald, in the spirit of Tooke himself, is choosing the libelous path—and implying that the answer to both sides of the question as posed is Yes: that the petition is both a libel *and* a just statement. Many in the audience will recall Tooke's toast to Burke's "libel." Some may remember the toasts at a recent Manchester Revolution Society banquet (reported in the *Gazetteer* of 12 November): "The Irish Jury, who declared Truth *not* to be a Libel,"[118] along with "The Liberty of the Press" and "Success to the Revolution in France."

First Oswald amplifies Tooke's charge of armed violence at elections:

> . . . And have we not seen the bludgeoned banditti of both factions (for between them both I am willing to divide equally the blame); have we not seen them marshalled under their respective leaders, block up every passage to the hustings, and rush to the combat like two contending armies in the field of battle? The timid, the moderate, and the prudent citizens in general, avoided a scene of violence and uproar; and cursed, from the bottom of their hearts, a brutal anarchy, more oppressive, if possible, than absolute despotism itself. In fine, Mr. Horne Tooke asserts, that the majority of seats in the House of Commons are bought and sold like stalls for cattle at a fair. And is not this a notorious fact . . . which till now, in the face of that corrupt and all-corrupting assembly, no man . . . has yet had the patriotic hardihood to assert.[119]

Oswald no longer sounds, as he sometimes did in the 1780s, like a Grub-Street apologist for Fox. He will soon lump together Fox and Pitt as both having a bad influence in the "confection" of the faulty first French Constitu-

Appendix B). The speech had been more immoderate than the ultimate printed version, since in preparing that he had "erased from the manuscript several facts and observations strictly true" which had displeased "some moderate men of my acquaintance." Then characteristically he laments that even so he may not "altogether escape the charge of violence; a censure which, in this age of sycophancy and circumlocution, a plain blunt man, who tries to advance in a straight line to the truth, cannot possibly avoid" (4). The "outlines" may have given the main lines of his review of the Constitution, but the speech as a critique of Burke's *Reflections* must have been written shortly before it was delivered.

118. The truth of a libel had no legal bearing until the law of 1843; it is still not an absolute defense.

119. Tooke had said, "seats for legislation are as notoriously rented and bought as the standings for cattle at a fair."

tion. (See note in *The Government of the People*, 8.) He now speaks as the
student of Rousseau; he has pushed past the physiocrats and taken what he
needs from his fellow Scot William Ogilvie, whose *Essay on the Right of Property
in Land* (London, 1781) he alludes to, recognized today as one of the pioneer documents on land reform and on socialism: [120] "But the representatives of
the people are the agents of the public: they manage the common stock . . . .
Every individual, therefore, should have a voice in the appointment of the common agents of all. No, say some with an air of triumph, those only should have
a right to vote who are men of property. But, pray, Is there any man without
property?" A startling question. Even the revolutionaries in France, at this
time, considered millions of citizens so propertyless they lacked the right to
vote or hold office. Not Oswald: "Is not the daily labour of the peasant, or the
mechanic, as much his property, and as precious to him, as the wide possessions or funded wealth of the landholder, or man of money?" (5).[121] Oswald's
account of the imposition of war, by "a weak or a wicked King, an ambitious
Minister, a rapacious Aristocracy," and its effect upon the poor, driven "to that
ferocity of wretchedness to which, to butcher a fellow-man, or to fall by his
hand, are alike unimportant," would make a prose accompaniment to Wordsworth's "Guilt and Sorrow":

> If, from the danger of war and perils of the deep also, he chances to escape, as soon
> as his service can be dispensed with he is sent ashore—to be hanged. He was guilty of
> theft, you will say: he committed robbery. But what could he do? He found himself
> thrown adrift upon the wide world . . . urged by hunger to overleap the iron barriers
> of property. . . . After a long and cheerless journey, he arrived at that humble cot from
> whence, a few months before, he had been dragged by the cruel hand of power. He
> approached his humble habitation; but his soul sunk with sad forebodings. . . . how
> fearfully silent is his fire-side! "Where art thou, my love!" he cries, with a faultering
> voice.—Alas! she was no more!—Torn from her husband . . . she bowed her gentle
> head and sunk into the grave. . . . she had seen her babe expire upon her breast. . . .[122]
>
> We may, therefore, I think, without presumption, assume it as a principle in a free
> State . . . That every man shall be actually represented. . . .
>
> And now, Where shall we find the representatives of the people of England? . . .
>
> Are the people represented by the Lords? No . . . . A Peer is a sort of political monster, who is born a law-giver, sucks from his nurse's breast the wisdom of legislation,
> and comes into Parliament to represent—himself. If he represents any body whatever,

120. On Ogilvie, see the article in the *Dictionary of Modern British Radicals* by Edward T.
Kosberg. On his socialism, see Beer, *A History of British Socialism*, 1:109ff.: "Ogilvie, a professor
of humanity at the Aberdeen University, and a successful agriculturist . . . regarded private property
in land as the source of all evil; the monopoly in land, 'by the operation of which the happiness of
mankind had been for ages more invaded and restrained than by all the tyranny of kings, the imposture of priests, and the chicane of lawyers taken together . . . .' The rumblings of the French
Revolution are distinctly heard in that denunciation."

121. In his "Observations on the Commercial Treaty with France," Ignotus had defined national
wealth as "the stock of labour" (*Herald*, 3:322).

122. The plot and sentiments may fit Oswald's own career and his feelings about his recently
entombed Louisa.

it must be those Danish, Saxon, or Norman pirates, who, at different periods, invaded this country . . . .

To Tax a man without his consent, is to plunder him. But is it not infinitely more tyrannical to forbid the operation of his mind . . . ? . . . a man comes forward, and putting round the neck of another man a red or blue ribbon, or affixing to his breast some glittering toy:—"Behold!" he exclaims, "a GREAT MAN! . . . call him your Lord, even if he should be the lowest lacquey [or] the veriest dunce . . . !" . . .

No sooner was the French nation fairly represented, than the order of the Noblesse was abolished; and whenever the people of this country shall obtain an equal representation, our Barons must also bid adieu to their political existence. (9–10, 12)

In the British Library copy of this pamphlet, a contemporary reader with the pen of a draftsman has made here a bracket and a pointing fist. The next fist points to a castigation of the regulation, cited in Tooke's petition, that limits the right of voting to men possessed of at least three hundred pounds per annum:

. . . the scandalous immorality of a regulation, which stigmatizes an honourable state of poverty, and which, by holding up to our view wealth as the criterion of worth, debauches the people, and impoisons the public mind with . . . an opinion that is the cause of almost all the disorders that disturb the peace of society . . . .

Are the flock to be represented by wolves? (14–15)

Several pages are floated on the logic of Burke's argument (in the *Reflections*) that "the very inequality of representation . . . is, perhaps, the very thing that prevents us from thinking or acting as Members for districts. Cornwall elects as many Members as all Scotland. But is Cornwall better taken care of than Scotland?" Oswald replies:

The meaning of this subtle argument, if it has any meaning at all, amounts to this: that the Members of Parliament, not being elected by the districts from which they are sent . . . do not consequently represent one district more than another; . . . we may with equal logic conclude, that neither do they represent one country more than another; England, more than France; nor the natives of Great-Britain, more than the negroes of Madagascar [Oswald's old friends, the Joannamen] . . . . (13–14)

The marking finger next points to his vision of "the human race rolling down the tide of ages" with "no beam of hope . . . their limbs, lean and distorted" and, riding high above, "a revel rout, fat and sleek, and shining with good cheer: on every side they throw their harpy hands; they seize the substance of the poor; they get drunk with his blood." The passage ends quoting Burke's already famous reply to the poor that "they must be taught their consolation in the final proportions of eternal justice." The Oswaldian twist is to look into "the deep mist of futurity" for that final justice: to see "the tyrant stretched upon the wheel" and hear "the shrieks of the sycophant"—for a lesson "that would deter from purposed wrong the sons of violence; the lords of the earth would learn justice, and reverence the will of God." In a footnote he gives the Latin, to remind us that he is countering Edmund Burke with Virgil (17–18).

Quoting Burke leads him around to Burke's "great masses of property" which, perpetuated in families, secure "the benevolent disposition" of their legislation. Here Oswald turns to his own political education by citing debates in Parliament that revealed such propertied greed as to make him a revolutionary. He cites the feeble debate (mentioned above) on a bill making cabbage cutting a crime for which the great masses of poor must be "hanged, like a dog, by the neck," and he recalls his "sensations" on that occasion and his "eyeing wishfully the lamp-irons which a provident architect has planted thick about the dark inlets of the House," identifying himself perhaps inadvertently, perhaps intentionally, as a Jacobin who knew how they managed these things in France.

A still clearer example, because a frequent occurrence, was the role of the Commons in legislating the "enclosure of the commons":

> I happened to be present, in the House of Commons, when [an enclosure] bill was brought into the House. Having left England at a very early age, and being engaged in a life too active to permit political enquiries, I had, like other young men, taken it for granted that the British Constitution was the very model of legislative wisdom. I therefore listened with much pleasure to the decorous preamble of the bill, which professed to have for its sole object the improvement of agriculture; and I imagined to myself, that the House of Commons were going to divide the common lands among the poor. But what was my astonishment and my indignation, when, by the after-clauses of the bill, I found that the poor and indigent were to be driven from the commons; and that the land which before was common to all, was now to become the exclusive property of the rich!—The honourable House of Commons vanished from my sight; and I saw in its stead a den of thieves, plotting in their midnight conspiracies the murder of the innocent, and the ruin of the fatherless and the widow! (20)

"The business of making laws," he resumes, "is committed to bullock-contractors, slave-merchants, gamblers, brokers, moneychangers." And he calls out, "Saviour of the World! When wilt thou arise?" (24).

In Coachmakers' Hall, two days before Christmas, perhaps he keeps silent a moment to let the ambiguity of "Saviour" dart backward or forward in people's minds—to the Christ who drove out the money changers, or to a Robespierre or a Napoleon—as yet undiscovered and unnamed. He then names the people as the militant savior, Blake's Orc: "When shall the PEOPLE expel, with a scourge, that impure herd of buyers and sellers, who have converted into a den of thieves, the sanctuary of the law?" And then, to shame the people of Britain, a horde of pedlars and lackeys who have even "debauched the female mind," Oswald argues that the people of France had stood for only half as much grief from their tyrants before overthrowing them. Speaking as a world traveler, he asserts that "one-half of the misery under which we groan would raise, in the most absolute governments of Asia, a cry of 'Vengeance!'":

I have travelled over a large portion of the empire of Turkey, one of the most despotic countries in the world . . . . In Turkey, I found that a peasant or labouring mechanic, by three or four days moderate labour in the week, could maintain two, and sometimes three or four, wives, and a numerous family of children.—In England . . . the peasant or mechanic is often deterred from marriage by the difficulty of obtaining bread . . . his coarse and scanty fare [includes] butter . . . very rarely . . . except, perhaps, that unwholesome and unpalatable species of butter which salt arrests in a certain state of putrefaction: cheese, except of the driest and most insipid sort . . . with a kind of corrupt water, called small beer . . . .

One can see how the rumor that Oswald had two wives was encouraged by his own remarks; perhaps it was true—at this point he could have had one wife in Deal, or London, and one in Paris—though that *Green-Room* report of meager living on the outskirts of Paris with two vegetarian sons does not mention any mother(s). Some moderns might be shocked to know that many in his debating club audience would have approved.[123]

But Oswald's speech finally settles down to its work on the "boasted Constitution" of Britain, in a manner calculated to shame anyone who would not prefer one grounded on "the natural and indefeasible *Rights* of *Man*." As our attention strays from grim accounts of pernicious rulers, biblical and Roman, or according to Burke's fancy, we are brought up suddenly by a startling report on King George:

> He is said to delight in the story of the frugality of Spartan royalty, and to admire, above all, the Constitution of the United States of America, where the Chief Magistrate is satisfied with a salary of five thousand pounds. . . . His Majesty, I am also informed, rejoices beyond measure in the late glorious Revolution in France, and pants for that happy day when he also shall become, like Louis XVI, the father of a regenerated people!

The speech the King is imagined to have made on that "glorious day" expresses his delight in deflecting the rivulet of wealth "from the broad stream of ministerial corruption" to extinguish the national debt and to free his subjects from the "band of public robbers." In a footnote Oswald assures us that the Commonwealth of France has risen "from the very sink of moral depravity" (36). The King is further imagined redistributing Burke's "great masses of property" and the "luxurious livings" of the bishops. But then Oswald lowers the boom:

123. That very season the subject of multiplicity of wives, or of lovers, was popular in the societies. The Coachmakers' Hall Society, on 17 February 1791, freely debated the question "Is a Lady justifiable in admitting of the addresses of two lovers at the same time?" City Debates, the same day, discussed a question introduced at the Coachmakers' on 20 January: "Would either of the following laws tend to prevent Seduction and Prostitution, viz. a law to compel every man to marry who has remained single at the age of 30, or to allow those who are fond of matrimony, to have two wives?" Blake's *Book of Thel* and *Visions of the Daughters of Albion* were then in gestation; his Oothoon is like the leading speaker in the January debate, a "Lady, who has lately perused the celebrated work of the Rev. Mr. Madan in favour of Polygamy, and who has made the causes of female ruin a subject of her particular attention. . . . She is desirous of knowing the opinion of an enlightened assembly upon the consequences of allowing in this country a plurality of wives" (*Gazetteer*, 20 January 1791). On Martin Madan's influence on Blake, see E. B. Murray, "Thel, *Thelyphthora*, and the Daughters of Albion," *Studies in Romanticism* 20 (1981): 275–97.

I return from this digression . . . to consider another important point of what is
called the Constitution . . . the non-responsibility of the Chief Magistrate. . . . The
King, you say, can do no wrong. Cannot the King make war? . . .[124]

Should the reason of your Chief Magistrate suffer an eclipse, and the royal maniac
should begin to sport a little too roughly with the maids of honour, and to kick the
titled lacqueys about his court, it would be thought necessary to put him in a strait
jacket.

Recently, of course, such antics had been reported of King George.

But why, ye deluded nation! are his arms unconfined, when urged by tenfold frenzy,
he unfurls the bloody banner of strife, lets loose the hounds of havoc, and whirling
furious in his hand the firebrand of war, involves in ruin and desolation half the hab-
itable globe?

Thanks to the glorious Revolution of France! Thanks to the enlightened labours of
the National Assembly! We may now hope to see the day when . . . the LAW, which is
the voice of the people . . . shall establish peace and good-will among men. (39)

Returning to "the real cause of all those wars which have so long agitated Europe," Oswald finds them

not a whit more respectable in their motives than those bloody contentions which
the slave-merchant, with the brandy-bottle in his hand, excites between the drunken
chiefs of Africa. In Europe, as in Africa, it is the proud intoxication of royalty, and the
cruel avarice of traffic, that plan together those scenes of murder . . . *to make slaves.*

In a word, the practice of almost every species of government in Europe is per-
versely opposite to . . . that sentiment of brotherhood which united mankind from
the beginning, and which was taught as the base of morals by Plato, Brimha, Con-
fucius, Jesus Christ, and . . . other immortal men . . . (40)

—reverberation of the Everlasting Gospel[125]—from Oswald's reading antino-
mian pamphlets of the seventeenth century; or from direct contact with that
republican tradition?

Oswald next turns to "that pretended salve for all the malversations of government . . . the responsibility of office." But he finds it in neither King, the
House of Lords, nor the House of Commons. Instead he discovers "a political
machine, cunningly contrived to elude responsibility, and to plunder the people
with impunity" (41). Now John Oswald, with his repast of roots and his sword
for settling arguments, recalls a story from ancient Greece: "The Athenians,
impelled by famine or gluttony, were desirous of tasting the flesh of the bull, an
animal consecrated . . . to the labours of the field, and which seems . . . to have

124. A debatelike essay in the *Political Herald* (2 : 203 – 5) by Gilbert Stuart ("Lucius") had apparently lodged in Oswald's mind. Stuart put the question "Is there a Situation where a King of
England is amenable for his Conduct?" and then declared, "That 'a king of England can do no
wrong,' is a maxim which was first suggested by the sages of the law; and they have endeavoured to
cover up very ingeniously the native folly or absurdity of the assertion." For the identification of
"Lucius," see Marken, "William Godwin," 532–33.

125. For the political implications, see Morton, *The Everlasting Gospel.*

escaped long the slaughter to which almost all other creatures had successively been doomed." Suddenly his fable takes on the contemporaneity of the Rowlandson cartoon in his *British Mercury*:

The Athenians wished ardently to feast upon the flesh and to drink the blood of John Bull; but, like a *wise* and *prudent* people, they desired, at the same time, to avoid the odium of the act, and to feast, if possible, with a quiet conscience. They contrived the business in this manner: they chose a number of virgins (*sweet innocent creatures who could do no wrong*) to bring water to whet the hatchet and the knife. As soon as those weapons were made sharp, one man delivered the axe, another struck the blow, a third cut the bullock's throat. Having *done the deed*, they skinned the animal; and all that were present feasted upon his flesh. After this, they sewed up the skin, stuffing it with straw; and having set it up, put a plow to its tail as if it still were alive, and in act to till the ground. Those who had been guilty of the deed were then called before the tribunal of justice to answer for themselves. The virgins . . . threw the blame on the persons who whetted the steel; those . . . shifted the responsibility on the man who delivered the hatchet; he impeached the person who struck the blow; and the latter accused the weapon; which, unable to answer for itself, was found guilty of murder, and cast into the sea.

What a wonderful resemblance between the Athenian and British sacrifice of the bull, even to the worming-out his bowels, and setting up a John Bull of straw! . . . In order that the sacrifice should be deemed good . . . it was necessary that the animal should advance without reluctance to the altar, and *submit* his throat to the knife. . . . the House of Commons, who *do not* fatten on the blood of the people . . . officiate as priest, and judge by the gesticulation of John Bull, whether he is or is not willing to be bled. It is curious to observe, that the political priest has never yet found that the patient animal shrunk from the operation.[126]

As he sums up, Oswald pushes aside any hope in gradual reform—even in 1787 he had paid little attention to a Reform Bill—and dares "to give utterance to that which every mind conceives," that "Our only hopes of renovation are suspended on a National Assembly."

He that does not foresee a grand revolution in the general system of European Governments, must shut his eyes to the evidence of things. On one hand, the public misery; on the other, the progress of reason and political information press forward. . . . The late glorious revolution in France holds forth an example . . . . Let not the Government of England fondly imagine that she alone shall stand unmoved. . . . The Irish . . . the Scots . . . numerous classes of the English nation . . . have clubbed together their common hatred, and conspired the ruin of their common oppressor. Already round her growls the storm that shall lay the *rotten fabric* in the dust.

Oswald's program is simple in its assumption: that the British people are ready for the step the French took in 1789—and logical in its proposed action:

126. You see they consider our House of Commons as "a semblance,"—"A form,"—"a theory,"—"a shadow,"—"a mockery," perhaps, "a nuisance." BURKE'S REFLECTIONS, &c, p. 83. [Oswald's note; Burke, in his "shadow" remark, was retorting upon Tooke.]

arm the people, making them independent enough to legislate; assemble them, to choose freely their representatives; and renew their local assemblies, to vote on laws proposed by these representatives. For John Oswald—as for his associates Camille Desmoulins and Nicolas Bonneville—the strategic significance of 14 July 1789 had been the arming of the people (who stormed the Bastille) and the formation of a national guard. He sums up:

> But no sooner had the nation taken arms (and no nation unarmed ever rescued their liberty, or long retained it in their hands); no sooner, I say, had the nation taken arms, and that public force was coupled with public opinion, when instantly all outrage ceased (for all resistance was in vain), and, like the thunder of Omnipotence, the VOICE OF THE PEOPLE commanded reverence and respect from one extremity of France to the other.

Granted that the invention of arms was pernicious, "let us use it like those poisons which, taken in copious draughts, are said to defeat the fatal effects of a smaller dose." This sounds like the logic behind the symbolism of Wordsworth's Oswald, who chooses among his simples the deadly nightshade. And the calculation is rather different from that remarked upon in the *British Mercury*. But Bonneville, the first proposer of a national guard, and the editor of a journal with a name like an ignited cannon, *Bouche de fer*, would understand. Oswald continues:

> As the age of iron was the last stage in the depravation of man, so neither in our upward progress in the circle of human mutability can we hope to arrive at the age of gold without passing through an age of iron. Let us therefore every man become a man of iron; let us rise up as one man, armed, to vindicate our right. . . . All that we desire at present, however, is a fair and equal representation.

We are back in Coachmakers' Hall. Oswald is confessing to a truly British conviction "that the best, and indeed the only good system of government is that which unites in one a pure democracy, a pure aristocracy, and a pure monarchy." And it comes down to the question of how to choose "the *best*." Answer: "By assembling the people, and electing, as the Jews did when they chose a king, those who are taller than the rest *by the head*; for such are the men whom God, Nature, and the fitness of things, have destined to hold the reins of government."

There is one final page, full of italics, small and large capitals, and a quotation of "the words of the *inspired* writer" who judged Belshazzar, here applied to the Constitution under review—with a hint at present rulers: "Thou art weighed in the balance, and art found wanting."

THE END.

The bravado of Oswald's concluding flourish must spring from the unmistakable fact that our Scottish poet and military theorist was *not* himself "taller by the head." I am not sure from which "biographers" André Lichtenberger culled his description of Oswald, but it sounds right: "a man of middle height, of noble carriage, heroic and grave face, sober manners, and a bit stiff."[127] William Thomson could never have mistaken Napoleon for Oswald if his friend had been a tall, burly man like Danton.

The debating societies almost never published the results of their discussions, though they always concluded by voting on the Question, but the published *Review of the Constitution* spread the fame of Oswald's ideas and oratory in both capitals during the following years. It was hailed by Bonneville in the *Chronique du mois*, and it was strongly recommended for Burke's edification by the English radical Thomas Cooper, in *A Reply to Mr. Burke's Invective . . . in the House of Commons, on the 30th of April, 1792.* Cooper, citing "that well written and animated pamphlet" (75n), was excepting Paine and Oswald from a sweeping complaint that no one had yet "talked of dividing the Wastes and the Commons—of abolishing Tythes—or rewarding population— of comfortably providing for the old age of the Labourer, the Manufacturer, the Artificer—of exonerating the poor for the indirect Taxes which they pay without knowing it . . . above all, of providing ample means of *Public Instruction* . . . ." Earlier in Cooper's own pamphlet, finding Burke's grasp of "the Controversy respecting the political Utility of privileged orders" faulty, he offered his opponent a reading list:

> In our Country, *Milton, Harrington,* and *Sydney,* have treated on the danger and Inutility of Monarchy; but the subject has been much more profoundly, as well as popularly discussed within these two Years. Those who will take the trouble of perusing the "Essai sur les Privileges," and the Sequel to it (Qu'est-ce que le Tiers-Etat) of the *Abbe Seyes,* Paine's "Rights of Man part 1 and 2," *Barlow's* "Advice to the privileged orders," and *Oswald's* "Review of the Constitution of Great Britain," will find almost every thing that the Subject affords on one Side of the Question . . . .[128]

127. "John Oswald Ecossais, Jacobin et Socialiste," 483. According to the Scottish *Lives,* 178, "Mr. Oswald was about the common stature, but of a very commanding appearance." For an idea of his looks we have only the Brain-Sucker caricature, with its vaguely Scottish profile (see Figure 4).

128. Cooper, *Reply,* 17n.

FIRST INTERCHAPTER
HANDS ACROSS THE
CHANNEL—OR ARMS?

(A chronological glance)

1688–1689

When a son was born to King James II, threatening a perpetuation of Stuart "tyranny," seven Whig nobles invited William of Orange, statholder, captain general, and admiral, to "invade" England. He landed in Devon with an army of fifteen thousand and advanced to London, meeting virtually no opposition. James was allowed to escape to France. Early in 1689, William summoned a Convention Parliament and accepted its offer of the crown jointly with his wife Mary, oldest daughter of King James II. The Glorious Revolution was thus accomplished in England without bloodshed, and it proved a decisive victory for Parliament. William was forced to accept the Bill of Rights in 1689.

1779

As the summer of the American Revolution approached, public opinion in France "was greatly excited by the expected invasion of England or, alternatively, Ireland by the French army. The entrance of Spain into the war seemed to assure naval superiority for such an operation. Patriotism ran high, and Necker believed this would permit him to issue his second major loan of life rentes" (i.e., public bonds).[1]

1788

4 and 5 November. A Revolution Jubilee celebrating the hundredth anniversary of the landing of William, Prince of Orange, in Torbay, to reestablish constitutional government in England, was held at Whittington and Chesterfield. A

1. Harris, *Necker*, 145.

dinner at the Revolution House in Whittington, where the British welcome of William's invasion had been planned,[2] was held on the 4th and a divine service at Whittington Church on the 5th (text: "This is the day, &c."), after which the eight Revolution Clubs marched with blue and orange colors bearing the cap of Liberty, representations of Liberty crowning Britannia, and various mottos declaring "Liberty, property, trade, manufactures"; "Liberty Secured"; "The Glorious Revolution 1688"; celebrating King William as "The Glorious Revolter from Tyranny 1688." The members of the clubs were estimated to be two thousand persons, each having a white wand in his hand. "The whole was conducted with order and regularity; for, notwithstanding there were fifty carriages, four hundred gentlemen on horseback, and an astonishing throng of spectators, not an accident happened." "In the evening a brilliant exhibition of fire-works was played off. . . . The day concluded with a ball, at which were present near 300 gentlemen and ladies."

To the eye of a philosopher (writing for the *Annual Register*) the composition of the assemblage was most impressive: descendants of the illustrious houses of Cavendish, Osborne, Boothe, and Darcy; a numerous and powerful gentry; a wealthy and respectable yeomanry; a hardy, yet decent and attentive peasantry; whose intelligent countenances shewed that they understood, and would be firm to preserve that blessing, for which they were assembled to return thanks.

—Annual Register for 1788; Appendix, 249–51.

1789

Thursday, 16 July, Paris. "Everybody since Monday has appeared with a cockade in his hat: at first green ribbons were worn but that being the colour of the Comte d'Artois's livery, red and white in honor of the Duc d'Orleans, have been substituted.

"Thus, My Lord, the greatest Revolution that we know anything of has been effected with, comparatively speaking, if the magnitude of the event is considered, the loss of very few lives: from this moment we may consider France as a free Country; the King a very limited Monarch, and the Nobility as reduced to a level with the rest of the Nation."

—The Duke of Dorset to the Duke of Leeds.[3]

*

When the English have helped revolutionary France to establish itself, writes Joseph Priestley in Birmingham, "we may see the nearer approach of those glorious and happy times, when wars shall cease to the ends of the earth, and

---

2. People were shown "the room called by the Anti-revolutionists 'The plotting parlour,' with the old armed-chair in which the earl of Devonshire is said to have sitten . . . ."

3. Oscar Browning, *Despatches from Paris, 1784–1790*, 2:243.

when the kingdoms of this world shall become the kingdoms of God and of his Christ."

—*Conduct to be Observed by Dissenters on the Repeal of the Corporation and Test Acts.*[4]

1790

May. In Paris "a set of Gentlemen, Britons, by birth, but by sentiment and principle, Universal Patriots," announce the publication of "an English Newspaper, entitled, *The Universal Patriot,*" to be published twice weekly in Paris and London, beginning on Monday, 3 May. The "late glorious Revolution" in France is attributed "in a great measure" to the French study of English authors and affairs. "The Revolution in France, in turn, it is hoped, will rouze from a state of political delusion the supine Englishmen of the present day and the French Nation will have the glory of giving a Lesson of Liberty to the people whose disciples they have been." "Subscriptions for the *Universal Patriot* are received by M. Oswald, at l'Hotel d'Angleterre, No. 243, rue Montmartre"; and by two booksellers in Paris, one in Calais, and two in London.

—Prospectus of an English Newspaper, printed at Paris.[5]

*

10 July. Joel Barlow and Paul Jones and two others sign a manifesto of international sympathy addressed to the National Assembly. Helen Maria Williams, on the first of many visits to France, arrives in time to join the great celebration on the 14th in the Champ-de-Mars. "Women of all ranks, from a princess to seamstresses, too, take part in preparing the Champ de Mars for the Federation, or Feast of Pikes."[6]

*

14 July. William Wordsworth and Robert Jones, having arrived at Calais the night before, find France "standing on the top of golden hours" and see "How bright a face is worn when joy of one / Is joy of tens of millions."[7]

*

August. The *Journal de la Société de 1789* welcomes "the two best poets of England," whom the society recognizes as Robert Merry the Rosicrucian, now "at work on a poem celebrating the French Revolution" (it will be ready for the *next* 14th of July, in London)—and William Hayley, who "in no way yields to his rival" (and, indeed, will by next February have written a play for the French stage, *Les préjugés abolis, ou l'Anglois juste envers les François*—who, not

4. Priestley, *Works*, 15:403–4.
5. Text in Appendix B.
6. Alger, *Glimpses*, 138.
7. Wordsworth, *Prelude*, 6.341–49.

that free, will reject Hayley's play because the presence of a courtesan in the plot offends the French code).[8]

*

4 September. John Oswald offers to the National Assembly "An Ode" not written for a brain-sucker but "Printed for the Author," to commemorate "The Triumph of Freedom!" on the glorious 14th. On the title page, the printer arranges an ascending parade of braggadocio (after "*By JOHN OSWALD*" in the largest type): "Late Lieutenant in the . . . Royal Highland," "Member of the Club des Jacobins," AND "Author of Poems, by SYLVESTER OTWAY, &c."

Here "Otway" seems to reach prophetic heights, with a quotation in Greek from the First Olympian Ode of Pindar. That Ode lauds the new ruler of Syracuse and predicts that his winning a horse race will lead to greater victory in the next chariot race (four horses). "As for me," reads the Pindaric moral Oswald quotes, "the Muse is preparing a weapon [βελος] most mighty in strength."

βελος can mean shaft, javelin, or, alas, terror. What Oswald means we may suppose to be his pen, now offered in the service of the Revolution. Yet he will soon, as we shall see, be advocating a people's weapon, the pike, as a shaft essential to revolutionary combat. It would be like him to have a pun in mind here.

*

4 November. The Revolution Society of Manchester, on the Anniversary of the Glorious Revolution of 1688, begins its thirty-four toasts with "The Majesty of the People" and includes such hopes for the near future as "A friendly Alliance between France and Great Britain, for perpetuating Peace, and making the World happy," and "The disfranchisement of *rotten* Boroughs, and a *speedy, full, and adequate* Reform of the Representation in Parliament." Some of the toasts sound like Blake's "Proverbs of Hell," for example: "Success to all Innovation that leads to Reformation" (cf. "What is now proved, was once only imagin'd").[9]

*

The London *Gazetteer* features a long "Letter from the Society of Friends of the Revolution of Limoges to the Club of Jacobins in Paris," now "transmitted to us from the Club of Jacobins" (by Oswald himself, perhaps) and published with the bold heading "UNION between ENGLAND and FRANCE."[10]

*

8. Alger, *Paris*, 346; Hayley, *Memoirs*, 1:410–13.
9. Blake, *The Marriage of Heaven and Hell* (1790–1793). The Manchester toasts were reported in the *Gazetteer* of 12 November.
10. *Gazetteer*, 4 November.

November to June. Bancal de Isarts is in London trying to set up a sister Cercle Social, to dispel the differences between the nations.[11]

1791

13 February. Lord Lansdowne writing to Morellet: "Your revolution is excessively hard upon individuals, but the effect it must have upon the whole world exceeds all power of imagination!"[12]

*

20 May. Samuel Romilly writing to Madame Genlis: "The impression which [Paine's *The Rights of Man*] has made in Ireland is, I am informed, hardly to be conceived . . . . If the enthusiasm which it has kindled should anywhere break out in acts of violence, it will certainly be first in Ireland."[13]

*

21 May. William Windham, still Foxite, "begins to be very much alarmed with the spirit of revolution which is spreading" through Britain, "a Constitutional Society lately established at Norwich . . . also at Manchester. . . . the Revolution or Constitutional Society in London . . . have hired Ranelagh for 14th July." Blended French and English flags, sent from Paris for the occasion, have been seized at the customs house as made of contraband materials.[14] "Sheridan's present intention is to attend this meeting. . . . he says if he should not go his absence may be imputed to timidity, and that if he is there he may possibly have it in his power to prevent mischief."[15]

*

June. A warm evening at Lady Malmesbury's, the youngsters hunting nightingales—hundreds singing; the adults sitting up half the night to talk over the news from France, and persuade themselves that they too are dancing on a volcano. (The French cook overhears, with his flute and his tame animals: fawn, owl, two pigeons.)[16]

*

July. The Cercle Social in Paris invades the Jacobin Club, bringing several ex-mesmerists and freemasons with British connections and sympathies. Bastille Day celebrations unite many friends of freedom in both nations.

Paine leaves Paris, not having learned to speak or even listen well in French, and hurries to London, ready with ringing words to be delivered, not at

11. Ellery, *Brissot de Warville*, 161n.
12. Fitzmaurice, *Life of Shelburne*, 3:325.
13. Romilly, *Memoirs*, 1:324–26.
14. So much for the treaty of "commerce"!
15. Minto, *Life and Letters*, 1:379.
16. Ibid., 1:387.

Ranelagh (that was either a false rumor or a squelched plan) but at the Whigs' Crown and Anchor Tavern. Arriving in Piccadilly on 13 July, he discovers such a brouhaha in the London press about his republican manifesto of 1 July that he stays in his hotel; "his presence at the meeting might connect it with movements across the Channel." [17] Pressure on the landlord cancels the Crown and Anchor meeting anyway. Paine a month later delivers a fresh manifesto at the Thatched House Tavern, regular meeting hall of a reform society founded by John Frost, a Winchester solicitor, in 1782. Tooke chairs the session.

*

25 October. News reaches England (and, about this time, France) of the insurrection of the slaves of St. Domingo on 2 August, massacring "2000 white colonists and 8000 of mixed blood" and setting fire to plantations. Edmund Burke sees this "shocking affair" as confirming his alarm about the Revolution. "But it is impossible that our people should learn any thing from it on either side of the House; or that the French should be in the smallest degree cured of their insanity by any experience of the consequences. As to the Gentlemen in England who favour this Revolution one answer is always ready:—'These Calamities must attend on all great Changes however proper in their principle or however well conducted.'" Burke sees "little probability" of reversing the course of events. [18]

*

29 November. All members of the Jacobin Club of Paris are invited to come to their hall at nine Tuesday morning to observe the instruction of children in the catechism of the Constitution—i.e., the *Almanach de père Gérard*, by Collot d'Herbois (immediately translated by John Oswald for the English-speaking world, with an added title—*The Spirit of the French Constitution*—and a subsidy from the London Society for Constitutional Information). [19]

*

1–5 December. Wordsworth tours Paris, from the parade ground of the Champ-de-Mars to both "clamorous Halls," the Assembly and the Jacobins. Retrospectively he will describe this as a period when "the revolution Power" was tossing "at anchor." [20]

*

13 December. Anacharsis Cloots, "orateur du genre humain," warns the Assembly that time is wasting. "Show Europe that we are not afraid of war, and we shall have peace; we shall see the émigrés scattered and resourceless." He proposes a time schedule. "Let us set a date, January 20, for the march of three

17. Conway, *Life of Paine*, 1:315.
18. Cobban and Smith, *Correspondence of Burke*, 6:439.
19. Williams (*Artisans and Sans-culottes*, 68) reports the subsidy.
20. *Prelude*, 9.51.

great armies, upon Brussels, upon Liège, and upon Coblentz: and I promise that by February 20 the tricolor cockade and the air *Ça ira* will rejoice twenty delivered peoples." (*Loud applause.*)[21]

*

16–18 December. A Constitutional Whig from London becomes the center of a joyous ritual of the fraternal and sororital embracings of the "Three Free Nations, France, Britain, and the United States of America," at the Jacobin Club.[22]

21. *Arch Parl*, 4:79.
22. See the next chapter.

5.
PARIS

The Glorious Fourteenth of July!

The belief that better communal thinking must produce a better society was an Idea whose time had come. Behind the events that exploded into the memorable "Days" in the calendar of the French Revolution, like waves bursting through ancient barriers, was the great tidal swell of social thinking defined as The Enlightenment. Readers of Voltaire, of the *Encyclopédie*, now clutched their Rousseau and Mably and Restif de la Bretonne and were ready for the speeches and pamphlets and journals of universal patriotism—and ready to assemble as citizens establishing their citizenship, to rewrite their social contract, to raise their hands to speak—to join hands in a dance of equality, fraternity, and their assertion of liberty.

As the Days advanced, the articulate, active leaders of whatever groups constituted or could be transformed into communities found themselves busied in committees, with a varying consensus as to the agenda of their progress, and drawn into combat with enslaving ideas that had had their day. By the time the National Convention, in late 1792, was ready to frame a constitution for representative or parliamentary government, the essentials of a counterdoctrine of direct democracy had gained wide popular support—among the people who were defined or defined themselves as Sans-culottes.[1]

1. Here I draw somewhat upon R. B. Rose, *The Making of the Sans-culottes*, 171. Rose continues: "Rooted originally in Rousseau's *Social Contract*, this counter-doctrine had nevertheless been modified and complemented by a generation of popular tribunes [the object of Rose's study] at grips with the day-to-day exigencies of practical politics: Martin, Dufourny, Babeuf, Fauchet, Girardin, Varlet, and a host of still more obscure leaders of opinion in district, popular society and section. The basic principles were: the inalienable embodiment of sovereignty in the primary assemblies of the people, popular legislation by referendum, binding mandates for the people's deputies and the constant right of recall; *in extremis* the reserved right of insurrection to dislodge usurping governments and to ensure the effective continuity of the sovereignty of the people. This fiercely intransigent interpretation of the meaning of democracy would remain a central feature of the *sans-culotte* movement during its period of greatest solidarity and influence, in 1793 and 1794" (171–72). Among the obscure but important leaders we must include Bonneville and Lanthenas, both cited elsewhere by Rose, and Oswald, not cited. Rose calls Lanthenas and François Sergent

Nicolas de Bonneville, while in London before the Revolution, had undertaken to prepare a French translation of a history of modern Europe which he liked, but he had come to feel it would be more to the point to write one himself.[2] In Paris in 1789 he found himself suddenly among people who were in a strong position to *make* history. That spring, when deputies of the Third Estate were being chosen by two electors from each of the Paris districts, Bonneville proved popular enough with the voters of his own district to be chosen as one of its electors. When, in June, the revolutionary impetus of the Estates General seemed to be stalled, the deputies of the Third Estate, in the famous oath of the Tennis Court, declared themselves *to be* the National Assembly of France.

The next day, Bonneville persuaded the Paris Assembly of Electors, not formally disbanded after the elections, to declare itself a permanent body—to declare that it was now, in effect, the municipal government, having been chosen by a primary assembly of the sovereign people. (Oswald would have argued the same way.)[3] Then, in July, Bonneville's participatory momentum enabled him to become one of the fourteen organizers of "The glorious Fourteenth!"

For the rest of his life Bonneville would boast of the motion he made for an armed guard of citizens—a motion he would often reprint, asking readers to look up the official journal of Jean Dusaulx for a true account of his role in those momentous days.[4]

It was on 25 June that the 120 Paris electors first met, displacing a wedding party in the hall du Musée, rue Dauphine, a sort of cabaret "which, like the Tennis Court of Versailles," says Dusaulx, "served as cradle of our nascent liberty." Overflowing the hall, they reassembled in the adjacent gardens, with a multitude "waiting impatiently around this enclosure." Agreeing to remain in permanent session, they moved into the Town Hall the next day. After that, says Dusaulx, everything prospered.[5]

On that first day, in a discussion of how to overcome the enemies of the people, "a young man, Mr. de Bonneville, who expressed himself on this subject with much sagacity and maturity, suddenly burst into a passion [*s'enflammant tout à coup*] and, foreseeing what was soon to happen to us, cried out, 'To arms! To arms!' Some trembled in horror, others laughed at him, and one of us replied: 'Young man, it is not yet time; put off this motion a couple of weeks.'" But his motion for a city guard was passed.[6]

Naturally only a handful of the electors gathered daily to tackle the urgent chores of governing the city. Bonneville as one of the responsible group was

(an engraver) "veterans of the popular society movement" (143) when noting their names among signers of a Jacobin call for a network of popular societies, 15 September 1791.

   2. Kates, "The Cercle Social," 21, citing Bonneville's *Lettre . . . à Mr. le Marquis de Condorcet*, 13, a prospectus for his intended history.

   3. Nicolas de Bonneville, "Aux Electeurs de la Commune de Paris," *Tribun du peuple*, no. 14, 145–53 (dated 21 June 1798).

   4. In the April 1792 *Chronique du mois*, for example, under the heading "Prise des armes."

   5. See "L'Oeuvre des Sept Jours," 138–50, for the following account.

   6. Dusaulx (ibid., 142) points out that Carra, no less decisive than Bonneville, had already in

charged with organizing the provisioning of Paris, and by all accounts he did it efficiently and successfully. It was from that first day, says Dusaulx, "that we began to know each other well, and to designate those who could be trusted to govern our vessel in the foul weather ahead." (Dusaulx, in fact, had known Bonneville well since the early 1780s when they had met at the home of d'Alembert, their Enlightenment mentor.)[7] He names six and recalls there were "about fifteen others of the same firm temper and who all spoke the language of liberty." Once settled in the Town Hall, they had about two weeks of relative calm, establishing rapport with fellow citizens and communication with all provinces of the realm, shaping that coalition of the people in the presence of which the ministerial troops and their masters, petrified as by the Medusa's head, let the Bastille fall and, with it, all the powers of tyranny. "Several of us had presentiment of the approaching tempest. On 11 July the vigilant Deleutres warned us to be on guard: the thirteenth could be a day of disaster."[8]

On the 12th, Sunday, Dusaulx gives credit to an unnamed young man (who sounds like Bonneville but was Camille Desmoulins, as the editors of Dusaulx have noted) for having responded to the alarm at rumors of Necker's dismissal by leaping upon a table in the Palais-Royal grounds and crying "To Arms!" while drawing a sword and flashing a pistol and a green cockade. The cry spread animation and excitement everywhere, says Dusaulx; signs of civil war appeared in all parts of the city, and people marched toward the Place Louis Quinze, which was filled with menacing troops.[9]

Bonneville's recollection is more dramatic: "On the night of July 12, Lambesc entered the Tuilieries; I flew to my post at the Hotel de Ville; did my duty. We found ourselves fourteen, and in that night of terror and hope I dared affirm that I was one-fourteenth part of the great organization [*plans*] of Union and insurrection which saved France." His own detail was to "convoy grain to save the starving."[10]

Dusaulx concurs in the count of exactly fourteen at the central moment:

> We decreed unanimously that the districts be convoked; be armed; and it was then that we resumed the motion made in the Musée by the young de Bonneville. . . . On the next day, the 13th of July, the Electors resumed their meeting, declared themselves

---

May raised the same suggestions, and that no one better than Carra had foreseen from the beginning the sequence of events of the Revolution: a successful revolution resulting from a well-timed uprising.

7. Kates, "The Cercle Social," 177.

8. "L'Oeuvre des Sept Jours," 140.

9. The account in Carlyle's *The French Revolution* (138–43) is largely an amplifying translation of Dusaulx, but Carlyle puts the June meeting (not dated) just before his account of 12 July, ignoring Bonneville and concentrating on Desmoulins, and then omits Dusaulx and his fourteen or so comrades, simply having the old twenty-six town councillors disappear and the new "Electoral Club" gather from nowhere and declare itself a "Provisional Municipality." Dusaulx's account was commissioned by the Assembly, wishing for a permanent record of the taking of the Bastille. Signing himself "Dusaulx, sexagenaire," he addressed it, on the first anniversary, to the patriot soldiers assembled in the Champ-de-Mars on 14 July 1790.

10. Bonneville, April *Cdm.*

Fig. 14. Camille Desmoulins in the Palais-Royal gardens on 12 July 1789, calling "To Arms!" (Abbott, *The French Revolution*, 1 : 109; SB.)

a "permanent committee" that would meet day and night, gather at the Town Hall, work, and "sur-le-champ" reestablish public tranquillity. One counted at first only fourteen members, who in the evening were augmented.

Fifty thousand pikes were forged in less than thirty-six hours; and they must be regarded as the principal instruments of our newborn liberty.

As a citizen of Rouen on the supply route to Paris, Bonneville would now have, as provision-master, responsibility for keeping open that bottleneck of shipping on the Seine. He had already taken on the responsibilities of a lieutenant colonel in the Rouen Volunteers, including helping to "put down" the sort of "bread riots"—actions directed toward getting bread to the needy—that were typical of the eighteenth century; he would help at the same task in Rouen in 1792.[11] And although the most recent restorers of Bonneville's reputation dwell on his patriotic efforts as a "man of letters" seeking to "unite two kinds of truth: . . . the type of truth one learned through the scientific method, but also a more democratic truth, coming from the general will of the people,"[12] there is

11. I have not found any detailed account of this action, but Bonneville is the sort of person who would have stepped into the "riot" to see that the bread, or whatever provisions, were distributed fairly, rather than the sort who would get the rioters jailed.

12. Kates, "The Cercle Social," 36; Kates, *The Cercle Social, the Girondins, and the French Revolution*, 56–57.

a tendency to overlook a concern he shared with Oswald (by his own declaration, as we shall see) for the democratizing of the "scientific" use of arms. In the autumn of 1791, when Bonneville was planning the *Chronique du mois* as a monthly magazine of scientific and democratic thought, he inevitably (I think) included John Oswald among the editors and contributors whose sum had to be the magic circular number: Fourteen! Only his own name and that of Jean Dusaulx provide an actual continuity with the Fourteen of 1789, so far as we know. But many of the other Grub-Street members of the *Chronique* had entered the fray at that time. Those so publicly involved as to become deputies from Paris to the Assembly in 1791 were Brissot, Broussonnet, Condorcet, Dusaulx, Fauchet, and Garan de Coulon; Kersaint was an elector who *may* have been among the Town Hall Fourteen.

Oswald was probably unable to get away from Parliament in 1789 until mid-August, but he must have spent part of the winter and much of the spring in France establishing the network of political and organizational connections that enabled him to launch the *Universal Patriot* as a newspaper for two cities by the first week in May 1790.[13] Bonneville, refraining from Assembly politics, thus had time to build the "masonry" that would welcome and support Oswald as universal journalist and pamphleteer—and also as organizer of a citizen army such as Bonneville had proposed. As president of the General Assembly of his own district,[14] Bonneville was becoming acquainted with the functional realities of the "direct democracy" of a "primary assembly" such as Oswald would advocate in his *Review of the Constitution* and, doubtless, in the "outlines" published in the *Universal Patriot* in May.

A more vocal district, that of the Cordeliers, led by Danton (whose support in 1792 would enable Oswald to be given command of the first battalion of Paris Volunteers), decreed in its own assembly that its delegates to the city-wide Assembly of Representatives could be recalled at the will of the district.[15] "All power comes from the People," proclaimed a Cordelier delegate to this Assembly in November 1789. And this speaker, Claude Fauchet, soon became its most popular leader, being elected Assembly president four times and attracting a corps of district leaders who were, like himself, young priests and writers. The publicist for this group was, in effect, Nicolas de Bonneville, who at the time of Fauchet's November speech quietly circulated a small pamphlet to members of the city Assembly only, inviting them to form a Cercle Social and revealing the influence of Rousseau and Mably in his suggestions for bridging "the gap between the people and their representatives."[16]

13. See details below.
14. Carmes Dechausée.
15. Kates, "The Cercle Social," 32, citing Bourne, "Improvising a Government in Paris in July 1789," 282–83, and Garrigues, *Les Districts des journaux et des journalistes de la Révolution française*, 135.
16. Kates, "The Cercle Social," 34; Kates, *The Cercle Social*, 56.

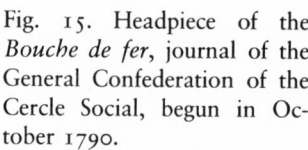 

Fig. 15. Headpiece of the *Bouche de fer*, journal of the General Confederation of the Cercle Social, begun in October 1790.

The bridging would involve an editorial function: if the people would submit written suggestions, complaints, denunciations, and also stories, and place them in a public box, the edited results would be published as the texts of the people's will. To emphasize how uproarious the vox populi might sometimes be, the box would be called the *bouche de fer*, its posting slot the open jaw of a cast-iron lion, i.e., the lion's mouth.[17]

Other publications would educate the legislators themselves and recruit additional leaders of the people. Bonneville and Oswald would launch a series of publications in 1790 and 1791 to supply both current political information and a variety of theoretical and practical discussions of the needs and prospects of the revolutionary situation.

In January 1790 a group calling itself the Cercle Social was announced in a new journal of the same name, a group of fifteen consisting of Bonneville as spokesman and an unnamed *quatorze* of directors. "Bonneville insisted on keeping the group 'few in numbers and composed of the most honored men.' Thus the first Cercle Social was something between an academy and a secret society."[18] Brissot, who may have contributed to the discussion, would have seen this development as an adaptation of his concept of a Lycée or school of politics.

Three months later, on 3 May, an unnamed "set of Gentlemen, Britons, by Birth," were prepared to publish, in Paris, London, and Calais, that "English Newspaper, Printed in Paris," the *Universal Patriot*, which seems to have been intended to function as a revived and liberated *British Mercury*. Indeed the definition of its board of patriots and even its inevitable mailing address, an English Hotel in Paris, anticipate the composition and location of the British Club of 1792.[19] In each case the public secretary turns out to be John Oswald.

The Universal Patriot, by title and language, also offered itself as a cross-Channel companion to Brissot's *Le Patriote françois*. It would dedicate itself to the cause of freedom "in every corner of the Globe," with specific attention to

17. Kates, "The Cercle Social," 35; idea first mentioned in Bonneville's *Tribun de peuple*, no. 13, 156.
18. Kates, "The Cercle Social," 36; Kates, *The Cercle Social*, 55.
19. See Prospectus, in Appendix B, below.

the exertions of sons of freedom in Ireland and in Scotland. In the candor and accuracy of its parliamentary reporting it anticipated no difficulty with the French Assembly, and it expected to manage uncensored reporting of the British Parliament, for the editor would be in Paris and "not have before his eyes the terror of the Pillory nor the dread of . . . prosecutions for libels."

In the Prospectus Oswald is given a Paris address; yet to report the debates of Parliament he would have had to put in much of his time in London—easily continuing to report them for the *Gazetteer*, if with more circumspection than he liked. It was not difficult to move back and forth between the two capitals, however, in 1790.[20] And he may have planned to have substitutes in one place or the other, when necessary. The *Patriot* obviously *was* suppressed, quickly, for not a single number survives.

It was, like Oswald's *Mercury*, to have its bagatelles: "Its slighter regards will run over the *quicquid agunt homines*, the pursuits, the amusements, the follies, the whole multifarious farago of human life." It would also, like *The Cry of Nature*, give due attention to the preference "which even Brutes" give to freedom.

We do know, of course, that the *Universal Patriot* published "in May" a draft version of Oswald's criticism of the British Constitution, and that its immediate reception in Paris was so favorable as to obtain for the editor the exceptional status of a British member of the Jacobin Club. The concept of universal patriotism may have done the trick; yet I know of no other Britons accepted by the Jacobins so early. There were several Britons in Paris at this time who might have been among the anonymous backers of the new journal, including travelers back and forth such as John Hurford Stone and David Williams; yet the prose even of the Prospectus sounds much like the blend of Oswaldian and Bonnevillean sentiments and rhetoric that we find later in their *Chronique du mois*.

During the summer of 1790 the Cercle Social busied itself in a campaign to defeat Bailly and Lafayette in elections for a new city government in August, but this first effort in practical politics was not successful. Pure democracy alarmed too many. The Fauchetists, however, immediately regrouped into a Fraternal Society of Former Representatives of the Paris Commune, which soon grew into a larger Confédération des Amis de la Vérité. Brissot and Condorcet were henceforth associated with the Cercle Social; Kates believes they were

20. An indication that Oswald was still garnering a few guineas from London Grub-Street in the autumn of 1790 is a series of love poems in a London newspaper, *The World*, 8, 12, and 30 July, signed "OSWALD"; a tongue-in-cheek letter to the "Adviser" on 10 August, signed "OTWAY" (asking how to earn a living in London: "Having, alas! read with rapture the pages of VIRGIL, of CICERO, and of HOMER, my mind has not learnt the practices of commerce. Instruct me, then, Mr. ADVISER, how to subsist, and the *World* shall be praised while a breath remains in the bosom of OTWAY"); followed by two more love poems, signed "Otway," 19 October; climaxing in a satiric sonnet 27 December, signed—as if to clinch the authorship—"SILVESTER OTWAY." (Discovered by David Worrall.)

among the original fifteen of January,[21] and they would be leading figures in the Quatorze of the *Chronique du mois*. Lanthenas, another of the future Quatorze, in the summer of 1790 founded a Society of the Friends of Harmony and Equality in Families, a reform lobby that attracted many Cercle members, among them Bonneville, Brissot, and Desmoulins. Oswald must certainly have attended the first public meeting of the Federation, which packed four thousand into the circus building of the Palais-Royal on the afternoon of 13 October and both initiated and ritualized the idea of bringing together all existing clubs, lodges, and societies, including those outside Paris and outside France, in one circle of humanity.[22]

As a memento of Anglo-Franc solidarity the Paris meeting was well timed: three weeks later, on 4 November, the Glorious Revolution of 1688 would be memorialized in London—by the Revolution Society (and by the Grand Lodge of Constitutional Whigs)—and also in Paris, by the National Assembly itself.[23] A few weeks later an emergency session of the British Parliament would be convened, and Oswald, thanks to his duty as reporter for the *Gazetteer*, would find himself at the ideological battlefront, where he would seize and hold up to public scrutiny and free debate the militant weaponry of Burke and Tooke, as we have seen.

And Oswald's published remarks can help us penetrate the semi-secrecy of the Cercle Social, or at least of Cercle socialism. Only with Robert Darnton's candid book, *Mesmerism and the End of the Enlightenment in France* (1968), and more recently James Billington's *Fire in the Minds of Men: Origins of the Revolutionary Faith* (1980)—to which we may now add Gary Kates's *The Cercle Social, the Girondins, and the French Revolution* (1985)[24]—are the nature and importance of the political philosophy and organizations of the Cercle publicists and intellectuals being brought into focus as meaningful social phenomena. Hypnotic magic (mesmerism) and Masonic conspiracies, treated as intolerable or insignificant by earlier historians, from Barruel to Nesta Webster, had distracted attention from the thought and functions of the Cercle Social which Marx and Engels considered sources of modern communism.[25] To quote Darnton:

21. "The Cercle Social," 41.
22. Billington (*Fire in the Minds of Men*, chapter 2) calls attention to the Palais-Royal as the central "space" for the Revolution; the "perfect point" within a "circle of friends" (in Masonic language); the Hyde Park or Forum; the locus in which nowhere (Utopia) first became somewhere. He finds Oswald there, of course (40).
23. See 4 November 1790, in the First Interchapter, above.
24. I have also made considerable use of Kates's dissertation of 1978, "The Cercle Social: French Intellectuals in the French Revolution."
25. Marx and Engels, *Die Heilige Familie* (1845), 186: "The revolutionary movement which began in 1789 with the Cercle Social, whose main representatives were to be Leclerc and Roux, and which ended in Babeuf's conspiracy, gave birth to the communist idea which Buonarotti, friend of Babeuf, reintroduced into France after the revolution of 1830." But Rose, "Socialism and the French Revolution," 141, argues that the direct linkage implied is in error—though "of the many

The political ideas of Bonneville and the Abbé Claude Fauchet, who founded the Cercle Social with him, derived from well-known authors like Rousseau and Mably, but they also showed kinship with Carra's and Court de Gébelin's ideal of primitive, natural society. Bonneville and Fauchet preached the communism of primitive Christians and primitives in general. . . . the redistribution of property by means of an agrarian law . . . .[26]

Billington extends the recognition of sources and followers to Restif de la Bretonne and Buonarotti and Babeuf. Let us now add Oswald.

The rallying idea of the Cercle was a universal society of free masons (builders) or friends of the Truth, uniting all peoples into a single family of love and humanity. The basic solution to all social and political questions was that all the able-bodied should receive the necessities of life from their work and all unable to work should receive them from the state. It required only that all acts of the state be guided by what is right—and that the state be governed by the general will of the people, to that effect.[27] These are the sort of "masonic" ideas that Bonneville absorbed before the Revolution and that Oswald spells out in his *Review* and *Plan*.

As Oswald left Paris in the autumn of 1790, there was growing resistance to such ideas within the Jacobin Club, and on 21 December, at the instance of Choderlos de Laclos, alarmed by the trend toward "republicanism" of Brissot and Bonneville, the Jacobins decreed that all affiliated societies should keep aloof from the Cercle Social.[28] After several more turns of Fortune's wheel, however, the Cercle leadership would become the Jacobin leadership.

Oswald does not appear in this phase of the dialectic, and it seems probable that while in Paris in the autumn he was less involved with the Bonneville-Fauchet group (he can hardly have got on well with Fauchet) than, as Sampson Perry recalled, "with Camille Desmoulins and Danton," in other words, the Cordeliers. In all likelihood, to keep his family alive, Oswald continued his parliamentary reporting for the *Gazetteer* until the end of the next session, 10 June 1791, though knowing that his employment was then ended unless he stayed in London for other chores. And there is no evidence of his presence in Paris that spring. This time the move would be permanent—and his arrival would coincide with a new lease on life for the Cercle Social and result in an expansion of his own revolutionary interests and of his acquaintance among French and British radicals in the storm center. Before we leave England with

---

political clubs and societies . . . in the early years of the revolution," the Cercle was responsible "for disseminating the ideas of the Philosophers in their most 'socialistic' aspect."

26. *Mesmerism*, 134–35. See the extensive account in Hatin, *Histoire politique et litteraire de La Presse en France*, 6:380–88. Hatin adds an Oswaldian point omitted by Darnton: "Bonneville forged his theory of perfect happiness: it must be attained . . . by two simple means: a fresh distribution of goods, and the community of women."

27. Fouchet, in Hatin, *Histoire*, 6:386.

28. Kates, "The Cercle Social," 60; Kates, *The Cercle Social*, 94–95.

him, however, it will be well to consider what other friends and associates he
was leaving behind—or would meet again in that center.

International Friends and Acquaintance

In October 1791 the Prospectus for the new Cercle Social monthly, *La
Chronique du mois*, would in describing its contributors describe John Oswald,
author of the excellent *Review of the British Constitution*, as "joining his
efforts with those of his illustrious friends, James Mackintosh, Thomas Paine,
David Williams, and John Horne-Tooke, to eradicate the ancient prejudices
which have so long sown discord and rivalry between the two nations truly dis-
tinguished by their love of justice and their enthusiasm for all that is beautiful
and honest."
   Of the illustrious "friends" named, Mackintosh would go his own way;
Williams would continue in close acquaintance with Oswald and Bonneville;
Horne Tooke, doubtless well acquainted with Oswald after his oration in
Tooke's defense, would remain indispensable for the support of any activity in
London.
   Before Oswald's speech, John Thelwall ("one of the acting members" of the
Society for Free Debate, according to his wife's *Life* of her husband) must have
felt confident of his abilities; after it their acquaintance may have grown. As for
Thomas Paine, his name would appear, after a few months, as one of the Fourteen on the masthead of the *Chronique*, when that of Collot d'Herbois was
dropped. Paine and Oswald, during the next year, would be among the handful
of "permanent" members of the British Club in Paris—as Redhead Yorke's anecdote about Paine's remark to Oswald signifies (we shall see). But they first
met in London.
   Helpful with information are the recollections of Thomas Rickman, a publisher and musical composer at whose London home Paine resided much of the
time between early July 1790 and March 1791. Among the "select few" of
Paine's "friends and acquaintance," Rickman names eighteen, including Horne
Tooke, of course, and Lord Edward Fitzgerald (who would join the British
Club), "Sharp the engraver" (Blake's radical friend), "Romney the painter, Mrs.
Wolstonecraft" (*sic*), Joel Barlow (who must at about this time have exchanged
symbolic ideas with Blake about the American Revolution), and then, neatly
grouped in Rickman's memory, "Col. Oswald, the Walking Stewart, Captain
Sampson Perry." [29]
   People must have wanted to put General Stewart and Colonel Oswald to-
gether (though Oswald would not be officially a colonel until October 1792,

---

29. Stewart was, indeed, an "old friend" and frequent companion of Paine. Conway, *Life of
Paine*, 1:321–32.

in the Paris Volunteers), for they had much in common as radicals, atheists, Brahmanic vegetarians—it was noted that Oswald drank wine while Stewart did not (a score for Stewart's "benevolence," it seemed to De Quincey)—and as officers who had served in India. Both were also "mad" pamphleteers.[30] They were reputed to be the only travelers who had lived with the Kurds in the highest mountains.[31] Both had traveled by land from India to England, only Stewart by foot, a walker in three continents.

About Oswald's acquaintance in Paris outside the Bonneville group, Captain Perry of the *Argus* seems our most reliable informant.[32]

Two other British radicals Oswald had encountered in London, but probably not at Rickman's, were Col. Norman Macleod of the Black Watch and John Hurford Stone. Macleod, who met his old duelist in a London theater and embraced him warmly, was in town as newly elected member for Inverness, making his maiden speech in the House of Commons on 17 December 1790, and another on the 21st. They *must* have met at this time. (Oswald may have reported the speech for the *Gazetteer*. It is pleasant to know that he had leisure and money to attend the theater.) And surely Macleod heard, or at least heard of, Oswald's debating speech that week: two-and-a-half years later he would defend Oswald's belief in the sovereignty of the people in the House of Commons, against Burke.

Both of Macleod's December speeches offered information and advice from his experiences in India, where war had resumed. He also made clear his Constitutional whiggery—and his agreement with Tooke as to Burke's impeachability. Citing Tippoo Sultan as a character witness to the effectiveness of Hastings—whom Tippoo could respect as "the greatest enemy he had in the world"—he dismissed Burke with a constitutional point: "Edmund Burke was constitutionally dead though alive; Edmund Burke died with the last parliament."[33] He would speak again, on the war with Tippoo on 2 March and in

30. De Quincey is unfair to Stewart when he says he read nothing but his own books. Biblical prophecy wells up in the books of both men; in Oswald enriched by learned allusions and notes citing classical, Hindu, and English historical and economic sources—as well as Rousseau and Sydney and Burke and Ogilvie.

31. *European Magazine* biography.

32. See excerpt in Chapter 1, above.

33. *Parl Hist*, 38:1021–22. Later in the debate (1190–91) Macleod explained that Tippoo's great abilities, unattached to the virtues of justice or humanity, made him a tyrant who should be exterminated. After his March speech the *Morning Chronicle* complained that he showed "a most forgiving disposition" toward those other Indians, the Mahrattas, and quoted the *Annual Register* of 1783 (see above) on the Mahrattas' attack on "Colonel Macleod, Colonel Humberstone, Major Shaw" after peace had been "concluded and ratified" (*MChron*, 10 March 1791, 3). The *Annual Register* account, based in part on Macleod's documentation, had of course made the point that news of the peace treaty had not reached the Mahrattas when they attacked the British so mortally. Macleod's present point, however, was that the Mahrattas "in their present state were not at all dangerous"; hence that removing Tippoo from the territory he had made conquest of would be "an act of justice to . . . the native princes, who had, in consequence of the usurpation, been reduced to the greatest distress and extremity" (*Parl Hist*, 28:1329–30).

favor of repealing the Test Act in Scotland (a major issue in the campaign for parliamentary reform) on 10 May 1791. Both Oswald and Macleod were developing as Horne Tooke's people and would have had much to talk about besides India.

Hurford Stone, a frequent Channel-crosser of critical importance in the promoting—and frustrating—of Oswald's career in France, was a master of the double entendre. Both men were members of what Bonneville would have called the "Directory" of the British Club in Paris in 1792–1793, which at times included Paine, Redhead Yorke, and Citizen (Lord) Fitzgerald. And many letters from Stone to his brother William in London survive, because the brother, as an available body, was tried in a British court in 1796 for high treason, with the correspondence as vital evidence.[34] The core of the messages was a continuous political weather report as to whether a revolutionary invasion of London or Ireland would successfully precipitate a British Revolution or come to disaster. The jury, having heard as character witnesses many eminent Whigs, including Sheridan and William Smith and Samuel Rogers and Lord Lauderdale, and both Lord Grenville and William Pitt, put an innocent construction upon these documents and voted Stone not guilty: his reporting to the French government the kind of welcome an invading army would receive might seem like treason, but his advising the enemy that it could *not* succeed had been a service to his native England.[35]

Actually, both Oswald and Stone, moving back and forth between London and Paris in the first years of the Revolution, seem to have been confident of its *ultimate* success. And both, in desperate moments, urged the people who had pulled down the Bastille to sail up the Thames and pull down the British prison called the Tower. Stone, however, hedged his commitments and must have troubled Oswald by his deviousness. He *was* in a sense a sort of double agent— not for either nation but for his and his brother's commercial interest—justified, he seems to have reasoned, by its coinciding with the interests of humanity.

A personal feud between Hurford Stone and David Williams must have troubled Oswald—though it may have been so one-sided that Williams was unaware of it. Stone apparently considered the Welshman as his rival in the backstage area of diplomatic conversations with the eminent politicians of both London and Paris. But since Williams confined his activities to seeking peaceful accommodations whereas Oswald was a moralist of extremes who was certain of the need of what Wordsworth called "philosophic war" (quite a different

---

34. Trial of William Stone, *State Trials* 25 (1818): 1155–1438.

35. This defense, led by Lord Erskine as Stone's attorney, seems to have convinced the editors of the *Biographical Dictionary of Modern British Radicals*, from which Stone is excluded. There are of course alternate possible explanations: (a) that he did not remain a radical; (b) that he was only a patriotic liberal, as his defense maintained; (c) that he was neither, but a government agent (single or double). Even category (a) should have got him into the *BDMBR*, however. In this matter Lionel Woodward, in 1931, was less sophistic; he found little difficulty decoding the relevant messages.

thing from Blake's "intellectual war"),[36] Stone must at times have been able to bring forth Oswald's sword in the just cause.

These general remarks are intended to reduce the need for commentary as our narrative proceeds. The details will be documented as we come to them.

Universal Patriots: A Widening Circle

Whether Oswald moved permanently to Paris in the spring of 1791, or not until the close of Parliament in early June, he would have found Tom Paine there, the logical person to assist him and Bonneville in drawing the friends of universal liberty into concerted publication. Bonneville's *Bouche de fer* was now flourishing as a thrice-weekly newspaper (having absorbed some of the functions of the *Universal Patriot*, but with no English edition). Oswald was by now probably acquainted with all the persons on Sampson Perry's list: Danton, with whom Paine had been on good terms since 1787, now a leader in the Cordeliers Club; the Rolands, at whose salon Paine and Bonneville were beginning a lifelong friendship; and Camille Desmoulins, now one of the directors or inner circle of the Fouchet-Bonneville Confédération des Amis de la Vérité, a membership organization which people joined by paying for subscriptions to the *Bouche de fer*.[37]

The membership and organization of the Cercle Social were now of sufficient strength to produce a major monthly journal, which would be announced in October as a *Chronique du mois*, with the names of fourteen authors—the inevitable number—filling the title page. Oswald and Bonneville were of course among them; seven were already declared members of the Confédération, and the Cercle now had its own printing press and publishing office, at No. 4, Rue du Théâtre Française, near the Cordelier headquarters. The Bonnevilles lived in rooms on the second floor, and Desmoulins lived across the street, writing his own weekly editorial pamphlet, *Les Révolutions de France et de Brabant*.[38] In

36. In *The Prelude* 9.415ff., Wordsworth identifies the soldier who taught him "philosophic war" as Michel Beaupuis, a French officer whose conversation was like that of Dion with Plato when planning a military overthrow of a Sicilian tyrant. Their armed invasion of Sicily was "philosophic war Led by Philosophers." Blake's "Mental War," on the contrary, signified "Art against Armies."

37. The membership was sustained at between four and five thousand in 1791. See Kates, *The Cercle Social*, 83 and appendix A. Public members of the Confédération by 1791 included Brissot, Cloots, Condorcet, Desmoulins, Grégoire, Lebrun, both the Rolands, the Englishman Rutledge (identified, as were Oswald and Brissot, as "publiciste"), and Siéyès. Meetings of the Cercle Social were held in "a hall in the Palais Royal, capable of seating some three thousand people. It had a large membership at a subscription of eight livres a month, and its motto, inscribed in prominent lettering above the speaker's head, was, 'Bring each a ray of light'" (*un trait de lumière*, i.e., a bright idea) (Hamel, *A Woman of the Revolution*, 158).

38. Kates, "The Cercle Social," 105; see also Kates, *The Cercle Social*, 88–89.

Fig. 16. Thomas Paine (1737–1809), extender of the circle of civilization. Portrait by Romney, engraved by A. Easto. (In Mary Agnes Best, *Thomas Paine*, 1927; SB.)

November, in apt symbolic language, mocking the panic of Choderlos, who feared the Cercle as a rival club, Desmoulins accused the directors of plagiarism, and dreaded that the Jacobins ("le Société des amis de la Constitution") and the club of 1789 would lose their identity in "flinging themselves into the ocean of the Great Universal Confederation through the mouth of the circus (perdre leur nom, en se jetant dans l'ocean de *la grande confédération* universelle, à l'embouchure du cirque)." [39]

Until recently the Cercle Social and its projects had been sustained largely by the interests and oratory of Claude Fauchet, but they were now more dependent on Bonneville's leadership—and the thinking of François Lanthenas, translator for Paine, who was composing a treatise on the nature and functions of clubs, both patriotic and popular. According to Lanthenas, who would agree with Oswald on the importance of "primary assemblies," the Jacobin Club was the prototype of the "patriotic" club, a group of "men from the comfortable class," mostly politicians and writers, who met to sponsor reforms or discuss issues. That sort of club had been adequate in the last years of the Ancien Régime and the first of the Revolution but must now give way to the type of "popular club" which was led by the same kind of men but drew its rank and

39. Desmoulins puns on the "Bouche" and the "Cercle"—and the "Cirque" (Circus) of the Palais-Royal. The passage is from Aulard, *The French Revolution*, 1:392, quoting Desmoulins' speech as printed in his *Revolutions*, no. 54.

file from the people, workers and artisans. In these clubs the thought of an agrarian law (redistribution of property!) would rear its head, but the Cercle leadership were happy to include in their Confédération of clubs an organization of unemployed wage earners, the Point Central des Arts et Métiers (a name using Masonic code images: two lodges in Paris were named "the perfect point" and "the circle of friends"),[40] and to campaign against Mayor Bailly's indifference to the funding of public workshops (*ateliers de charité*) for the unemployed.

Oswald's egalitarian ideas about property in the *Universal Patriot* of 1790, which so pleased the Jacobins, would have been particularly attractive to the Cercle strategists a year later, as they campaigned for greater economic equality. Passage of a modified inheritance bill in March had been celebrated at a meeting of the Confédération chaired by Etta Palm, the feminist leader.[41] And a campaign for universal suffrage, without property qualifications, was under way. But resistance to the growing power of the popular clubs was increasing, and in May the National Assembly passed a decree to deflate their petition campaigns by banning all collective petitions and recognizing only individual petitions signed by "active" citizens, i.e., property owners.[42]

On 17 June 1791, Bonneville prepared a defiant petition, for the Confédération, in the collective names of a dozen clubs which were, in effect, primary assemblies, declaring to the National Assembly that "the day which sees the beginning of primary assemblies will be the signal of universal reclamation" and that meanwhile people who obey laws "which they have not approved or sanctioned are slaves." This was posted "in all the streets of the city" but not acknowledged by the Assembly.[43]

According to Lanthenas' definitions, the Assembly itself was behaving like the "old kind of club" which "had the audacity to remain isolated, to have special rules," and "to praise itself as the most enlightened." But events were now

40. Kates, "The Cercle Social," 113, 109; Kates, *The Cercle Social*, 89–93; Billington, *Fire in the Minds of Men*, 24.

41. "One of the first of the clubs to see a woman on its platform was the Cercle Sociale" (Hamel, *A Woman of the Revolution*, 158). On 26 November 1790, a rather inept speaker, Charles Louis Rousseau, attempting to discuss the kind of *lumière* that women might bring to politics, was cut short by the president, whereupon "a woman of commanding figure rose and asked a question in ringing tones, plainly heard through the hall. 'Gentlemen,' she said, 'is it possible that the Revolution, which has for its object the attainment of the rights of man, can be the cause of Frenchmen showing injustice and dishonesty to women? . . . I demand, in the name of the women citizens present, that M. Rousseau be allowed to proceed.' At these remarks there was general applause. The speaker was asked herself to continue." The few words she spoke were so much to the point that there was "a general desire amongst them to elect her *présidente*, but she refused. This woman, Etta Palm by name, of Dutch extraction . . . worked as well or even better than Théroigne in her sisters' cause. . . . Etta placed herself at the head of those who pleaded for civic and intellectual education" (ibid., 161–62).

42. Conway, *Life of Paine*, 1:443; see Kates, *The Cercle Social*, 141–45.

43. *Bouche de fer*, 17 June 1791, reporting also a petition against property qualifications, by "Some Active Citizens," i.e., the Section Théâtre-Français.

hastening the day of "the new club," which "would shudder at the stubborn-ness of their senior to remain separate" and "would like *all* their members to support the establishment of popular societies."[44] Events to that effect included an increase of unemployment, strife in the Jacobin Club, and the June crisis caused by the royal flight to Varennes. The King's capture and return impelled most of the Cercle participants into more active political engagement—some toward theoretical intensity, others toward struggle; Oswald, perhaps as soon as he came onto the scene, into both.

To republicans like Paine and Brissot, the King's flight had seemed good rid-dance; his return, however, revived the hopes of old clubbers for a monarchical Constitution rather than a republican one. Brissot could be counted on to blow hot and cold. On 1 July, Paine and Condorcet and Achille Duchatelet, "proba-bly also Brissot, and Nicolas Bonneville"[45]—probably also John Oswald—placarded Paris with the manifesto of a new or newly visible Société Républi-caine "which was even nailed on the door of the National Assembly" (shades of Martin Luther). Paine soon sailed back across the Channel to celebrate the Glorious Fourteenth in London (at some risk: see First Interchapter, above). And on 15 July "a crowd from the Social Circle headed by the Cordeliers" in-vaded the Jacobins, who then "agreed to sign a new petition requesting the Assembly to replace Louis—'By all constitutional means,' added Brissot, who drafted the text the next day."[46]

In the continuing crisis the Cercle "Directory" went into permanent session, keeping the lion's mouth open for primary input. And the *Bouche de fer* was changed to an eight-page daily, giving its space to current politics and local issues, rather than "debates on the role of Jesus Christ in an upcoming civil religion."[47] For a moment the Cercle Social had become "one of the most im-portant republican cadres in the capital."[48] Soon, however, on 17 July, the pri-mary assemblies lost in blood their battle for the rights of petitioners. The Cor-deliers had objected to Brissot's phrase about "constitutional means," which would leave the door open for a regent, e.g. the Duke of Orleans, but when the Assembly accepted Louis himself as a constitutional king, the Jacobins dropped the petition idea. Whereupon the Cordeliers proceeded without Jacobin help to rally the citizens, "active" or not, to sign a new petition on the Altar of the Fatherland in the Champ-de-Mars. The "Massacre of the Champ-de-Mars" followed, as National Guards under Lafayette's command hoisted the red flag of martial law and fired upon the republican petitioners.

44. *Patriote françois*, 28 February 1791, 178; Kates, *The Cercle Social*, 155–57.
45. Conway, *Life of Paine*, 1:311; also 308.
46. Lefebvre, *The Coming of the French Revolution*, 209; Aulard, ed., *Recueil des Documents . . . des Jacobins*, 3:231; Kates, "The Cercle Social," 130; Kates, *The Cercle Social*, 167. Mathiez, *Autour de Danton*, 117, described the 15 July meeting of the Confédération, its last, as a "great republican demonstration."
47. Kates, "The Cercle Social," 117: "In short, this . . . academic journal became a popular newspaper." See also Kates, *The Cercle Social*, 160.
48. Kates, "The Cercle Social," 131.

This was the beginning of the end for Lafayette, but the radicals temporarily panicked; the Cordeliers shut down for several weeks; Danton fled to England; Desmoulins halted publication of his *Révolutions*. The Jacobins agreed to listen to a letter from Bonneville, but then rejected it as dangerously republican. On 19 July, Etta Palm was arrested; on the 21st the *Bouche de fer* announced that the Confédération would "instantly close its tribune at the circus arena." [49] And by the end of the month the *Bouche* itself was closed. Lafayette, misjudging the forces involved, confidently offered himself to the "active" voters of Paris in the autumn elections for mayor, only to be soundly defeated by a Jacobin, Jerome Pétion.

Gary Kates, who assembles a detailed account of the permanent collapse of the Confédération, seems correct in ascribing it to "a fundamental identity crisis":

> How could Bonneville and Lanthenas scold the Jacobins for being elitist when they kept membership dues at the exorbitant twenty-seven livres per year? On the other hand, how could they expect to maintain the philosophical discussion and fraternal atmosphere of the club if they opened it up to everyone? The seeds of the Confederation's destruction were not embedded within the nature of the institution, as much as in the growing acceptance among its leaders of the ideology of popular sovereignty.
>
> Fauchet and Bonneville had created the Confederation to give their discredited political faction an organized form until its members could gain enough public support to re-enter the political scene. The king's flight to Varennes gave them this opportunity. Cercle Social leaders became popular and highly visible in Parisian politics. With elections to the Legislative Assembly to be held in August 1791, Cercle Social leaders looked forward to acquiring offices at the national level.
>
> Finally, while Bonneville's suggestion for a merger between the Cercle Social and the Jacobins was not taken seriously by anyone at the time, that is in fact precisely what occurred during the months following the massacre at the Champ-de-Mars. [50]

In the autumn both Brissot and Fauchet, of the Cercle, were elected to the Legislative Assembly (which by agreement was to have no carryovers from the Constituent Assembly). Bonneville was not elected but gained a commissioner's post. And then—could Oswald's long-standing Jacobin membership have had anything to do with this?—practically all the Cercle leaders joined the Jacobin Club and "quickly became" *its* leaders. "In the following weeks Bancal, Broussonet, Lanthenas, Louvet, and Roland all were elected to Jacobin leadership," Brissot having been elected the president for October, succeeded by Fauchet and Condorcet. [51]

One of the first Jacobin agenda items manifesting the Enlightenment ideas of the Cercle was a motion of 19 September that a prize be offered "for the almanach that should be found the best adapted to explain to the people the spirit

49. Kates, *The Cercle Social,* 170.
50. "The Cercle Social," 132–33; *The Cercle Social,* 172.
51. Kates, *The Cercle Social,* 199.

and principles of the French constitution." These are John Oswald's words, in the preface to his English translation of the prizewinning *Almanach du Père Gérard*, written by Collot d'Herbois (who had only just joined the Cercle), of which we shall hear more later. Five of the six contest judges were Cercle members.[52] Collot's French text was published by the Jacobin Club; Oswald's translation, entitled *The Spirit of the French Constitution*, was published in Paris by the Imprimerie du Cercle Social, with a subvention from the London Society for Constitutional Information: the connection being presumably through Horne Tooke.[53]

The Spirit of a Constitutional Compromise

By the time the King came formally to accept the Constitution, few people believed that he was sincere in doing so.[54] And by the time Collot and Oswald had prepared their popularization of that Constitution as an "Almanach" of lessons by an elder Jacobin instructing the simplest citizens, the new Legislative Assembly was elected and in session—and one of its responsibilities was to draft a better Constitution—for a republic.

Collot enjoyed and made great platform capital out of his prize winning but kept silent about Oswald's involvement and did not mention the English translation publicly. Yet Oswald probably preferred not to share this kind of applause; for him this would have seemed little more than another Grub-Street chore, already somewhat anachronistic in its politics as it left the press in November or December.[55] He did, however, manage, in the process of translating, to modify some of the specious "royalism" of the text. And in any case the *Almanach* of constitutional instruction seems worth looking into as a symptomatic document of this "ship-tossing-at-anchor" interlude (Wordsworth's image of the Revolution at this period). Also, since Collot and Oswald will emerge as a pair of sparring partners in the Jacobin debates, this collaboration is of interest as testimony to Oswald's ability to take Collot's measure.

Since the French and English editions seem to have been published simultaneously, in late November, it is possible that author and translator worked together that autumn, not only on the translation but on the final draft of the original. Oswald's English is generally faithful to the French; yet though neither version evinces enthusiasm over the plum of a monarch in this constitutional pudding, some passages in the English lean more forcefully upon the absurdity of this aspect.

52. Clavière, Condorcet, Dusaulx, Grégoire, Lanthenas; the sixth was Polverelle.
53. Or dealings directly with Ridgway? The title page wording: "Translated by John Oswald. Sold by Ridgway Bookseller, London, and At the Printing Office of the Social Circle, Paris, 1791."
54. Roberts, *The French Revolution*, 42.
55. The earliest advertisement in the *Moniteur* appeared on 18 December.

As readers—or as listening subliterates hearing these twelve homely "conversations" read aloud—we are to imagine the "economy of the family": a monthly dispensation of wisdom by the "venerable old man," an "honest peasant of Brittany" whom we all remember, who having served his turn in the National Assembly of 1789 is now explaining at his fireside or on the village green—an Oswaldian extrapolation—the excellencies (and apparent contradictions) of our new Constitution. There was an actual Citizen Gérard, who had sat in the Jacobin Club and left warm memories behind him.[56]

The *Almanach of Father Gerard* has been dismissed as a "royalist fiction" on the one hand; on the other, Oswald's prefix has got *The Spirit of the French Constitution* into bibliographies as if there were a separate treatise on that subject by Collot.

The Constitution of 1791–1792 is of course "royalist" in having still a king—hence the preface hopes "this little work may tend to spread and to corroborate the principles of liberty in the *Kingdoms* of Great Britain and Ireland" (my emphasis)—but our Goodman explains that the "Legislative Power of the National Assembly is as it were the head" while "the King . . . is as it were the arm which executes that which the head has resolved" and "the People are as it were the blood," the real source of warmth and life. (A marvelous bouleversement of the traditional head/heart/limbs cliché.) The Constitution does, in short, "secure our welfare and that of our children!" The first conversation is quite solemn, but the second ends with "a laugh." Gerard has been explaining that the King has to be free to choose his agents so that he cannot blame the Nation if the agents prove guilty of folly. A peasant replies: "Why yes to be sure if they must be guilty of folly, it is better that they should be chosen by the King; that is just as it should be." And some things about the new Constitution make Gerard "a little embarrassed" (here the English text differs a bit from the French) but he urges that they be respected until amended, which requires only that we "consult our hearts." ("Bravo, Goodman Gerard!")

56. Michel Gérard (1737–1815) had been prominent in the Assembly of 1789. Collot's book made their mutual fame, and Gérard was painted by David and others. He also got into English literature, in the writings of Helen Maria Williams (*Letters*, 1790–1795) and William Wordsworth (*Prose Works*, 1 : 59) and Conan Doyle (whose Brigadier Gérard derives certain aspects from Pére Gérard—according to Molly Lefebure, who notes that Doyle's mother was French and that Doyle himself was widely read in French).

In the Jacobin session of Sunday, 23 October, with Fauchet presiding, Dusaulx announced the award of the prize to Collot. The entire hall resounded with applause; the president embraced Collot. And Collot, mounting to the tribune to thank the committee, congratulated them on their choice: "I have no false modesty, he says, the prize indicates I came closer to the target than any others—and that my work has merit. It does; it has the merit of being directed to country people with a voice that can carry authority, that of a virtuous elder who has sat among us and whose absence we regret, father Gérard." He was quickly persuaded to read some excerpts, and then to announce, philanthropically, that of the prize money he would assign 100 pounds to found a benefit fund; 200 to the unfortunate prisoners of Chateaux-Vieux of the Brest galleys (which he was making into a cause célèbre); and 300 for a new edition, to be sold at profit for the same victims of ministerial oppression. (Applause.)

Gerard, a member of the Assembly, is a part of the head, consulting the heart, the peasants—who are severe on him about the continuation of slavery, for instance. (One of the societies in which Brissot and Kersaint and other Cercle members were active, with quite revolutionary consequences, was the Friends of the Blacks: *Amis des Noirs.*)

In short, the Jacobin acceptance of the Constitution is provisional and open to popular revising.[57]

Conversation Third, "Of the Law," comes by the calendar in March, but it alludes to the New Year and also to a Twelfth Night custom (employing the old reckoning, of the peasants not the church or the state, whereby the year begins in March). As the peasant sees it, if we have to speak of kings, we should "draw for King Together." The French were still fond of the ceremony of choosing a mock sovereign by the lottery method of "finding the bean in the cake" (*la fève au gateau*). Says Gerard: "Why not? I love that antient custom; to decide by lot who shall be King by drawing for a bean is a very pleasant custom (he laughs with good natured simplicity) ha! ha! our forefathers then were not such fools ha! ha!"[58] (Royalist fiction indeed.)[59]

In Conversation Fifth, "Of Property," Collot and Oswald agree that "it is not material possessions alone . . . that constitute property;—industry, and the love of labour are also mines of wealth of which the produce forms a property, perhaps of all others the most precious." And the language of the Goodman— "He who does nothing is unworthy to be reckoned among the number of citizens"—is, in English translation, the language Redhead Yorke attributed to Oswald when he drew his sword in that dispute about Ireland.[60]

> Peasant: What is it that the priests call Spiritual?
> Gerard: The Spiritual, my friend, signifies the tythes . . . .

But the peasants discover that God too has gained by the Revolution. At the end of the Sixth Conversation, "The curate and Protestant minister embrace each other," and "The Catholic and Protestant peasants embrace each other also." This is a reenactment of the glorious Fourteenth of July, and—this is the Goodman's contribution—"Every year on the 14 of July all law-suits should terminate . . . and every good citizen should see in every man around him the

---

57. These qualifyings were not sufficient for Jacobin editor Prudhomme, however, who had disapproved from the beginning of the club's plan to publicize a feeble constitution (*Révolutions de Paris*, 17–24 September, 10–17 December 1791). A modern historian has called the *Almanach* "a sort of *Reader's Digest* Enlightenment" (Williams, *Artisans and Sans-culottes*, 31).

58. This custom, I am told, continues even at the end of the twentieth century, in France *and* in Britain.

59. Collot was a side-changer, as everyone knew, and here we see him preparing to shift. Brissot, in a pamphlet of 1792 published by the Cercle Social, cites Collot's theater pieces such as *Nostradamus en Provence* (in honor of so-styled Monsieur) for extremes of sycophantic royalism. Today (1792) Collot is one of those republicans, says Brissot, who yesterday knelt before princes, whom they called "suns of most resplendent glory" (*À Tous les Républicains de France*, 14).

60. This paragraph draws upon *Almanach*, 38–39; the next upon 43–63.

face of a brother and a friend." In Conversation Tenth the Goodman is pleased at the peasants' "readiness to serve in the army or the National Guard in defense of their country: ' . . . the Nation have declared that they will attack no one; but if they are attacked . . . .'" But when a married peasant with four children says he is "ready to march" and "A Child About Ten Years Old, tossing his firelock," says, "I can prime and load in twelve motions," it is too much for Father Gerard. Let these children know "that warlike valour does not supply the place of every virtue, for then the military spirit would become dangerous. There are other virtues . . . ." [61]

Cahiers for a New Revolution—by a New Fourteen!

The *Bouche de fer* was closed; the Cercle had opened wide. In October it would announce its new monthly review, of philosophical, political, economic, tactical, poetical essays as well as analyses of legislative debates, by leading friends of truth and freedom on both sides of the Channel. On 16 November the Jacobin Club committee of correspondence (members included Lanthenas and Bonneville) would officially endorse *La Chronique du mois* (still in the press), which historians have come to recognize as "among the most important and most enduring journals of the Revolution" and "certainly the most successful of those published by the Cercle Social." [62]

For Bonneville this represented the culmination of his ambition to be influential among the glorious Fourteen leading the "march of the peoples." For Oswald it was an opportunity to make that march "scientific." His making less of it than he might have done, with his pen, must be attributed to his being compelled to listen again to the call of war's alarms. We do not know exactly when he undertook to erase the petitioners' blood from the Champ-de-Mars, by drilling Parisian volunteers in tactics for the people's victory, but months before the *Chronique* came to its end he had marched his ragamuffins off toward Brest—probably with a dream of leading them by ship to London, which perished in the no-win battles of the Vendée.

In the original planning of the *Chronique du mois*, Oswald's *Chronicle* and *Gazetteer* experience seems to have been of some help, though it would be Lanthenas, an actual Assembly delegate, who undertook the brief parliamentary

---

61. The *Almanach* survives in many copies of several editions (I have located thirteen copies, none identical, some with illustrations and other added features, some for very small pockets). The English editions and some of the French editions have "The Triumph of Freedom, an Ode . . . by John Oswald" at the back, alone or with other, unsigned, poems. The French editions usually have a calendar of saints' days and quarters of the moon. Both author and translator of the Ridgway edition are identified as members of the Jacobin Club. The Advertisement says that forty-two competitors submitted manuscripts, and that the committee "decided unanimously in favour" of this work.

62. Reinhard, *Chûte*, 190; Kates, *The Cercle Social*, 173–74.

summaries. At any rate the *Chronique* was impressively successful, supplying its subscribers with twenty-two monthly issues and many long Annexes. It was not primarily a chronicle, nor was it another *British Mercury*. It had no room for Oswald's jests and "bagatelles," nor for caricature. But it did print a good many poems by Bonneville, which Oswald probably admired, since their heroic stance was like that of Macpherson. Bonneville wrote bardic chants, sometimes in cadenced prose, also chantlike transformations of passages from Shakespeare's *Julius Caesar*: the times might require a Brutus! Each monthly issue beginning with the third (January 1792) was headed by the portrait of a hero of revolutionary valor or truth (Condorcet could represent both as the subject for January). And the editorial prose was occasionally allowed to assume a marching cadence—once, at least, with the help of Oswald's pen.

It was, however, self-consciously a "chronicle" in the revolutionary sense that *ideas* are expected to become, or seen to become, *events*. If Oswald was, in Wordsworth's sense, a "philosophical" warrior, Condorcet was a philosophical journalist. Nor does it seem unlikely that Oswald and Condorcet were responsible for the new journal's name and proposed objectives. Oswald had got his training on the *London Chronicle*; Condorcet had moved his own daily journalistic attention to *La Chronique de Paris* (on 17 November 1791), a newspaper which in its first month defined itself as "modeled on the London Chronicle" and as "true, free, impartial."[63]

The subtitle of the *Chronique du mois*, *Cahiers patriotiques*, is followed by the names of the fourteen authors, not listed alphabetically but scrambled as a paradigm of republican equality.[64] And of course the phrase recalls the cahiers of 1789 that were delivered from primary assemblies to the Estates General in Versailles by elected delegates. The November Prospectus also suggests an equality of eminence. It is worth summarizing (with parenthetical comment):

Prospectus for the Chronique du mois

These authors who have joined forces consist of *hommes célèbres*, some members of the legislature, others who may become such. The monthly is to be like the English monthly Reviews or Chronicles, but not a mere compilation of clippings—and not open to enemies of the people. It is to contain the genuine ideas and critiques and sketches (*desseins*) of distinguished writers. Each number will have two parts: the first a review of legislation and publications, the second What is to be done (*ce qu'il faut faire*).

Clavière undertakes to deal with the critical state of our finances, and the fact that Mirabeau (of the previous regime) looked up to him as a master

63. Hatin, *Histoire*, 5:234, 238.
64. For the first four issues the title read: *La* CHRONIQUE du mois ou les CAHIERS PATRIOTIQUES de E. Clavière, C. Condorcet, L. Mercier, A. Auger, J. Oswald, N. Bonneville, J. Bidermann, A. Broussonet, A. Guy-Kersaint, J. P. Brissot, J. Ph. Garran de Coulon, J. Dussaulx [*sic*], F. Lanthenas et Collot-d'Herbois . . . A PARIS. De L'Imprimerie du Cercle Social.

should inspire confidence. Condorcet will furnish observations on legislation and on citizen education. Mercier will deal with public welfare. Auger, celebrated translator of Demosthenes and Cicero, has promised comparative studies of ancient and modern constitutions. Bonneville's specialty will be the diplomatic scene. (We shall find him taking on other departments, a serialized digest of legislative proceedings since 1789 about as compact as, and perhaps suggested by, those of Oswald in the *British Mercury*, as well as Ossianic poetry, the march of freedom, and reminders of the glorious Fourteenth of July!) Oswald himself gets the largest paragraph in the Prospectus:

> JOHN OSWALD, auteur d'une excellente *révision de la constitution d'Angleterre*, dont on imprime actuellement à Londres, une troisième édition, réuniera ses efforts à ceux de ses illustres amis, MACKINTOSH, PAYNE, WILLIAMS et HORNE-TOOKE, pour détruire les préjugés populaires qui ont semé si long temps la discorde et la rivalité entre deux nations vraiment distinguées par leur amour pour la justice, et par leur enthusiasme pour tout ce qui est beau et honnête.[65]

Bidermann gets almost as much space, and an extravagant assertion that nothing on the great subject of national commerce will be printed without his comment, because of his experience and purest patriotism. None of the other thirteen is given such controlling authority. The explanation is that Bidermann's talents include the possession of five or six European and oriental banks, seven or eight merchant ships, and a diversity of manufactures. This is clearly to be a bourgeois-guided revolution, after all.

Broussonet will deal with rural business, Kersaint with maritime legislation. Brissot will supply several of his eloquent speeches on our rights, which he knows so well how to defend. (He does supply nine items, mostly speeches printed elsewhere, but as promised.) Garran de Coulon will treat of the great questions of jurisprudence with which the National Assembly is to be concerned. Finally, we are asked to be interested in seeing the names of Lanthenas, Dusaulx, and Collot-d'Herbois—who evidently have not been pinned down to anything specific—the last of whom has just received a prize for his *Almanach du Père Gérard*, to instruct the people. These cahiers of the month will appear on the first of each month, subscription 15 pounds a year, in Paris, or 8 pounds for six months, at the press of the Cercle Social, Rue du Théâtre-François, no. 4.

The Portraits

Of the twenty monthly frontispiece portraits in *La Chronique du mois*, eighteen were designed by François Bonneville, a cousin of Nicolas.[66] Eight portray

---

65. Translation: "John Oswald, author of an excellent *Review of the Constitution of Great Britain*, now in the press in London, a third edition, will join his efforts to those of his illustrious friends, Mackintosh, Paine, Williams and Horne-Tooke, to destroy the general prejudices which have so long spread discord and rivalry between the two nations truly distinguished by their love of justice and by their enthusiasm for everything that is beautiful and honest."
66. François Bonneville is said to have engraved "hundreds" of portraits, most of them designed

members of the editorial group (which included sixteen persons over the twenty-two months). Oswald is not among those thus honored, but neither is Bonneville nor Lanthenas: these were the working team.

An annotated list of the twenty portraits will give us a calendar-maker's panorama of witnesses or heroes of the Revolution, from January 1792 through August 1793 (the last issue of the *Chronique* and the last full month of Oswald's existence). The printed captions single out the prestigious governmental functions of the individuals in this pantheon; I shall add other characterizing information, designating members of the Quatorze with *Q* and those who had been open members of the Cercle Confédération with *C*.

1792

January. *M. J. A. N. Condorcet.* (Q,C) "Deputy of Paris to the National Assembly in 1791, year 3 of Liberty." A volcano hid under snow, to Carlyle. Secretary to the Academy of Sciences; probabilist in mathematics. Oswald must have liked his ideas (published posthumously, but no doubt expressed to colleagues) on the history of the progress of the human mind—a progress calculated to arrive at a glorious culmination. (He committed suicide, 2 June 1793, to cheat the guillotine.)

February. *Claude Fauchet.* (C) "Deputy of the National Assembly in 1791, year 3 of Liberty, and Bishop of Calvados." Guru of the Cercle Social. (Guillotined with Girondins, 31 October 1793.)

March. *Louis Mercier.* (Q,C) Mesmerist plus; satirical writer; editor with Carra of *Annales Patriotiques* since 1789 and on the staff of *Journal d'Etat et du Citoyen.*

April. *Athanase Auger, abbé.* (Q,C) Venerable classics scholar; "died at Paris 1 February 1792." The Cercle had just published his pamphlet *Sur les gouvernements en général et en particular sur celui que nous courient,* and other works including *De la police du senat Roman,* announced in the March issue, with an obituary by Bonneville.[67]

---

by himself, over a period of twenty-five years: "the entire royal family and several foreign sovereigns, Paul I among them; ministers such as Maurepas or Necker; the most visible members of the Assemblies, Robespierre and Danton, Brissot or Clavière; the generals of the Republic from Dumouriez and Custine to Kléber and Menou; the Directors, the Consuls, sages like Laplace, philanthropists like the Abbé de l'Épée, the Septembrizers, the Vendéens, etc." In Oswald's time his shop was at No. 4 de la Rue du Théâtre-Français (Hamy, "Notre sur Diverses Gravures de Bonneville . . .," 41).

67. The *Chronique* calls attention to a petition addressed by Auger to the Assembly in October 1791 and now before its Legislative Committee, which "could change the face of the world." It concerns a law about successions—succession to the crown, or inheritance of property. (And we are told that Bonneville, as author of *l'Esprit des Religions,* was assured by Auger that he had "discovered the principle of social perfection, natural, successive, almost impartial, and had given in his work the solution to a problem that had never even been imagined"—*Cdm,* February 1792, no. 1.)

May. *Jean Philippe Garran* (i.e., Garran de Coulon). (Q,C) "Grand procurator of the Nation: Deputy of Paris in the National Assembly in 1791, year 3 of Liberty." Head of the National High Court of Justice at Orleans; a very fussy lawyer, who would do Brissot's bidding (Dumont, *Souvenirs sur Mirabeau*, 225).

June. *Thomas Paine*. (Q) "Secretary of Congress in the department of foreign affairs during the American War, author of Common Sense and of replies to Burke."

July. *J. P. Brissot*. (Q,C) "Deputy of the Department of Paris to the First Legislature, Year 3 of Liberty." "Restless, scheming, scribbling" (Carlyle). Works for Clavière; needs no introduction but July was the month to *move*: could Brissot truly lead?

August. *John Horne Tooke*. Portrait "sent from England in 1792 to the Cercle Social." Maverick radical since John Wilkes's day; busiest desk in the English movement. (If only his correspondence had survived! It was probably marked "burn this!")

September. *Etienne Clavière*. (Q) "Born at Geneva . . . ." Swiss banker, republican, speculator; rival of banker Necker and the Genevan aristocrats; founder with Condorcet of *Le Moniteur*. Finance minister. "Brain of a man, heart of a child" (Mme Roland).

October. *J. M. Roland*. (Both Rolands: C) Feckless in his second ministery; an honest republican, not good at sharing power; on his way to the fatal "iron chest" episode (a Caleb who inspired Godwin's *Things as They Are*).

November. *Armand Guy-Kersaint*. (Q) "Chief of division of the naval army, and member of the Department of Paris" (*Cdm*, March 1792, 3). Deputy since April. Writes on marine laws, colonies; a naval officer, frustrated in efforts for reform in the navy; is writing a pamphlet on peace in our colonies—and organizing the Friends of the Blacks (Amis des Noirs).

December. *Jos. Ant. Joach. Cerutti*. "Born at Turin June 13 1738, died at Paris Feb 3, 1792, 1st year of the French Republic." He had given the funeral oration for Mirabeau, 4 April 1791, dedicating the Pantheon. (Early member of Assembly of Representatives of the Communes of Paris.)

1793

January. *J. Ankarstrom*. "The Swedish Brutus. The Year one of the Republic . . . portrait sent from Sweden to the Cercle Social." With Louis on the way to the guillotine, it was macabre to publish this portrait of the assassin of Gustavus III of Sweden (who had restored absolutism in 1772 and recently been overthrown by a conspiracy of nobles—which did *not achieve* a Swedish republic; Gustavus IV would prove only a fiercer tyrant).

February. *Charles François Dumouriez*. "General in chief of the Armies of the Republic." "Drawn from nature by F. Bonneville." Trusting him had been one of Roland's less inspired ideas; he would defect in March.

March. *Georges Jacq. Danton.* "Deputy to the National Convention." Probably responsible for Oswald's prominence in the volunteer army of Paris. This was the month Oswald marched off to war in the Vendée.

April. *L. M. LePelletier St. Fargeau.* "Deputy to the National Convention in 1792. Assassinated Jan. 20 1793 [by one Pâris of the old King's-Guard] for having voted death to the tyrant. Deposited in the Pantheon 24 Germinal, Year 2 of the Republic."

May. *Adam Philippe Custine.* "General in Chief of the Army of the Rhine. . . . Entered the service in 1747. Colonel in 1762. Adjutant at the Siege of Mestricht in 1748. Drawn from nature by F. Bonneville." (Guillotined at the end of August: not a Girondist but accused of harshness, perfidiousness; "found guilty . . . of one thing, unsuccessfulness"—Carlyle.)

June. *Armand Gensonné.* "Deputy of the Department of the Gironde, to the National Convention year 1 of the French Republic." Publishing at this time a portrait of one of the three actual "Girondistes" was a strong act of defiance for the *Chronique*, which was often itself given that label.

Since February, all names had been omitted from the title page. A list of accused, in this June issue, included Brissot, Dusaulx, and Lanthenas of the Quatorze, as well as Gensonné and twenty others; actually arrested, of these I have named, were Brissot and Gensonné, on 2 June.

July. *Alexandre Beauharnois.* "Commander in Chief, Army of the Moselle. Year 2 of the French Republic." (Soon to die, a man "who shall get Kings though he be none"—Carlyle.)

August. *F. C. Kellermann.* "Commander in Chief of the Army of the Alps. Born at Strasbourg in 1737." Heroic leader at Valmy; on his way now to the Vendée.

If the *Chronique* had survived to have a September issue, possibly it would have contained the portrait of General Miranda which François Bonneville engraved, typifying positively the liberating "Général des Armées de la Republique."

Other Members of the Quatorze

I add here a list of the unpictured members of the *Chronique* team, except for Bonneville and Oswald, of whom no portraits survive but who will remain on stage:

J. Bidermann, the big shipping merchant mentioned above, a Swiss banker whose Paris home was a rendezvous for Clavière and Brissot and others. One of the suppliers of arms to the Revolution.[68]

68. J. Bidermann's function in the purchasing committee (Le Directoire des Achats: 1792–1793) is described in Charles Poisson, *Les Fournisseurs aux Armées sous la Révolution Française*; his own firm was a big supplier of military material. Kates, *The Cercle Social,* draws on the Poisson study but confuses J. Bidermann with his relative, Antoine. (And Dumont spells the name *Bidder-*

A. Broussonet, a Paris deputy, interested in rural economy and manufacturing.

François Lanthenas. (C) Deputy from Rhone et Loire, in 1784 an "enthusiastic disciple of mesmerism and physiognomy," who introduced Manon Roland to the mysteries of hypnosis; a businessman interested in languages and anatomy, he entered the study of medicine but remained a perpetual student, indolent, melancholy, weak-willed; he had a secret passion for Manon. However, he functioned well in the Cercle.[69]

Jean Dusaulx, elderly deputy of Paris to the National Assembly; he had been a member of the Commune of Paris with Brissot; one of Bonneville's original "fourteen"; dismissed later by Marat as "too old a dotard to be a party leader."[70]

Collot-d'Herbois, often on stage with Oswald in the Jacobin Club. Carlyle: "Collot d'Herbois, tearing a passion to rags, pauses on the Thespian boards; listens, with that black bushy head, to the sound of the world's drama: shall the Mimetic become Real?" Carlyle captures Collot perfectly; he requires a portrait, however (see Fig. 17).[71]

The Cahiers

Many of the political essays in the twenty-two numbers of the *Chronique* were of great importance at the time, and some remain of considerable interest today, though not attracting attention as a group until quite recently. Keeping our attention on articles that concern French and British relations, or were contributed by those friends whose work Oswald promised to obtain, we shall be

---

mann.) There is a fine portrait of Jacques Bidermann (1751–1817) in Poisson, which may have been intended, too late, for the *Chronique*. J. Bidermann and Clavière had been leaders of the successful revolution in Geneva in 1782; he had then moved to Brussels and established a manufacturing firm, with help from Necker, reestablished in January 1789 as a multinational corporation (see Poisson, 37–40, for the ramifications in seven cities, including two in India). Correspondence between Clavière and Dumont, cited by Poisson, 48–50, suggests that Bidermann played a role in setting up the *Chronique* and put himself in a position to pontificate upon commerce—yet had little intention of doing so. Clavière suspected a bit of charlatanry since Bidermann was not fluent in French.

69. Lanthenas, a mesmerist before the Revolution, is thought to have shared Brissot's wisdom of 1791: "Liberty . . . is the principle of health."

70. His name is sometimes spelled *Dussaulx*. Carlyle finds him attempting to harangue the mob engaged in the September Massacres in 1792: "'Good Citizens, you see before you a man who loves his country, who is the Translator of Juvenal.' . . . 'Juvenal?' interrupts Sanculottism: 'Who the devil is Juvenal?'" (502). Literary history records Dusaulx as "solide et lourd" yet among "les plus originaux" writers for the *Journal des Debats* (Des Granges, 714).

71. Collot's relations with Oswald were at times symbiotic, but he was less a collaborator than a parasite. A trained actor, he could be counted on to leap to the stage whenever he saw a chance for instant glory. He would be the first to move the abolition of the monarchy, 20 September 1792; the first to vote the death of the king "sans sursis" in January. A Girondist in 1791, he would be the first to denounce Brissot and other Girondists in April 1793; yet he would fall in the Thermidorian reaction and be deported to French Guiana, where he died in 1796.

Fig. 17. Collot d'Herbois (1750–1796). Portrait by Raffet in Lamartine, *Histoire des Girondins*, 7:175. (SB)

disappointed in our expectations even though in the case of Oswald we can see what happened.[72]

The first issue, November 1791, consists of a forty-five-page article by Clavière on the present state of French finances, and in a note announces a matching article on British finances expected from David Williams, author of *Lessons to a Young Prince* (1791: in French given a title identifying him as the prince of Wales: *des leçons au prince de Galles*). The next issue is given almost wholly to Clavière again, on What is to be done. Still nothing from Williams.

The January issue (136 pages) splendidly presents six articles along the lines promised, by Bonneville, Condorcet (two), Mercier (*Du Courage National*), Kersaint, and Bidermann. The February issue, even larger, presents eight essays—by Condorcet, Bonneville, Kersaint, and Clavière—and four appendices.

Only in the March issue do we find the drumbeat of Oswald, who has, by that time, begun to concentrate his attention not on writing but on military tactics—drilling volunteers in the Champ-de-Mars—or on efforts within the Jacobin Club to forge bonds of international solidarity with the British, at home and abroad. It was ominous that portraits of army generals finally took over the frontispieces of the *Chronique*; we shall find a parallel editorial development when we hear war and its revolutionary and historical implications and tactics march right into the cadenced prose of the cahiers, with the assistance chiefly of Bonneville, somewhat of Lanthenas, and collaboratively and allusively of Oswald. Meanwhile it is advisable to turn back to the autumn of 1791 for the growth of a peaceful internationalism that reached its Jacobin Club climax at about the time the drums began to beat, in the spring.

The purposes and expectations announced by the Cercle press as publisher and distributor, however, must not be overlooked. In its first issue, the press offered for sale a list of twenty-two books, topped by Bonneville's *De l'Esprit des Réligions* and including works by Mirabeau, Regnault, Condorcet, Marsillac (Doctor of Medicine), and Thiery, and a comedy by Mercier, *Le ci-devant Noble*; most of the others were anonymous. In January the Cercle would begin publishing the *Journal of Natural History*, by Lamarck and others.

In February it required eighteen pages to tell of the many new Cercle publications, with a joyous prediction from the business office (words by Bonneville—or Oswald) of the great opening up of international exchanges of manuscripts and books, and the ultimate prospect of a universal confederation of Friends of Truth. Authors hitherto cheated, betrayed, and insulted in their poverty by wealthy dealers would at last draw income from their work.

---

72. Paine, however, would actually become one of the Fourteen in March, replacing Collot, and in the issues from May to July would make a three-part Response (translated by Condorcet) to four questions on legislative and executive powers. Oswald, perhaps by agreement and encouragement, would devote his writing time to a major, independent document so that when in February 1793 the National Convention published a *PLAN de Constitution* Oswald would top it with his *PLAN or Sketch of a Constitution for the Universal Commonwealth*.

Farewell, Grub-Street! In this February announcement, Oswald's English translation of Collot's chapbook is presented as symbolic of the new international commerce in the arts of peace:

> Our publishing is still in its infancy. Fortunately there are members of the National Assembly who recognize that it will produce riches for France. This translation of the *Almanach of Goodman Gerard*, by John Oswald, a young writer of great talent, was printed by the Social Circle press for shipment to England, and we are keeping some copies here. We hope to see this sort of venture encouraged by the founders and administrators of family wealth (*les instituteurs et les péres de famille*), for when the French introduce into their national education the study of their great works which we are translating and printing in all languages, our principles and our laws and all that can unite us in trust, interest, and friendship with our neighbors will imperceptibly steal past the bayonets and the censors into all libraries. Thus our neighbors will be enthralled by our zeal in assisting their instruction; we shall increase our trade with them in publications; and we shall repeat the process, having tried it once and gained their confidence.

The purposes of the *Chronique* were spelled out broadly. It would be "indispensable to those whom the constitution calls to the management of affairs; to members of the national assembly who, too close to thorny questions, need to look at them from every point of view and fear being misled by pernicious talent on the rostrum." The cahiers would be "useful" to bankers and merchants "who need to know the state of the interior and exterior" and to those who need general ideas about agriculture. "Finally, we hope that the patriotic cahiers will be equally useful to the Societies of Friends of the Constitution [the Jacobin Clubs] whose patriotism, in more than one place, needs to be clarified by those who have pondered, in their study, the basic elements of public prosperity."[73]

Though not mentioned in this early announcement, the *Chronique* would also serve as a journal of support for antislavery groups including the Société des Amis des Noirs, of which six of the original Quatorze were members.[74] To apply the inspiration and thought of the Enlightenment to every sort of mental and moral and physical slavery, in ever-widening circles of free human society, remained the educational and political purpose of the Friends of the Truth.[75] But there were other means besides essays and almanachs. To many persons in other countries and to many persons in France, for example, it seemed of immense importance that the French and the British should meet together, feeling each other's humanity; not only exchanging addresses and toasts, but cere-

73. "P.S. The typefaces of the press of the Social Circle are Baskerville, de Waflard, and de Mignonait, and one may always distinguish works from our presses, having the seal of the press affixed to the title-page, from counterfeits produced by typographical highway robbery."

74. Kates, *The Cercle Social*, 217. For more details about the contents of the *Chronique*, see Delsaux, *Condorcet Journaliste*, 275, 319–20.

75. I.e., those who wrote and distributed the produce of the printing house where the Bonnevilles lived and the Cercle directors met.

monially engaging in a *commerce des lumières*—a complex image used by the Jacobin schoolteacher Léonard Bourdon in a context allowing a blend of meanings: the meeting of luminaries, by mutual recognition of one another's auras; exchanges of knowledge, insight, bright ideas.[76] By the autumn of 1791 there was a multitudinous posting back and forth of correspondence among "Jacobin" and other societies, of France and Britain. And many British friends of freedom had traveled to and in France. But the first strongly Jacobinical Channel-crossing that involved and inspired strong ceremonial bonding (*etreintes*) was that of Jérôme Pétion in November 1791.

Paris to London: Commerce des Lumières

Let us suppose that John Oswald watched the evolving of this symbolic drama from its beginning, which I think we can trace to the Paris home of Pétion, where in July the bright idea (*lumière*) of announcing a Société des Républicaines and publishing a journal *Le Républicain* occurred to Paine and Bonneville and other Cercle revolutionaries. The project was brainstormed, according to Manon Roland, at such a meeting. The *Républicain* ceased after four issues, but when Pétion in the purity of his heart (and with other attractive persuasions) chose to be absent from Paris during the mayoral campaign in which he was to run against Lafayette—and which he would win—he staged an elaborate social commerce with Horne Tooke's people in London, arriving in time to attend the 4 November banquet of the Revolution Society as its guest of honor.

The correspondence with the London society of the newly forming French societies (using the magic word *Constitution* in their names) had begun as early as August 1789; George Veitch in 1913 found that fifty-three French societies had written to the Revolution Society by December 1791.[77] Many French—and British—had been inspired by the famous (or infamous) British welcome to the Revolution delivered by Richard Price in the society in 1789. Lord Stanhope, in the chair, had forwarded Price's sermon/address to his friend the Duke de la Rochefoucauld-Liancourt, who read it to the National Assembly on 25 November, praising Stanhope and Price as great scientists and as zealots for popular liberty. This philosophic gesture from London produced in the Assembly "a great sensation, manifested by repeated applause,"[78] and

---

76. "A thought has suddenly struck me," wrote Bonneville, in his *De l'Esprit des Religions* now on the press of the Cercle Social, "which scatters in my head like thousands and thousands of bright thoughts [*traits de lumière*]. It fills me with ideas and sentiments that cause me to hope that there is now being born for future generations a sensitive being who, in the happy delirium of a tender heart, will present the truth to mankind in images a hundred times more sublime than those that have dressed out lies and false wisdom" (130).

77. *The Genesis of Parliamentary Reform,* 357–59.

78. A century later this declaration of a common cause uniting the French Assembly and the

the French duke was instructed to write to the English earl—as they continued to do.

After London's Bastille Day of 1790—again reported by Stanhope to La Rochefoucauld—with a meeting of Revolution Society and other Whigs being chaired by Stanhope and addressed by Price and then toasting "extinction of all jealousy between France and England" and advocating an Anglo-French alliance (plus Holland and the United States: such was the thrust of Price's speech), tears of joy came to the eyes of the listening Jacobins. Seventeen provincial clubs wrote seeking "intimate union" with the London society, and the club of Nantes "reacted especially enthusiastically to the English overtures. On 23 August 1790, it hosted a 'magnificent fête' for all British subjects" in its department and then sent its president and "a municipal officer" to London to meet Stanhope and dine with the society on 29 September. The Nanteans proudly told their London brothers of the Anglo-Franc festival they had just left, featuring the joined flags of the two nations—an idea which thus reached London before it had reached Paris.[79]

In October the Limoges club, while urging the "mother society" of Paris to proclaim opposition to war, proposed a group deputation to London—an idea that was approved by twenty-seven of the corresponding clubs during the next weeks. The Paris club did announce that a questionnaire would be circulated through the entire network of French clubs, but no evidence has been found that the peace mission to London "ever became more than a dream."[80]

Pétion's visit to London a year later was a meager token indeed; yet it led to the December response, anonymous yet epochal. Stanhope, meanwhile, having withdrawn from the Revolution Society, was notably absent from the 4 November banquet in 1790 and again in 1791, when he arranged to meet Pétion on the 5th.[81] The rival banquet of the Constitutional Whigs at the Intrepid Fox *may* have attracted him, or at least the intention of that group may have been to lure him to join the Foxites. Their own final toast was clearly in the spirit of Citizen Stanhope: "May the example of one revolution preclude the necessity

---

British Revolution Society would be singled out, by a French historian, as the precipitating cause—since it enraged Edmund Burke—of the ensuing decades of war that ravaged Europe (Pariset, "La Société des amis de la Révolution de Londres," 297–325). More recently the Revolution Society's having congratulated the National Assembly for having vanquished "aristocracy and despotism" has been called "one of the principal causes of the foundation of the Paris Jacobins" (Kennedy, *The Jacobin Clubs*, 234). Perhaps so. The Jacobin responses in turn encouraged the "Corresponding" societies of London and more than a score of other British towns, in early 1792.

79. Kennedy, *The Jacobin Clubs*, 236. London entertained the Nanteans with an opera "on the Federation of Frenchmen at the Champ de Mars." Carlyle (279) supposed the original Champ-de-Mars "Feast of Pikes" to have been "the highest stretch attained by the Thespian Art on this Planet."

80. Kennedy, *The Jacobin Clubs*, 239.

81. Stanhope had withdrawn in disapproval of an undemocratic procedure comparable to Oswald's disapproval of having any "representative" do his thinking or voting for him. Stanhope's name had been signed on published resolutions on which he had not voted. But he entered active politics all the more intensely.

for another!" Six weeks later the Paris Jacobins would welcome a mysteriously unnamed "Constitutional Whig" with sweet embraces inspired by Pétion's spirited *"commerce."*

The political event which precipitated these more dramatic exchanges was King Louis's involuntary oath of allegiance to the French Constitution on 14 September, for which the Jacobins received deserved acclaim, since it signaled the dissolution of the Constituent Assembly and its replacement by the Legislative, a crucial forward stride of the Revolution. At this joyous moment, the two busiest and most trusted Montagnard leaders at this time, Pétion and Robespierre, seeing that the new Assembly was off to a good start, took needed vacations. Robespierre went home to Arras. Pétion, now candidate for mayor of Paris, traveled abroad with Mme de Genlis and an entourage of young women, visiting London between 24 October and 11 November.[82]

Pétion kept a diary of this London trip, unknown to his contemporaries but discovered and published by Marcel Reinhard in 1970. A high point in this experiment in mutuality between Paris and London was the long, sympathetic conversation with Stanhope, who spoke pure French (Pétion knew no English) and pure egalitarian sentiments (while yet praising Sheridan highly).[83] At the London Tavern banquet the night before, Pétion had seen Priestley and chatted with Tom Paine—perhaps his liaison with the Revolution Society, if he had needed any—and had been deeply impressed by the orchestra's playing *Ça ira;* by the much greater applause for the French Revolution than for the ancient English one; and by a "symbol of alliance" (which he had failed to notice but was told about): English and French flags draped together with garlands, and a crown on top. (Neat ambiguity: a royal crown, or a civic crown of popular sovereignty?) In December the draped flags and the Constitutional Whig were on their way to Paris.

Persons Pétion liked well enough to correspond with later included David Williams and John Hurford Stone and Thomas Christie (later of the British Club in Paris); also, of course, Horne Tooke, whose desk was a clearing center for egalitarian communications; and Thomas Cooper and James Watt, Jr., of the Manchester Constitutional Society, who called upon him at his hotel and who would be the British participants in April of a large public ceremony spon-

82. Legend has it that Pétion through Masonic connections was assisting a scheme to marry Princess Adelaide d'Orleans to one of the sons of George III, perhaps ultimately to bring two "free nations" under one constitutional crown. Princess Adelaide and her sister Pamela were the charges of Mme de Genlis, who went on with them to Bath. (See Ellis and Turquan, *La Belle Pamela*, 218–23, for whom the whole Revolution was a Masonic plot "organised and subsidised in France by the King of Prussia and the Duke of Brunswick, Grand Master of all European freemasonry.") Mme de Genlis, mistress of the Duke of Orleans, is described by Billington (*Fire in the Minds of Men*, 29) as "a kind of princess among the prostitutes" of the Palais-Royal, "as well as a 'governess of princes.'"

83. Pétion was delighted with the elegance of Stanhope's town house and his and his wife's elegant, learned, and beautifully nuanced conversation of "four hours," though shocked at the presence of *pots de chambre* in the dining room.

Fig. 18. Jérôme Pétion (1756–1794), elected mayor of Paris 16 November 1791, defeating Lafayette. Portrait by Raffet, in Lamartine, *Histoire des Girondins*, 3:27. (SB)

sored by the Jacobins which the British (even Burke, with alarm) would see as epochal.[84]

Back in Paris in time to enjoy his election as mayor on 16 November, defeating Lafayette two to one, Pétion was greeted by the Jacobin Club on the 18th. Asked to tell about his visit to the Revolution Society, he described the British toast to the French Revolution, and his own toast to the union, sincere and durable, of the two peoples, as equally received "with transport." He told of the entwined flags in the hall; at a later meeting the Jacobins decided to go their English friends one better by displaying the joined flags of *three* free peoples, British, French, and American.

It was on the 18th, after Dusaulx, speaking from the heart, had descended from the tribune and embraced Pétion, that Bourdon identified the London visit as having been made "pour y faire commerce des lumières." Carlyle's historical imagination (388) is delighted by "Pétion the virtuous" (lawyer, violinist, full of self-confidence) in London "harangued and haranguing, pledging the wine-cup with Constitutional Reform-Clubs, in solemn tavern-dinner." At the later meeting, on the 30th, the club not only voted to hang the three entwined flags in the vaults of the hall, but also proposed that a letter about this be sent to the London society and to the United States of America, though not without approval by the Committee of Correspondence. A small point, but right in the zone where Oswald in later months will find suspicion and bitter strife before shouted sentiments are trusted to the written word.

On this occasion all was sunshine when someone proposed that, to the fraternal letters to Britain and America, the committee should add copies of the *Almanach du Père Gérard*. Since the presiding officer on this day was Collot, the author himself, there was a gesture of evading the motion, but "finally, pressed by further urging: 'As President,' says he, 'Gentlemen, my modesty suffers, but I assure you that you give me great pleasure.'" This frankness is covered with applause. The motion is unanimous.[85]

Douce Etreintes: *London Embraces Paris*

The December communication of the London Society of Constitutional Whigs with the revolutionary citizens of France was made in writing and in person. Bonneville's summary in the February *Chronique du mois* dwells on

---

84. William Godwin too was with Pétion on several of these occasions, as we learn from Godwin's diary, but he is not mentioned in Pétion's.

85. Aulard, ed., *Recueil des Documents . . . des Jacobins*, 3:256–57. It may be noted that even on the day of Pétion's election, 16 November, a "Letter to Affiliated Societies" had been approved and signed by Bourdon, president, and a long list including Fauchet, Desmoulins, Lanthenas, and Broussonet, all Cercle stalwarts. To the printed copy of the *Letter* in the Bibliothèque Nationale someone added by hand, one of the Quatorze probably, this note: "N.B. The surest way to triumph

the Whigs' message offering "alliance et fraternité" to the French nation, read in the Assembly on 8 December, and inserted in its proceedings. It was to be sent to press immediately and distributed to all departments of France. And it was to be replied to formally by the Assembly president. Presumably the president's reply was the decree of 19 December, which we shall hear more of.

On 18 December, a Sunday, one "Wigh constitutionel" appeared in person to convey the warmth of living sentiments and received it, in the Jacobin Club. He had arrived from England a few days earlier, holding several informal conversations though remaining incognito in public. (A fairly easy thing to manage in the days before photography.) I believe that this Whig was Citizen Stanhope himself, but since the anonymity was sustained, the point is not material in the present context.[86]

On Friday, the 16th—a day memorable in the revolutionary calendar as the anniversary of the English Declaration of Rights of 1689—there had been a planning session for the Sunday visit, and the proceedings reveal that there had been various preparatory exchanges between London and Paris, including the delivery of a special British flag from the Whig Society, and the enlistment of a corps of women to prepare the twined flags, in imitation of the London draping. These were the women who customarily sat in the galleries (*les citoyennes habituées aux tribunes*); there was also to be a special deputation from the affiliated women's society: the *orateur* who would interpret the role of the visiting Whig, and the young innocents who would hand him the ikons.[87]

Carlyle takes us into the Jacobin Club at this period by borrowing an eyewitness description of the hall from the Marquis de Toulongeon and conflating several occasions in a way that calls attention—appropriate to our purposes—to the theatrical potentialities of the transformed church where the ritual of bonding was solemnized:

> The nave of the Jacobins Church is changed into a vast Circus, the seats of which mount up circularly like an amphitheatre to the very groin of the domed roof. A high Pyramid of black marble built against one of the walls, which was formerly a funeral monument, has alone been left standing: it serves now as back to the Office-bearers' Bureau. Here on an elevated Platform sit President and Secretaries, behind and above them the white Busts of Mirabeau, of Franklin, and various others, nay finally of Marat. Facing this is the Tribune, raised till it is midway between floor and groin of the dome, so that the speaker's voice may be in the centre. From that point thunder

over persecution by aristocrats and priests is to spread good books among all classes of people; and we recommend to you especially the *Lettre* of Creuze la Touche, the *Esprit des réligions*, by M Bonneville, and the *Chronique du mois*" (ibid., 3:251–53).

86. My deduction that the mysterious Whig was Stanhope himself rests on circumstantial evidence spelled out in my "Citizen Stanhope and the French Revolution." For one thing, Stanhope was being a stickler for direct representation at this time, as I doubt any of the Intrepid Fox trenchermen would have been.

87. For some of this, see Aulard, ed., *Recueil des Documents . . . des Jacobins*, 4:290; my interpretation requires also the *Journal des Débats* for 16 and 18 December.

the voices which shake all Europe: down below, in silence, are forging the thunder-bolts and the firebrands. Penetrating into this huge circuit, where all is out of mea-sure, gigantic, the mind cannot repress some movement of terror and wonder; the imagination recalls those dread temples which Poetry, of old, had consecrated to the Avenging Deities.

Scenes too are in this Jacobin Amphitheatre,—had History time for them. Flags of the "Three Free Peoples of the Universe," trinal brotherly flags of England, America, France, have been waved here in concert; by London Deputation, of Whigs or *Wighs* and the Club, on this hand, and by young French Citoyennes on that; beautiful sweet-tongued Female Citizens, who solemnly send over salutation and brotherhood, also Tricolor stitched by their own needle, and finally Ears of Wheat; while the dome rebellows with *Vivent les trois peuple libres!* from all throats: a most dramatic scene.[88]

History might have had time for these scenes if the connection between the flag waving and the thunderbolts had been more than rhetorically recognized. In the Jacobin Club proceedings the Constitutional Whig is said to have deliv-ered the sentiments of "his class of free British" (not further defined)[89] before the National Assembly, but I find no trace in the Assembly proceedings.[90]

On Sunday, when called upon to speak, our Constitutional Whig assures his

88. Carlyle, *The French Revolution*, 422. Some scholars have criticized my use of Carlyle's book as a historical source, even though I do so critically (see the next footnotes). Yet Carlyle was often closer to authentic sources than many later historians (who, for instance, tend to ignore such things as the daily *Journal des Débats* because it is a "printed" not a "manuscript" source). Indeed, *The French Revolution* "has withstood a century and a half of historical criticism; so that when we want to know what storming the Bastille or stopping the King at Varennes or living in Paris during the Terror was really like we turn, not to the statisticians and the retrospective sociologists, but to Carlyle." So says John Clive in his review of Fred Kaplan's recent *Thomas Carlyle: A Biography*, in *TLS*, 20 April 1984, 419–20. And John Clubbe, also in 1984, in "Carlyle as Epic Historian" (120), recognizes the historical value of *The French Revolution* as "by no means negligible," quot-ing John Stuart Mill, who hailed it as "an epic poem" and also "the truest of histories."

89. *Journal des Débats* (Jacobins, 1791, no. 113). This daily journal is extant only in scattered numbers. When I tracked down this issue, I was shocked to find that Aulard had omitted more than two-thirds of the bulk of the proceedings of 18 December. Later, however, I found that this material *was* given, quoted from the *Journal Des Débats*, in Carlyle's source, Buchez et Roux, *Histoire Par-lementaire*, 12:376–81. More shocking still, I find that Aulard even cites the preceding editorial pages in Buchez et Roux, but with no comment on the omission *he* chose to make.

Somehow, nevertheless, Carlyle was misled into citing plural Whigs; there was only one, who stressed that he was alone, "moi-même." And Buchez et Roux had it right!

Brissot's brief report in the *Patriote* (paraphrased in Alger, *Englishmen*, 45–46) dwells on the "very effusive scene," omits the context, and concludes: "he could only make himself understood with tears of compassion; it was in this moment the language of all friends of the constitution." The Whig was able to say quite a bit, however, according to the *Débats*: he said that he had already sent to England detailed reports of his reception (i.e., in private talks) and had received some replies from England, but none from his society, since it had not had time to meet; that his feelings for the Jacobins were not the work of a day, but "well that of a year, ever since the month when my society wrote to M. Pétion"—a communication which Pétion has now told him was never received. Does this mean that the Whigs wrote to Pétion a year earlier, in that memorable month of November?

90. Curiously enough, on the 18th the Assembly and Collot d'Herbois (who did not attend the Jacobins, apparently: that was not going to be *his* show) busied themselves with mutual laudations over the success of Collot's *Almanach*. He persuaded them to recommend it to their Committee of

French brothers and sisters that his society (*ma société*) has charged him in person to express their sentiments, and that he will in turn give a faithful account of their good reception by the Jacobins but is not prepared to make any formal speech. The reason he gives is characteristic of the Stanhope who had resigned from the Revolution Society when they put his name on a resolution he had not been present to vote upon: he was authorized by his society to represent them in person, *moi-même*, he said, but there had not been "time for it to meet" to authorize an oration.

Since arriving in Paris he has been talking informally with several of the Jacobins, we learn from the female citizen who ritually introduces him as "a brother, an Englishman." During the last few days he has been "the object of your sweetest bondings [*douces etreintes*]." Applause from the Jacobins and the galleries. The Sunday ceremony, then, is a bonding of the hearts and minds of men and women and nations. "Today," she explains to the Jacobins, "you are giving to this brother (and to your selves) a new enjoyment; you have hung in the vault of your temple three flags, American, English, French." On all sides: "Vivent les trois nations! Vive la liberté!" And the ceremony proceeds with the solemnity of a wedding. "The union of the three free peoples is now to be cemented." The Jacobins must contribute something, she exhorts: their pure sentiments. The civic crown serves as a wedding ring. Stepping forward, the *jeune citoyenne* offers it: "Accept a crown, free Englishman"; and then, probably aided by sisters: "Accept another from the hands of innocence." And then the covenant: "Receive, in the name of the *citoyennes françaises* who are here, an Ark of the Alliance which you are to take to our brothers, the Constitutional Whigs." In short, "three flags, a national concord, and the words, in two languages: Live free or die!" (The entire hall resounds: "Vivre libre ou mourir!") [91]

After these rites of confederation, Bourdon delivers an appropriate political sermon, congratulating the Jacobins on having kept a wall of bronze between corruption and their disinterested love of liberty, creating "the circumstances which have brought about the ceremony which unites us today." He credits Pétion, "whom all France has styled the incorruptible," with having sought out this "new means of public prosperity for France" by going to London, "the

National Instruction. (In neither Club nor Assembly was there any mention of Oswald's English translation. In the *Moniteur* that day—perfectly timed—Collot's *Almanach* is prominently advertised, in various formats and prices.) Yet the delegates were not exactly happy with Collot's self-aggrandizement. On Monday in the Assembly (*Moniteur*, 20 December, 1479) someone noted that M. Collot had been heard to extend his name by adding "d'Herbois," and by Assembly vote this aristocratic extension was ordered to be removed as a violation of the Constitution.

91. The National Assembly session on the 16th had opened with a dispute as to whether the proper oath was "la Constitution ou la mort" or "la Liberté ou la mort" and reached no agreement; the latter would be the popular slogan for the coming season, climaxing in the adventure of the five hundred volunteers from Marseille who "knew how to die," 10 August. No open doubts were expressed in the Jacobin debates.

home of a people long habituated to liberty." Banners, formerly symbols of murder and carnage, are today emblems of friendship and peace. The cause of free men is alive; the blindfold on the eyes of nations is about to fall. The ties which the three nations are forming today, uniting as a true family, shall never be weakened by time nor severed by the daggers of tyrants.

Like Wordsworth eleven years later, Bourdon wishes that a great English republican—in this case Richard Price of the Revolution Society, who had died in April—were living at this hour. "Price, Franklin, Mirabeau," he addresses as one man. "O you evangelist of peace, apostle of liberty, why are you not, all of you, among us? . . . Today, when Britain, America, and France unite, presenting the gage of universal peace . . . may your sacred spirits share the happiness which this union promises; may they come to dwell among us; may they warm us incessantly with the sacred fire which burns in your hearts." And he makes a motion "that the busts of Doctor Price, and of Doctor Franklin be placed beside those of Mirabeau and that there be works to that effect by a voluntary subscription."

Others propose adding busts of Rousseau and Mably and the British martyr, Algernon Sidney. The sculptor Dufourny at once offers a bust he has made of Franklin. At this point a secretary brings forth a fine damascene sword, proposed by its maker to be given to the first French general who shall fell an enemy of the Revolution. President Isnard brandishes it—and Robespierre begs the assembly to cool off the bellicosity.[92]

Roederer then, however, insists as calmly as possible on discussing the question that must be faced (which Aulard dismisses as "observations on the special nature of the next war" and does not print—perhaps because Roederer would turn Feuillant). The question is not, he argues, whether to attack or not to attack, whether to make war or to make peace. "We are already in a secret war . . . the war of the nobles against the people; of all the tyrants against liberty and personal security." Roederer favors an open declaration of war—with assurance that France shall never make conquests.

These remarks draw still stronger language from Robespierre, giving "new developments to the motives which he has already revealed for not declaring war." Brissot has his name put on the next day's agenda, to dispute Robespierre's objections—but does not appear for the rest of the week. When their debate resumes, with Brissot speaking on 30 December and Robespierre replying on 2 and 11 January, and Brissot calling a halt on the 20th, both assume a

---

92. Aulard leaves all this out, as not proper history; Buchez and Roux (*Histoire parlementaire*, 12:365) do quote Isnard, however, as matter for the history of oratory. Yet they drop the word *libres* from his concluding phrase: "Le peuple français poussera un grand cri, et tous les autres peuples répondront à sa voix; la terre se couvrira de combattans, et tous les ennemis de la liberté seront effacés de la liste des hommes libres." (I quote the *Débats*. It strikes me suddenly that Redhead Yorke's quoting of Oswald's remark when he draws his sword—"You are unfit to live in a civilized society!"—has a similar ring: both speakers pull back from murder and imply banishment.)

necessity to fight the external enemies of the Revolution, but disagree as to the nation's preparedness, and consequently about priorities.

Carlyle may have perfectly captured the ambiguities of the scene with his allusion to the forging of thunderbolts and firebrands "down below, in silence," suggesting the warlike backstage discussion and dispute (though some had been on stage before the historians deleted it). Curious that both Carlyle and Aulard delete talk of war, secret or open, from their reports of this "historical" occasion, though "History" would have all too much room for it. Curious also that about a year later the British spy Captain Monro would report the Constitutional Whigs as a group "particularly industrious in endeavouring to corrupt the soldiery"[93]—who would, thereby, be inspired to fight for and not against the Revolution.[94]

The First Festival Truly Civic

On 18 December, the day of the visiting Whig, and again on the following Thursday, the 22nd, Earl and Citizen Charles Stanhope wrote to his friend La Rochefoucauld, who was not in Paris at the time. And his friend replied that he recognized in these letters Stanhope's "unchanging support for the cause of liberty and humanity."[95] Clearly, whoever that anonymous Whig had been, Stanhope was keeping in touch with the Friends of the Constitution. He may have refrained from public participation in the dispute about "the nature of the coming war," but we may be sure he was busy making his pacific views known among the thunderbolt wielders, offstage, especially the influential ones. In February a London correspondent of *Le Journal général*, a Parisian anti-Jacobin daily, complained that while he had been in Paris recently—perhaps he traveled back and forth frequently—he had been told again and again (*mainte*

93. Goodwin, *The Friends of Liberty*, 501n.

94. The Jacobins' embracing the Constitutional Whig and the National Assembly's circulating the Whig address to all departments were not looked upon as epochmaking in all quarters. Most skeptical perhaps were the newspaper reporters. The London correspondent of the Paris *Moniteur* reported on 13 November that the Revolution Society had drawn a crowd of 250 to its 4 November banquet, and drunk 32 toasts, whereas the Grand Constitutional Lodge of the Whigs of England had drawn only 123 diners, drunk only 25 toasts. The more fully informed London *Times*, two days before Christmas, in a column of scorn for the French and for "Democracy," laughed at the Assembly for having "dignified with a letter of thanks" a club "first set up by Sam. House, in order to draw company to his ale-house [the Intrepid Fox] at the time of Sir Cecil Wray's first contest with Mr. Fox, for Westminster" in 1784, and assured its readers that the society had soon "dwindled to about fourteen Members, the most respectable of whom were journeymen Barbers," and that "The beveridge is porter and crank." On this cue the *Moniteur*, on 30 December, rebuked the Assembly for treating so insignificant a crew as if really "the direct descendants of the founders of *our* liberty" (my italics: the London correspondent was evidently British) "as well as its most illustrious defenders." (Veitch, in 1913, reports some of this—but not the London *Times*—and adds his own contempt [*The Genesis of Parliamentary Reform*, 214].)

95. La Rochefoucauld, 14 January 1792, quoted in Gooch and Stanhope, *Life of Stanhope*, 111.

et mainte fois) by those "factious" dreamers that milord Stanhope was of their party, failing to understand his adherence to no party.[96]

France did not declare war against the emperor until 20 April, and until then Stanhope busied himself in peacemaking efforts, first hopefully and then desperately, with Talleyrand and with David Williams, both active intermediaries since that London Tavern meeting in the autumn. At Stanhope's suggestion, Talleyrand, via Dumouriez, obtained from Louis XVI a confidential letter to George III thanking him for not joining the coalition against France and urging that "united we ought to assure the peace of Europe." On his own side of the Channel, assured by Talleyrand that the French were willing to propose King George as arbitrator of the points in dispute between France and Austria, Stanhope (as he told the radical Major Cartwright years later) went to his cousin Lord Grenville in the British Cabinet. "He told me generally that he was only one, and that he must consult others. I then went to my brother-in-law, Mr. Pitt. I made a full communication of what had passed between M. Talleyrand and myself, and I expressed the high satisfaction I felt at my having it in my power to give him such pleasing information. Mr. Pitt, without a moment's hesitation, rejected the idea totally. I urged with great earnestness . . . but wholly without effect." [97] The windfall prospects for Britain, should France be torn or tear itself apart, were already more than a gleam in Pitt's eye.[98]

If we were to join the game of singling out what caused the European wars that ensued, we might point to Pitt's deliberate rejection of negotiation. The event some historians point to, however, is the Jacobin Club sequel to the flag-twining and fraternizing of December. This time the demonstration and celebration of British-American-French solidarity culminated in a spectacular gathering of two to three hundred thousand Parisians and visitors, watching and joining in a parade, with banners and statues (including this time a bust of Sidney brought over from London), on Sunday, 15 April 1792.

96. *Journal général de France*, 7 March 1792, 266; dateline, "De Londres, le 28 février 1792." In the House of Lords, Stanhope had refused to join the Whigs in a motion censuring the Pitt administration for arming against Russia. His characteristic argument was that the administration ought rather to be congratulated for deciding not to go to war after all—since that indicated that the British constitution *did* work on the side of peace. Such political generosity didn't fit the journalist's stereotypes.

97. Gooch and Stanhope, *Life of Stanhope*, 117–19, quoting Pallain, *La Mission de Talleyrand*, 146–47. Stanhope to Cartwright, 3 January 1809 (Gooch quotes in full).

98. Peace between France and Austria would, of course, halt the counterrevolutionary impetus. And Pitt himself, as John Ehrman observes in a long chapter on "The End of Peace," was "apparently impressed by the prospect . . . of an easy seizure of the French West Indies" and aware that "public opinion 'was disposed for war, which might not be the case six weeks hence'" (*The Younger Pitt*, 2:253). Ehrman does mention that there were indications at this time that the French were "prepared to meet the substance of the British case" (251) and does express bewilderment at Pitt's "chilly" response to a French communication via William Miles, but he cites David Williams's peace mission only in a footnote, and makes no mention of Stanhope's mission. He saves his hero's honor by asserting, as a strictly documentary historian, that "there is no sign from other documents [than the one communicated by Miles] that the French Government would have backed . . .

This time there were two English guests, who scorned anonymity and were proud to be known as Thomas Cooper and James Watt of the Manchester Society for Constitutional Information—later, alas, to serve as target for the tirades of Edmund Burke. Cooper was a chemist and ultimately a judge (in Pennsylvania). He had read the second edition of Oswald's *Review of the Constitution of Great Britain* and would praise it in his brave reply to Burke. James Watt, Jr., was an old friend of Wordsworth, who would remember him vividly, saying years later that when he "went over to Paris at the time of the Revolution in 1792 and 1793, and so was 'pretty hot in it,' . . . he found Mr. Watt there before him, and quite as hot in the same cause." [99]

They seem not to have been in Paris together for any length of time, but Watt could have visited Wordsworth in Orleans or Blois, or Wordsworth could have made a brief visit or two to Paris. He certainly got to know a good deal about Oswald and quite possibly met him in Paris. It is fanciful, but not farfetched, to imagine that when Cooper and Watt visited the Jacobin Club on 13 and 15 April, Wordsworth and Oswald were there to share in the festivities. Annette Vallon, only a month pregnant, could have been with them.

The two "Constitutional" British in this parade served to focus the celebration as the anonymous Whig had done in December—but this time Collot d'Herbois supplied the raison d'être: to celebrate the success of one of his political causes, the release of sixty Swiss survivors of a court-martialed military company who had struck for pay in September 1790 and been chained at the oars of a French galley in Brest harbor, victims of surviving Ancien Régime legality. [100] Here is a highly colored account of the parade by Burke; the British flag is conspicuous:

> Messrs. Cooper and Watt had presented an address, and carried the British colors in a procession, and on what occasion? The most infamous that ever disgraced the

---

concessions" (257). Presumably the Talleyrand document survives only by hearsay and the Stanhope only as reported conversation: as such they can give "no signs" to the "scientific" historian.

99. Muirhead, *Life of James Watt*, 478. Notice the recollection of "1792 and 1793." Wordsworth scholars today incline to accept the evidence that, having left Paris for London in late November or early December 1792, Wordsworth made a brief return visit in October 1793. Besides wanting to visit Annette and Caroline, can he have been trying to help report the state of revolutionary sentiment in London or trying, like Hurford Stone, to keep abreast of developments on both sides of the channel? (See my "Wordsworth as Heartsworth.") It is also time to recognize that being "pretty hot in it" was likely to mean not simply sharing the fraternal enthusiasm, but sharing the interest of the British in Paris in candid discussion, sub rosa plans, and the offering of themselves in military or other support of the cause. (Watt cannot have been the strange Whig of December 1791; for his itinerary, see Robinson, "An English Jacobin," 351, 353.)

100. The strike of these mercenaries, the Swiss "of Châteauvieux," was of course treated as mutiny; even Lafayette, at the time a revolutionary commander, had supported his colleague, the Marquis de Bouillé, "who subdued the rebels in a pitched battle, had several insurgents executed, and sent forty-one Swiss from Châteauvieux to the galleys." The action tarnished Lafayette's credibility in the Assembly, especially when it learned that Bouillé "was treating all partisans of the Revolution as suspects" (Lefebvre, 144). By the time Collot came to the rescue, the forty-one had become sixty.

name of government. A set of soldiers had been tried by a court martial, and condemned to the gallies. These were fit men for the republicans of Paris. They might be useful—though bad soldiers, they might be good murderers. They were released in contempt of the Assembly then sitting, brought to Paris, and paraded in triumph through the hall. On this detestable occasion, Mr. Cooper and Mr. Watt carried the British colors. They were locked in the fraternizing embrace. They received the fraternizing kiss. They went from the Hall of the Assembly to the Hall of the Jacobins, where they kissed the bloody cheek of Marat . . . .[101]

This passage is excerpted, not from Burke's first but from his second parliamentary allusion to the affair, on 4 March 1793, when France and Britain were formally at war. He went on to cite Brissot and Pétion as benefactors of the "massacre of the 10th of August," then Sheridan's dagger "trick" to dismiss the horror of Dr. Maxwell's order for thousands of daggers, and finally "some publication by a Mr. Oswald, now in Paris, who expressed his hopes that all government by representation would soon be at an end, and that France would be freed from the iron yoke of property" (a phrase at the conclusion of Oswald's *Government of the People*). "The sovereignty of the people," exclaimed Burke, "was the most false, wicked, and mischievous doctrine that ever could be preached to them."

Burke's earlier allusion to the civic festival, less dramatic but more accusatory, was made in a debate on 30 April 1792, only a fortnight after the Jacobin parade. Burke's charge then, as gathered by Cooper from reports in London newspapers, was

> That there were in this country, men who scrupled not to enter into an alliance with a set in France of the worst traitors and regicides that had ever been heard of, the club of the Jacobins. Agents had been sent from this country, to enter into a foederation with that iniquitous club, and those were men of some consideration here, the names he alluded to were Thomas Cooper and James Watt, (here Mr. Burke read the address . . .). . . . He likewise could name others . . . Mr. Walker of Manchester. . . . they spoke, and were sworn into this foederation, in the name of the people of England. This led him to state, that, however upright the motives of the Honourable Gentlemen near him [e.g., Fox and Sheridan] might be, they must necessarily, in order to succeed in their object, unite themselves with some of the worst men in the kingdom.[102]

Before he had seen Burke's charge, Cooper described the affair in a letter to Thomas Walker of Manchester "as a meeting of two hundred thousand sober, orderly, and at the same time enthusiastic citizens, 'the first festival truly civic that Europe has seen,'" a definition that concludes a long unsigned account[103] begun in the *Manchester Herald* 28 April and continued 5 May:

101. *Parl Hist*, 30:552–54. Burke simplifies in saying that Cooper and Watt carried British colors. One carried a flag, the other the bust of Sidney that had been requested in December of the next London representative.

102. Cooper, *A Reply*, 4, citing the *Morning Chronicle* and the *General Evening Post*.

103. By Watt perhaps, or possibly by Watt and Cooper with help from Oswald for the background story and some of the epigrammatic passages. We shall come to his involvement shortly.

The processions of France have hitherto been processions contrived by the priests, for the purpose of superstition—this was contrived by the people to honor the defenders of their country; heretofore such a number of people meeting together, and bearing not only patiently, but chearfully and joyously, the fatigues of a long day, in hot weather, a long march, on dusty roads [they began near the place of the Bastille at 7 a.m. and reached a waiting crowd in the Champs-de-Mars about 8 p.m. for an hour of singing] with little or no refreshment, with no tumult or disturbance, no drunkenness or ribaldry, no quarrels among themselves, or *provoking expressions to their adversaries*, would be deemed next to miraculous, and for the first time in Europe the French nation . . . gave an example *of the peaceable spirit of true liberty*. . . .—This therefore was the first festival, truly civic, that Europe has seen.[104]

This from the supplemental report; the earlier is more clearly Cooper's, though unsigned: "I saw at least 50,000 people dancing at once to *Ça ira*—I heard repeatedly 100,000 voices cry out *Vivent les Anglois*. . . . though near 300,000 people were assembled in the Champ de Mars alone, not a single accident happened to blot the triumph of this glorious day . . ." (*Manchester Herald*, 28 April).

The 5 May *Herald* also condemned Burke's "invectives, against those persons who form, in our opinion, the pride and ornament of the country," summarizing Burke's charges and giving Sheridan's reply "vindicating the character" of Walker and Cooper and Watt, with his *tu quoque* rebuke to Burke: wondering what might sanction this "correspondence which had taken place . . . between unauthorized individuals" in England and France, Sheridan had suggested that "it could find a sanction . . . in the correspondence of Mr. Burke, during the contest with certain individuals in America."

Cooper, returning to London in early summer, dismissed reports of Burke's contribution to "the hue and cry of Ignorance and Inattention" as "ridiculous fears and intemperate Invectives." Within a fortnight, however, finding Burke's slanders retailed by "a herd of parliamentary Orators," he penned *A Reply to Mr. Burke's Invective against Mr. Cooper, and Mr. Watt in the House of Commons on the 30th of April, 1792*, in which incidentally he praised Oswald's *Review of the Constitution*, perhaps first lodging Oswald's name in Burke's mind—or reminding him of the Coachmakers' Hall attack on his *Reflections*.[105]

Cooper quietly explained that he and Watt had been in France on "Commercial Concerns"—which was true—and, far from being "sent" to the Jacobin Club, had been in Paris about a month before receiving a "Deputation" from Manchester to address the club. This was disingenuous. From Flanders, on

104. On 12 May the *Herald* printed a translation of the Address signed in Paris by Cooper and Watt—and a letter of 8 May by Walker and Jackson for the Manchester Constitutional Society announcing that the society has "no *secret* correspondence" and is glad that Cooper and Watt, "in Paris upon private business," initiated a correspondence with the Jacobin Society which both societies agree to.

105. The *Reply* was written after 16 June 1792 (see 98); Oswald's work is cited, 17n.

Fig. 19. Edmund Burke (1729–1797), who in the House of Commons in March 1793 accuses Oswald of spreading democracy. Portrait by Reynolds, in Philip M. Magnus, *Edmund Burke: A Life*, frontispiece. (SB)

Fig. 20. Thomas Cooper (1759–1839), who had advised Burke to bring his political wisdom up to date by reading Oswald and others. Engraving from portrait in Cooper's *Lectures on Political Economy*, 1831. (SB)

their way to Paris, Watt had written on 6 March to Thomas Walker, his employer but also chairman of the Manchester society, reminding Walker of his wish to establish formal correspondence with the French societies, asking Walker for authorization from the Manchester society to act as delegates to the Jacobin clubs of Paris and Nantes and Bordeaux—but also declaring that he and Cooper would assume the character of delegates without waiting for formal authorization.[106] Walker had already supplied them with letters of introduction, including one to Pétion, whom they looked up as soon as they reached Paris, reminding him of the London Tavern reception of the previous November.[107] Pétion was not the only planner of the April ceremony aware of

106. Goodwin, *The Friends of Liberty*, 202.

107. Cooper, already an admiring reader of Oswald, may have met him during if not before the April festival. Watt, writing home to his father on 22 March 1792, indicated that he and Cooper were indeed on a business trip, Watt as a salesman for Thomas Walker, "while acting also as an agent for his father's copying machines, but that the people they looked up were more interested in politics" (Robinson, "An English Jacobin," 349–55). "The only persons of any note that we have been to see yet are Mr Pethion the Mayor Mr de la Rochefacauld & Mr Lavoisier"—Stanhope's friends, and Cercle Social people. (The Cercle was publishing Lamarck's *Journal of Natural His-*

and concerned to sustain the continuity of interchange. For the April parade the three flags were temporarily separated, so that a Manchester delegate could march with one, while American and French representatives were chosen to carry the others. Then they were carefully retwined after the march.[108]

Plans for the festival were discussed and disputed for weeks beforehand. Most of the popular societies in or near Paris were involved, including the sister societies of Amies de la Liberté (though barely mentioned in Aulard). On the final day of planning, 13 April, Robespierre presented the Manchester deputies and requested and obtained a vote for their participation in the session in order to seek affiliation. The minutes say nothing more, but in the *Patriote françois* that day were printed the brief "Discourse of Cooper and Watt" and the response of J. L. Carra, *Annales* editor, occupying the chair in the absence of the president.[109] The discourse is said to have been read (*prononcé*) at the society, and since Cooper could not speak French but Watt fluently could, Watt was obviously the reader—unless someone else delivered it for him.

This question is of interest because years later the tale was told, and passed along by Cooper's biographer,

> that Cooper told Robespierre that he had written an address which Watt had trans-
> lated, and that he asked the Jacobin leader to deliver it for him, as he spoke French
> badly. This Robespierre promised to do. At the club, however, when the crowd called
> for the speech of Citoyen Gouappè [Cooper], which had been formally announced,
> Robespierre refused to budge. Whereupon Citoyen Gouappè, after a remonstrance,
> said, "Citoyen Robespierre, vous êtes un coquin!" and with that mounted the plat-
> form and delivered the address, which was received with great enthusiasm![110]

This lively but false anecdote was constructed not quite out of whole cloth but from a scribal error in the minutes of the Jacobin session of 27 May, when Oswald—not Watt—battled with Robespierre, verbally, for the right to read aloud a letter of greetings from a London society—which he gained after tumult in the hall. In the minutes, though not in the transcript of his remarks, Oswald was identified as "M Waths of Manchester." Not a surprising mistake, since the London letter, addressed to "Brothers and Citizens of the World," began thus: "Our worthy compatriots, Messrs Cooper and Watt, Members of the Society of Manchester, and associated with ours, have informed us of the cor-

___

tory/Journal d'histoire naturelle.) "Dr Priestley gave us letters to Mr de la Rochefaucauld and he introduced us to Mr Lavoisier who has been very civil to us. We met Messrs. Morveau, Fourcroy, Hassenfratz, and other first rate Chemists at his house, but not a word of Chemistry was there spoken, they are all mad with politics we have not met anywhere with such a set of *enragés*, except Mr Lavoisier who assumes the character of a *modéré* probably from prudential motives." (Note the "Mr" for La Rochefaucauld.)

108. Aulard, ed., *Recueil des Documents . . . des Jacobins*, 3:502–4.

109. Ibid., 3:496ff.

110. Malone, *Life of Cooper*, 35–36, citing "Table Talk" in Duyckinck, *Cyclopaedia*, 2:322 (not located).

dial and fraternal reception with which you have honored them." One difficulty with this tale is that it was Watt who could speak French; Cooper could not. So Watt's biographer, Muirhead, transferred the tale to Watt, in the role of a young enthusiast not yet ready to deplore the "violence of revolutionary rage" but sufficiently British to foresee "he must in future deplore" it:

> Robespierre having . . . insinuated in one of his addresses at the Club of the Jacobins, that Cooper and his compatriot were emissaries of Pitt, Mr. J. Watt, with the same fearlessness with which he had previously supported a cause which he imagined to be just, took an instant opportunity of confronting that monster in his own arena: he indignantly sprang on the tribune, from which by main force he ejected the truculent orator, and in a brief but impassioned harangue, delivered in French, which he spoke with perfect fluency and an excellent accent, completely silenced his formidable antagonist, carrying with him the feelings of the rest of the audience, who expressed their sense of his honest British spirit, in a loud burst of applause![111]

This sounds something like the Robespierre-Oswald battle of the 27 May session, which we shall come to, though that was fought with verbal nuances, not acrobatics. But nothing could be further from the spirit of the April session and the civic festival it preceded.

111. *Life of James Watt*, 479–80. Then Muirhead loses his grip: "On returning home, having learned, by sure intelligence from one deep in the secrets of his dangerous foe, that his life was no longer safe for a day, he [Watt] instantly quitted Paris, without even a passport." Not true; he did not leave Paris until 7 October, and Robinson notes that as late as September Watt wrote to his father mentioning Robespierre, Payne, Priestley, Condorcet, Siéyès, Rabaut, and Pétion as men "universally distinguished for their patriotism or their talents," and observes that Watt's asking his father to keep his journey to Italy secret was probably from fear of royalist persecution in Naples ("An English Jacobin," 353).

SECOND INTERCHAPTER
LIBERTY OR DEATH

On 20 April 1792, the war toward which the nations were heading was begun by a Declaration of the French Assembly, still anchored to a constitutional
monarch, against Austria, in the person of Emperor Francis II. Oswald and his
friends would have agreed with the historian Georges Lefebvre about the fatal
gap between words and action:

> The war of defence and of ideology preached by the Girondins undeniably worked
> its charms upon the revolutionary imagination, and its aura outshone any image of
> the disaster it would invoke. Those who promoted it are still admired because they
> seem to embody the young nation freshly delivered, proud to extend liberty to its
> "sisters." They failed *not because their plans were rash* [my italics] but because they
> did not execute them properly. For in waging war they intended to unmask and strike
> down traitors: "Let us designate the place for traitors beforehand, and let it be the
> scaffold," cried Gaudet on January 14, 1792; and Brissot had already announced,
> "We need spectacular treason cases; the people are ready!" "But you, representatives
> of the people," countered Robespierre, "aren't you ready too? . . ."[1]

Let us begin our Almanach with that Jacobin sword-brandisher, Isnard:

1792

5 January. Isnard, in the National Assembly, expresses the hope that a national language may be heard in every country. Herbert Marsh of Oriel College,
watching for sinister intent in every French utterance, detects in this a special

---

1. *The Coming of the French Revolution*, 219; but this puts too much blame on "the Girondins." As Furet observes (*Interpreting the French Revolution*, 125–26), "the outbreak of the war
between the French Revolution and the rest of Europe is probably one of the most important and
telling *problems* [my emphasis] in the history of the Revolution. The war . . . was accepted rather
than desired by the European monarchies, despite pressure from the *émigrés* and the French royal
family. By contrast, it was desired in France by the court and the social forces that hankered after
the Ancien Régime; but in the winter of 1791–2 those forces were far too weak . . . . In reality it
was the Revolution that, over Robespierre's objections, wanted to go to war against the kings. The
Revolution, yes, but here again, which one?"

"attention to the people of England, who, in consequence of their political liberty, were considered as fitter subjects for French intrigue than the inhabitants of any other country."[2]

*

16 February. The second part of Paine's *The Rights of Man* is published in London, proposing "an alliance between England, France and America" which will bring "freedom and happiness to all nations."[3] (Also contrasting the British Constitution unfavorably with the other two, but conveying to all the prospect of greatly reduced taxation, by removing the administrative costs of tyrannic government.) Gouverneur Morris reads it at once and tells Paine "he really will be punished." But Paine "seems to laugh at this . . . . He seems Cock Sure of bringing about a Revolution in Great Britain, and I think it quite as likely that he will be promoted to the Pillory."[4]

*

Talleyrand, former bishop of Autun, is in London this month, encouraged by Pétion and Stanhope to seek an alliance between France and Britain. Christie and Hurford Stone (future members of the British Club in Paris) advise him against hoping anything from Pitt.[5]

*

9 March. Horne Tooke nominates Barlow and Mackintosh to membership in the Society for Constitutional Information, which now holds weekly meetings and "seems to have taken over from the London Revolution Society as the chief channel of communication between the English radicals and their French counterparts."[6] This Friday the meeting "was held at the Secretary's [house], Took's Court, Chancery Lane, and there were present Richard Sharpe Esq (in the chair), Dr Edwards, Mr M Bush, Mr Fewell, Capt. Tooke Harwood, Mr J Adams, Mr J L Batley, Mr A Bush, Mr Hollis, Mr Frost and Mr J H Tooke." A letter was read "from Mr Oswald requesting the consent of this Society to dedicate to them his translation of [Collot's] Almanach du Pere Gerard. Ordered that the Secry return him an answer expressing their rediness to accept the

2. Marsh, *History of the Politicks of Great Britain and France*, 51n.

3. A recurring theme in Paine's thought, over the years, was that every establishment of peace between nations previously at war was an extension of the "circle of civilization" that could lead ultimately to a world association of nations. I imagine that when he talked with Bonneville or Oswald they would find that the Cercle Social concept was only a variant formulation and that they were all engaged in a true *commerce des lumières*. See "The Circle of Civilization," chapter 18 in A. Owen Aldridge, *Thomas Paine's American Ideology*.

4. Morris, *A Diary of the French Revolution*, 2:368.

5. For Talleyrand's efforts at this time, see Gooch and Stanhope, 110–19.

6. Goodwin, *The Friends of Liberty*, 216.

same."[7] (In a perhaps unrelated gesture, Tooke's portrait would be sent to the Cercle Social in time for the August issue of its *Chronique*.)

*

18 March. "Six weeks after the British Parliament had reduced the sailors and marines to be employed that year to *sixteen thousand*, Theodore Lameth, in the name of the Committee for Naval Affairs, delivered a report . . . that about *eighty thousand* sailors would be necessary, in order to man the vessels now at the disposition of the state, and which the honour of the nation, as well as the interest of its commerce, *does not permit us to reduce*."[8]

*

24 March. After dining at the Star and Garter, the "party club" where Fox and Grey and Sheridan dined every Friday during the sitting of Parliament, Sir Gilbert Elliot wrote to his wife that there was now "an appearance of greater moderation" about the French Revolution and the British Constitution "than there seemed to be last year.

"The conduct of France is not commended in *everything* as it was, by *anybody* that I have met with, and Fox spoke as ill of Payne's book yesterday as other people, which he did not do last Parliament of Payne's first book." There were always some people desirous of confusion, but "that matter is now in the hands of Horne Tooke and such persons, who will probably never be able to raise even a mob of the populace, but will certainly make no revolution. Francis, however, I am sorry to say, is very furious, and, I think, wrong-headed on these points, and seems to have no objection to a convulsion. Sheridan is also one of those who think they might gain by confusion, and I am persuaded that he wishes to stir the lower ranks of the people even by the hope of plundering their betters. But I class him in a form very little above Horne Tooke in character and estimation, and therefore in *effect* in this country."[9]

*

31 March. The first issue of the weekly *Manchester Herald* appears (at 1 1/2d), "unequivocally radical in its commitment to 'the cause of the public'" and soon "the organ of the radical movement throughout the industrial North-West." With "trenchant articles contributed by Thomas Cooper, under the pseudonym of 'Sydney'"—Cooper must have been the one who marched with the bust of Sidney in the April festival—the journal is "Painite, in its scurrilous attacks on the Crown, the aristocracy and the House of Commons and in its

7. PRO TS 11/962/3508. Presumably Oswald had already received the SCI subsidy, mentioned above.
8. Marsh, *History of the Politicks*, 77–78; his emphasis.
9. *Life and Letters of Sir Gilbert Elliot*, 3 : 1–3.

unrestrained admiration for the French revolution" (according to Albert Goodwin). It will even publish a "special apology for and defence of the September Massacres" on 10 September, "based on eye-witness reports from correspondents in Paris," presumably including Watt.[10]

*

3 April. The more temperate but "most original and significant radical publication to issue from the provincial press" (in Goodwin's judgment), the Sheffield *Patriot, or Political, Moral and Philosophical Repository,* is launched as a fortnightly paper for "the middle and lower ranks of the people."[11]

*

11 April. A society of The Friends of the People (not the people themselves) is formed by the Foxite Whigs (without Fox himself), as a sort of diversionary "evolution" of Masonic or Social circularity. On the 19th they publish a resolution for (mild) constitutional reform, with one hundred signatures, among them only two of the future members of the British Club, but important ones: J. Hurford Stone, esq., and Rt. Hon. Lord Edw. Fitzgerald—all with proper titles. Also in the list of Friends are such radical reformers as Major Cartwright and Wordsworth's radical friend John Tweddell (brother of Francis Tweddell of the British Club) and James Losh; also English visitors to Paris such as Mackintosh (characteristically acting in *both* the SCI and the Friends) and Christie, Arthur Piggot, Samuel Rogers, John Towgood, R. Knight, esq.,[12] and William Smith, esq. M.P.

Smith, spokesman for the Unitarian interest in Parliament, will be sounded out a year later by Stone as to what the British response would be if France were to invade. Smith's answer: "We should only wrap our Cloak tighter around us, like the man in the Storm, and refuse every offer of Fraternity that came to us in so questionable a shape."[13]

*

"*ah! ça va mal.*"

In a satiric cartoon of this period (Fig. 21) we are asked to see the mad capers of the *enragés* in the Jacobin Club as caused by "the *émigrés* and the foreign powers" in the basement "stirring the flames and giving the deputies assembled at the Jacobin Club a hot time." We may consider this an analogue or variant of Toulongeon's description, quoted earlier, from Carlyle, which imagines thunderbolts and firebrands being forged "down below, in silence."

10. Goodwin, *The Friends of Liberty,* 228–30 and n.
11. Ibid., 223–24.
12. Probably not Richard Payne Knight but Robert Knight of the Society for Constitutional Information.
13. Goodwin, *The Friends of Liberty,* 324, quoting *State Trials,* 25:1263.

Fig. 21. *ah! ça va mal*. Flames of counterrevolutionary war madden the Enragés in the Jacobin Club. Contemporary satiric print, reprinted in Henderson, *Symbol and Satire in the French Revolution*, plate 100. (SB)

In a table below the picture are twenty-eight numbered identifications of the numbered figures. In the center, with bell, is Condorcet, calling for silence. In clerical black, directly below the bell, is Fauchet. Brissot is waving and shouting at us, hat held high, just below the balcony at the right. One of those in the top gallery is "Gorsas"; it must be the press gallery. At the left in the middle gallery, two women surrounding an unidentified man are called "Theroigne" and "Stael" (at left and right). Just below Théroigne is Merlin, being irascible, to use Carlyle's term for him.

*

20 April. France, seizing the initiative, declares war against Austria.

*

25 April. The first guillotine made is used on one Pelletier, a highway robber.

*

In April, David Williams sends ten pounds to Oswald in Paris, via Gillet (a London printer), and in May ten guineas. The latter is a grant from the Literary Fund—recently established through the efforts of David Williams—for the relief of Oswald and his family, approved at the 4 May meeting of the Fund. Possi-

bly the April payment came from the same source. (George Mead was inter-
mediary between Gillet and Oswald in these transactions, according to the
sequence of signatures.) Visits between Oswald and Williams may have occurred this spring, in Paris or London, or even possibly in Williams's home in
Wales, though these transactions did not require them.[14]

*

11 May. William Jackson, future British Club member, submits to the French
Assembly a proposal for rapid telecommunication, something like the sema-
phore system later invented by Chappe. The Assembly is not interested.

This day in London, the SCI, having heard from Cooper and Watt of their
warm reception by the Jacobins in April, vote to send to Paris the letter of response which (in the next chapter) we shall see Oswald struggling to present to
the Jacobins on 27 May. (When prosecuting Horne Tooke in 1794, the British
government will charge that this letter incited the French to embark on a policy
of exporting revolution.)[15]

*

14 May. Paine's London printer, Jordan, is summonsed. Paine will appear in
court on 8 June, when his trial will be postponed to December in the hope that
London will then be cooler or Paine will have left the country—an accurate
prediction.

*

21 May. The Pitt ministry issues its famous Proclamation against Seditious
Writings and Meetings, recognized by Gillray at least—see above—as a logical
sequel to the Royal Proclamation of June 1787; by most people as aimed at
Paine's book, with the political effect of embarrassing and dividing the Whigs.
If, says Marsh, such publications had been "any longer treated with indul-
gence, the revolution, which soon after deprived the King of France of his

---

14. Gillet (and the Stone brothers) had probably been involved in the Cercle Social publications
of Bonneville which Oswald arranged to translate and print for distribution to the Free Welsh, Free
Irish, and Free Scottish in 1790–1791. By the summer of 1792 Gillet would be busy printing Os-
wald's *Review of the Constitution of Great Britain* at his "English Press," to be sold by the Cercle
in Paris. In May Gillet was serving, in effect, as a London banker for Oswald. Later, Gillet and
Hurford Stone would have visions of obtaining nearly all the business banking for British and
French merchants, exchanging negotiable bills of the two nations. (See *State Trials*, 25:1210–13.
The April note is in Ms. 10333 fol. 49, the National Library of Wales. The May receipt is in the
Archives of the Royal Literary Fund, Case File no. 15. James Dybikowski, who is writing a life of
David Williams, kindly supplied this information about the Fund—which later became the Royal
Literary Fund—and the transactions between Gillet and Oswald.) Madeleine B. Stern, of New York
City, notes that in 1802 Joseph Acerbi's *Travels* through Sweden, Finland, and Lapland, to the
North Cape were printed by T. Gillet of Salisbury Square for Joseph Mawman, and that Caritat had
handled Acerbi for "The English Press" earlier. In 1805 James Beattie's *The Minstrel* was "Printed
for J. Mawman by T. Gillet."

15. Goodwin, *The Friends of Liberty*, 217.

throne, would . . . have extended itself to Great Britain." (Here a contemporary reader of Marsh's tract, who apparently would have welcomed that consequence, penciled in the margin: "Exactly so." His comment on the text of the proclamation is, "What a burlesque.")[16]

*

In the May issue of the *Chronique du mois* the name of Thos. Payne appears on the title page, replacing that of Collot d'Herbois, who disapproves of the war policy of the Brissotins.

*

5 June. The *London Chronicle* reports that on Friday, 1 June, "Two officers, on information, at Dover followed a gentleman to Canterbury, who came from France, and was informed to have seditious papers. Search revealed a packet addressed to the President of the Constitutional Whig Club in London. It contained some professions of friendship of the Jacobin Club of Thoulouse." The order is given: "Search all suspected persons."

*

7 July. Tom Wedgwood to his father from Paris: "I lodge here in the same house with young Watt—he is a furious democrat. . . . Watt says that a new revolution must inevitably take place, and that it will in all probability be fatal to the King, Fayette, and some hundred others. The 14th of this month will probably be eventful. He means to join the French Army in case of any civil rupture." Wedgwood is disappointed that there are no democrats in his hotel: "The English here are all Aristocrats, and I do not intend to dine again at the Table d'Hote."[17]

*

12 July. King Louis: "Why, it is a revolt, then?" Liancourt: "No, sire; it is a revolution."

*

14 July. The Reverend Joseph Fawcett, model for the "Solitary" in Wordsworth's *The Excursion* twenty years later, is a participant in the Parisian ceremony which Fawcett celebrates in his "Ode on the Commemoration of the French Revolution in the Champ de Mars, July 14, 1792."

*

25 July. The Duke of Brunswick, generalissimo of the Austrian and Prussian forces poised to invade France, signs the famous Manifesto which "was to

16. Marsh, *History of the Politicks*, 93n, 103.
17. Litchfield, *Tom Wedgwood*, 25.

prove the most deceptive and counter-productive ultimatum of modern times." It fuses the "democratic forces in both countries into a common front of political solidarity."[18]

*

31 July. A *citoyenne* admitted to the bar of the Assembly displays a pike with a liberty cap on its tip and asks permission to arm herself and her companions. Lecointe-Puyraveau calls for sending the request to the military committee. Says Thuriot: "I oppose the transfer and ask the Assembly to proceed with the order of the day, on the grounds that no law prohibits women from taking up arms."[19]

*

10 August. An uprising in Paris overthrows the monarchy. A National Convention is summoned. The primary assemblies, the Sections, purge the Paris Commune. This "second Revolution" secures universal suffrage and arms the "passive" citizens.

*

14 August. Four days after the King's fall, Lafayette abandons his attempt to suppress the aroused people; he flees. On this very day "several Englishmen" appear before the Assembly with an address of sympathy and solidarity—"which is of interest," says Alger, "inasmuch as it was drawn up by James Watt, jun., the son of the great Watt."[20] It bears the names of Watt and two, perhaps three, who will be members of the British Club. One is James Gamble, engraver and papermaker who is part owner of White's Hotel, where the club will meet. Another is Robert Rayment, an economist who recently presented the Assembly with his new book on British national income and expenditure.[21] The third name has been transcribed as *W. Arnviside* or *William Amvifide*—perhaps a brother of the British Club's Thomas Armfield—but perhaps William Wordsworth.[22]

18. "According to Thomas Hardy" of the London Corresponding Society, "the Brunsick manifesto 'was the cause of the friends of liberty in this country addressing the Convention and promising assistance . . .'" (Goodwin, *The Friends of Liberty*, 241n).

19. *Arch Parl*, 48 : 121.

20. Alger, *Paris*, 324; see *Arch Parl*, 48 : 121.

21. *The Corn Trade of Great Britain, from 1748 to 1765, compared with the Eighteen Years, from 1771 to 1788; shewing the National Loss in the latter Period to have been about Twenty Millions of Money*. A microeconomist! (Reviewed in *Gentleman's Magazine*, 61, part 1, February 1791, 154.)

22. Wordsworth might have thus disguised and at the same time punned upon his own name—and predicament. He would do both in calling his fictional self, in the early *Prelude*, Vaudracour (Heartsworth: *Il vaut de la coeur*). And we know he enjoyed Latin puns on his name. I can imagine his giving out the name *Ambifide* or *Amphifide* (of double faith or worth) and its being written down *Amvifide* (thus Aulard; Alger, often careless, reads *W. Arnviside*, perhaps confusing *f* for *s*). Since we must find Watt and Wordsworth together somewhere in this period (Watt will leave Paris 7

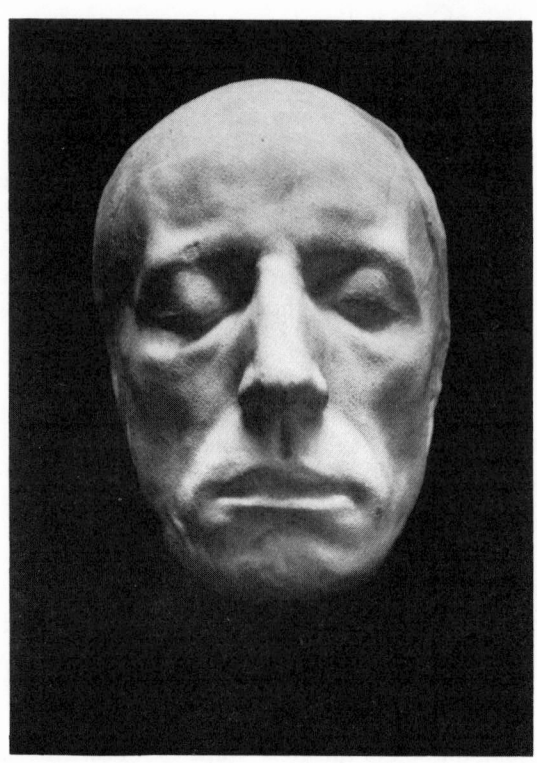

Fig. 22. Life mask of Wordsworth, by B. R. Haydon, 1815.
Wordsworth was indeed in
Paris—but it is difficult to discover just what and whom he
saw there. (National Portrait
Gallery, London)

These Englishmen congratulate the French on the energy shown on 10 August to recover their republican liberty. They deposit a sum to aid widows and
orphans of men who died that day. (*Vifs applaudissements.*) And, in a sentence
which someone erased but Alger managed to read, say: "May this great and
terrible event teach the tyrants of the earth to respect the will of the people;
may it teach the nations surrounding you to know and exercise their impre-
scriptible duties." "Some of Watt's companions had apparently objected to this
passage," notes Alger, "which obviously advocated a revolution in England." [23]
The next day several English, viewing the situation rather differently, demand
their passports and are referred to the Security Committee of the Paris Commune. A week later [24] deputy Nicolas Beaupuy of Dordogne gives his cross of
Saint Louis (*vifs applaudissements*) to be made into a medal for the next distin-

October, not to return), it is conceivable that Wordsworth came up from Blois for a day or so,
dividing his loyalties between Annette and the Republic. He is thought to have been attending
meetings of the Jacobin Club of Blois since February. See Reed, *Chronology*, 130. (Possibly what
was given to the reporter was "William, Ambleside.")
    23. Alger, *Paris*, 324.
    24. *Arch Parl*, loc. cit.

guished act by a revolutionary soldier. (His brother, Wordsworth's companion Michel Beaupuy, left Blois for the Rhine on 27 July; his regiment, the 32d, famous for its surviving the siege of Mainz [Mayence] will be fighting near Oswald's a year later, in the Vendée.)

*

22 August. Oswald proposes to the Jacobin Club an address to the societies of England, Scotland, and Ireland. (See the next chapter.)

6.
MARCH OF THE SPIRIT

———➤————————————————————————————

Dancing our ronde patriotique

Even as the peaceful federation of nations advanced, the probability of war increased and with it the struggle to find the right words and the right weapons to advance the great cause and defend it against enemies within and armies from without. The simplest answer was pikes, the weapons of citizens, the glorious homemade pikes that had conquered the Bastille, the pikes of the women who had marched to Versailles in October 1789 and brought the king to Paris.

When the men had been at a loss for words to define their deeds, the women had seized these eloquently physical ikons of freedom. Théroigne de Méricourt—who had been living in Versailles to be close to the debates of the National Assembly, which she observed with a keen mind—was inspired by the militant spirit of these Parisian women and would be involved, in 1792, in efforts to organize a Paris battalion of women warriors.[1] At the end of the year

---

1. The "real" Théroigne was evidently "a striking figure, passionate, eloquent, determined, fearless, and loyal; a lover of liberty, the people's friend, and an advocate of her sisters' cause," as Fanny Hamel deduces from her careful examination of the evidence (*A Woman of the Revolution*, 1911). But "Mademoiselle Théroigne," from her first public act—embracing and haranguing the marching women of 1789 at Versailles, apparently—was largely an invention of the royalist press, whose fabrications were accepted by Carlyle and other historians—and further romanticized by Lamartine. Hamel has a helpful appendix on "Théroigne and the Royalist Press"; she also reproduces nine of the many "Portraits of Théroigne de Méricourt," including a profile drawing by Gabriel made in 1816 when Théroigne was mad, alas, "the only authentic portrait." Fortunately some of her own speeches were reported soberly; her own "Confessions" are of value; and several sympathetic records exist. Ellis and Turquan, in *La Belle Pamela*, 176–78, compare portraits and accounts of Théroigne and of their heroine, Pamela, who became the wife of Citizen Fitzgerald. "Pamela was small and very well made; Théroigne likewise: 'Five foot high, a waist that you could span with your ten fingers,'" according to one witness, who declared that their coloring "was very much alike; both had chestnut hair inclining to black, and an ivory-white complexion: 'On distingue au milieu de ses soeurs de bataille / La blancheur de son teint et le fut de sa taille' writes Barthélemy about Théroigne. . . . Thiébault, who saw her . . . makes the following little sketch of her: ' . . . A woman wearing a black felt hat, turned up in Henri IV style, attired in a blue cloth riding habit and having a pair of pistols and a dagger at her waist-band; a *brunette twenty years old* and, I say it with a sort of horror, pretty, *very* pretty, her beauty even embellished by her excitement . . . .'" She was actually twenty-eight when he saw her.

Fig. 23. Théroigne de Mericourt (1762–1817), armed organizer and orator of the Revolution. Portrait by Raffet, in Lamartine, *Histoire des Girondins*, 2:367. (SB)

we shall find her associated with Oswald; they shared many interests and beliefs, and since both had friends who were aware of these they probably met soon after her return to Paris in January, after nearly two years' absence (suffering imprisonment in an Austrian jail "for the sake of liberty"—but outside the realm of our tale).

Hailed as a martyr, "wearing a short skirt, a soldier's jacket, and a hat with a long feather," she shook hands as she made her way to the Jacobin Club on 26 January. When she burst in, one of the members was describing "an Englishman's scheme for putting the people through certain new tactical exercises which in six weeks were guaranteed to render them equal to trained troops"[2]— manifestly Oswald's proposal of tactics for the people (see below). She was welcomed by "a tumultuous uproar"; spoke in thrilling tones; was given a second ovation. And a week later, by request, she read an account of her imprisonment; "declared that the patriots had friends and partisans everywhere—in the Low Countries, in Germany, even in Leopold II.'s palace"; and urged the lovers of liberty "to bring war against the rebels and despots who menace us with hostilities, and yet fear them more than we do"[3]—to the great delight of Brissot, and the Abbé Siéyès, and Lanthenas.

The latter rose to address thanks to her in person, for having "accomplished something useful in the advancement of universal freedom."[4] Oswald may not have been present in the club that day; but Théroigne's wish to organize a Paris battalion of women warriors cannot have escaped his attention. On 27 February a letter signed by over three hundred "women patriots" and printed and distributed by Tallien as president of La Société Fraternelle séante aux Minimes, of which Théroigne was a member, was addressed to the Assembly.

These were the women's demands:

> We hope to obtain from your justice and equity, firstly, permission to procure pikes, pistols, and sabres, even guns, for those who have strength to use them . . . ; secondly, to assemble on fête days and Sundays in the Champ de la Fédération, or other convenient place, to exercise and manoeuvre with the said arms; and thirdly, to name as our commanders certain former French Guards, always in conformity to the regulations prescribed by the wisdom of the mayor [Théroigne's good friend Pétion] for good behaviour and public tranquillity.[5]

Those women of the Jacobin Club galleries who embraced the English visitor in December 1791 and found words when he could not even find a name— were they not, even at that time perhaps, drilling with Oswald's volunteers or some other group of citizens who would become official battalions this summer? A tale survives, not in Aulard nor in Brissot's *Patriote* but in some news-

2. Hamel, *A Woman of the Revolution*, 266.
3. Ibid., 266–71, quoting the *Patriote françois* of 4 February 1792.
4. Ibid., 272.
5. Ibid., 280.

papers, including the cynical anti-Jacobin *Journal général* of 8 March 1792, which tells of the women's initiative in preparations for the great Civic Federation of April, and also of their pragmatic militancy: on 6 March "Madamoiselle Théroigne, forever celebrated in the follies of the revolution, left the Cordeliers club with many other *citoyennes*. Arrived at the Jacobin Club, these women presented their plan for a superb festival to receive the soldiers of Château-Vieux when they arrive from Brest."[6]

Hamel notes that Théroigne had been busy organizing this from the beginning of the month: "On March 1st Gorsas wrote to Palloy saying: 'Mlle Théroigne wishes to see you and talk with you, comrade. Please fix a day and hour when I can accompany her to your house. She particularly wishes to speak to you of a proposed fête for Châteauvieux.'"[7] Apparently Cooper and Watt were unaware of the women's involvement: their reports do not mention it. The *Journal* account quotes a variant version of the 27 February letter as the remarks of the speaker to the club, and then quotes the presiding Jacobin, Prieur of Dijon, as recalling the poets he had read in his youth. "Ladies," he says, "you kindle by your example the ardor of the soldiers of the nation: you know how to unite on your brows the myrtle and the laurel."[8]

In February, meanwhile, Bonneville and Oswald had been preparing the following manifesto for the March issue of the *Chronique du mois*, to make clear how the Enlightenment aims of the Cercle Social were related to the arming of citizens and, specifically, to call attention to the message of a proposal of Oswald's which lay buried in an Assembly committee but which in early March he placarded on city walls, attracting most attention in the Faubourg St. Antoine, near the ruined Bastille.

The manifesto has a title page giving Bonneville as author:

DE LA MARCHE UNIVERSELLE.

———

Of the Universal March of the Human Spirit toward
Social Perfection.
And of a New Means of Rendering it More Certain and
Swift.
By N. Bonneville.

6. Carlyle sees Théroigne entering the Jacobin Club "leaning on the arm of Joseph Chénier, Poet Chénier, to demand Liberty for the Hapless Swiss of Château-Vieux" (*FR*, 422). Both Marie Joseph Chénier and André Chénier were poets; Joseph supported this cause; André wrote a poem *against* "Les Suisses de Châteauvieux."

7. *A Woman of the Revolution*, 296.

8. Dijon had an "auxiliary" Jacobin club, Amies de la Constitution, of four hundred members; in September they had persuaded the men's club to print and send to all affiliates the women's *Address* stressing the need for feminine societies in all parts of the nation, with their own network of correspondence. In July the Dijon club would host a ball on the Fourteenth at which a huge crowd danced forty quadrilles (Kennedy, *The Jacobin Clubs*, 96–97).

But the four sections that follow are numbered, and a note explains that "the first section was printed before the revolution" and that "the second was also printed in London in 1786, in a letter to Condorcet"—letting us know that way back then, in London and Paris, a commerce of luminaries was active, involving at least two of the present Quatorze.

The note then explains that the third and fourth sections are by John Oswald, drawn from his mistakenly neglected "communication to the Committee on Petitions." Why, then, is the joint authorship not indicated in the heading? Because Oswald characteristically preferred not to share the limelight. Bonneville, and later Lanthenas, would perfectly well express to readers of *La Chronique* the ideas he shared with them about the present danger and the necessity for an armed citizenry, democratic alternative to that ancient evil, a standing army.

Here are the four sections of the manifesto; two of Bonneville's followed by, blending into, two of Oswald's:

1. Universal March.

A universal march is beginning, one feels it.

Cherish the peace and happiness of all mankind. You have need of them to be *yourselves* more happy.

Thanks to the invention of the printing press—which will little by little render wholly familiar to the human race *in general* the most refined knowledge acquired after centuries of groping in the dark—no more shall horrible wars annihilate entire nations nor make us afraid that the humans remaining on the face of the earth will lose even a single step in their universal march toward social perfection. Nor fear that genius, always scarce, always calumniated, always persecuted—but always indefatigable—shall cease to manifest itself in a thousand varied forms and, after so long a time, to all the peoples—some of whom have happily commenced to open an eye which searches and which finds. Perhaps, despite the labors of the sages, we shall always see convulsive movements in society?

Can it be a law of nature, that the force of humanity shall triumph over the centuries?

Observe already the benefits which we owe to the friends of truth. Although many violent, treacherous shocks disturb society, although individuals attracted by the universal disorder clash against one another, and often, one must admit, precious works are destroyed in the confusion; yet the storms of politics, like those of the atmosphere, are not forever; despite particular losses, general order soon reestablishes itself. Thus, when a heavy cloud comes to ravage the Seine or the Thames with its downpour, the sage hastens to reassure the inexperienced who take alarm at seeing a muddy impurity rise to befoul the river. A stream naturally pure and fertile, when the storm passes, regains its fertile course and the salutary transparency which enables the skillful pilot to avoid the sandbars or to break them up.[9]

9. Apt image for Bonneville, commissioner of Seine traffic.

2. Of the Fall of Tyrants.

I can no longer doubt it. The Nations are awaking. They are uniting.

The more the nations are united, the more they will feel the need to unite more firmly, to unite forever. Mankind is beginning to *comprehend* life!

In vain has tyranny attempted to thicken the shades of ignorance in which it has enveloped us. From time to time bursts of light announce to the villain that somewhere the lightning is collecting to make a great example. The earth, enraged, springs up from the sleep of lethargy in which she was sunken, and like the sleeping bull whom the reptiles, thinking him dead, have begun to defile with their poisons, she shakes her old bones and flings every which way the insects which besmirched her.

3. Force and Right Are but One.

The force of the people, that is, of the human race, consists in the indestructible principle of the rights of man rooted in his conscience. Or perhaps it is nature herself, in her force and in her justice, who stirs imperiously with us. For it is in her that we live, that we act, that we have ONE existence. From which follows this truth, so long heralded and so badly understood, that the will of God and the will of the people are but one; for in the true language of nature, force and right are but one, and in the social contract of the federated nations, force is the basis of right.

The force of nations, or of the people, is often circumvented by fraud. Of all frauds the most fatal is the invention of arms.

Since it is no longer possible to plunge into oblivion this pernicious invention which has set the part against the whole, today we must arm the whole against the part, to reverse the despotism of the few and enable ourselves after that to disarm altogether.

4. Of the Tactics of the People.

Up to now we have had only the tactics of the tyrants, an obscure system, far from the reach of the man of the people, passive instrument of their hangmen.

The means of paralysing this other sort of fraud, by which the few have been able to prevail over the undisciplined multitude, will be to instruct the man of the people in a simple and easy principle of evolutions.[10] This will restore to the human race its primitive force, its primitive liberty! Its original happiness!

The *Journal général de France*, of 6 March, was furious to find a great number of Oswald's placards in the Faubourg St. Antoine, a quarter aflame with not only "incendiary placards" but also "civic ceremonies" of pagan inspiration, "especially on Sundays"—the *Journal* editor sounds like Wilberforce or George the Third—and "abundant distribution of pikes and patriotic pamphlets . . . to seduce, to alarm, the honest citizens."[11]

The *Journal* is certain that pikes can be intended only for internal enemies, because "that terrible and frightful weapon . . . has been useless against the

---

10. The movement troops make to march in a new direction.
11. *Journal général*, 6 March 1792, p. 262, under "Mélanges."

external enemy since the invention of fire arms." "We are nevertheless, on this point, in opposition to M. John Oswald, former officer in the British service." In his placard Oswald not only boasts that his secret discovery of a people's tactic, if adopted, can "put six hundred thousand men of the people" within six weeks into better fighting condition than "the best disciplined troops in Europe." He also explains his advocacy of pikes against armies with a simple syllogism. Any army "which moves with the greatest speed and which strikes with the greatest force is always sure of bearing the victory." His new method of maneuvering on the battlefield will enable his troops to attack "in half the time with double the force." "Therefore, ARMED WITH A SIMPLE PIKE, the people, always master of their home ground, will have no trouble repelling their enemies, that is to say, crushing their tyrants." Q.E.D.[12]

Bonneville ends his *Chronique* note with a promise to return "to John Oswald, to the course of popular tactics which he proposes, and to the means of instruction to encourage the forging of pikes, and to make sure they cannot be turned against the country and against brothers, the pikes! the immortal pikes of July 14!" How would a people arming to repel the invading armies of tyrants be able to escape being turned into another such army? Rapidity of arming—as much of the current discussion made clear, muskets were in short supply but pikes could be made overnight—and simplicity of training were of the essence. One reason Oswald did not write much for the *Chronique* was that he had set himself the task of preparing a complete *Tactique du peuple*, of which only a twelve-page "Première Partie" survives—perhaps all that he wrote.[13] And it had a strong effect. According to Sampson Perry, Oswald's "new evolutions . . . were highly esteemed by the French general officers," who presumably were willing to believe that "they saved time in the movements" (evolutions) and occupied "less space in the performance." Moreover, some such support from experienced officers must have enabled Danton and Servan to appoint Oswald as commandant of the First Battalion of Volunteers, "Piquiers," on 1 October 1792. The clubs and journals were aswarm with the makers and advocates of pikes, but Oswald's grasp of the subject was impressive. I can see him, with pencil on paper, taking Danton through a sequence of military evolutions with such verve as to dispel any dubieties.[14]

12. The *Journal général* firmly insinuates that John Oswald knows very well this is nonsense, and that he expects his agitation, glorifying pikes, will prepare the people, when "it reaches a point of maturity," to "push fully armed against those called the enemies within."
13. *La Tactique du Peuple*, par John Oswald, Anglois, membre de la société des Amis de la Constitution séante aux Jacobins. / Première Partie. / A Paris, / Chez Gueffier, Imprimeur-Libraire, quai des Augustins, No. 17. (Not by the Cercle press; no date given. I translate the subtitle: "New principle for military evolutions, by which the people may easily learn to combat by themselves and for themselves, without the dangerous assistance of regular troops.")
14. When Anderson, in the *Scottish Nation*, probably drawing on David Stewart, stated that Oswald "attempted to substitute for the musket a pike of superior construction" and the soldiers mutinied, refusing "to be trained in its use," he must have been confusing Stewart's report of near mutiny in India when Oswald was adjutant with some conjecture about what happened to Oswald

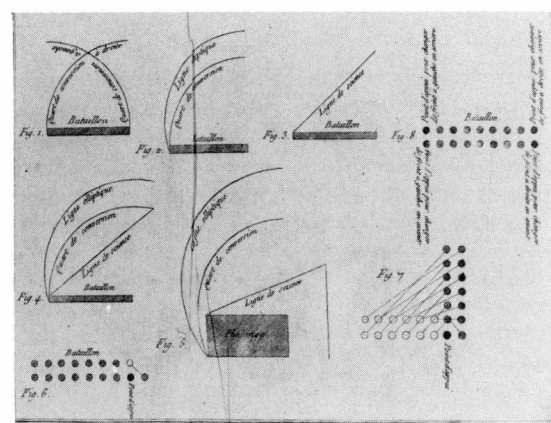

Fig. 24. Marching diagram from Oswald's *Le Tactique du Peuple*. (USC: in Brochures Diverses 044/B863)

The extant chapter of his book, headed "Nouveau Principe du Tactique," with eight diagrams, offered enough instruction for people to learn easily to halve the time and double the force of marching in traditional turns. In the missing chapters he was to teach evolutions impossible by conventional rules—for example, the corner, the pincers, the rhomb (*le coin, la tenaille, le rhombe*).

Learning to march in Oswald's egalitarian "line of science"—instead of the aristocratically imposed *marche circulaire* with its hazardous vacillations, loss of equilibrium, and resistance to instinctual marching—involves following natural instinct by marching in *une ligne droite* directed by a fixed point, at one and the same time giving "to each individual his own particular route" yet following "an absolute necessity," which relieves the individual soldier from having to calculate his relative speed. The line of Oswald's invention gives better striking capacity, whether in advance or retreat—"and *whether the troops are equipped with musket and bayonet or with the pike*" (my emphasis). We should not be surprised to find that when marching off to war a year later his battalion "addressed the Convention to allow them to change their pikes for firelocks . . . and colonel Oswald, with his corps, filed through the Convention."[15] His battalion records show supplies of guns and sabers, but no pikes.

The author's education in military drill is surveyed in the "Advertisement" of *La Tactique du Peuple*: "I entered the army early in life. I set myself to the study of tactics with the enthusiasm of a young man who hopes to discover

---

on the battlefield in 1793 in the Vendee. (Wordsworth had apparently heard the rumor that he was slain by his own men.) The *Green-Room* account sounds right for the summer of 1792: "He proposed . . . the use of the pike, not only in the Army, but among the Mob. This proposal being accepted, he had under tuition an immense concourse of both sexes, to instruct in the use of that instrument"—probably not long after war had begun.

15. Sampson Perry, in his *Argus*.

thereby the true principles of a science of the first utility." Predictably, for Oswald, he was

> quite astonished to find it full of a ridiculous jargon and of military rules that had no sense. I gave myself the task of discovering a principle of movements, simple, easy, and natural, which could be applied to every sort of evolution. After long search and many wild experiences, I have finally arrived at my goal. Here is the discovery which I offer today to the good sense of the French people; may it become, in their hands, a powerful means of destroying all the despotisms and all the aristocracies on earth.

The crescendo of the last clause is characteristic of the rhetoric of the clubs, yet breathtaking in its encirclement of the globe. Christian millennialists were currently preaching universal salvation, but not agreeing as to whether Christ would offer it to all peoples or the peoples must achieve it. When William Thomson saw the armies of Napoleon sweeping Europe, did he correctly identify Buonaparte's goals as Oswaldian, or was he quite mistaken about his Grub-Street friend? Or about Napoleon?

In the second part of his manual on tactics, Oswald may have discussed the symbolic significance of the pike, whether he was discussing its history or its use.[16] Since Roman times, it was supposed, the people in insurrectionary mood always knew what to do: "railings are torn up; hammered into pikes; chains themselves shall be welded together into pikes," writes Carlyle, alluding to August 1792.[17] "The force of arms was [an] important attribute of popular sovereignty for which the sans-culottes repeatedly demanded recognition," observes Soboul. "The pike became the object of lavish praise—the 'holy pike'—and was finally identified with the sans-culottes themselves."[18]

The holiness goes back to antiquity, whence it was solemnly translated on 14 July 1790 to serve as the symbolic center of the first Feast of Federation, a sixty-foot pike standing upright on a high mound and topped by a Phrygian cap (which became the *bonnet rouge*).[19] In July 1792 it was a Federation Feast of Pikes. "It is true that the cap of liberty had been a symbol employed from the outset of the Revolution," remarks Alger, but it was Robert Piggot, another Anglo-Jacobin, and vegetarian, "who made it an article of dress."[20]

16. In Bombay, Oswald may have been edified by, or contributed to, a running discussion among his commanding officers about the relative importance of cold steel or powder and shot, in close fighting. He would have agreed with those who argued that what "distinguishes good soldiers" is their "trusting to the bayonet instead of powder" and that "when the bayonet can be used . . . a shot should not be fired" (D. Stewart, *Sketches*, 221–22). Among steel weapons, the long-handled pike was clearly superior to the stubby bayonet, whether or not detachable from the musket barrel, and to the sword. In Paris, of course, Oswald also had in mind the political implications.

17. *FR*, 480.

18. *The Parisian Sans-culottes*, 105.

19. The shape adopted for sans-culottes to wear somewhat resembled the conventional cap worn by French workmen, except that it was red. For clarification of the confused history of the liberty cap as a symbol in the eighteenth-century revolutionary context, see the forthcoming study by Yvonne Korshak, "The Liberty Cap as a Revolutionary Symbol in France and America."

20. *Paris in 1789–94*, 44, 47.

Fig. 25. Pike-bearing sans-culottes. At left: *Vainqueur de la Bastille* ("Paix aux chaumieres; guerre aux châteaus!"). At right: *Françoises devenues Libres* ("Libertas Hastata Victrix! 14ᵉ Juillet"). Reprinted in Henderson, *Symbol and Satire in the French Revolution*, plates 36 and 67. (SB)

An early manual of pike construction and use was published in the *Annales politique*, 20 October 1791, and reprinted in Brissot's *Patriote*, 26 October, which again in February 1792 stressed the revolutionary importance of pike-bearing citizens.[21] Many of the old-clubbers among the Jacobins, however, viewed these arms with alarm. The context of Brissot's reprint shows him coming down on the popular side of a teetering balance. I digest Gerard Walter's account:[22]

In the session of 7 February, a poor locksmith who wished to bestow upon

21. Ellery, *Brissot de Warville*, 281.
22. *Histoire des Jacobins*, 239–41.

the society four pikes constructed by himself had them put into the order of the day. Doctor Doppet, a Jacobin militant, was his interpreter and persuaded the assembly to have him present himself. The pikes were brought forth. The man appeared and, visibly moved, could not speak. Doppet came to his rescue: "Gentlemen, this citizen is a locksmith. Do not expect a fine discourse from him. He knows about pikes, knows how to make them, and certainly, gentlemen, these four 'phrases' which we now present are worth more than all the speeches of the Feuillants and the ministerials." [23]

After some amiable words from the president, the pikes are accepted for deposit in the archives of the society. Three days later Brissot's article appears, declaring the need of pikes to hold the court to its duty. "Pikes began the revolution, pikes will finish it." For days, in the club and out of it, one hears of nothing but pikes. They reappear, in a manner totally unexpected, on the 19th. Just as the president, Bazire, is approaching the order of the day, a group enters bearing pikes. Bazire declares the rules do not permit anyone to come in armed; the pikes must be deposited at the door. Another member, wishing perhaps to excuse this blunder of the president, suggests that the deputation cannot be admitted because unannounced. The delegation manifests no eagerness to be relieved of its glorious arms. A proposal to have the pikes deposited at the side of the president receives a divided vote. One member insists it is important "not to turn citizens into malcontents."

It is Danton who resolves the matter, with his characteristic energy: "No doubt we wish to observe the rule which requires that citizens while discussing either their views or the public interest should be unarmed. But look at those flags; they are mounted on lances; no one has contested their being here. I demand that as a sign of an indissoluble alliance between the force of the regular army and the popular force, that is, between the citizens who bear bayonets and the citizens who bear pikes, there be a pike added to each of these flags."

The society adopts his proposal "amid lively applause," and the pikes are installed on each side of the president. He embraces the members of the deputation, who protest their attachment to the Constitution and swear to live free or die. Those flags are the twined flags of the three free nations, installed on the occasion of the Constitutional Whig's visit. We shall find Oswald the Anglo-Jacobin alluding to them dramatically when he speaks from the dais which faces the tribune from across the hall. More room in the National Assembly makes possible even the war dance of Amazons that Carlyle sings about, apparently in reference to the appeal to the Assembly which Théroigne and her Cordelier group told the Jacobins they intended to make:

> Deputation of Women, pleading that they also may be allowed to take Pikes, and exercise in the Champ-de-Mars. Why not, ye Amazons, if it be in you? Then occa-

23. On the interchangeability of words and pikes, see Oswald's quotation from Pindar (above, p. 105).

Fig. 26. Georges Jacques Danton (1759–1794). Portrait by Raffet in Lamartine, *Histoire des Girondins*, 3:321. (SB)

sionally, having done our message and got answer, we "defile through the hall, singing *ça-ira*"; or rather roll and whirl through it, "dancing our *ronde patriotique* the while,"—our new Carmagnole, or Pyrrhic war-dance and liberty-dance.[24]

La Patrie en Danger

The declaration of war on 20 April, though directed simply against the King of Bohemia and Hungary (i.e., against Austria, not the Empire), was presented as a "Manifesto to Europe," prepared by Cercle members Condorcet and Gensonné, for King Louis's formal, deadpan reading, and the Assembly's almost unanimous vote. It repeated the vow of a unanimous Assembly decree of December that the French nation renounced any war of conquest. And it welcomed all strangers who would abjure the cause of the enemies of France and join the French people.

The only strangers likely to approach were armies, however. Dumouriez improvised a plan to attack on the frontiers, but nine days after the bold Manifesto, at the first sight of Austrian troops, two of the French generals ordered a

24. *FR*, 418.

retreat and the men disbanded, killing one, General Dillon; within a month the remaining heads of armies met and declared an offensive impossible. One of these was Lafayette, who would soon try to turn his army against the Paris Jacobins and, failing, would flee to Austria.

Bonneville, in an appendix to the *Chronique* of May, which was said to have been posted in the capital "two days before war was declared . . . against the enemies of equality," urges the meeting of force with force, to make the people's destiny as great as the tyrants' has been, and points out that the words *anciens Francs* can mean both French and free. The remnant of free people (*Peuple-Franc*) in all the nations must now awaken at the voice of free men. "Never forget the sound advice of the friends of truth [namely the Quatorze] 'Love of conquest is not what should guide the Nations today; the French People, moreover, have solemnly renounced it . . . our courage has been proved.'" Yet "Tyrans, vous demandez la guerre!—Vous l'aurez!" Bonneville also reprinted his "Call to arms" of 1789 and offered a "War Chant" for distribution by the armies.[25]

It was high time to build up some armies, a large patriot body with patriot officers, and to find arms that could be supplied swiftly. There was naturally some backlash in the Assembly, such as "A voice: 'That's enough about pikes!' (Clamour)." Another: "Pikes are worthless against cannons!" and "Send it to the Military Committee!"[26] But the military committee included people who were positive about pikes, and about John Oswald.

The most important of these was Lazare Carnot, a military engineer later famous as the general who "organized victory" for the French armies, season after season. His brother was also a member of the committee; another was Michel Beaupuy, who had been instructing Wordsworth in "philosophic war." One agenda item, dated "May-September" in the summary published 4 September, was a "Plan of organization for battalions of pike-bearers, prepared by minister Servan."[27] Since Oswald was formally appointed commandant of the first battalion of pike-bearers in October, he probably had begun active duty of some sort as early as May.

Joseph Servan, the minister of war, was a professor of military science and author of books on his subject which Oswald may have read. His *Soldat Citoyen* (1780) condemns standing armies (as does Oswald's *Tactique*) and opposes the traditional brutalities of military discipline. His *Seconde aux Grands* (1789) in true revolutionary spirit makes a penetrating attack on measures taken since 1762 to sustain the hierarchy of aristocratic officers.

Politically Servan was a shadowy figure in the milieu of Danton and the Rolands, and in that quarter we may explore the politics surrounding Oswald's appointment. In Sampson Perry's account of his career we note that the focus is not on Paine or Brissot or any of the Cercle Social, but on Desmoulins, Danton,

25. This appendix was partly reprinted from the *Bouche de fer* of 1790.
26. Assembly debates, 23 April and after.
27. Déprez, *Les Volontaires Nationaux (1791–1793)*, 244–45.

and the Rolands. The Rolands made his acquaintance in 1791, but he does not figure largely in their story. Early in 1792, however, they drew the vigorous Marseilles Jacobin, Charles Barbaroux, into their orbit, and during February and March, during the mounting enthusiasm for pikes, the Jacobins of Marseilles gained fame for their active crushing of opposition throughout Provence, sometimes with armed force. In late April, Manon Roland seized upon Rouget de Lisle's "War Song for the Rhine Army," written 26 April, as a fine marching song for the sans-culottes of Marseilles; and in May when Dumouriez as minister of foreign affairs was looking for a few manageable Brissotins for his new cabinet, Mme Roland, troubled by the indolence of her husband and most of his friends, proposed Servan. She knew he was reliable and industrious. As an inspector of manufacturing he had been innovative and conscientious; the forging of pikes and casting of cannon called for steady application to detail.

The cabinet had resigned on 10 March. General Dumouriez, given carte blanche to form a new one, kept its composition moderate but included the unknown Roland as minister of the interior and his friend Clavière, of the Quatorze, as minister of finance. With Dumouriez in charge there seemed no hurry about a minister of war, until the actual declaration of war. Like Roget's war song, Servan's industry was Manon Roland's gift to the federates.

A measure "initiated by Servan" on 6 June doubtless grew out of discussion in the war office and at the Rolands', but it happens to match some of the ideas in Oswald's *Le Gouvernement du Peuple, ou Plan de Constitution Pour la République Universelle*, in the title page of which the author is announced as "Anglo-Franc, Commandant du Premier Bataillon de Piquiers."[28] Servan's order proposed summoning a camp of twenty thousand National Volunteers, five out of each canton, "picked Patriots, for Roland has charge of the Interior: they shall assemble here in Paris; and be for a defence, cunningly-devised, against foreign Austrians and domestic *Austrian Committee* alike."[29] Without the king's approval, a decree was sent out on 8 June. Immediately "the royalist staff of the National Guard . . . literally drummed up a *Petition of 8,000* against it. The Guard, still organised in its original 60 battalions, . . . cherished some socially exclusive elite units. . . . Military and para-military forces were mobilising around the Tuileries, and on 13 June Louis dismissed the Brissotin ministers," including Roland, Clavière, and Servan.[30] (Shortly afterward, Dumouriez resigned and rejoined the Army of the North.) "On 20 June the 'infected' Guard of two Paris Sections, with a crowd of men carrying pikes, and of

28. I usually refer to this by its English title, *The Government of the People*. The date of the English version is "First Year of the French Republic" (which began in September) but that of the French is 1793, and it was probably published that January. It was obviously long in gestation. Oswald could have presented it as a series of articles in the *Chronique du mois*, but he was a book man, not an article man. As with his speaking, he preferred to hold back until his thoughts were prepared to strike the readers with double force, if not in half the time.

29. Carlyle, *FR*, 429.

30. Williams, *Artisans and Sans-culottes*, 33–34, for this and the next two paragraphs.

women and children, marched to the Assembly and then broke into the Tuileries, where they cornered Louis, plonked a *bonnet rouge* on his head and demanded withdrawal of his vetoes."[31] The royalists countered with a mobilization *notaires* to produce a *Petition of 20,000*.

Gwyn Williams, whom I shall continue to quote as the first historian to rival Carlyle in the combining of accuracy and insight, describes the ensuing tumult in the Section assemblies:

> "Passive citizens" disappeared as the mobilised sans-culottes (defiantly adopting the jeer as a title) established their moral hegemony and tried to extend it over Paris. Section Mauconseil tried to abolish the uniform of the National Guard and merge it into the armed people. The arrival of the *fédérés* was decisive. In an atmosphere of patriotic-revolutionary exaltation which one can still catch in *Marseillaise* and *Carmagnole* these formidable men, infinitely more radical than their Girondin sponsors, began to "contaminate" the National Guard. The air was loud with collective oaths to "*vivre libre ou mourir*." . . . When at the end of July two Sections formally abolished the distinction between active and passive citizens, and were acknowledged by the Assembly, it was merely the "phonetic shadow" of a deed which had already been done in the streets and in men's hearts.
>
> Equally crucial was the desperate Assembly's decree, on 11 July, of *La Patrie en Danger*. At the prompting of the Commune's radical group they dramatised it. [With proddings no doubt from such *Amies de la Liberté* as Demoiselle Théroigne.] Platforms were erected in the streets for public recruitment; the effect was electric. Between 12 and 22 July some 350 volunteers had come forward. Within three days of the new publicity's going into effect 4,500 men had volunteered in four centres alone. In scenes of mass enthusiasm women offered themselves for the armies and 15,000 men were raised. . . . Decree after decree flowed from "regenerated" Sections, with the Assembly trailing patriotically behind.

The Federate National Volunteers did arrive from various parts of the nation, holding a new Federation-Festival, or Feast of Pikes, in Paris on the Fourteenth. And we may imagine Bonneville and Oswald enjoying this occasion, but we have no record of it. But to encourage, and cope with, the influx of volunteers, Carnot and the Assembly's military committee and Servan have been busy preparing a multimedia presentation, from the war office and for the Assembly, for the arming and organizing of these citizen troops. The initial, soft-sell phase of the presentation is made to the National Assembly on 25 July when Brossard, municipal officer of Paris, pays homage to the Assembly with a translation of Cicero's *On Duty*, received with acclaim and sent to the archives. M. Scot, captain of dragoons, decorated with a cross of Saint-Louis, is admitted and explains himself. (I have abridged the speeches that follow.)[32]

> In these times of danger to *la patrie*, to defend her and to offer of one's resources are the duties of a good citizen. I've done the first by signing up for the frontier. I'll do

31. The King had claimed to respect freedom as an ideal; he was now being compelled to try it on literally.
32. *Arch Parl*, 47:121–23.

the second by making some suggestions. Since cavalry are our enemies' most redoubtable means of attack against us, I propose that we offer compensation to young men who ride, to postillions, and to pike-bearers, and we may have thousands of cavalry ranged under the banners of liberty. And to obtain horses, I propose that the Assembly decree that all luxury horses be turned over to the nation, no matter whom they belong to. (*Lively applause.*)

By the way, before I leave, I have a second idea: the making of pikes for all soldiers who lack arms. I leave with you something I have written: *Manual for Citizens Armed with Pikes.* (*Further applause.*)

The hard-sell phase followed immediately:

> *Carnot the elder* mounts to the tribune.
> (*Several voices*:) Send it to the committee!
> M. *Laureau*: It's ridiculous to pit pikes against cannons. Carnot is a military man; he'll explain how absurd it is; listen to him combat this proposition.
> *Carnot.* Not at all; I'm here to defend this marvelous idea. [His talk, six columns in small print, must have filled a score of manuscript pages.]
> Gentlemen, you demand a means of arming your troops, of arming them promptly, and of arming them well: the means exist; it is simple; and if you weren't the slaves of old routines, you would have acted upon this long ago.
> It is not just my opinion, Gentlemen, that I am about to give you, but that of almost all the generals of any fame: the Condés, the Turennes, the Montecucullis, the de Saxes, the Follards. I'll quote you their exact words, and I'll prove to you with facts, that this is a very fast way to arm your troops, much better than they've ever been armed, and at much less expense, and almost in a moment—the essential and principal clause, because in effect we haven't a moment to lose.

It's the pike, of course, and he does quote the authorities. Then he makes a proposal: pikemen and musketeers intermixed, as in the old days; or a row of pikers and a row of gunners, leaving it up to the generals how to arrange them, as circumstances require. And of course the *piquiers* are to have short swords or pistols, as of old, in case the pike gets broken. It will mean two hundred thousand armed men instead of one hundred thousand, in this instant—since we have pikes but no guns.

His proposed decree spells out the distribution and manufacture of pikes, training arrangements, instruction manuals. But the opposition does not subside at once. Laureau remarks ironically that without paying too much attention to this dreary recital he catches the drift, and he will arm himself from Carnot's own arsenal, the experience of the past. He runs through Carnot's great names, and more, and dismisses the weapon of savages from modern use. "Now it is proposed we adopt a new arm, therefore a new instruction, new tactics. That's exactly how we lost to the great Frederick at Rosbach" (in 1757). (*Murmures.*)

The discussion gets heated, explosive, studded with *bruit, rires à droite; murmures à gauche*; and *applaudissments des tribunes*. The left, we note, is firm for the pike. But the project is finally sent back to committee, to be reported out the next day—though in fact delayed till August.

On 1 August the Manifesto of the Duke of Brunswick—threatening to reduce Paris to dust—reached the Assembly, which then went into continuous session for three days. Carnot's brother opened the session with a revised report. The war office had discovered that for the present there were actually enough guns to go around, if issued to frontier troops only.[33] So no pikes were to be attempted at the frontier, for the time being, but they would be used by citizens defending their own homes. The report further emphasized the need of citizen officers. Rousseau, it noted, insists that the citizen should be a soldier only when duty calls and never as a professional. Duty now was calling loud and clear, of course. A homelier maxim was offered by Citizen Rouyer: "Il ne faut pas séparer l'homme libre de son fusil, c'est sa second maitresse." However, the nine articles of the decree finally voted dealt entirely with the making of pikes and the mobilization of citizens in their use.

Barbaroux, meanwhile, encouraged by the Rolands, had appealed to his Marseillois brothers to send six hundred men to Paris "who know how to die." They arrived to lead the van in the storming of the Tuileries on 10 August, the "second revolution"—which suspended the King, compelled an election by the Assembly of a new Executive Council, and brought Danton, a unity candidate, to the top. Camille Desmoulins, elected with him, "truthfully put it [that] he was 'Minister of Justice by the grace of cannon.'"[34]

Servan, somehow not present, was to be minister of war again. Monge served until he returned on 21 August and set to work—circulating that *Plan* a month late. Oswald's companies of *piquiers* were doubtless present in the table of thirty new battalions of Paris volunteers—his battalion would be the First in the final listing—which Servan sent to the Assembly on 27 August to be forwarded to the military committee.[35]

The *Plan* as circulated did not draw back from Oswaldian recommendation of the pike's superiority as a weapon, even against guns—except for one grim observation. After calculating from the firing range of a gun, the number of shots per minute, and the speed of a marching battalion, that a battalion of *piquiers* risk no more than four gun shots in 180 paces, it shrugs: "Hé! quel Français refuserait d'assurer la victoire au prix d'un si faible danger?"[36] But the *Plan* was not circulated until 4 September. Mme Roland seems to have overestimated the staying power of her friend Servan. In the panic session of 1–3 September it was Danton who gave the directions: "A portion of the population [i.e., the regular army] will proceed to the frontiers; another section will dig trenches, and a third, armed with pikes, will defend the interior of our

33. Had the claim that there were not enough guns been a mistake—or a calculated precaution?
34. Madelin, *Danton*, 188.
35. *Arch Parl*, 49:26.
36. By Oswald's calculations, assuring doubled speed, there would be only *two* gun shots to dodge before you reached the gunner and his feeble bayonet.

towns."[37] And the defense would be against resident "aristocrats" as well as any invading army. It is frequently made clear that the pike was the traditional revolutionary weapon of citizens.[38]

In Paris the first visible action of the adjutant general of the First Legion of the Parisian National Guard, Debalaune, in response to the Servan-Carnot order to organize battalions of *piquiers*, was the posting of the city on 18 September with a large placard representing a battalion ready to charge the enemy, with the caption "I'll give up my gun for a pike."[39] Servan's name is signed to the major statement on the placard, offering to trade in *his* gun and suggesting that his brothers-in-arms do the same. A "me-too" endorsement is signed by the chief of the First Legion; another, by brewer/general Santerre, perhaps already Oswald's commander. The official date of the embodiment of the First Battalion of Pike-bearers with John Oswald as commandant was 1 October—but no names are given in the Assembly minutes for that day, or in the *Moniteur*. The minutes for 3 October carry, unsigned, a stirring address which Oswald, for the Jacobin Club, directed to the societies of Britain (see the next chapter). On the same day, before the Assembly, a letter of resignation by Servan was read. Servan, of course, may have had little to do with Oswald's appointment, since it was Danton who actually ran the war office, spending more of his time in Servan's office than in that of Lebrun, minister of foreign affairs. "I have been Adjutant-General to the Minister of War as much as I have been Minister of Justice!" Danton would exclaim. He was "perpetually on the heels of Servan," since "the conduct of the war was practically in his hands."[40] Yet Oswald may also have had a good deal of support at this time from other active advocates of international revolution.[41]

It may not have been purely coincidental that it was also this September that the American Eleazer Oswald, already a colonel, was being assigned to the army of Dumouriez in northern France—as a mutual friend reported to General Miranda: "He will be employed, I fancy, in the artillery—it is unfortunate for him, that he does not speak a word of French: he is a brave good officer and will, I trust, do us honour, should the war continue . . . ."[42] Curious that neither he nor Paine, to whom he had been assigned as secret-service aide, managed to learn the French language. His next actual assignment, however, scarcely required it, for he soon turned up, not in the army but in London, apparently investigating the British readiness for revolution while also on the lookout for printing equipment! (See the spy report quoted below in Chapter 8.)

37. Madelin, *Danton*, 188.
38. It is hardly surprising that the British radicals who were giving close attention to the French are reported frequently to have discussed the procuring of pikes and their use and effect. See, for example, the *Second Report of the Committee of Secrecy* of the House of Lords, 7 June 1794.
39. Chassin and Hennet, *Les Volontaires Nationaux Pendant la Révolution*, 2:348.
40. Madelin, *Danton*, 203–4.
41. It may be worthy of note that Servan's *Lettre* to the Assembly about his accounts, dated 8 July 1792, was issued from the Press of the Cercle Social (Mathiez, *Autour de Danton*, 144n).
42. *Archivo del Miranda*, 7:443–44.

Quite surprising, to those not in the know, was the collapse of Servan and his reputation at this time, one obvious effect being the deflection of any public interest in his command appointments, including those of both Oswalds. Manon Roland, with a surprising *faut de lumière*, had chosen Servan as "an honest man, in the fullest signification of the term . . . with all the austerity of a philosopher, and . . . in need of nothing, but a more sober imagination, and a more flexible mind."[43] A nonentity? Perhaps worse than that. Mathiez has a chapter of scandalous goings-on under Servan as manager of military procurement. Found to have signed some very disadvantageous contracts with notorious merchants of guns and grain and horses, Servan seems to have survived a legislative investigation despite great losses to the treasury, possibly at gain to his own account. The committee in July had brought before the Assembly evidence of irregularities and misdeeds, but no one had protested, either in the Assembly or in the press. No one had come to Servan's defense either, and he himself had only babbled excuses and cited extenuating circumstances concerning the bad contracts. Yet the Assembly, after the distracting crisis of 10 August, trusted him once again with the ministerial portfolio. "La politique a de ces mystères," observes Mathiez.[44] Danton protected the notorious supplier who had compromised Servan, as long as he could.

Perhaps it was not simply rapid aging (as he claimed) that led Servan to resign suddenly, at the end of September. In letters read before the Assembly on 25 September and 3 October, he protested that his health was making him so feeble that he could hardly sign his name and would be grateful to be replaced at once. He was. Possibly the last thing on his mind was the formal inauguration of the first pike battalion;[45] perhaps it was not a moment when public attention by the departing minister of war could have benefited the new commander. In the visionary history of Thomas Carlyle, however, Mme Roland's friend is "austere Servan, the able Engineer-Officer," elevated to the post of Difficulty.

Servan's resignation seemed to do wonders for his health. Soon after, he hurried to the south of France—and took active command of the army of the Pyrenees.[46]

The *Chronique du mois*, keeping abreast of efforts to establish and maintain the people's control over military force, included a twenty-four-page supple-

43. *An Appeal to Impartial Posterity* (1789), 1:82. Yet Servan had written a *Discourse* vividly arguing the superiority of citizen soldiers to mercenaries (99–100). (Madame Roland had long agitated for an armed camp of volunteers to protect the revolutionary center.) And Servan survived this crisis to be a strong supporter of General Miranda.

44. *Autour de Danton*, chapter 5.

45. According to the sketchy accounts Danton turned over to the Committee of Finance in early October 1792, however, Servan had paid Santerre thirty thousand *livres* for pikes—with no record of how many were delivered, or even how many were ordered. Santerre could have kept the money, even while abandoning the plan to use pikes in military combat. See Madelin, *Danton*, 225–27.

46. In December Mme Roland was writing to Servan as commander of the army of the Pyrenees (May, *Madame Roland*, 251).

ment by Lanthenas on the *Nécessité et Moyens d'Établir la Force Publique,* with a plan for avoiding standing armies or encrusted legislatures by "continual rotation" and proportional representation, again stressing that new force was powerless without new law.

Freedom's Language

While armed struggle was urged at this moment as essential to the Revolution, Oswald and Bonneville and Lanthenas never ceased to attend to the urgency of universal *lumière.* Oswald had managed even to make marching in armed squadrons an exercise in democracy. Bonneville, while serving as an officer in a volunteer battalion, maintained a search for effective ways of exercising the deadness out of the words in which social institutions were encoded. "Analyze languages. Decompose words. The study of language throws great light on the mysteries of nature,"[47] he had advised Condorcet in a public *Lettre* to him in 1786.[48] Words can regenerate and purify, but "prejudices graft themselves onto words" and must be removed by education. In times like the present, education includes reconstructing the ceremonies of popular religion.[49]

On the Fourteenth of July, in this "Fourth Year of Liberty," Bonneville published, as an appendix to a second edition of *The Spirit of Religions* (at the Press of the Cercle Social), a sermon "On the Theory of Insurrections."[50] Oswald's attacks in 1787 on the cruelty of "Sun-days" without play were hurled as thunderbolts in this mental war. Bonneville's advice is to bring out the sunshine by deconstructing the name of the "Lord's day." Democracy requires frequent meetings of "primary assemblies." The insurrection called for in this essay will return to the people that "grand day of Sunday" when the majority are already in the habit of assembling.

On the Theory of Insurrections.

With dignity, and haste, replace the processions of fanatics with national and universal festivals, of which we may make excellent use to establish equality and confound hypocrites—a much wiser course than to make fun of them; for the jesting of a magistrate, however well intended, may seem intolerance and cruelty.

If you wish to occupy yourselves fraternally in the cure of fanatics who are sick and the punishment, when needed, of hypocrites and devourers, who mislead people, these processions which are so numerous will be useful to you.

47. This was an interest of Oswald's during his early study of languages; he probably shared it with Bonneville during their London acquaintance. Note his finding the Priapic center of such words as *Baal Peor,* and in his treatises the idea that *love* and *law* and *will* and *Liberty* share a common root (*Government of the People*: see below, p. 295).

48. *Lettre,* 51, quoted in Kates, "The Cercle Social," 166, with related texts from *Bouche de fer,* 1 February 1791, 194.

49. *De l'Esprit des réligions,* part 2, p. 17.

50. Appendix, 129–31.

Let a magistrate, beloved of the people, present himself with dignity before the canopy of the Sacrament. Let him say to the worshipping people: "Friends, here is the image of the Sun which ripens the harvest. Here is the image of the bread which the rich owe to the poor! The time has come to exchange the symbols of truth for the truth itself! It is blessed Liberty who divests the great ones of the earth of their surplus, to give to the man who labors his daily bread. Long live Liberty!"

The Lord of the priests and kings shall no longer play the chief role in their processions.

We might say that no one has quite realized that the majority of the people and perhaps of nations is regularly assembled fifty two times each year.

Those who originally changed the simple name "sabbath" or "assembly" to "Lord's day" knew very well that by doing so they were advancing their own interests.

Day of the Lord.—The day of the master.—Of the All-powerful.—The day of light.—The day of the sun, Dimanche, Sonntag—Sunday.

On the grand day of sunday when the majority of the people are assembled, let the institutions of the new legislature insensibly substitute the cult of the new law, and the sovereignty of the national will establish itself universally, without commotions, without demands on the part of the people. Thus far:

Be careful how you handle an angry people, . . . Putting yourselves between them and their Gods!

*

The new law must succeed, as in the time of the son of Mary, to the old law. This new law requires a new cult; a true cult; the cult of the law.

Is it possible to have, in one state, two sorts of laws? Absolutely not.

For your rapid success, rely on the imposing appearance of the tables of the law. See how, already, the people command your respect when the Image of Liberty goes by.

The ancients used to inscribe the law "of the master," of the "all-powerful" on their garments and in their temples. Will it then be so difficult to have inscribed on our banners:

All men are born free and equal in rights.

*

Brothers and Friends, our constituent legislators have well been forced to recognize the national sovereignty, demanded for three years by the invisible galleries of the people, but they have not taken any effective steps to assure its exercise; must you then still longer meditate upon the theory of insurrections? I refer you, for this important study, to the theoretical and practical means of accomplishment which the *Bouche de fer* has developed.

You have doubtless heard it talked about.[51]

51. In a postscript Bonneville speaks of the hostile reception of the *Bouche de fer*, which is of no use to "the factions" since it "fights neither for Caesar nor for Pompey," and of its having fought for the people "in absentia, in the middle of an assembly of four or five thousand spectators, applauding to the verge of delirium," but then admitting that she (*La Bouche*) has been well understood "by a rather large number of enlightened citizens." He then quotes a praiseful review by "a very esteemed writer." And he is comforted that, while he busies himself "here" (at his desk) "with a definitive reckoning with all the priests, past, present, and to come," i.e., revising his *De l'Esprit des réligions*, "people are busy reprinting select issues of the *Bouche de fer*."

7.
AT THE JACOBIN CLUB
ELOQUENCE AND ENERGY

"He was a long time there."

The era that began on 21 September 1792 with a new Convention and a new calendar for the Year One of the Republic almost offered John Oswald two official careers, as commander of volunteers and as legislator. The terminating Legislative Assembly on 26 August had conferred French citizenship and hence eligibility for office upon a score of foreigners including James Mackintosh, David Williams, Thomas Clarkson, William Wilberforce, George Washington, John Hamilton, James Madison, and Thomas Paine (who was soon elected as deputy for Calais). John Hurford Stone, busy courier between the two capitals, advising Sheridan in London and Brissot in Paris, had suggested some of these names, or at least that of Mackintosh, but severely criticized the inclusion of others. Just back from London the next day, seeing the Paris newspapers, Stone wrote to his brother William reproaching the Assembly "for having wished to confer citizenship on Wilberforce, who refused it with indignation; on David Williams, who didn't deserve it; and on Clarkson, who took no interest in politics."[1]

Stone apparently made his disapproval known to Brissot, who advanced a second list in the Convention on 25 September, presumably more to Stone's liking. It added the names of Thomas Cooper, Horne Tooke, John Oswald, Thomas Christie, Joel Barlow, and two others—all fine choices for the British Club in Paris which Stone and Oswald would soon be organizing.

Procedure in the Convention was not as direct as it had been in the Assembly, however, and these names were referred to a committee. Brissot's *Patriote françois* published the list; Hébert's *Courier de l'Egalité* (his *Père Duchesne* rebaptized) gave some details but employed a conditional verb:[2]

---

1. In Stone's pragmatic view, there was nothing "political" about Clarkson's antislavery activity. Stone's hostility to Williams, on the other hand, was that of a rival negotiator between courts (Stone to his brother, 27 August 1792; *State Trials*, 25 : 1297).

2. *Patriote* and *Courier* of 25 September 1792. Hébert, on the 23rd, had already welcomed the

Fig. 27. Exterior of the Jacobin Club in Paris. Of many surviving sketches, this seems the most realistic in its proportions, although the occasion depicted, the closing of the club by government decree in 1794, is beyond our scope. From a Dutch engraving reprinted in Henderson, *Symbol and Satire in the French Revolution*, plate 52. (SB)

List of English to whom the National Convention May Give the title of Citizen of France:

Thomas Cooper, author of several works in favor of the blacks, and on the true principles of government, published before the French Revolution, containing all the fundamental propositions of the rights of the human race; previously deputy of the Constitutional Society of Manchester to the Jacobins at Paris; he is author of the *Judicious Replies to Burke's Invectives* [*sic*].

John Horne Tooke, known for having supported the Rights of Man for twenty years, and for his opposition to the arbitrary measures of the dominant faction of aristocrats in the British Government.

John Oswald, author of the *Review of the Constitution of Great Britain*, in which he supports the French Revolution with eloquence and energy.

---

brave English with sweet embraces: "I have this morning embraced the savant Thomas Payne, who has just arrived for the National Convention."

George Rous, author of two works in reply to the attacks of Burke on the French Revolution.[3]

Joel Barlow, American, author of *Advice to the Privileged Orders*, almost equal in merit to the work on the rights of man by M. Paine.[4]

Thomas Christie, author of a well-written exposé in favor of the French Revolution.[5]

Doctor Warner, known for his energetic speeches, in which he deploys his love of liberty and hatred for kings.

Names, including Sheridan's, were still being proposed two months later, but by that time Stone, sensitive to shifts in the political atmosphere, had changed his advice and persuaded Brissot to delay confirmation.[6] Barlow, with special support from Paine and Grégoire, and now the elected representative of the new department of Savoy, finally received French citizenship in February. I believe none of the others did, except Williams, who had been given it earlier—perhaps even at Stone's suggestion, hoping it would do him harm.

Oswald was already a de facto French citizen, in the Jacobin Club and the citizen army. And he probably had little interest in these formalities—except that he made clear that he wished to consider himself and be considered a true Anglo-Franc, a citizen of *both* countries and in person a symbol of their human identity of interests. In the Jacobin Club of Paris, though he boasted of his membership in his title pages, he seems, like the anonymous Whig of December, to have done most of his serious talking in private groups. Even in May 1792, as we have seen, the shorthand reporters could make a mistake about his name. Yet at least five times his energy blossomed into eloquence in the Jacobin debates: we have substantial reports of four of them in Aulard's collection from the *Procès-Verbaux* of the society, reaching from 27 May to 30 September 1792, and of a fifth, the speech of 4 February 1793, that was sent off to be printed for international circulation.

On the third of these occasions, Oswald opened his remarks by saying (as

---

3. George Rous (1744–1802) was counsel for the East India Company. He published two pamphlet replies to Burke: *Thoughts on Government* (ca. December 1790) and *Letter to . . . Edmund Burke a reply to his Appeal from the New to the Old Whigs* (1791).

4. Joel Barlow's writing and principles were praised by Paine in the Convention on 17 November 1792, and Grégoire proposed his name again for citizenship. The proposal was not reported out of the Diplomatic Committee until 17 February; yet Barlow was presumed a citizen when he was elected in January, from Savoy, to the Convention and was made one of the commissioners to annex the new department of Mont Blanc (incorporating Savoy), whereupon he was elected *its* deputy, with a seventy-four-gun salute (for the seventy-fourth department) (Woodress, *A Yankee's Odyssey*, 129–33). If Oswald had tried, with similar backing including Stone's, he might have gone a similar route. On Stone's shifting, see below.

5. Christie's *Letters on the Revolution in France*, in response to Burke's *Reflections*, appeared in the spring of 1791 "at approximately the same time" as Mackintosh's *Vindiciae Gallicae: A Defense of the French Revolution*. At the time, Christie and Mackintosh were inseparable (according to *Public Characters of 1806*, 225), and Werkmeister, who cites this note, conjectures that it was Christie who inspired Mackintosh to write (*London Daily Press*, 341).

6. See below, pp. 232, 235.

though he hadn't been talking French for years): "I should never have had the hardihood to speak to you in a language which is not very familiar to me, if a sense of duty had not ordered me to do so."[7] He had made a similar apology when called to the platform in Coachmakers' Hall. In the prefaces to his works he was inclined to insist that he appeared in public only under strong compulsion. And no doubt it was true. The occasions for his recorded speeches are indeed such as to have invoked his sense of a binding duty to speak up when the ties between the French and the British required repair or improvement. There must have been a good deal of off-the-record strong talk. "He was . . . a long time there without being distinguished by any thing but his violent speeches," declares the *Green-Room* biography.[8] On the other hand, the *Scottish Poets* biography reports it as "the common opinion of the English, then resident in Paris, that after Mr. Oswald had acquired consideration in the Jacobin Club, there was not a transaction of any note emanating from that body in which he had not a leading part."[9]

Indeed his speeches and activities may not have become violent (i.e., insurrectionary) until the approach of war. The earlier mood in the club was often jubilant and celebrative and harmonious, and I see Oswald playing a "green-room" role as impresario in some of the scenes which he himself, standing back a moment, could have recognized as "operatical" if not "farces"—to recall the language of *The Humours of John Bull*. I believe he must frequently have served as a sort of liaison officer when fraternal visitors from Britain were being either casually or theatrically entertained and embraced. I refer to the occasion of the Constitutional Whig and, more certainly, to the civic festival that featured Cooper, already an admirer, and Watt.

On 27 May 1792, remarks by Oswald were first put into the club record. His verbal dispute with Robespierre on that occasion was attributed by careless biographers to Watt and Cooper, respectively, since it did after all concern their Manchester society.[10] An earlier reference to Manchester on 7 May will help us understand the reporters' and biographers' confusion—and also the members' easily aroused suspicion of messages or messengers from Britain; worse yet, of communications from affiliated French societies—of which by this time there were nearly a thousand.[11]

Oswald's remarks of 27 May, however, grew out of the confusion of a previous meeting seventeen days earlier; so it is advisable to make our first visit to the club on that occasion.

7. Aulard, ed., *Recueil des Documents . . . des Jacobins*, 3 : 653. Here, as elsewhere in the proceedings, Oswald's speeches are given in good French. They seem sometimes prepared in advance, sometimes not. His mastery of the language is hardly all the work of good reporters.

8. Haslewood, *Secret History of the Green-Room*, 165–66.

9. *Lives of the Scottish Poets*, 175–76.

10. See above, pp. 154–55.

11. A table in Kennedy, *The Jacobin Clubs*, 362, shows 921 French cities with clubs by July 1791, counting "every patriotic society which secured affiliation or engaged in correspondence with the Paris Jacobins or one of its affiliates."

*At the Jacobins, Thursday, 10 May 1792, Merlin of
Thionville presiding*

The tone of this tumultuous session is set early by a crackpot proposal (the
term is Carlylean but appropriate) from Saint-Hurugue to break up the aristocrats' clubs by rushing into them swinging bulls' pizzles (a better weapon than
pikes).[12] Reporter picks up Merlin's aside: "I hear Saint-Hurugue talking about
liquidating with bulls' pizzles!" *Voices on the platform:* "That's great! That's
great!" There is frequently "violent tumult in the hall" amid futile efforts of
Merlin and others to calm Robespierre, who is beside himself about a letter
from the Douai Club (founded two years ago) calling him a vile calumniator
and Lafayette a hero!
Merlin tries to get on to "more interesting" topics. In a parenthesis we learn
that while Robespierre is still discussing the Douai letter, Messrs. Deperret and
Collot d'Herbois engage in a discussion about the wording of an address to be
sent to the society of Manchester.
One wonders whether this was simply an overdue response to the society
whose representatives had marched in the parade—or whether Collot (prod-
ded by Oswald, presumably) had seen newspaper reports of Burke's invective in
Parliament, 30 April, against the "foederation" of Cooper and Watt.
Suddenly Robespierre asks what Collot and Deperret are about, and a member explains that "they can't agree on the text of a proposed letter to Manchester and will have to get together to compose another draft." Robespierre,
having apparently seen the letter they are fussing over, comes down hard: "I
declare that if the letter must be sent in the spirit which has dictated it"—does
he mean the spirit of discord?—does he suppose or know it has been drafted by
Oswald?—"it will serve the purposes of this Society ill: for it is improper, on
vague rumors, to meddle in the affairs of foreigners. It would be dangerous to
give the impression that we wish to interfere with what concerns a neighboring power." He is very alert to the danger of supplying more fuel to Burke's
counterrevolutionary fire. "I demand that the Society not communicate with
anyone at all in a foreign country." France is now at war, though not yet with
Britain.
Robespierre makes no further comment, according to the record, but shortly
afterward Chabot tries to call a halt to the absurd discussion, demanding that
all divisive letters be interred in the archives. The meeting votes that only letters
dealing with the state of our frontiers and military objectives in the interior be
read. After lunch, Danton scolds the assemblage for having been violent
against Robespierre—off the record, apparently—who "has never exercised
here any despotism but that of reason."
We shall discover a curious pattern of camaraderie and cross-purposes recur-

12. Aulard, *Recueil des Documents . . . des Jacobins,* 3:571–76. The allusion to pikes is mine.

Fig. 28. The Jacobin Club, with Robespierre at the tribune. (From an engraving by Masquelier, 1791, reprinted in Thompson, *English Witnesses of the French Revolution*, 1:113; SB.)

ring between Oswald and Collot, which sometimes includes Deperret. Since Oswald's translation of Collot's *Almanach*, Collot, a trained actor, has been behaving like a character in a farce by Oswald who turns against the author. In the business of Cooper and Watt, it becomes clear that Oswald considers himself in duty bound—as Horne Tooke would wish—to affirm and enlarge all fraternal visits and communications from Britain. And it is also clear that Collot makes a point of keeping abreast of such developments—not necessarily to foster them.

At the Jacobins, Sunday, 27 May 1792, Merlin presiding[13]

This ambiguous collaboration between Collot and Oswald comes into the open on 27 May, when confusion develops around Oswald's request to read out a letter to the Jacobins, as "Brothers and Citizens of the World," from the London Society for Constitutional Information, which this spring "seems to have

13. Ibid., 3:612–23. I translate freely, and digest, using quotation marks only where the translation is full.

taken over from the London Revolution Society as the chief channel of communication between the English radicals and their French counterparts."[14] The London society had voted approval of the letter on 11 May, and Horne Tooke had transmitted it to Oswald.[15] Its opening words, alluding to "Messrs. Cooper and Watt, Members of the Society of Manchester," had produced the confusion. When it was shown to the writer of the agenda, he apparently jotted simply "Manchester."

Before that point on the agenda is reached, a heated debate about affiliation with suspect societies has charged the atmosphere with negativity. Oswald might have waited for a calmer time, but his sense of duty in the interest of the fraternal good will of all societies compels him to speak out.

Trouble begins with the report of Deflers, for the Correspondence Committee, which calls for the affiliation of five societies, and also that of Sables-d'Olonne, proposed by three Assembly deputies. Bylaws indicate that this is sufficient, but several members oppose the latter affiliation. Then Robespierre speaks. "For a long time now, many of the affiliated Societies have become in the hands of certain persons a means of misleading public opinion. I move that affiliations be suspended until the Society reestablishes its own order." Chabot: "I agree perfectly with M. Robespierre, but I wish he would make his proposition less sweeping. I would distinguish two sorts of Societies. In the towns they are mostly moderate (*feuillant*) because they are composed of bourgeois, merchants, who detest the sans-culottes. But I know that those in the country desire nothing more than perfect equality." Chabot proposes (1) renovating the primitive spirit in all the societies, and (2) suspending new affiliations from the cities, while accepting promptly those from the country, since it is so important that instruction spread among these. (*Tumult.*)

Chenier calls for the order of the day.

Robespierre makes a long speech, despite calls for order. He worries over the intriguing minority in the societies, who work for themselves, who "divulge our secrets to the court." (*Tumult.*)

Lasource then speaks for positive encouragement by deeds, not self-doubt. The majority-minority splitting he doesn't want to believe. "I like to believe that the citizens who come here wish to attain the public good. But I believe that Robespierre didn't really mean to say that intriguers come here."

> *Several voices.* Yes, they do come here!
>
> *Lasource.* Robespierre has told you that people introduce themselves here to divulge the secrets of the Society to the court. I cannot think . . . . (*Tumult.*)
>
> *The President.* Certainly those who have passed along to Bertrand and Montmorin what has been uttered from this tribune are intriguers and rogues. (*Applause.*)

14. Goodwin, *The Friends of Liberty*, 216.

15. As we have seen, the society in March had formally accepted Oswald's dedication to them of his translation of Collot's *Almanach*—a translation for which they had paid him something. In a perhaps unrelated gesture, Tooke's portrait would be sent to the Cercle Social in time for the August issue of the *Chronique*.

Fig. 29. Robespierre speaks. Portrait by Raffet in Lamartine, *Histoire des Girondins*, 8:200. (SB)

> *Lasource.* I do not think there exist any secrets in this Society! (*Applause; tumult.*)
> For our sessions are public. (*Tumult.*)

Lasource goes on, with some applause, for some time. Then suddenly, he announces a plot involving two former deputies in a murderous conspiracy in the Midi. "That's what I want to denounce before the Society." The relevance is unclear.

Daubigny, explaining that some previously admitted societies are unworthy, calls for immediate suspension of the Correspondence Committee. Chabot calls for the order of the day, adjourning these questions. Collot d'Herbois calls for immediate action suspending affiliations. Parliamentary disagreements follow and take some time to resolve. Finally Robespierre's motion, making no exception for country societies, is put and passed, with a time limit of eight days to settle upon a new mode of affiliation. Oswald has the floor next.

> I will take care not to make you waste precious time. The proposal I am about to make is of the utmost importance: it concerns knowing whether you will retain affiliation with the foreign societies. Keep clear of all relations with corrupt governments and venal parliaments; but do not refuse the communications offered you by foreign citizens, zealous for universal liberty, for the propagation of knowledge and the principles of humanity. I insist that we go to a voice vote on whether to hear the address read which I have been charged with presenting to you. (*Vote! vote!*)

Robespierre rises to speak; it raises a great tumult. The society resolves that M. Robespierre shall be heard.

The president wishes to give him the floor, seeing no objection. M. Corroller demands a vote. (Presumably he gets it.) Robespierre: "It is with keen regrets that I occupy the Society's attention at this moment."

A *censeur* (sergeant-at-arms) complains that since the start of the session the people around him have been insolent. Merlin summons him to come and name the interrupters and turns to the order of the day. (*Uproar.*)

> *Lulier.* The censors are still being insulted; I demand the calling of the question.
> *Montaut.* I have been here since two o'clock to hear discussion of matters useful to the nation, and I see nothing that relates to that. I demand that the President be called to order . . . . Instead of serving the public you do it a disservice every day with the tumult that reigns here.

The president observes that, by the vote, the floor belongs to M. Robespierre, who ought to be heard.

> *Robespierre* [sounding like Oswald]. Nothing appears more interesting to me than the observation of M. Montaut, for I see nothing more obnoxious than these endless idle discussions. If I have asked to speak it is because people have wanted despotically to shut me up. I have believed that it was good to resist oppression, and I have believed that it was useful to give an example to my country of serving her despite all these distasteful matters.
> I have wanted to say that the advice of M. Corroller [who called for a vote] seems

contrary to his objective. If it is necessary to strengthen the ties among all the Societies, then it is fitting to hear them without objections. Since the deputy of the Society of Manchester had been introduced, and had been given the floor, it was absurd to demand a vote to know whether he was to be heard. (*Applause!*) I am willing to pass over this difficulty, ridiculous as it may be; but I know also that a calumnious intention is hidden in it. I know that such a deputy, whose words are prepared in advance, is revenging himself upon those who attend while he disseminates here the libels against the patriotic Societies of France which are concerted among foreigners.

The double-bind thinking reflected here has prompted some to call Robespierre paranoid, others Machiavellian.

> *The President* [presumably gesturing]. I attest by the banners hung above my head that the Society of Manchester is affiliated with ours. It is doing an injury to demand a vote before they may be heard.
> *Oswald*. It is *not* an address of the Society of Manchester that I ask to read to you, but one from the Society of *London*. First, having been maligned, I wish to respond to M. Robespierre, who says that I have concerted this address. . . .

There is an elision in the transcript: perhaps Oswald said more than this; perhaps he was interrupted. Robespierre demands the floor, and after an uproar he obtains it.

> *Robespierre*. I believe that it is easy to spare the Society another incident; and, when I said that libels concerted with foreigners are distributed in this Society, I designated no one. It is not to the previous speaker that I was referring. And I have nothing to reproach him with.
> *Oswald*. I shall not respond to the suspicions which M. Robespierre has cast upon me, nor to those from any other member. I am too far above them.

Above the suspicions—or the members? A neat double entendre. "This speaker," Oswald presumably, "then reads the address, in which are recalled the great maxims of natural and political right."

> *Oswald*. It is not the vain ceremonial of courts which the peoples should take as models. The principles of humanity, equality, and liberty must form the basis of their relations. The authors of the address cite this immemorial verse: "Kings are passersby, the people is eternal." (*Applause!*)
> *President Merlin*. Britain has given us the example of scorning tyrants, protectors, and above all presidents of congress. Tell our friends that we are proud of them. (*Applause*.) •

The printing of the London letter is called for and approved, and nothing more is said in the society about a message *to* Manchester. But when we look at the printed four-page pamphlet (by the press of Brissot's *Patriote françois*, without date) we see that Merlin is a deep one.[16] The "Addresse" of the London

16. The *Patriote* text is reprinted in Aulard, *Recueil des Documents . . . des Jacobins*, 3:621–23; Marsh, *History of the Politicks*, 96–97n, prints an English version. The *Patriote* text

Constitutional Society is followed by a "Réponse du Président" greeting the British as among the free, peacemaking peoples of the world, desiring the brethren of London to invite all brothers to attend the Jacobin sessions, and stating the club's order to send this printed message to all affiliated societies. It is signed by Merlin, Chabot, and five others—including Collot, who has veered round to Oswald's support.

We know, then, what Merlin is thinking of when he says, "Tell our friends," and when he waves toward the flags that will be immortalized in Burke's invective. Neither Cooper nor Watt nor Oswald engaged in bodily combat with Robespierre on this occasion. But Oswald had succeeded in keeping affiliations firm.[17]

At the Jacobins, Monday, 4 June 1792, Chabot presiding[18]

Eight days after the uproarious "Manchester" session, John Oswald is given the floor as the first order of business. Robespierre is absent. Collot is present to help—and hinder. Despite Merlin's compromise, Robespierre's "demand" that no communications are to be made to anyone in a foreign country apparently remains in force. Stern duty calls our citizen of the world:

> *Oswald*: I ask your indulgence for a few minutes. I should never have had the hardihood to speak to you, in an unfamiliar language, if my sense of duty had not obliged me to do so.
>
> I need not remind you how important it is to cultivate the friendship of the English nation by the mediation of the popular Societies. The British have had the glory of making, in respect to you, the first moves toward that fraternal alliance which is going to overthrow the tyrants and establish, upon an indestructible base, the liberty and happiness of the human race.
>
> Animated by this spirit, the Manchester club sent you deputies Cooper and Watt as evidence of the vital interest it takes in your patriotic efforts, and to unite itself with you.
>
> The British government shook with rage on learning that ties of friendship were forming between the two nations whose mutual hatred facilitated its piracy. Messrs Cooper and Watt have been denounced in the British Parliament [i.e., by Edmund Burke], heaped with calumny, and pursued with an atrocious hatred. In consequence

---

repeats the mistake of having the letter "Lué par m. Waths, Membre de Celle de Manchester." Aulard uses the Oswald name correctly in his transcript; but Goodwin, *The Friends of Liberty*, 216, continues the error.

17. Both Cooper's and Watt's biographers wrote for audiences that would recognize Robespierre as the villain of the French Revolution and appreciate true British spirit in those who had been aroused to spurn him as such. The most dramatic of Robespierre's combative encounters in the Jacobin Club is probably that with his old friend Camille Desmoulins, in January 1794, which became at once legendary. (For a compact version, see Methley, *Desmoulins*, 256–61.)

18. Aulard, *Recueil des Documents . . . des Jacobins*, 3:653–57.

you have resolved to send to your brothers in Manchester a letter of commiseration and encouragement.

Since that resolve, however, you have been told it is improper to write to the Manchester club unless you shall have received from it an official notification of the persecutions it has experienced; and you have decided, in effect, that it is not possible to write. Since when has this etiquette been established among the Jacobins? Why! your brother has just fallen over a precipice, and you aren't willing to run forward at his cry of pain! You stay with your arms folded and say with sang-froid: "He should send me an official note to inform me of the accident which has just befallen him."

That is not the way the popular clubs of England behave; it is not the way the club of Manchester acts, today under indictment of the minister for having extended a fraternal greeting to you. Messrs Cooper and Watt, both endowed with ardent and patriotic hearts, have exposed themselves and their fortunes to great danger in order to strengthen the bonds of friendship between the two nations. Mr Cooper, pursued by ministerial spies, may today be languishing in a dungeon; perhaps a mob misguided by agents of a perfidious minister is setting fire to our friend's home, his fortune is ruined, perhaps his blood is being shed, and you have the tranquillity to say it is not possible to write a word of consolation to your brothers of Manchester!

Here Oswald, tactician of the people, refers to the pikes installed at Danton's suggestion in February to hold the flags sent from London with the Constitutional Whig in December and carried by the Manchester delegates in the April festival.

In mercy, brothers and friends, repair your wrong; erase from your books a resolution which will tarnish this coronal of unity and make these banners droop, these flags which were not set up here, with their respective pikes, to serve as a frivolous decoration for your meeting hall but as reminders of the solemn engagement which the three nations [including the United States] have taken to be prompt in reciprocal aid and to combat despotism side by side.

Next he attributes the recent assurances of neutrality exchanged between the British and French governments to Pitt's awareness of the peaceful sentiments of the people:

At this very moment the popular clubs of Britain have just rendered an important service to French liberty; for, Gentlemen, you must not suppose that the neutrality declared by the King of England should be attributed to the speech of your ambassadors and still less to the benevolence of the English minister, but rather to the solidarity of the British clubs, who have compelled the government to listen to reason. I am then inclined to hope that the motion which I am about to make will receive no contradiction, being entirely free of all personal interest and of all partisan spirit. Indeed, when I return to my native country (to which, soon, the perilous events of a revolution aborning will be calling every good English patriot), I shall have the extreme satisfaction of saying to my compatriots: "Be assured, my brothers, the Jacobins are with you; you can count on their amity and their support."

I demand then that the letter already resolved upon for the club of Manchester be sent without delay.

Note Oswald's open declaration of belief in an approaching English revolution—a belief underlying his attempt four months later to persuade the National Convention to organize an invasion of London, not so much to precipitate an uprising there as to assist one. The metaphor in Collot's immediate response may reflect a pulling back from such "perilous events."

> *Collot d'Herbois*: Certainly the previous speaker [that's a cool response to an old comrade of the Quatorze—but Collot needed to have everyone know he was steering his own course] has well defined our principles when he says that each of us would be ready to help his brothers of Manchester. But the precipice down which he supposes them hurled is only a pretty figure of speech to entrap our emotions. The danger may be real enough, but a letter is not what will save them from the precipice. Besides, it *is* rather surprising that they haven't written to us and that we receive their news only through the public papers. Is it prudent that, upon these vague rumors, we should bypass all the political considerations to be observed between two great nations?
>
> I know one must do the right thing without fussing over what to say; but I don't see what great use it will be to those of Manchester, if they are being persecuted, to get a letter from the Jacobins of Paris. Besides, if the letter which we voted to send to our brothers has not been sent, you must blame it all on the draft we had to work with, which was not suitable for Jacobins writing to the English.

The draft (*rédaction*) must be what Collot and Deperret had been muttering over on 10 May; I suspect it was supplied by Oswald. And Collot goes on to imply that it is not his own zeal that has slackened, but that of the Jacobins in the hall: "Blame it also perhaps on a reluctance to appear to be exercising a political influence that has contributed to your slackening of zeal. Whatever it is, I suggest that you write another letter than the one you have had read and, first of all, that you wait for news from Manchester before you write." The next speaker returns directly to Oswald's demand:

> *Real*. I certainly go along with the proposal you have made. It is not the criticism which M. Collot d'Herbois has put that prompts me to speak: I find it against the principles we have regularly followed. The question is not whether to respond to the news of the persecutions of our Manchester brothers; we must console them, saying to them "There are still on the earth free and sympathetic men, who take part in your misfortunes." Never was it a question of writing in these terms: "How are you? Have you need of consolation? Write us about it so that we can write to you."
>
> *Collot*. That's intentionally heaping ridicule on my views.
>
> *Real*. If I had such intention, it would be calumny. I agree with you that it is pointless to write vain declamations. [No copy of that draft letter is in the *Procès-Verbaux*; one wonders how declamatory it may have been.] I don't presume to put myself forward as a model, but if I had such a letter to write, I would say: "Brothers and friends, you suffer, you are persecuted; have patience, we are taking a lively interest in your plight."
>
> But, you say, we must beware of calumny. Well, so far calumny has done us a lot of good; and, if we were not being calumniated by the rogues, we would not be applauded by the honest. Don't think, if you are writing to a Society, that the force of

the letter depends on having an army of Jacobins at the ready. That ridiculous assumption could only enter the head of a Leopold.   ·

Or an Oswald? But the discussion is now terminated by that hero of the Bastille, Carlyle's "Cattle-butcher Legendre," who will this coming Sunday, 10 June, be threatened by the bayonets of the aristocrats and, ten days later, lead the van of the revolution of the sans-culottes in the "second revolution," first parading with pikes into the Assembly, with "tall sonorous Santerre and tall sonorous Saint-Hurugue," and then storming the royal apartments.

> *Legendre.* I am far from accusing the English citizen who has appeared at your tribune. But either you [the Paris Jacobins] are affiliated with the Society of Manchester, or you are not. If you are, why don't they write to you that they are persecuted? Haven't they the right to confide in you their miseries? If one wrote to them on the vow of one person, what good could it do? I demand that we pass to the order of the day. (*It is so ordered.*)

At the Jacobins, Wednesday, 6 June, Chabot presiding

Two days later Legendre storms into the Jacobin meeting again. There is a war going on, and he finds the club occupied with a self-righteous argument about the good faith of M. d'Orleans: "It is astonishing that, when the country is in danger, we find ourselves occupied with one individual." This gives rise to a great agitation. It is moved that Legendre is not to be heard.

> *Legendre.* You don't need to put that to a vote, Mister President. This Society is a bunch of slaves.
> *Robespierre.* The speaker may have used improper terms in treating the calumnies of a defender of liberty, but hearing his opinions might furnish us with excellent ideas: he must be heard; and nobody here has the right to violate the freedom of debate. (*Applause.*)

But someone demands that Legendre be called to order for saying of Chabot, presiding, "I have no respect for that legislator." Legendre slams down his card on the desk. Several applaud. Chabot puts on his hat, signal of closing discussion. "It is indecent," he cries, "to applaud an act of bad humor by a member who is so firm a patriot." Robespierre also scolds the fickle membership, and Legendre, welcomed back by "universal applause," explains the state of mind that accounts for his snapping at "an English citizen" (Oswald). Yesterday there had been an English tourist here, calumniating the English nation in the Jacobin Club, and "going out in a rage along the streets when he left." Legendre, in a huff, trailed the raging visitor, who said, "Yes, what I've been told is true, these Jacobins have sold out!" "I followed him with my friends," says Legendre, "and we found that he lives with usher Damiens." No one comments;

Oswald has already left.[19] The session ends with news that the Assembly has just approved Servan's proposal to summon to Paris a camp of twenty thousand patriot volunteers.

At the Jacobins, Sunday, 10 June, Chabot presiding

Oswald again takes the floor, having done some homework and found a way to the bosom of old Legendre—who has recently had a close call with a crowd of spies (*mouchards*) who attacked him for failing to doff his hat to a religious procession.

Busy as Oswald must have been in these fateful days—for I do not find the legend that he took part in the affrays of August and September improbable— he returns to his task of keeping open the channels of fraternal communication between French and British Jacobins. He has "just been reading" the published *Journal* of the debate of 6 June, and he has something to add to Legendre's question, made after Oswald had left, about a certain "voyageur anglais qui est l'intime de l'huissier Damiens."

> *Oswald.* I assure the Society that this intimate friend of usher Damiens is not En- glish at all, and that the English patriots have nothing to do with him. He is French, and his name is Guédon.—He has lived for several years in London, where he deni- grates the French nation, though he now calumniates the English nation. Such with- out doubt is the holy mission he has been assigned as a spy in both courts. I demand that he never be admitted to the sessions of this Society; if he shows up again, I prom- ise to remove his mask.

Legendre himself is present and is so delighted to have had his attempt "to enlighten my fellow citizens" taken seriously that he now makes bold to en- lighten them further with the personal but also Jacobinical story of his close call among the National Guardsmen on the 7th. It is a brave story, that goes on for several pages, the point being that the Parisian National Guard, still riddled with faith in Lafayette though he is betraying the Revolution, are strife-torn— one sympathetic battalion commander helped Legendre get word to the Jacobins and other societies to have him rescued by patriots—and are particu- larly wrought up at the prospect of those twenty thousand patriots coming to the capital. The more personal point is that our butcher had to get to the mar- ket at Poissy, to earn his living.[20]

As soon as Legendre sits down, Citizen Martin shows the society a letter from London, "which tells of several insurrections taking place there. They have had to bring troops up to the city." He also has a letter from a Jacobin of

19. Ibid., 3:661–63.
20. On 29 June, Legendre was assigned a personal bodyguard.

Toulouse who had been searched at Dover by customs officers who confiscated
a packet intended for the Constitutional Society of London. Oswald's presence
in the Jacobin Club seems to succeed, even in small details, in focusing attention on the precarious but heartening London-Paris connection.

At the Jacobins, Wednesday, 22 August, Choudieu presiding

Twelve days after the glorious 10th of August, the "Second Revolution" that
would make France a republic instead of a constitutional monarchy, Oswald
resumes his effort, this time successfully, to persuade the French sans-culottes
to pay more attention to their British correspondents.[21] Given the floor, he proposes an address to *all* the popular clubs in England, Scotland, and Ireland—to
offset adverse publicity in the London press, biased, as he knew, by government
pressures, about the new French insurrection. One supposes he had a draft
ready. Perhaps he had already tested it on potential quibblers; but the occasion
and the message rose above them in any case.

Official British reaction to the deposition of Louis on the 10th had been to
recall Lord Gower, the ambassador at Paris, while advising Lebrun that King
George would maintain British neutrality.[22] This was a "sudden" act, of course,
as the fall of Louis had been.

> *Oswald.* I know not whether the sudden departure of the British ambassador
> threatens France with any hostile measures on the part of the court of Saint James;[23]
> but what is quite certain is that all the English journals, paid for some time out of the
> civil list of the court of London, and that of the Tuileries, to besmirch the French
> Revolution, have been presenting in the most atrocious colors the events of the
> glorious day of August 10. It is to be hoped that the English people will not be duped
> by these perfidious tales, and that the court of Saint James will not by that means lead
> them into an undertaking ruinous to liberty. It is thus most urgent to undeceive the
> British nation and to baffle the infernal plots of these royal tigers who have always
> sought and will forever seek to set two generous nations at each others' throats. It is a
> duty forced upon us by the interests of France, of England, and of the welfare of the
> human race. In consequence, I propose:
>   1st. That the Society of Friends of Equality [revised name of the Jacobin Club] send

21. Aulard, *Recueil des Documents . . . des Jacobins*, 4:229–33.
22. Bisset, *History of the Reign of George III*, 2:403–4.
23. Bland Burgess in London writing to Lord Auckland, ambassador to Holland, supplies one
answer to Oswald's question as to the significance of the recall of Gower. Pitt's government is still
greatly interested in Englishmen in Paris: "I have sent a very good man to look about him in Paris
after they [Gower and his aide Lindsay] come away, and who will let us know from day to day what
passes" (Alger, *Paris in 1789–94*, 329, quoting Burgess, 17 August 1792). The good man was
Capt. George Monro, to whose surviving reports we are indebted for much of our information. He
will move into the British Club headquarters, White's Hotel, and send a copy of the unedited list of
toasts for the dinner of 18 November to London—perhaps the list that reached Burke. For the
Jacobins' decision to send Oswald's suggested message to the British, by unanimous vote, see below,
pp. 208–9. For the text see Appendix C, pp. 301–3.

Fig. 30. The Jacobin Club platform simplified. How it was
when Oswald spoke (we may
guess). From Abbott, *The
French Revolution*, 1 : 212. (SB)

to the British nation an address in which will be exposed the conspiracy of the traitor
Louis XVI, and all the outrages which provoked the holy insurrection of August 10;

2nd. That this address be sent to all the popular clubs of England, Scotland, and
Ireland, with a request to have it reprinted and distributed through the whole extent
of the British empire.

By this means you will dispel the aristocratic clouds which have begun to darken
the air of Great Britain, you will revive the courage of our English brothers and patriots, shackled by royal proclamations and tyrannized by all the odious arts of a con-
spiratorial minister; and soon perhaps England, disencumbered of her tyrants, will
come to lend you a strong arm to uproot aristocracy and royalty, and to achieve with
you the revolution of Europe, of the human race, of "l'homme tout entier."

After some discussion the proposition of M. Oswald was carried, with an
amendment proposed by M. Boisguyon to add to this message the minutes of
the session of 10 August of the National Assembly, and several samples of the
papers found in the desk of the King. The notorious "iron chest" of papers fully
incriminating Louis would not be discovered until 20 November.[24]

In the subsequent discussions everywhere, especially in the decisive ones in
the societies, the Commune, the outgoing Assembly, and soon (20 September)

24. The iron chest opened in November contained such incriminating correspondence by the
King that his death was, after that, merely a matter of time and debate. But Roland, who first
opened the chest, lacked the foresight to have witnesses with him and so could be suspected of
tampering, selecting . . . in short, it ended his political career. William Godwin's *Things as They
Are, or The Adventures of Caleb Williams* (1794) must have been recognized at the time as making
use of the same situation in his plot; for when the novel was made into a play, it was given the title
of *The Iron Chest*. The connection, however, seems not to have been noted in modern times.

in the new, convening Convention—which, hearing the news of royalist defeat at Valmy, voted to abolish the monarchy and declare 21 September the first day of Year One—standing armies were still anathema. War was only justified by self-defense, and most of the language spelling that out admitted several possible scenarios: (1) success of the French against invading armies would encourage the people of the Netherlands, of Italy, of Germany, of Great Britain, to throw off their kings and emperor; (2) some of those people, those nations, might succeed before the French—and be able to send citizen armies to assist them; (3) the French succeeding first (now a possibility, on sunny days) might be called in by struggling nations to assist their revolutions.

On 9 October, secret agent Noel reported to Lebrun, French minister of foreign affairs, that a declaration of war by Britain would precipitate a British revolution. *That* might explain King George's caution about responses to 10 August.[25]

At the Jacobins, Sunday, 30 September, Year One of the Republic, Pétion presiding[26]

Five days after being named honorary French citizen (confirmation pending) and on the eve of his official appointment as commander of the First Battalion of Paris Volunteers, Oswald took the floor again at the Jacobin Club and spoke his mind. Better than that, he carried his audience with him, either by extemporary adroitness or because he had acquired a following. Several of the speakers seem to have come prepared with supporting documentation of the case he puts. Several times in his remarks he seems to speak with the tone of a Coleridgean "commanding genius" with full confidence in the virtue of a volunteer army and also in the future of the revolutionary cause.

The whole sessional report is worth quoting. It gives us Oswald in his glory. And, dramatically, a volunteer soldier takes the roof off the meeting by coming in, not before Oswald has carried his point, with a climax-capping burst of good news from the battlefront.

The usual reading of a digest of correspondence opens the meeting. A volunteer from Orleans denounces a curate of that city, and the society names two commissaries to examine the papers supporting the denunciation.

Oswald is given the floor.

> Citizens, I am going to communicate to the Society a fact received from London a few days ago.
>
> Several English patriots, seeing that the French lacked arms, had resolved to send

25. Goodwin, *The Friends of Liberty*, 257. Gower's office in Paris may have discovered this report.
26. Aulard, *Recueil des Documents . . . des Jacobins*, 4:345ff. My free translation.

them some from the manufacture of Birmingham and Sheffield. For this purpose they published in the papers an invitation to all who favored the cause of liberty in France, against the infamous conspiracy of crowned brigands, to assemble on September 12 at two o'clock at the residence of Mr Maxwell in Portland-square. This Mr Maxwell is a patriot of good faith, though his courage, as the event proved, was not equal to the task he had undertaken. Early on September 12 there came to Maxwell's house a colonel named Glover, a lackey of the court, the same who some years ago in Paris prosecuted a lawsuit against the duchess of Kingston, famous lesbian associate [*tribade*] of Marie-Antoinette.

This fellow addressed Maxwell in the name of his royal master: "You have," said he, "announced an assemblage at your house to give arms to the infamous regicides, the Jacobins; but I warn you, if you dare to hold this assemblage, you'll be burned alive in your own home; moreover, if you don't decamp this instant, I'm going to cut off your nose and ears." Maxwell did not wait to test these threats, for a crowd of hirelings had already surrounded his house, preparing to repeat the scene of Birmingham [i.e., the burning of the homes of Priestley and other English dissenters in 1791]. The patriots arrived at the appointed hour, but what was their astonishment when, instead of a welcome from their brother, they were met by this knight of the dagger at the head of his spies, who overwhelmed them with insults and menaces! It is well to remark that these spies are for the most part nonjuring priests and émigré former nobles who infest England these days, as once the locusts devastated and poisoned Egypt.

Nevertheless the patriots convened elsewhere, and they began a large subscription, which is increasing daily. The business is now in the hands of Horne Tooke, a true Jacobin, whose resolve will not be shaken by royal threats nor weakened by the bribes of the civil list.

At Manchester also our brothers have begun a subscription which is increasing daily despite the animosity of the aristocrats.

I have felt it important to communicate to you these details, which disconcert the spirit of the London court and at the same time prove how impossible it is to unite the two nations *until an English revolution* brings to our brothers the rights of man.[27]

Frenchmen, you have driven from your own house the monster royalty; but as long as this ferocious beast crouches in your neighbors' field, can you live without alarms? Can you believe that the king of England is not in league with the elector of Hanover? [Both the same person, of course, George the Third.] Can you believe that he who

---

27. My italics. The news about Maxwell was first reported in Hébert's *Courier de l'Egalité* on 23 September (299) in a paragraph about the evil French who have fled to England. The "tableaux affreux" summoned by Dr. Maynell (*sic*) when he tried to raise money to aid the embattled French people is cited as an example of the ferocity of the British terror. "Brave English," Hébert pleads, "don't believe all the absurd tales they tell you on our account: they want to embroil us to rape liberty." On the 24th (308) Hébert had the details (and Maxwell's name):

I spoke yesterday . . . of the doctor Maymell; read *Mexwel*. The menaces made to him against a gathering of friends of the French Revolution at his house, for a subscription, had no effect. Colonel Glover, the aristocrat, had intimidated him and threatened him with roasting and assassination, but that big bully was himself obliged to flee and the subscription to furnish us arms is going on at the home of Horne Took, living in Jean Street Sohosquare. There has been a considerable order for arms from Birmingham. O Liberty, these are your prodigies! A bit more time and the English, our true friends, shall be but one people with the Francs.

engineered the enslavement of Holland, that he who to enslave the Americans has pitilessly caused the death of so many thousands of his faithful subjects (as he has the impudence to call our English brothers), can you, I say, suppose that this man, tyrant and sanguinary, is able to watch calmly the revolution of France which is going to crush kings everywhere and topple royalty?

Scarcely having escaped the madhouse, where he should have spent the rest of his days, this mad king wishes to hurl the thunderbolts of war and shed the blood of the two fraternal peoples. The stubborn opposition of the English democrats has up to now prevented this evil.

However, efforts are being made to bewilder public opinion about everything that concerns France, and thereby to prepare the English nation to support the bloody views of this royal tiger. For this purpose use is made not only of the lies of the émigrés but also of the incivism and aristocracy of the agents of the French nation. I am referring to the French consul in London, Monsieur Thellusson. That fellow is pleased to calumniate the French Revolution in the most atrocious manner. He slyly spreads the most damaging rumors and the gloomiest forecasts. He has several times rebuffed the proposals of English negotiators who wanted to furnish arms to France,[28] telling them that he will take good care not to send arms to such butchers as the French. He is involved in everything most traitorous among the émigrés in London. He is often admitted to secret conferences at the house of Mr Pitt, the minister.

Upon such considerations, I urge today the sending of that fraternal address to the British nation which you have held up for quite some time.

Oswald has learned that to be taken seriously in a revolutionary forum it helps to make an accusation. But who was Peter Thellusson, what kind of target?

Peter Isaac Thellusson (1761–1808) was a director of the Bank of England and a merchant in London and Paris; in 1793, as soon as war is declared, we shall find him organizing a privateering campaign against French shipping.[29] His father Peter (Pierre) (1737–1797) was an international banker with a brother George in Paris and was head of the Swiss firm in which Necker was a partner (rivals in Geneva to the more republican Clavière of the Quatorze). We learn from a letter of 24 September 1792 from the Prince of Wales to the Duke of York that one of the Thellussons (George, perhaps) is relied upon for information about French military and political affairs.[30] I suspect that Oswald may

28. Oswald's involvement in the negotiations between Servan and Maxwell is glimpsed here. Robert Thornton, in *William Maxwell to Robert Burns*, 66–75, gives a detailed account of Maxwell's efforts to supply arms to the French—and the efforts of the British government to frustrate those efforts. Unfortunately Thornton at times garbles his information; in quoting Oswald's speech in the Jacobin Club he calls it the National Assembly; and his characterization of Oswald rests on the contemptuous comments of Redhead Yorke. Thornton assumes (70–71, 96) that Oswald's remarks "sullied" Maxwell's name; hence that Maxwell must have been unable "to sit down in the same room with John Oswald [as he often obviously did] without some . . . shudder."

29. See below. For a close investigation of the profiteering of privateering in the 18th century (in earlier wars) see Betty Rizzo, "John Sherratt, Negociator."

30. By one account Necker was originally clerk to George Thellusson and met his future wife when she was governess to the children of one of Thellusson's sisters. See Aspinall, *Correspondence of . . . Prince of Wales*, 2:659 and notes at 251 and 695; also Alger, *Napoleon's British Visitors*, 44.

have been aware of privateer Thellusson ever since the Grub-Street days of attacks on "commercial intercourse" between Britain and France. Here was a target of maximum international visibility. Moreover, as Oswald, advised by Paine and Frost, must have realized, action upon this accusation would be likely to initiate a series of perilous diplomatic events that might lead to war—and an English Revolution.

As soon as Oswald stopped speaking, the first person on his feet was Jean-François Boursault, a crony of Collot's who had turned from law to the theater, and now to politics.

> *Boursault.* The previous speaker has just denounced the consul Thellusson; I support with my own testimony the facts which he has given you; I will add also that this man is perhaps the greatest enemy the French Revolution has in England, where the services he renders as consul for the commerce of France are absolutely nil. But, in this regard, he shares these failings with all his colleagues. My many travels to what are called the principal courts of Europe[31] have put me in a position to judge that, wherever the French reside for a long time they denaturalize themselves, so to speak, and lose the true French character which has made us embrace with ardor the cult of liberty.
>
> All the ambassadors, the envoys, the chargés d'affaires, the consuls commissioned by the old regime, naturalized in the land of slavery, cannot taste or appreciate the fruits of a land which has purged itself of the venom of royalty; so I take this occasion to demand that they all be recalled.

Had Oswald expected, or planned, this escalation?

> *Saint-Hurugue.* If a witness is lacking to produce the recall of Thellusson, I assure you, myself, that he is the greatest aristocrat, the plainest rogue, the most . . . (*universal laughter*).
>
> *Laugier.* It would be without doubt most useful that the Jacobins could have all the consuls recalled; but this object, extremely important from one point of view, must not cause us to lose sight of the very important proposition which Oswald has made to us, that of sending an address which, in exposing the truth of the events of the revolution of August 10, should dispose the English to love us, that is to say, to know us.
>
> *Moenne.* Neither one nor the other of these objects should be lost sight of, and, without putting off the subject of the address, which I believe very important and which I support with all my power, I demand that the persons who have been making grave allegations against Thellusson should sign their denunciation, so that it may

---

31. Boursault had directed theater troupes in the courts of Europe since 1772. At the outbreak of the Revolution he was directing a theater in Marseilles and became head of the Jacobin movement there; moving to Paris, he had a theater built called La Salle Molière, which opened in June 1791. Apparently he gave too much attention to politics to keep it running. He took part in the Day of June 20 and in the September massacres. His section named him elector and captain of the National Guard; at the end of 1792 he would be driven out of the Jacobin Club for his friendship with Brissot and others of that ilk, which beclouded his career in the Convention, but he survived to reopen his theater in 1806 and to purchase the Opéra Comique in 1829 and enjoy a ripe retirement until 1842 (*DBF*).

promptly be presented to the minister of foreign affairs, who doubtless would not wish to entrust the interests of France to unreliable hands.

Deperret. If there was ever a time when it was important to enlighten our English brothers, it is without denial during this moment of crisis when the papers in the pay of the civil list of that court are confusing public opinion, even to printing that at the Palais-Royal people are dining on patées made of the flesh of the Swiss.

The number of émigrés in London is immense, a horde of refractory priests have joined them, and they contribute by the air of persecution they assume to confusing once more the public attitude toward the Revolution. Fortunately all Roman Catholic priests affect an air of superiority toward those of that country and disdain the Protestants. This is clearly the time to put into execution the project of the address proposed by Oswald.

Boisset. It is shameful for free France to trust her interests to men gangrenous with all the prejudices of aristocracy and royalty; I support, then, the proposal to demand the recall of all the consuls, envoys and ambassadors in foreign courts.

Taschereau. To give you an idea of the civic spirit of Thellusson and prove to you just how far his attachment to the French nation carries, it will suffice, I believe, to inform you that, during the last war, he had two armed privateers in action, for his profit, against the French.

Oswald. The witnesses to the facts I have advanced are Thomas Paine and [John] Frost.

A nicely orchestrated presentation. And Oswald for the benefit of doubters in the Jacobin Club now makes public his sources of information: Horne Tooke, of the London society and another new citizen of France; Tom Paine, French citizen since August and now an elected delegate to the Convention (for Calais, quickest step from London); also the attorney John Frost, Tooke's SCI colleague—who would be pilloried and jailed on his return to England early in 1793, for appearing to serve as an English delegate to the French Convention and clinching that impression by saying in a Marylebone coffeehouse: "I am for equality . . . . Why, no kings!" [32] That Oswald fails to mention Maxwell himself as a source (who had already returned to Paris, leaving further British efforts to Tooke) is perhaps simply a matter of discretion. [33]

Bourdon. I entirely approve of the desire which the Society manifests to see the interests of France confided to clean hands in a foreign country. Nevertheless, the proposal to demand purely and simply the recall of all our agents in the different courts of Europe appears to me to be of too great importance to be adopted without mature examination. You all know that when a power recalls its ambassadors from a foreign court the recall amounts to a declaration of war; yet that is not our intention. [34] I will demand then that instead of insisting on the recall of all our agents, it be proposed, solely to the executive power, to act in their regard as the national Convention has

32. On Frost, see Thompson, *The Making of the English Working Class*, 110–11, 114; but also Werkmeister, *Newspaper History*, 276.
33. Goodwin, *The Friends of Liberty*, 243.
34. A point on which the Jacobins were not in agreement.

acted in regard to the interior administrations of which it has ordered the renovation.

Boursault. Entering into the views of the previous speaker about getting to the root of the question, I will propose particularly to avoid the bad choices which the ministers are always exposed to making, surrounded incessantly by intriguing suppliants, that the nomination of these agents be transferred to the legislative body.

Bourdon. Let us be careful, citizens, about adopting this measure: first because it would take up precious time of the national Convention to be forced to busy itself with all these nominations; second because in adopting it you would relieve the ministers of the burden of responsibility, without placing it anywhere else, for an Assembly which nominates by a plurality of votes cannot be responsible.

Jeanbon Saint-André. It is important, citizens, to distinguish two classes of political agents: agents purely political, and agents of commerce.

It is necessary to vow that, the politics of courts no longer existing, the interests of nations being everywhere the same, we shall soon be relieved entirely of ministers who serve only to dupe us; but, until we have reached this point of perfection, it is essential to change those who are presently employed, and the care for such changing should not be confided only to the ministers, because, as the previous speaker has wisely observed, the executive power alone must be responsible.

As for the consuls, from what little one has observed of the services they pretend to render to commerce, one is soon convinced that stock-jobbing and the work of advancing their own fortune by brokerage and protection which they charge to the merchants, are their principal occupations, even if not their only ones. It is surprising that, in this century of enlightened innovation, the government still clings to agents as useless as they are dangerous: I demand then the recall of consuls be attended to.

A Volunteer. I have come from Metz, and I must tell you that the question you treat of is absolutely pointless, for in six days you will have no more enemies in France. The position of their armies and that of our own is such that they shan't be able to hold on for six days, and that they will be able to escape only by a miracle. If they retreat, then we shall enter Germany, the Brabant, the Savoy, and our armies are the only ambassadors we will be sending. I demand then that there is nothing to do but send the ambassadors from here in a few days and await developments which must soon change entirely the measures to be taken.

Amid the agitation produced in the Assembly by the news from this volunteer [no one says anything about stopping at the borders], the motion was repeated which had already been made, to name the commissioners to indite the address to the English people.

This motion, supported and put to a vote, was adopted unanimously.

Likewise adopted was the adjournment of the question of the recall of consuls, envoys, and other political agents.

Aside from Boursault, who were those supporting and opposing Oswald's manifesto?

Léonard Bourdon, schoolteacher, was a radical who worked with Deperret and Collot but a squelcher of extreme proposals, or men (see his ferreting out of Roux).[35] Deperret, supporting Oswald, is the Girondin deputy, Carlyle's Du-

35. After having been one of the most sanguinary proconsuls of the Convention, Bourdon would be employed in the military hospital of the Emperor and die at Breslaw just before the Peace of

perret, who will arise, during a tumultuous quarrel in the Convention between the Mountain and the Gironde on 11 April 1793,

> rushing on one another with clenched right-hands, and even with pistols in them; when, behold, the Girondin Duperret drew a sword! Shriek of horror rose . . . whereupon Duperret returned it to the leather again:—confessing that he did indeed draw it, being instigated by a kind of sacred madness, "sainte fureur," and pistols held at him; but that if he parricidally had chanced to scratch the outmost skin of National Representation with it, he too carried pistols, and would have blown his brains out on the spot.

A splendid companion for Oswald; in Barbaroux's opinion "républicain ardent, honnête homme, bon père, bon ami; il a toutes les qualités qui doivent concilier l'estime publique."[36]

Boisset, a lawyer, was a feeble, versatile character easily influenced. He was one of the first to accuse the Girondins; made a demonstration of voting the death of the King *sans appel ni sursis* (as did Collot); survived several denunciations himself. Jeanbon Saint-André was a steady montagnard, inconspicuous; yet he and Collot would be among "the twelve who ruled" during the Terror.[37]

Laugier, heading the committee to indite the manifesto proposed by Oswald, was a former justice of the peace in the Section de la Fontaine-de-Grenelle. In April when several sections were petitioning for the disarmament of the rich, he was one who "went further still";[38] two years later he was accused of having proposed that the rich, rentiers, financiers, and bankers, should all be dispatched as enemies of the Republic.

The laughter that breaks in upon the remarks of Saint-Hurugue had become the habitual response to that clown—and patriotic dancer. Carlyle describes him as he emerged in 1789:

> Tall shaggy Marquis Saint-Hurugue, a man that has had losses, and has deserved them, is seen eminent, and also heard. "Bellowing" is the character of his voice, like that of a Bull of Bashan; voice which drowns all voices, which causes frequently the hearts of men to leap. Cracked or half-cracked is this tall Marquis's head; uncracked are his lungs; the cracked and the uncracked shall alike avail him.

In April 1792 Carlyle describes him as "the Saint-Christopher of the *Carmagnole*," defiling through the Jacobin Club in the midst of a cheery group of sans-culottes "singing many-voiced their *ça-ira*, dancing their *ronde patriotique*."[39]

Tilsit. See Gwyn Williams, *Artisans and Sans-culottes*, 51; Louis Ternaux, *Histoire de la Terreur*, 2:450.

36. Carlyle, *FR*, 590; Barbaroux, *Mémoires*, 173.

37. Palmer, *Twelve Who Ruled*, 1, defines Jeanbon as "Protestant minister, one time ship's captain, diligent, masterful." Collot, also of the Twelve, is "self-made, crude, excitable."

38. Soboul, *The Parisian Sans-culottes*, 28.

39. *FR*, 187, 428.

At the Jacobins, Wednesday, 3 October, Pétion presiding[40]

We may be sure that Oswald was on the commission that met to write the address he had called for—indeed, that he had a draft ready for them. What they quickly agreed upon was printed in the minutes of this Wednesday session. There was no further dallying. The secretary summarized the whole meeting thus:

> The Society solicits the citizens of Paris to lodge the volunteers that are passing through the city, as they had lodged the fédérés.—*Gaston* and *Merlin* give news of the armies.—*Dessieux* complains that the Commune of Paris has decided that the next election of the mayor of Paris should be by secret ballot.—*Chabot* rises to oppose maintaining a single mayor at the head of a municipality as populous as Paris. A long debate ensues on the subject.—It is resolved to send to the popular Societies of Britain the address presented anew by *Laugier*.

The text of the "*Circulaire*"—Bonneville would have been pleased at the term—"of the Society of Jacobins of Paris, to the Patriotic Societies of England, Scotland and Ireland," is then printed in full. It is the main business of the day.

It surveys the crimes of "Louis the Last" and the events and meaning of 10 August. It assures the British people that there is now such a blossoming of republican virtues among the hitherto servile French that both peoples can share in a fraternal rejoicing.[41]

Oswald will not speak again in the Jacobin Club until 4 February 1793, after the declaration of war against Britain and Holland. But in that February speech which history has not been aware of, because it was sent off to the printer, Oswald reveals that his efforts this October ("four months earlier") were directed not only to persuading the Jacobins to circulate their enlightening words among the patriotic societies of Britain, but also to persuading them to give armed support to the forthcoming revolution in England. It would require, he estimated, an army of sixty thousand volunteers who "knew how to die"—and the alerting of the sans-culottes of Britain with some kind of tocsin. I imagine the attack on Thellusson and the attempt to have the French consuls recalled was meant to ring one kind of alarm. Consider Jeanbon's remark that now, "the politics of courts no longer existing, the interests of nations [are] everywhere the same."

Oswald says he had thought he had convinced an effective group of Jacobins who were members of the Convention, and that they were to have there proposed the immediate planning of a descent on London, but that Brissot had dissuaded them from the idea.

---

40. Aulard, *Recueil des Documents . . . des Jacobins*, 4:355–56; text of the Circular, 356–59.
41. Text in Appendix C, below.

The February speech will be discussed in its own context in Chapter 9 (see pp. 255ff.), but the light (or shadow) it casts upon the origins of the British Club can only be seen in accurate perspective when we adapt our organs of perception to the peculiar climate of opinion in France and England during this first month of the Year One of the Republic of France.

THIRD INTERCHAPTER
ARMING AND DISARMING

1792

15 September. A customs officer at Dover confiscates the proofs Tom Paine is carrying of his *Address to the Addressers*, calling for a British Convention. This

> parting shot was . . . followed by the "miracles" of Valmy and Jemappes and the "sans-culottes" sweeping into Brussels. At this moment Paine was as important in his person as in his books. For this one moment, a new expression of the British libertarian tradition and a new French democratic republic were not merely related, they were identified. And it was at this point, *two years after the offence*, that political artisans took public umbrage at being called a "swinish multitude." For they saw the future and it worked.[1]

*

Arthur Young in May had proposed "arming the property of the Kingdom in a sort of horse militia." This autumn his idea of building up a volunteer army was being adopted, but with unforeseen results. Near the end of his life, Young would recall that his proposal to arm in defense of property had made the biggest public impression of his long public life.[2] "The scheme took with astonishing celerity," but it also got out of hand "and became the parent of a measure of a very different complexion, which was putting arms into the hands of thousands without property, and upon whose allegiance and constitutional principle but little reliance could be placed. Government received demands for arms to the amount of above 700,000 men. The Ministers were alarmed, and saw too late the consequence . . . ."[3] Did Britain seem to be arming its own people in blind preparation for a future liberation *from* "property"?

*

1. Williams, *Artisans and Sans-culottes*, 70.
2. Young first published his alarmist papers in the *Annals of Agriculture* and expanded them into his famous pamphlet, *The Example of France a Warning to England*, late in the year.
3. Young, *Autobiography*, 203–6.

10 September. The *Manchester Herald* defends the September massacres, with eyewitness reports from Paris, probably sent by Watt.

*

15 September. Margarot, president of the London Corresponding Society, suggests privately to Horne Tooke that, instead of raising money à la Maxwell to send the French arms—or in addition to raising money for the French—all the radical societies be asked to assent to "an Animated (but safe) Declaration" of friendship and British neutrality. In a follow-up letter Hardy suggests that "Ten or Twenty thousand signatures would have more weight than as many thousand pounds, for ten men might subscribe that sum";[4] obtaining thousands of signatures seemed no problem.

*

24 September. Antoine Gorsas, whose journal is read by Wordsworth, exhorts the Convention to put war at the top of its agenda:

> The National Convention has distinguished its labor with great and useful measures. It has opened the book of nature; it has read there that fine principle that it requires no constitution but that which is accepted by the people. It has opened the red book of tyrants; it has seen there . . . that the history of kings is the martyrology of Nations, and each of its members has become a Brutus. We have already obtained the recognition of the people. . . . The laws must be maturely and thoroughly deliberated. We must get busy to save the Republic, before proposing a constitution for it. I propose that all the laws, except for the most urgent, be adjourned to more tranquil times, and that the war be the order of the day. (Applause.)[5]

*

27 September. Margarot and Hardy of the London Corresponding Society begin to solicit authorizations from the Manchester Constitutional and Reformation Societies, the Norwich Revolution Society, and the London "Constitutional Whigs, Independent and Friends of the People." The sponsors amount to "a few thousands" (five, in the final count) of "indignant" British citizens who profess themselves "united in one common cause; namely the obtaining a fair, equal, and impartial Representation in Parliament." Their "Address to the French National Convention" avows a "sacred" and "inviolable Friendship" to the French "champions of human happiness"—and gratitude to the French egalitarians for helping the British to discover "our real enemies" in an "all-consuming Aristocracy."[6]

4. Goodwin, *The Friends of Liberty*, 244 and note 160.
5. *Moniteur*, 1137. Wordsworth may or may not have heard Gorsas speak; he would have read his *Courrier*, one of the two papers subscribed to by the Jacobins of Blois (the other being Carra's more popular *Annales patriotiques*). Kennedy, *The Jacobin Clubs*, 365; 66.
6. The fine tuning of this declaration, to the effect that we British find these enemies "in our bosom" and "feel ourselves inwardly torn," is lost in the French translation, where the enemies are

Conveyed at Hardy's advice via Chauvelin, the French consul in London, the joint address will finally be read in the Convention on 7 November (see below). A postscript explains that obtaining "the concurrence of different Country Societies to this Address has occasioned a month's delay in presenting it" and that "this testimony of friendship" was uttered *before* the arms of the Republic had been successful.

*

Early October. Chancelleries reverberate with anticipations of a war that might produce insurrections in Britain.[7]

*

Some time in October. William Wordsworth moves from Orleans to Paris, having probably helped the Jacobins of Orleans celebrate the birth of the Republic on 21 September.

The September Massacres were hardly more than a month old and newsboys were hawking through the streets the account of Louvet's denunciation of Robespierre, with its accusation that the Massacres were part of a bloody and pre-conceived scheme for seizing supreme power. Public opinion, at first favorable to Louvet, manifested itself throughout the following week with demands for Robespierre's head and with the burning of his effigy. But at this crucial juncture, on Monday, November 5, the "Incorruptible" struck back with a speech which swung the tide completely in his favor. Small wonder then that Wordsworth, looking back at his stay in Paris from the viewpoint of historical hindsight and increased conservatism, described himself as having difficulty in falling asleep in his "high and lonely" room, because the city

Seem'd a place of fear
Unfit for the repose which night requires,
Defenceless as a wood where tigers roam.

But I suspect Wordsworth's truer feelings at the time are reflected in those extraordinary lines which describe his emotions as he watched the struggle for power between Robespierre and his opponents:

Yet did I grieve, nor only griev'd, but thought
Of opposition and of remedies,
An insignificant Stranger, and obscure,
Mean as I was, and little graced with power
Of eloquence even in my native speech,
And all unfit for tumult or intrigue,
Yet would I willingly have taken up
A service at this time for cause so great,

---

found "dans les partisans de cette aristocratie dévorante." The English version suggests the symbolic ambiguity of *The Adventures of Caleb Williams*.

7. Goodwin, *The Friends of Liberty*, 257.

However dangerous. Inly I revolv'd
How much the destiny of man had still
Hung upon single persons . . . .[8] (*Prelude* 10.80–82, 129–39)

Wordsworth much later had such strong sympathy with republican France that he "grieved for Buonaparte," its unsuccessful savior. He seems here to grieve for his own lost opportunity—not to slay Robespierre but to enter the struggle, à la Oswald; to be a humane Buonaparte, or a successful Robespierre —or at least to join his fellow British in Paris who were speaking up as a sympathetic group. He may well have been still as "hot" in revolutionary spirit as his friend Watt had found him—though Watt had left Paris by 7 October.

*

26 October. London. *The Times*: "It is certain that the Jacobins in this capital make no scruple to say that there will be an insurrection here this winter, resembling that of Paris." Evidence: a report of a strange man running about London with "bayonets, poignards, and other small instruments of assassination" which he sells at a low price: "here are the arms with which the French have obtained their Liberty."

*

26 October. Paris. Edward Fitzgerald arrives at White's Hotel, dropping the "milord" as in his toast at the British Club affair next month, and writes to his mother: "I lodge with my friend Paine; we breakfast, dine and sup together. . . . I pass my time very quietly; read, walk, and go quietly to the play. . . . I go a good deal to the Assembly [*sc.*, Convention]—they improve much in speaking."[9]

This is an eloquent cover story. Lord Fitzgerald might have added that Paine and Stone have introduced him to Madame Genlis and to her ward Pamela (whom Pétion had escorted to London the year before and who will soon become Mrs. Fitzgerald). Historians, knowing this and reading the letter, take it as evidence that Fitzgerald only much later became a serious Irish revolutionist.

A confidential communication from Paine to Lebrun, however, in February, reveals that during their meals together Paine and Fitzgerald had been engaged in seeking covert assistance from the French government for a Dublin insurrection coordinated with a French invasion. This is the impersonal report: "Toward the end of 1792 an important Irishman, whose name is in the margin [Fitzgerald, written upside down in Greek], came to Paris uniquely to see Paine and to tell him that if he could find three months' subsistence for 40,000 volunteers, who would not of course actually assemble for more than a day, a revolution would be inevitable."[10]

8. Walling, "Wordsworth's *The Borderers*," 91–92.
9. Moore, *The Life and Death of Edward Fitzgerald*, 87–88.
10. Woodward, *Un adherente Anglaise*, 101, my translation. (Papers in the Quai d'Orsay ar-

*

2 November. Lebrun's secret agent reports that Ireland is "ripe for revolution," that Scotland is causing much anxiety, that French principles are rapidly spreading in England and the government is "now suspended on a volcano." [11]

*

4 November. William Rickets of the British navy—and shortly to join the British Club—asks the Convention to permit him to join the French navy. Later he will offer to equip a vessel under his own command. [12]

*

5 November. For the annual meeting of the London Revolution Society (perhaps its last) five hundred Friends of Liberty dine at the London Tavern—and a thousand more are turned away. Tooke and Christie sit on the left and right of the chairman. An "Address or Congratulation" to the Convention is acclaimed (and delivered 1 December). More than forty toasts are drunk (an all-time record), interspersed with singing of the Marseillaise (copies of which have been sent over by Minister Lebrun). [13]

*

7 November. Paine presents to the Convention a copy of Barlow's *Advice to the Privileged Orders . . . the Necessity and Propriety of a General Revolution in the Principle of Government*, part 1. On the same day an address of the united societies of London, Manchester, and Norwich, dated 27 September, vows inviolable friendship "to a Nation proceeding on the plan which you have adopted," of a free people without monarch or aristocrats. "Frenchmen, you are already free, and Britons are preparing to become so." [14]

---

chives.) Elliott, alone I believe among modern historians, discusses this document but as inoperative in the context of Paine's lack of an Irish base and Lebrun's lack of any follow-up except perhaps authorizing Eleazar Oswald's reassuringly giving the same details to United Irishmen in Dublin in May 1793, at a time when they were not in a position to take advantage of French aid (*Partners in Revolution*, 60–61). McDowell (*Ireland in the Age of Imperialism and Revolution*, 478–79, 503) is unaware of these documents and sees Lord Edward in 1792 as a giddy youth "swept off his feet" only to the extent of donating the price of a musket to the French cause—and not seeking "French assistance for a radical insurrection" until 1796.
11. Goodwin, *The Friends of Liberty*, 257.
12. Alger, *Englishmen*, 451.
13. Goodwin, *The Friends of Liberty*, 247; Goodwin believes this gesture was "the swan song of the society, for no further traces of its activities or . . . existence have survived." "This effort to assimilate the principles, not merely of 1789, but also of 1792, to those of the English revolution of 1688 may have been called for by the occasion . . . but the specific apologia for 10 August and the encomium of French republican institutions must have seemed, to less biased observers [he means to negatively biased ones], unnecessarily provocative of English conservative opinion."
14. Goodwin (in ibid., 501–6) transcribes the English manuscript and quotes variants in the French text which gave it a "more uncompromisingly caustic or implacable" tone; also variants in an English retranslation that made it a significantly "loaded variation of the original." This loaded version was printed for Reeves' Association (see 20 November, below) "probably at Treasury ex-

*

18 November. The English, Scotch, and Irish resident and domiciled in Paris, soon known as the British Club, hold a great Sunday rally at White's Hotel, Rue des Piques. (See Chapter 7.)

*

19 November. The Convention adopts the following manifesto, "to be printed in all languages": "The National Convention declares, in the name of the French Nation, that it will accord fraternity and assistance to every nation which wishes to recover its liberty; and charges the executive power to give the generals the necessary orders to bring aid to such peoples and to defend citizens who shall have been oppressed [*vexés*] or who may become so in the cause of liberty." [15] It is passed "with enthusiasm," though Brissot will later call it "an absurd and impolitic decree which justly caused disquiet in foreign cabinets." [16]

*

20 November. An Association for the Preservation of Liberty and Property against Republicans and Levellers is formed in London by John Reeves, "a former justice of Newfoundland and monopolist, if there ever was one, of lucrative public offices." [17] This Crown and Anchor Association began a concerted attack, with the cooperation of Lord Grenville in the Home Office, upon clubs, newspapers, and individuals suspected of French sympathies.

Among publishers and printers indicted for libel by the attorney-general, on the 28th, was James Ridgway; among the commissioned officers who were cashiered on the 30th for corresponding "with the Friends of Freedom in France" were Edward Fitzgerald (for attending the dinner at White's Hotel and toasting the abolition of titles) and Norman Macleod (for "heading a party of Jacobins" and other indications of "his *fixed* principles"). [18] Was Macleod keeping in touch with Oswald still?

---

pense," in time to bias members of Parliament against Sheridan's motion (4 March 1793—not 28 February as stated) for an inquiry into the alleged sedition of the reform societies.

15. This decree was, in effect, a declaration (to use Carlyle's language for it) "That any Nation which might see good to shake off the fetters of Despotism was thereby, so to speak, the Sister of France, and should have help and countenance. A Decree much noised of by Diplomatists, Editors, International Lawyers; such a Decree as no living Fetter of Despotism, nor Person in Authority anywhere, can approve of!" (*FR*, 549). The shape of this declaration implied that it constituted a reply, sixteen months delayed, to the Declaration of Pillnitz, in which emperor and king offered to help other sovereigns who might see good to reapply the fetters their subjects were throwing off. (Curiously enough, modern history books rarely mention it.)

16. Brissot, *À ses commettans*, 68. In the *Chronique du mois* for January 1793, 11, Lanthenas misdates this decree "18 novembre," perhaps confusing it with the Sunday meeting at White's.

17. Goodwin, *The Friends of Liberty*, 264.

18. Werkmeister, *Newspaper History*, 140–41.

*

28 November. Two British addresses are read before the National Convention. One, by the three British nations gathered at White's Hotel and dated the
24th, is in part a response to the manifesto of the 19th; it strongly focuses on
revolutionary war, and it significantly speaks not for "Great Britain" but for its
component nations. The other, brought in person by Frost and Barlow as formally elected delegates of the London Society for Constitutional Information,
elicits a response that reminds us of the "douces etreintes" of the previous
December.

Grégoire, presiding, hails the addressers as citizens of the world and agrees
that "Royalty in Europe is either destroyed, or on the point of perishing on the
ruins of feudalism," since the Declaration of Rights is "a devouring fire, which
will consume them." Barlow explains that the SCI has long hoped for this day
and that there are now similar societies throughout England: "After the example which France has lately given, revolutions will be rendered easy; and it
will not be extraordinary if, in a short time, addresses of congratulation will be
sent to a *National Convention of England*." [19] Grégoire gives Barlow and Frost
"the kiss of fraternity," drawing "tears from a crowded assembly" (according to
Barlow's letter to his wife).[20]

*

6 December. An order is issued for the arrest of John Frost, absent in Paris;
he is outlawed two days later. On the same day Sampson Perry, under indictment since July for a "libel" in his *Argus*, is tried in absentia and outlawed, and
his paper is suppressed; whereupon a government paper rejoices "that Mr.
Horne Tooke has lost the use of one of his limbs." [21]

*

13 December. Both houses of Parliament are convened in an emergency session to vote on a warlike manifesto called the King's Speech, authorizing "a due
provision" for "some augmentation of my naval and military force." The legislators are bludgeoned with invented accounts of insurrections in London (!),
Dublin, and Scotland. (Charles Fox: If we need an insurrection, it's better to
have it in Scotland.)

In the debate on the speech, Lord Grenville says he is holding "in his hand no
less than ten addresses presented to the National Convention of France" by
subjects of Britain.[22]

19. *Arch Parl*, 53:636.
20. Woodress, *A Yankee's Odyssey*, 181.
21. Werkmeister, *Newspaper History*, 151.
22. Grenville was not exaggerating. Goodwin (*The Friends of Liberty*, 508–9) tabulates eleven
addresses actually read in the National Convention between 7 November and early December,
from eleven different societies or groups of societies.

*

Early December. In Dublin a "Convention, representing the entire Catholic population, commenced its sittings with all the forms of a Legislative Assembly," having been chosen by primary assemblies in "all the counties and many of the great towns and districts of Ireland." An armed association of the United Irishmen, calling themselves the First National Battalion and bearing for their device an Irish harp, without a crown, surmounted by a cap of Liberty, had sent out summonses for a meeting of their corps, which was prevented by a government proclamation. Their name suggests a fraternal emulation of Oswald's First Battalion of National Volunteers, which Fitzgerald could have told them about.[23]

*

20 December, Paris. Thomas Christie of the London Corresponding Society, a member of the British Club who had been nominated with Oswald for French citizenship in September, now agent of a British firm selling flour to Paris, writes to General Miranda, now of the revolutionary Army of the North, conveying his sober thoughts about the present crisis in the revolutionary movement in both Paris and London. What strikes Christie about the present French leadership is "a feebleness and even *defaut de lumières*." People coming to the fore in the Convention are mediocrities, "*sans lumières*." Those who have "never perfectioned a single idea" now talk of "humbling the *Aristocracy of Knowledge*."

In France, if the party of Robespierre and Marat get uppermost, "a *third* revolution must take place & an agrarian law, & as they have not heads to manage the state, it is probable that Anarchy will take place & Despotism succeed to close the dreadful scene."

In England, "a spirit of sober & temperate reform" had been "gradually gaining ground." But suddenly, during that insurrection which wasn't,

> the Court became alarmed & associations to keep up every abuse were formed by their Emissaries & Dependants. They held it forth that there was a plan formed to overturn the Constitution, & to introduce all the disorder & confusion that reigned in France. They operated artfully on the fears & weakness of the rich Proprietors, & have turned them all against any change whatever for the present, lest the system itself should be overturned. The People however murmur secretly. Paine's works continue to sell by thousands & the silent progress of truth must in time produce a conviction that will overwhelm all the power & reign of Error.

(Is Christie here implying the obverse of a "reign of Terror"?) The British court would like to make war

> to check the progress of republican principles. Nothing can prevent a war but their fear that the nations will not heartily concur in it.

23. Moore, *Life and Death of Fitzgerald*, 105–7.

But, should it blow over for the present, I am clear that peace cannot long continue between the two Nations. A great Republic & a great Monarchy cannot long exist at the side of one another. Their principles will either destroy our Prejudices, or our Prejudices will overwhelm their Principles. The American Republic extended its influence over the Atlantic Ocean & made the Revolution of France. The French Republic will much more easily transmit its Principles across the Channel & make a new English Revolution.

These thoughts were confirmed by the people Christie talked with at "a Sans-Culotte dinner yesterday where I was much amused. We had Mlle. Théroigne, John Oswald Commandant de 1er. Battaillon de Piques" (people well known to Miranda and Christie).[24] "They all agreed that the French Repub. could not be safe while the Eng. Monarchy was so near it. Our Court reasons in the same way on their side & the consequence is that WAR IS INEVITABLE. What will be consequences of such a war God only knows.[25] They are incalculable." P.S.: "Mr. Paine sends his compts to you."

*

20 December. Richard Ferris, a member of the revolutionary committee of Ireland, who has been deputed to the French government, is presented to Lebrun in Paris, at Lebrun's request, in the name of the Executive Council.

In July 1793, Ferris will report on his successes in pursuing Lebrun's suggestion that officers for a proper insurrectionary force should be recruited from among the Irish presently serving in various European armies. Ferris will have found the Irish officers in the service of ci-devant English princes well disposed. He will assure Lebrun that there are "80,000 volunteers in Ireland ready to rise," and that the Scottish will not be slow to follow the example of Ireland.[26]

*

28 December. Burke, in a House of Commons debate on the Alien Bill, favored passage as a means of keeping terrorists out of England. Probably no more than two hundred persons in France did all the murdering. (Here I draw upon Robert Thornton's summary in *Maxwell to Burns*, 91–92.) Only about nineteen in Great Britain were likely to be affected by the bill. All of these indi-

24. General Miranda had been in Paris in early November but joined the French army in Brussels by the 17th. When he returned to Paris next May he resumed a busy social interchange with his British friends. Records of visiting Mr. and Mrs. Christie, Miss Wollstonecraft, and others occur for May and June (*Archivo*, 13:77–78, 84–86), and in July 1795 there would be a reunion of Miranda's friends in the house of "our friends" Mlle Williams and Mr. Stone (*Archivo*, 13: 122–23).

25. *Archivo*, 13:38–39. Even so, Christie's letter ends with the revolutionary slogans, "*Guerre aux Châteaux, paix au chaumières* [cottages]"! And as soon as war did break out, a British spy reporting on a meeting of the London Corresponding Society on 23 February 1793 would note that "Mr Christie, of Devonshire Square," was sending fifty pounds to the Convention "for supporting the Warr; tis supposed he has meetings"—fund-raising dinners? Rendezvous with French agents? (Thale, *Selections*, 53.)

26. Woodward, "Projets," 9.

viduals were known by the dagger. Burke mentioned that three thousand daggers had been bespoken at Birmingham by an Englishman, of which seventy had been delivered. It had not been ascertained how many of these were intended for home consumption. Here he drew out a dagger which he had kept concealed[27] and "with much vehemence threw it on the floor":

> This, said he, pointing to the dagger, is what you are to gain by an alliance with France; wherever their principles are introduced, their practice must follow. You must guard against the principles; you must proscribe their persons. He then held the dagger up to public view, which he said never would have been intended for fair and open war, but solely for murderous purposes. It is my object, said he, to keep the French infection from this country; their principles from our minds, and their daggers from our hearts. I vote for this bill, because I consider it the means of saving my life and all our lives, from the hands of assassins. When the French smile, I see blood trickling down their faces, all their cajoling is—blood!

Sheridan's comment was, "You have shown us the knife; where is the fork?" And Burke was unable to continue until the House "had resumed its wonted seriousness and dignity."

Sunday papers, 30 December, quoted facetious advice to Burke warning him that Sheffield and Manchester were preparing three thousand buttons with the motto "Liberty and Equality," to make the celebration of the Queen's coming birthday "a Bloody day and not a Birthday." James Gillray's famous caricature of the time, "The Dagger Scene:—or The Plot Discovered," was widely circulated. William Blake, in the Preludium of his political prophecy *Europe*, pictured Burke lurking in the cave of Parliament to waylay Everyman on his pilgrimage, Fox wrapped in shady woe—i.e., in Bunyan's Slough of Despond —and a symbolic black slave, chained with a heavy weight, hurtling into the abyss.[28]

27. Burke had obtained the dagger from Henry Dundas the day before the speech; it had been the "pattern dagger" taken from one of Maxwell's Birmingham suppliers. Details in Thornton, *Maxwell to Burns*, 92ff.

28. Gillray, in a separate caricature, depicts Fox as the pilgrim mired with his "Gospel of Liberty" in the Slough, while facing the Celestial Gate of Libertas—behind which a stepladder aimed toward the moon could never reach it. (Blake, in *The Gates of Paradise*, parodies Gillray with a ladder reaching the moon and no gate in the way. For Blake, "The Desire being Infinite, the Possession is Infinite.")

8.
THE BRITISH CLUB

Unsquaring the Circle

The discovery of the Year One of the Republic was made suddenly, in the afternoon of 21 September 1792, and the Oswaldian covenant of hope, the *Circulaire* to English, Scottish, and Irish brethren (agreed upon and launched from the Patriot press within a fortnight) was one bright consequence. It is a striking historical phenomenon that almost simultaneously (as fast as the news was carried) the founding of the French Republic created a qualitatively new excitement. The fall of the Bastille had been a glorious happening, but this was a transformation. The members of the Assembly, suddenly looking around, saw that the quorum present had the authority to constitute themselves the new Convention, "an assembly of philosophers" (said Manuel) "occupied with preparing the happiness of the world."[1] No lack now of luminaries!

Bonneville's hope for an incarnation of the Enlightenment seemed to be coming true. Yet the meeting nearly adjourned without action. A decree to abolish royalty was proposed, then postponed. Collot, president of the Electors of Paris, flashed the urgent message: this is "a matter that you cannot put off till tomorrow; that you cannot put off till this evening"; yet they did. On the following day, however, illumination came from without. Hearing people in the streets cry "Vive la République!" the elected citizens suddenly realized that its birth was near—that they were "about to proclaim the republic"—no solemn declaration, a whisper to test the world's response. Definitions?

On the 25th Danton moved to declare that "the French Republic is one and indivisible." Hesitation continued until the Convention was deluged by enthusiastic addresses from forty-two of the eighty-three departments, with no protests. "Dumouriez wrote to the Minister of Finance, Clavière, on September 26th: 'I am enchanted to know that we have taken the leap and become a republic.'" (A great leap indeed from that timorous alarm at the republican placard of Paine and Lanthenas in June 1791.)

1. Aulard, ed., *Recueil des Documents . . . des Jacobins,* 147, 156–57.

223

On the 29th the Convention established a committee to write a constitution for the Republic; its members (chosen 11 October) were Siéyès, Paine, Brissot (presently replaced by Barbaroux), Pétion, Vergniaud, Gensonné, Barère, Danton, and Condorcet. Eight days later the Jacobins began to form an "Auxiliary Committee of Constitution," including Collot, Robespierre, and Danton, which would not be completed or activated until the Condorcet committee reported in February 1793. Paine had come over from England in mid-September, recommending to the British people, as he left Dover, that they summon a Convention too.

Paine apparently thought that the British were also ready for a great leap. The impact of this Second Revolution, followed soon by French victories against royalist armies, was indeed clearly registered in the thinking and in the popularity of the British societies. Gwyn Williams in his *Artisans and Sans-culottes* (1969) defines these changes with precision and much detail, which I draw upon briefly here. Before the leap the second part of Paine's *Rights of Man*, published in February, had an enormous sale, not only inspiring many British at home and abroad but stimulating many statements by the popular societies in Britain, though these made "very little direct reference to France" and expressed "much abhorrence of levelling and violence," the specter of "an agrarian law" or socialism, which also haunted most French bourgeois revolutionaries. In England Paine's ideas had alarmed the Whigs enough to inspire them to form in April a society of "Friends of the People" to combat Painite "reformism." "Paine became the touchstone; this was what marked off the Friends from what they all too typically called 'Horne Tooke's people.'"[2]

The *Rights of Man* did inspire many new societies, which clustered around Tooke's Society for Constitutional Information. And this brought new life to the SCI. "Losing old members wholesale, it gained new, more radical ones, some of whom were to play a part in the popular societies—men like Thomas Holcroft . . . ." The membership of the London Corresponding Society also jumped to a couple of hundred in April, but then leveled off. The French Revolution was "an energising myth," but "it stood at some distance from the British popular movement." Then suddenly "that distance abruptly disappeared." In late September "men began to pour into the divisions. Throughout October and November the society was literally in almost continuous tumult."[3]

> During November, said Hardy years later, 300–400 signed on every week. This could be an old man's fancy, but in fact, a well-informed spy reported 26 "societies" packed to the doors on 24 November (the LCS recorded 27 divisions on 27 November) and said that 350 had joined in the past week . . . .
> Moreover what was happening in London was happening in every society which was unmistakably "popular," precisely at that moment when "respectable" sympa-

2. Williams, *Artisans and Sans-culottes*, 58.
3. Ibid., 67–71, for this and the next three paragraphs.

thisers were falling away in droves. This was the point of breakthrough. For the British popular movement, the French Revolution which counted was that of 10 August 1792. . . . First came Paine with . . . a fundamental challenge to a country "with no constitution." Then came 10 August, a French Convention and a Republic based on manhood suffrage, with a sans-culotte as its most vivid image . . . .

To the head of the movement, displacing the SCI, swept the London Corresponding Society, Burke's "Mother of all Mischief." Its constitution was almost *Rousseauist* in its direct democracy and unlimited numbers, its penny weekly subscription, local division, its members' right to recall delegates and to ratify committee decisions. Members took it seriously . . . .

Oswald and Stone and Christie and other British radicals in Paris must have felt right in the midst of this upsurge, for an increase in the numbers and the commitment of British visitors was a part of the same breakthrough. A few had come over at each stage of the Revolution, to watch the excitement or share in it. But Paine and Frost this September were the crest of a large wave. By November 1792 there were in Paris enough English republicans—a suitable term for the common spirit among them—to form themselves into a British Club with, in Cercle Social language, a directory, in which John Oswald served at times as secretary. And we must not suppose (as my focus may have suggested) that in his preparation of the Jacobin international manifesto of 30 September (3 October) Oswald was acting only with Frenchmen. By this time he was in the thick of British-French collaboration. Now perhaps more than at any other time the idea of a confederation of free peoples encircling the earth seemed within reach. And even the use of military force, directed of course only against tyrants, required the joint efforts of clearheaded organizers of governmental power and thousands of willing volunteers who were becoming trained tacticians. Paine would help write a republican Constitution. Maxwell would offer material and personal military assistance. Paine would also cooperate with the war office to supply French assistance for an insurrection in Dublin, and Maxwell would vote and sign the group manifesto of the British Club. Oswald was now officially drilling volunteers, and probably instructing other drillmasters. He could also find time to introduce Dr. William Maxwell to Minister of War Servan, in late August.

Maxwell, a friend of Horne Tooke, was delegated to Paris by the Society for Constitutional Information and the London Corresponding Society. Obtaining an interview with Servan, he offered to equip a company of sharpshooters with rifle-bored guns—as he explained later in a letter to Servan's successor Pache, 7 November:[4]

4. Goodwin, *The Friends of Liberty*, 342, note 153. Goodwin (21) puts Maxwell and Oswald in a list of "militant enthusiasts prepared to dabble in treason in collusion with the French," which includes Paine, Barlow, Fitzgerald, Duckett, Madgett, and Muir. He is unaware of Lichtenberger's long essay of 1897 on Oswald and cites only his brief note in the *Revue encyclopédique* of 1896, mistaking it for "a rehash of the article in the *Dictionary of National Biography*" (1882), upon which Goodwin himself seems to rely.

Servan had agreed and promised to give Maxwell command of the company, on condition that payment for the rifles should be deferred till the end of the war. In the same interview Maxwell had also suggested the utility of a formation of commando-type troops, equipped with pikes, daggers and small shields. One in ten could be given light sporting guns to provide the skirmishers with fire cover, while the daggers were intended for hand-to-hand combat at close quarters. Such improvised irregular forces could, Maxwell contended, operate with advantage "in the rain, in the dark, or when disorder had spread to the enemy ranks." Each man should carry a blanket which could be used with a pike to form a tent, while ship's biscuits would provide the necessary iron rations.

Daggers were suspect as aristocratic weapons in Paris, but Maxwell returned to England "to negotiate in Birmingham for the supply of pikes, guns and daggers."[5] By 21 September the mayor of Birmingham was reporting to the Home Office that swordmaking firms in the town had supplied Maxwell with patterns for daggers at a price of 22s. per dozen. To raise the cash for this venture, Maxwell announced the public meeting at his London house in Great Portland Street, for 12 September, about which Oswald exhorted the Jacobin Club on the 30th, as we have seen.

Dancing upon a Volcano

The British in Paris whose revolutionary sumpathies led them to club together in the Year One of the Republic ranged widely in commitment, from military involvement to amateur or official spying. (Among those who had to stay at home but expressed their sympathy concretely was Robert Burns, who tried to send cannon.)[6] Serious discussions in the well-known salons of Helen Maria Williams (and her lover, John Hurford Stone) and of whiggish Parisians such as Lavoisier and Manon Roland are seldom more than sketchily reported; knowing that Watt and Oswald visited them tells us little of what they talked about. But when a British group formally organized themselves in November as "The Friends of the Rights of Man associated at Paris," informally the "British Club," they left a fair amount of evidence of their views—though rather little of their intentions. Oswald's public declaration in February 1793 that a group of French Jacobins had been planning an invasion of England in October implies that there were British among them.

5. For an extensive and fascinating documentation of Maxwell's efforts to send arms to the French, see Thornton, *William Maxwell to Robert Burns*, passim.
6. "The poet Burns (February 1792) sent some guns, the equipment of a smuggling vessel which he had helped to capture, and had bought at the auction; but both letter and guns were stopped at Dover. Burns was in danger of dismissal from the Excise for this, but escaped with a reprimand" (Alger, *Englishmen*, 51). For a sympathetic account of Burns's revolutionary sympathies, and of the role of his "most intimate friend" Dr. William Maxwell during his last years, see Thornton, *Maxwell to Burns*, chapters 6 and 7.

British spy reports of September and October, however, focus on what may have seemed to many a more serious threat: books and pamphlets that would spread the terrifying concept of egalitarian democracy. A letter (misdated 4 September, since it deals with October events) from spy-watcher James Bland Burgess at Whitehall to Lord Auckland, ambassador to Holland, names some of Oswald's compatriots and is evidently a digest of several spy reports from the storm center:

> Tom Paine is at Paris and has just been appointed to some post in the executive government [the Constitution Committee, formed October 11]. Dr Priestley is also there [not true], and is looked upon as the great adviser to the present ministers, being consulted by them on all occasions[!] There are also 8 or 10 other English and Scotch who work with the Jacobins and in great measure conduct their present manoeuvres. I understand these gentlemen at present are employed in writing a justification of democracy and an invective against monarchy which is to be printed at Paris, and dispersed through England and Ireland. The names of some of them are Watts and Wilson, of Manchester; Oswald, a Scotsman; Stone, an Englishman, and Mackintosh who wrote against Burke.[7]

The spies had got some of the right names—though Priestley and Mackintosh were, in a sense, merely names in the citizenship proposals of August and September.[8] But what were these advisers to the Jacobins preparing to publish? The Oswaldian manifesto justifying the Revolution doubtless occupied several such gentlemen, but actually the work that was being printed in English—and advertised in the *Chronique du mois* for August and September—was the revised "Third Edition" of John Oswald's *Review of the Constitution of Great Britain*, "printed at the English press by Gillet" (an associate of J. H. Stone, who later would use the "English Press" rubric for a shop of his own).[9] Indeed, Oswald's book seems the only likely project these gentlemen were concerned in

---

7. Auckland, *Correspondence*, 2:207–8.

8. Wilson was "Captain Wilson, a half-pay officer, perhaps the Scotchman who ultimately married Wolfe Tone's widow." He "offered a seven-barrelled gun, all the barrels of which could be discharged simultaneously" (Alger, *Englishmen*, 51).

9. Oswald's *Government of the People* bears the imprint "Paris: printed at the English Press, no 1412, rue Notre Dame des Champs" and must have been printed by 4 March 1793, when Burke quoted it in the House of Commons. And the English version of his *Review of the Constitution* is imprinted "Paris, printed at the English Press by Gillet." Yet Gillet remained in London (see letters of 1793 and 1794 in *State Trials*, 25:1212, 1223, etc.); and Stone seems to have been only setting up a Paris press in December 1793 (1212), consulting Gillet in London about his foreman, etc. Madeleine B. Stern ("The English Press in Paris," 316) deduces that Stone's first "English Press" book printed in Paris was Joel Barlow's *Vision of Columbus*, published in July 1793. Allusions, in Stone's correspondence with his brother, to the cheaper cost of shipping unbound sheets (see *State Trials*, 25:1210) may afford a clue. Gillet, in London, can have printed either or both of Oswald's books in London and shipped them unbound to Paris. There the title pages may have been printed and added. We gather from the correspondence that only the outbreak of war compelled Stone to move his printing operations to Paris. Stern remarks, "Even the location where John Hurford Stone established his English Press is mysterious"; the addresses she does find do not include that on the title page of *Government of the People*.

printing for dispersal "through England and Ireland," the zones of potential revolution, during this autumn. It may even be that some of the summarized spy reports did specify both the title and the author's name, thus lighting the fuse that fired Burke's outcry in Parliament the following March against the dissemination by John Oswald of the doctrine of "democracy" and liberation from "the yoke of property." By that time, however, Burke would have been alarmed to find these ideas presented still more uncompromisingly in Oswald's sequel, *The Government of the People*, published in January 1793, probably with benefit of criticism from fellow conspirators.

Another person involved in the printing scheme of October 1792, as I read the evidence, was Eleazer Oswald, whose search in London for certain special types, for the title page perhaps, was reported in a memorandum dated 22 October by an informer named Charles Ross, who had gained the mistaken confidence of Paine's friend Rickman: "Memorandum—I have been inform'd by Mr. Rickman that Colonel Oswald / late of the American Army / was a Bookseller & Printer at a Town in or near Philadelphia, also Editor of a Paper—when in London, a few weeks since, he purchased new Types—I cannot learn whether he is the Author of any Publication.—"[10]

Perhaps this report came too late for Burgess's summary, or perhaps he saw no connection. But let us return to the reasons for the tremendous urgency felt by the British friends of the French revolutionaries at this moment.

It has been difficult for British historians to imagine that there could have been any honest British citizens whose enthusiasm or even sympathy for the French Revolution had not been dashed irrevocably by the September Massacres—so shocking, so outrageous, and so unwise, when viewed at a distance of time or place. To sympathizers close to the scene, however, here was reassuring evidence that there were bold citizens in Paris who would respond with unhesitating force to anything that smelled of counterrevolution. John Oswald's manifesto explains the violence as a panic response by the Parisians to imminent invasion and a suspected royalist uprising, when "our men" were out of the city fighting the Austrians for liberty or death. The Muirhead anecdote of Watt as a young enthusiast, who "foresaw he must in future" deplore revolutionary violence, nicely illustrates the historical biographer's succumbing to revisionism, since we have a carefully discriminated record of Watt's actual feelings at the time. Having witnessed some of the massacre of prisoners that had begun 2 September, he wrote to his father on the 5th describing the particularly horrid treatment of the Princess de Lamballe, dragged naked through the streets and her head "stuck upon a Pike . . . and shown to the King & Queen, who are in hourly expectation of the same fate." And his comment was, "I am filled with involuntary horror at the scenes which pass before me and wish they could have been avoided, but at the same time I allow the absolute necessity of

10. PRO TS 11 965/3510 A 2, discovered by Nicholas Roe.

them. In some instances the vengeance of the people has been savage & inhuman." [11] On that same day the armed citizens who had gone out to fight the Austrians for liberty or death had outfought them at Verdun (by superior artillery fire, not pikes), and by the 20th the balance of the world had changed. Cheering news came to Paris that the fighting was nearly over. By November a future of peace, if not relaxation, seemed assured. Here Carlyle succeeds, in language culled from the contemporary record, in being extremely faithful to what we now call the "perception" of what was happening, to the enthusiasm that inspired the British in Paris to call for a celebration:

> The Sixth of November 1792 was a great day for the Republic; outwardly, over the Frontiers; inwardly, in the *Salle de Manège* [meeting hall of the Convention].
> Outwardly: for Dumouriez, overrunning the Netherlands, did, on that day, come in contact with Saxe-Teschen and the Austrians; and Dumouriez wide-winged, they wide-winged; at and around the village of Jemappes, near Mons. And fire-hail is whistling far and wide there, the great guns playing, and the small; so many green Heights getting fringed and maned with red Fire. And Dumouriez is swept back on this wing, and swept back on that, and is like to be swept back utterly; when he rushes up in person, the prompt Polymetis; speaks a prompt word or two; and then, with clear tenor-pipe, "uplifts the Hymn of the Marseillese, *entonna la Marsellaise*," ten-thousand tenor or bass pipes joining; or say, some Forty-thousand in all; for every heart leaps at the sound; and so with rhythmic march-melody, waxing ever quicker, to double and to treble quick, they rally, they advance, they rush, death-defying, man-devouring; carry batteries, redoutes, whatsoever is to be carried; and, like the fire-whirlwind, sweep all manner of Austrians from the scene of action. Thus, through the hands of Dumouriez, may Rouget de Lille . . . be said to have gained . . . a Victory of Jemappes; and conquered the Low Countries. [12]

When the news of victory reached the Hall of the National Convention, a committee was reporting on "the Crimes of Louis." When it reached the British living in Paris, they issued a call for a celebration on Sunday the 18th at White's Hotel. There they sang, danced, drank toasts—and signed a manifesto of solidarity to be read to the Convention. [13] This British manifesto can be recognized as a response by the fraternal nations to the Oswaldian Jacobin manifesto of 3 October. By a coincidence of timing, however, when it was made public it appeared to be an immediate answer, by those assembled at White's, to a De-

---

11. Muirhead's reshaping gives a further twist to the tale (see above, p. 155) by putting Watt's supposed wrestling match with Robespierre just after 10 August—not even waiting for the September massacres—with this climax: "On returning home, having learned, by sure intelligence from one deep in the secrets of his dangerous foe, that his life was no longer safe for a day, he instantly quitted Paris, without even a passport." Alas for veracity: Watt did not leave Paris until 7 October; he was still praising Robespierre and others to his father on 12 September; when he did leave Paris to visit Italy, he asked his father to keep the journey secret, apparently from fear of royalist persecution in Naples (Robinson, "An English Jacobin," 351–53; Muirhead, *Life of Watt*, 479–80).
12. *FR*, 538–39.
13. On the 28th, as it happened.

cree issued to the world by the Convention on Monday, 19 November, offering brotherhood and assistance to all peoples seeking freedom.

The toasts were not fourteen (the French magic number) but thirteen (the American),[14] though there were meant to be fourteen. I number them for convenience:

(1) The French Republic, founded on the rights of man; (2) the French armies, and the destruction of tyrants and tyranny; (3) the National Convention; (4) *the coming Convention of England and Ireland* [my italics]; (5) the union of France, Great Britain, and Belgium, and may neighbouring nations join in the same sentiments; (6) the Republic of Men, accompanied by an English song to the air of the "Marseillaise," composed by an English lady (probably Helen Maria Williams); (7) the dissolution of the Germanic Circle[15] and may their inhabitants be free; (8) abolition of hereditary titles throughout the world (proposed by Lord Edward Fitzgerald and Sir R. Smyth); (9) Lord E. Fitzgerald and Sir R. Smyth; (10) Thomas Paine, and the new way of making good books known by royal proclamations and by prosecuting the authors in the King's Bench; (11) the Women of Great Britain, particularly those who have distinguished themselves by their writings in favour of the French revolution, Mrs. (Charlotte) Smith and Miss H. M. Williams; (12) the Women of France, especially those who have had the courage to take up arms to defend the cause of liberty, *citoyennes* Fernig, Anselm, &c [this would have to include Etta Palm and Théroigne]; and (13) Universal Peace, based on universal liberty.[16]

The fourth toast was followed by a singing of the "Marseillaise," doubtless arousing a proper do-or-die spirit for the fifth. The missing fourteenth toast, canceled by agreement among the directors, would produce a political sensation when it was disclosed; we shall come to it later.[17]

The most formal action of the banquet at White's Hotel was the signing of an address to the National Convention by fifty British citizens resident in Paris, chosen by votes of the whole group. (Alger guesses there were a hundred or

---

14. Consider the London gentleman who said "he hoped to see the 13 Stripes wave in every England harbour, from a federal union; nay, be quartered by our posterity, if we were so obstinately foolish, as not to do it ourselves, on the British ensign." These fighting, federational words were widely supported in a Westminster Forum debate—in April 1780; the sentiment was very much alive in 1792 (*Short History of the Westminster Forum*, 2:181).

15. Note the circle image.

16. Text in *Patriote françois*, 21 November 1792, as translated in Alger, *Paris in 1789–94*, 326.

17. In Moore's *Life of Fitzgerald* (p. 88, 1855 edition) the "announcement" said to have "made its appearance in the papers of Paris and London" reports only four of the toasts, in rather different language and interesting for the further detail: (our no. 2:) "The armies of France: may the example of its citizen soldiers be followed by all enslaved countries, till tyrants and tyranny be extinct"; (no. 6:) "by Sir R. Smith and Lord E. Fitzgerald . . . : 'May the patriotic airs of the German Legion [i.e., of the French army] (Ça Ira, the Carmagnole, Marseillaise March, &c) soon become the favourite music of every army, and may the soldier and the citizen join in the chorus'"; (no. 8:) "Sir Robert Smith and Lord E. Fitzgerald renounced their titles; and a toast proposed by the former was drank:—'The speedy abolition of all hereditary titles and feudal distinctions'"; (not on our list:) "General Dillon proposed 'The people of Ireland; and may government profit by the example of France, and Reform prevent Revolution.'"

more, Goodwin about eighty.) [18] Among those not nominated we are certain of the presence of Paine, not chosen since he was a member of the Convention being addressed, Helen Maria Williams, who sang, and Henry Redhead Yorke. Almost certainly Sampson Perry was there, and Thomas Christie, possibly William Wordsworth, but not Mary Wollstonecraft (who arrived in Paris too late). Here is a report by the British spy Capt. George Monro, summarized by Goodwin: [19]

> Dumouriez's entry into Brussels on 14 November . . . was celebrated on Sunday 18 November at White's Hotel in Paris by a dinner attended by about eighty English, Irish and Scottish residents, who appear to have held advanced democratic or republican views. Captain George Monro, a Scottish spy in the pay of the English government who arrived in the French capital on the following day, reported that the moving spirits in this heterogeneous group of enthusiasts were a future leader of the United Irishmen—Lord Edward Fitzgerald, a disgruntled former MP for Cholchester—Sir Robert Smyth,[20] and J. H. Stone, now settled in Paris as a manufacturer and printer. Dr. Maxwell, who had brought with him a first consignment of "rifle-barrelled guns" from Birmingham, was also present. The toasts drunk at this dinner were chivalrous, egalitarian and treasonable . . . .

Monro reported that Maxwell, "a man of violent principles," was still negotiating with the war minister for the command of a company in the French service, but Monro had not apparently learned that among the several French officers and deputies at the banquet was the Irish general Arthur Dillon, of the French war office, in contact with Stone and Paine and, probably, Oswald. In January Oswald would advocate an invasion of London, in confidence to the war office—probably the proposal Redhead Yorke said Oswald had communicated to the French government. Oswald and Dillon were agreed on the figure of sixty thousand troops.[21]

The address as signed and presented to the National Convention is extant, with its fifty signatures (those of J. H. Stone and Robert May O'Reilly repeated below as president and secretary, respectively), including that of Frost, who missed the meeting but reached Paris in time to assist Barlow in the presenta-

18. Alger's conjecture is the more credible. Goodwin seems, at times, influenced by his bias against the idea that any true English could have been such "militant enthusiasts prepared to dabble [*sic*] in treason in collusion with the French on the eve of, and even after the outbreak of war." He notes, "Most of these 'traitors' had American, Irish or Scottish associations, e.g. Paine, Joel Barlow, John Oswald, Lord Edward Fitzgerald, William Duckett, Nicolas Madgett, Dr. Maxwell and Thomas Muir. Most of them at one time or another found political refuge in Paris" (21 and note). (We have noted that he regards Oswald as an "exile"—as he has been from British history.) Of the fifty names on the English Club document, more than half seem to be English.

19. Goodwin, *The Friends of Liberty*, 249; Alger, *Paris in 1789–94*, 325; Alger, "English Eyewitnesses," 164—conjectural about Perry, who "arrived in Paris just in time." Wordsworth's presence is only a bare possibility; the date of his leaving for London is between mid-November and mid-December.

20. Smyth, on ceasing to represent Colchester in 1790, had settled in Paris as a banker.

21. See below, p. 260, item 4.

tion.[22] Oswald and Stone were almost certainly the main movers of the club, though Stone pretended, for the record in England, that he had not let himself be involved.[23]

At least a dozen of the other signers will appear or at least be mentioned in this tale of Oswald. The tactics and strategy of the directory or steering committee can be made out clearly at times, but even among the better known of the other members it is seldom clear how serious or how concerted were the actions which they talked about or engaged in. Their communications with ministers of war and eminent politicians, in France and Britain, are often ambiguous or ambiguously reported, and they seem not always to have been candid with one another.

To take a relatively easy example, because we know a good deal about the persons involved: when Paine and Fitzgerald by careful arrangement held a cryptic conference within a merry social routine (see Third Interchapter, 26 October), were they making sober plans for insurrection or were their words to each other straws in uncertain winds—or was their main concern the need to find by some kind of straw poll of "sources" just how the winds blew? Possibly all of the above, plus subliminal communication of deep doubts, desperation, overriding enthusiasm?

The fraternal sympathies expressed in the address contain no mysteries, but the immediate occasion for the banquet, the celebration of French victories climaxing in the recent battle of Jemappes, with the conquest of all Belgium, introduced a drumbeat into their thinking. Lefebvre's summary is apt:

> In France and through Europe this continuation of French success had a profound effect. Jemappes, echoing Valmy, was a true revolutionary victory; it had been won in an open attack without astute manoeuvres and by the sans-culottes, who rushed the enemy to the martial strains of the *Marseillaise* and the *Carmagnole*, swamping the adversary with sheer force of numbers. Their achievement gave birth to the ideas of mass levy and a popular war which required neither military science nor formal organization.[24]

Savoy, now to be represented by the Anglo-American Barlow, had been liberated; Belgium too. What of Ireland and Scotland—and Wales—and England!?

22. See the alphabetical list of signatures in Appendix E below.

23. Writing to his brother William in London, who would not see his signatures on the document, Stone reported thus, on the eve of the presentation (*State Trials*, cols. 1299, 1305): "*Paris, Nov. 26th, 1792.* Here's Frost & ---- [Barlow] come over with an address; I have taken care to inform the leaders with the leading features of these gentlemen. I was appointed to present one myself to-morrow, but I shall decline it from a variety of motives. I have prevented Fox and Sheridan's citizenship, and my own, and I hope every one's else at this time." "*Paris, Nov. 27th, 1792.* I believe that I mentioned to you that we had a dinner on Sunday se'nnight to celebrate the French victories, and that an address was to be presented to the assembly: that is to be done this morning: I was chosen president and orator, but I have declined both." His leaving his signature, as president, on the document, for the benefit of the Convention who would receive it, allowed him to have it both ways.

24. *The Coming of the French Revolution, 1789,* 261.

"Let us hope," the address declares, "that the victorious troops of liberty will lay down their arms only when there are no more tyrants or slaves," and expresses impatience "to see the happy moment of this great change, in the hope that it will no sooner arrive than we shall see the formation of a close union between the French republic and the English, Scotch, and Irish nations." Confidence is also expressed in the belief that "the great majority of our countrymen" would manifest the same sentiments "if public opinion were consulted, as it ought to be, in a national convention."

It was an Irishman, John Sheares, signing beside his quiet brother Henry, who had proposed this address; later in an English tavern they would express confidence in the early downfall of King George—and escape to Dublin to play a tragic role in the Irish movement. The dramatic use of the term *national convention*, signifying an anti-Parliament and implying that somehow the British may simply leap into the position the French are now in (with their King on his way to the guillotine), is more than a mere courtesy of reference to the National Convention to whom the address is presented. The SCI address read by Barlow at the same time even declares that "it will not be extraordinary if, in a short time, addresses of congratulation will be sent to a National Convention of England."[25] There is perhaps more courtesy than confidence, though, in President Grégoire's reply, that "The defenders of our liberty will one day become the defenders of your own.—The shades of Pym, of Sidney, hover over your heads" and that the people of France will soon be congratulating "the National Convention of Great Britain." Barlow's announcement that the London society is now sending footwear diverts attention from Maxwell's provocative offer of British guns and daggers; yet this too is equipment for continuing warfare: a thousand pairs of shoes for the soldiers of France have already arrived at Calais, and a thousand a week are promised for about six weeks.[26]

The president is ordered to write to the London society with the Convention's unanimous greetings (times have changed since Oswald's struggle in the Jacobin Club), and then Guy Kersaint, of the *Chronique* fourteen, urges encouragement to those British who have extended the fight against tyranny to a concern for the slavery of the blacks and the improvement of agriculture. To this effort the French should lend assistance, and his motion is to be sent to jog the committees concerned with commerce. Léonard Bourdon, the schoolmaster, thinks that the best response to these British advances will be to get on with the trial of Louis. (The incriminating evidence found on 20 November when the King's notorious iron chest was opened has given this question a push off dead center, and everybody has a swift idea how to proceed—evening meetings for one thing, stipulation of guilt rather than trial, for another. The discussion rolls on.)

25. *Arch Parl*, 53:636.
26. Goodwin, *The Friends of Liberty*, 510–12.

The Canceled Toast

Among the fifty nominated to sign the address, Oswald stood modestly thirty-fourth in line. In a long news report in the *Manchester Herald*, 1 December, about the "ENGLISH CIVIC FEAST at PARIS—November 18," however, the fifteen names singled out as newsworthy begin with Thomas Paine, Lieut. Col. Oswald, H. J. Stone, Robert Merry, Edward Fitzgerald—a fairly accurate list of the central revolutionary committee.

Another indicator of Oswald's importance on the committee was given prominence in the publicity about the canceled toast, which was to have hailed "The Patriots of England, especially those who have distinguished themselves by their writings and speeches in propagating the doctrines of the French Revolution, Fox, Sheridan, Cooper, Barlow, Tooke, and Mackintosh." A mixture of three Whigs and two radicals, which "was evidently objected to and omitted," notes Alger, "for when Burke in the House of Commons twitted Fox and Sheridan with having been toasted at this dinner, Sheridan referred him to a letter in which Oswald said: "We did not drink those toasts, nor could we do so without falling into a signal absurdity. Met to celebrate the rapid progress of the eternal principles of liberty and equality, how could we think of cringing to the heads or tools of any party? How could we pronounce the names of Fox, Sheridan, and Mackintosh?"

Oswald's letter had appeared five days after the banquet, in Brissot's *Patriote*. But the exchange between Burke and Sheridan took place the following 12 February, in the heat of the decisive debate "on the King's Message respecting the Declaration of War with France." Burke, reading an account of the address and banquet in the *Moniteur*, reacted as though Fox and his friends, being toasted and toasting, were accepting the embrace of regicides and fattening themselves on wine and food in Paris, "like swine to be killed to-morrow, and to become the easier prey to our enemies."[27]

In reply, Sheridan accused Burke of heating and misleading the House "by a spirit of vengeance and quixotism," since Burke knew that the French were undertaking the war "upon principles, and for purposes diametrically opposite to" his allegations. As an example of Burke's distortion of evidence, Sheridan cited his handling of the address and toasts "of an idle dinner of English and others, at White's in Paris." Here was a man "who ransacked every corner of every French paper for any thing that would make for his purpose," but had somehow "overlooked a formal contradiction of such toasts having been given, inserted by authority in the *Patriote françois*." Here, Sheridan continued, Burke was trying to insinuate that he and Fox were, "in Paris at least, considered as republicans; while the actual reason given for not drinking their healths

27. *Parl Hist*, 30:378ff.; 387–94.

was, that, though friends to the reform of abuses, they were considered as expressly against all idea of revolution in England, and known to be attached to the form of the existing constitution."

As Sheridan insinuated, it suited Burke's purpose not to have noticed the letter of correction which Sheridan quoted from the *Patriote* of 26 November, but it is worth our scrutiny. For one thing, it documents Oswald's secretarial status in the club; it is signed "Oswald" and opens and closes with the formal assertion that "I am authorized by the society of English, Scottish and Irish meeting at White's hotel" to rectify an error in papers of 21 November. And it tells us that a business meeting, at which this letter to the editor was decided upon, was held at White's on 23 November.

Taken as a statement of Oswald's own views (agreed to by the club and not necessarily formulated by him), it is consistent in retaining no sympathy for the Foxite Whigs, whose campaign against French intercourse he had publicized in his Grub-Street days. Taken as a proclamation by the British in Paris, it insists that reform can be no substitute for "revolution in England." But considered in the well-documented context of John Stone's thoughts and actions at the time, this "Oswald" letter indicates a more complicated purpose or function. Stone had presided at the White's Hotel meeting of the 20th, and he had been "chosen president, orator, &c" (he wrote his brother), that is, to be the official to present and read the Address to the Assembly. But then he declined both, for reasons his brother would understand.[28] Oswald's signature on this public letter of correction served to relieve Stone from public commitment. For Stone at this very time was in communication with Sheridan—and with Brissot. In August and September, when he had criticized the list of honorary citizens and made his own additional recommendations, Stone had shared the general feeling that this ritual bestowing was in the spirit of reconciliation of all nations, that could lead to a universal fraternity of Mankind: Hands across the Channel. But by November, following the declarations and proclamations that in effect reasserted national distinctions, he appears to have regarded French citizenship as a designation harmful to the cause in England—and to his own reliability as a forecaster of developments. The reform Whigs and any other prominent British political figures who he hoped might lead Britain into friendship, rather than war, with France would be isolated from their constituencies by the mounting zenophobia. Hence Stone busily argued with Sheridan against accepting French citizenship, and in Paris he urged Brissot to withdraw British names proposed now or earlier but not yet acted upon. Thus, before the British Club address was made public, he was pleased to have "prevented Fox and Sheridan's citizenship, and my own," as he told his brother, "and I hope everyone else's"—including Oswald's presumably.[29]

28. *State Trials*, 25:1305.
29. Woodward, *Un adherente Anglais*, 70 and notes 17–22. See also Alger, *Englishmen*, 64. And see *State Trials* cited above.

And Brissot did act upon Stone's suggestion. We do not know what reasons were urged, but the reasons Stone gave Sheridan (and Mackintosh) were devious. A plausible one was political: that the distinction would only give a handle to the Tories. But Stone reinforced that with sycophantic ad hominem arguments, that "obscure and vulgar men and scoundrels" having been given honorary citizenship, it was beneath the dignity of Fox or Sheridan to accept it. The "scoundrels" were presumably those he had disapproved of in August, Wilberforce, David Williams, and Clarkson. At the present stage of negotiations, with war more probable than peace, Stone would have seen Williams as overly committed to the cause of reconciliation and absurdly hostile to the alternative prospect of revolutionary war, which the British Club activists saw approaching rapidly.[30]

Stone, in short, was struggling to preserve the liberal Whigs' reputations for the future, when at a critical point in the English revolution they must emerge as *British* citizens to clasp hands with the *French*. On the French side of the Channel, meanwhile, Stone made every effort to encourage the French to launch their invasion of England *only* when times were auspicious.

We know about these matters in considerable detail from the record of the 1796 trial of William Stone in London, in which Hurford Stone's letters from Paris are quoted extensively. With staunch Whig support he was acquitted of the charge of attempting to destroy the King and giving counsel to the Enemy.[31] Sheridan and other Whigs in the Stones' defense demonstrated convincingly that the counsel given France was *against* invading England, upon which Erskine based a successful plea that to advise an enemy against invading was not to act against the king.

One must not underestimate the character of Stone, however, warns Woodward,[32] and the warning must apply to our estimation of his importance in Oswald's career. Younger than Oswald, born in Tiverton, Devonshire, he became a coal merchant in London and later a printer in Paris. Early a member of Price's congregation, he was involved in Revolution Society affairs. According to family history he was present at the capture of the Bastille. In 1790 he chaired the dinner held by the London Corresponding Society to entertain two delegates from Nantes—who described him as "a young man well acquainted with the languages and literature of all European nations, and himself a literary man."[33] By 1792 he was shuttling between capitals with welcome advice for the ears of decisionmakers—supplemented by a good deal of correspondence in both directions when spies were close—which eventuated in trials in both countries.

30. Oswald cannot have shared or liked Stone's contempt for Williams, a friend Oswald had been proud to announce in the *Chronique du mois* prospectus.

31. More exactly, "treacherously conspiring with his brother, John Hurford Stone, now in France, to destroy the life of the King and to raise a rebellion in his realms." *State Trials*, 25: 1155–1438. Summary in Alger, *Paris in 1789–94*, 66.

32. *Un adherente Anglais*, 69.

33. Alger, *Paris in 1789–94*, 356.

Stone's early acquaintance with Brissot in London could have included some association with Oswald. Stone was apparently superb in ballrooms and drawing rooms. Whether he proposed them or not, the first several toasts at White's Hotel suited his combining of military power with the embrace of nations: To the French armies and the destruction of tyrants; To the coming convention of Britain and Ireland; To the union of France, Great Britain, and Belgium. And Stone would have beamed during other toasts: To the Women of Britain whose writings support the Revolution; To the Women of France who have taken to arms in defense of it. One of these women, Helen Maria Williams, quickly attached herself to Stone, in a most amicable and effectual entente.

Stone was also a complete believer in the Revolution as an opener of the wealth of nations to an enterprising entrepreneur. To Pitt and company the Revolution was a fatal illness in the military power of a competitor nation that afforded a golden opportunity for the British to seize sugar islands and Channel ports, and perhaps obtain a permanent grip on France itself. Stone saw good investment possibilities, first in the decline of property values (one could buy cheap in France); then in expanding business opportunities. The printing business in Paris could offset the decline of the coal business in London. He saw France, because of its espousal of liberal democracy, as the ultimate winner. At times the only chance seemed to be an armistice of conciliation; at others, the French seemed able to liberate Britain, whereupon its buyers and sellers would form a common market with all Europeans and finally all peoples of the world. The coming sunrise he could always see somewhere: what comfort and cheer his words brought to Brissot or Sheridan or the Dutch ambassador! No wonder the Whigs flocked to his brother's legal defense with a firm conviction that the Stones' aims had always been to do the world more good.[34]

Misinformation and Disinformation

With historical hindsight it is easy to conclude that those in France or England who congratulated each other on the close approach of a union of free, peaceful nations were unrealistic, i.e., blind or stupid, or at least badly misinformed. Future historians may easily draw similar conclusions about the peace movements of the present. The air, indeed, was full of misinformation—and anxiety about it. In the White's Hotel address we may note particularly the confidence in majority British sentiment, combined with a need to have a poll of that opinion. Stone's attempts to keep informed of the state of the political weather were paralleled in the meetings of the guiding spirits of the British Club, who again and again decided (a) that a British revolution was inevitable, and (b) that Stone, or Eleazer Oswald, or Frost or Sheares—or Wordsworth?—

34. Wherever he is today, Stone must be smiling at the solemn debates over whether it was or was not a "bourgeois" revolution! He certainly was confident it would be.

should hurry back to London, or Dublin, and poll the societies and the statesmen.

It will put this problem into a neglected perspective if we examine in some detail the barrage of misinformation and what we today call disinformation that was instigated and organized in November 1792 by the British government, with the help of the Reeves Association. Its tactical purpose was to establish legal grounds for calling an emergency session of Parliament before the middle of December, but it had the powerful side effect of convincing many British and many French that an English revolution had already begun!

The Pitt cabinet's reason for calling an early session of Parliament was to obtain authorization for arming against France. In January, when the government seemed to have ruled out the possibility of war with France, Parliament had made the first of what was intended to be a series of budget cuts for the army and navy; by November, however, it was known that the army was being augmented and that barracks were being constructed in many cities—even though billeting soldiers in homes was a British tradition which guaranteed that the army would remain a thing of the people.[35] By the time the two houses of Parliament were convened, 13 December, such an atmosphere of alarm about sedition had been created that they were persuaded to vote approval of a warlike manifesto called the King's Speech, which authorized "a due provision" for "some augmentation of my naval and military force."[36]

To demonstrate that there was an emergency, the king had had to call out the county militias, which he did on 1 December on the grounds that the government had "discovered an infernal plot, planned by some foreigners," nicely vague and legally proper, who had already begun storming the Bank and the Tower, poisoning the Thames, and setting the city in flames. Within a week, the newspapers recognized these were false reports, but the pollution of the political atmosphere was real. An impressive summary of the "evidence" was circulated in a pamphlet which Bishop Herbert Marsh, writing in 1800 and completely credulous, quoted in colorful detail.[37] Marsh himself would not vouch for the "circumstances" but was convinced that the French Convention had

---

35. In a revolutionary situation, things worked out rather differently. The Third Amendment to the United States Constitution treats the home billeting of soldiers as an evil.

36. A similar maneuver had persuaded Parliament in December 1774 to vote preparations for war with the American Colonies. William Blake, in *America a Prophecy*, 1793 (canceled plates b & c), conflates the December sessions of 1774 and 1792, showing the king in "Angel form" weeping, dividing the House, and getting himself armed in "gold." See Erdman, "Blake and the Night Sky: Art against Armies."

37. Marsh, in his *History of the Politicks*, in 1800, had no difficulty interpreting all French political and military activity as having been aimed at invasion and all British public or private expressions of sympathy with the French, even advocacy of reform of the British Constitution, as invitations to French invasion. A contemporary purchaser of the copy of Marsh's book now in the Stony Brook University Library, however, wrote beside this passage: "This sounds more like humbug than anything I ever read," and, at other places, "Pish!" and "This sounds like a lot of fol-lol-de-rol!"

"co-operated in the plan to overturn the British Constitution." We may suppose that if this was believed for a week, by London editors, there were many in France, especially in the popular societies, and among the British and Irish resident in Paris, who were thus encouraged to believe in the insurrectionary potential of the London sans-culottes—and the Scottish, for on 11–13 December a Convention of the Associated Friends of the People was held in Edinburgh, attended by 180 delegates from 80 reform societies, including Colonel Macleod from the Constitutional Society.[38]

There was indeed a riot at that time, a counterrevolutionary one in Manchester by a Church-and-King mob who rioted for two days following a public meeting to preserve the Constitution against "incendiaries." So "enthusiastic" were these anti-incendiaries that "on the way home" they "attacked all the dissenters in the area, finally burning to the ground the homes of Thomas Cooper and Thomas Walker. James Watt was still on the Continent."[39]

Here are Marsh's excerpts from the contemporary pamphlet reporting what the king "knew" when he decided to declare an emergency:

The King of England knew the leaders, the agents, the societies, the correspondences, the emissaries, the periods of their meeting, their journeys, and their resolutions. He knew that the plan was laid to seize the Tower, to plunder the arsenal, to break open the prisons, to pillage the public buildings and the houses of the rich, and to cut off at one stroke the several branches of the constitution. His Majesty knew that the execution of the plan was fixed for Saturday, the first, or Monday the third of December: he saw likewise a model of the daggers with which the insurgents were to be armed, and this model was found in the hands of a Frenchman. He knew where twenty-thousand pounds of iron lay, in such a state of readiness, that in the space of six and thirty hours the whole could be forged into pikes. He knew what member of the National Convention complained, that the plot was not conducted with sufficient vigour; who wrote to one of the agents, that he did not work as he ought, and that he did not earn the money of the republic. His Majesty knew what other members of the French Convention formed a plan for the insurrection and the arming of the negroes, to ruin the English colonies, and to annihilate, whatever it might cost, the power of England. He knew what emissary, after remaining only four and twenty hours in London, set off for the Hague, with orders to revolutionize Holland. He knew what other emissary wrote to France in the middle of November, with assurances that the insurrection should soon break out, but wrote again in the middle of December, that all hopes of an insurrection were lost. His Majesty knew which of the emissaries warned his agents to take care, as the first attempt had failed, how they engaged in a second. He knew the number and the names of the French cannoniers, who being no longer of use in England, after the plot had failed, were ordered to embark for Ireland on Mon-

38. *State Trials*, 24:796. See also Thale, *Selections from the Papers of the LCS*, 327n, listing Norman Macleod's *Letters to the People of North Britain* among the tracts republished by the London Corresponding Society.
39. Werkmeister, *A Newspaper History*, 146. Of course the violent words and deeds of the mob rioting *against* suspected revolutionaries supplied further evidence of a revolutionary potential.

day, the 17th of December: he knew which of the leaders recalled this order, and sent them to France, whither he repaired also himself.[40]

It required only an escalation of disinformation to assert that (unnoticed by any of the citizens) the Bank and Tower *had* been stormed, à la the storming of the Bastille and, say, the Tuileries. The evidence adduced in Parliament, however, consisted of Lord Grenville's showing (see Third Interchapter) that more and more British addresses were reaching the French Convention (or the British spies).[41] The French, on the other side, were hearing of an elected Convention of Catholics in Ireland, and armed battalions. And the British who had rejoiced at the destruction of the Bastille could now hear the French alluding to the Tower of London as a similarly threatened emblem of tyranny.

In an atmosphere thus filled with real and imaginary messages, including the newspapers' gullible or planted reports of that invisible London insurrection, the British and Irish residing in Paris were inspired to further organization and propaganda, even to the extent of pasting up an Oswaldian placard dated "Paris, December 4" on *London* dead-walls—doubtless soon "known to his

---

40. *History of the Politicks*, 224–26. The pamphlet he quotes was apparently published in late 1792 or early 1793; Marsh finds it in a *Collection des Meilleurs Ouvrages qui ont été publiés pour la défense de Louis XVI* (Paris, 1793, 2:251–86). Pitt's disingenuous explanation to his cabinet survives in a Downing Street letter of 1 December to one of them, Lord Gower, the marquess of Stafford, which is a masterpiece of "words to the wise": "The *accounts* of the continued Industry of the Promoters of Mischief in all Parts, and the apparent necessity of sending *in case of* further Riots a greater Force to Scotland . . . have made us think it necessary to take the step of calling out some Part of the Militia . . . ." And then he explains the beauty part: "It is, I think, a *fortunate Circumstance* that the Measure obliges us, as the Law stands, to assemble Parliament within 14 days. . . . I have no doubt we shall obtain a very decided concurrence from Parliament . . . . The present Measure will, I flatter myself, immediately raise the spirits of the Friends of Peace and Order" (Browning, *The Despatches of Earl Gower*, 1:61; my italics). Ehrman, in what purports to be a thorough account of the negotiations and calculations of Pitt's ministry at this period (*The Younger Pitt*, 2:206–58), takes us no closer to Pitt's awareness of the considerations in this letter, which is not even mentioned, than the summary remark that, "as Pitt knew," the ministry "was on debatable ground in embodying militia without explicit proof of an insurrection" as "was required by law" (238). No hint that there was any misinformation about.

Another recent work, with a title that reflects the author's sympathies, *For King, Constitution, & Country: The English Loyalists and the French Revolution*, by Robert R. Dozier, represents Pitt's government as having "had no choice but to act as if the most alarming interpretations were valid," since there *were* rumors and "its intelligence-gathering resources" were inadequate (32–34). Neither Ehrman nor Dozier seems to have had the resources to obtain and read the full and judicious account of "The Insurrection Which Wasn't" and the effect on "The Convocation of Parliament," two quite detailed chapters in Werkmeister, *A Newspaper History*, 134–41, 142–51. The government, in short, is said by Dozier and Ehrman to have been justified in going to war with France—on the basis of false intelligence which its own "resources" had planted.

41. Sheridan's motion in March 1793 would be an attempt to correct the record, but the fact that war *had* now developed with revolutionary France served to harden the assumption, of politicians and editorial writers, that sedition *had* been abroad in London and Scotland in December. Macleod, after protesting Burke's exclusion of "the living mass of humanity" from the Constitution, utterly rejected the government's claim that there had been "insurrections" in Scotland. These "insurrections, which had been stated as the cause of the late extraordinary measures, were totally unknown to the fifteen judges of Scotland, till signified to them by the proclamation, which they could not believe, till confirmed by the debates in parliament" (*Parl Hist*, 30:555 [4 March 1793]).

Majesty."[42] The emphasis is upon communicating essential information, and I call it Oswaldian because the thinking has a Cercle Social quality—and because he took his secretarial duties seriously and is likely to have arranged for the printing (by Gillet in London perhaps):

> Friends of the Rights of Man associated at Paris, December 4, first year of the French Republic.
>
> We whose names are subscribed to this declaration, for the greater part natives of Great Britain and Ireland, and now resident in Paris, sensible of the duties we owe to our countrymen, as well as to the general cause of liberty and happiness through the world, have formed ourselves into a society for the express purpose of collecting political information and extending it to the people at large in the several nations to which we belong.
>
> We are happy that our temporary residence in this enlightened and regenerated capital enables us to become the organ of communicating knowledge on the most interesting subjects, of administering to the moral improvement and social happiness of a considerable portion of our fellow-men, and of undeceiving the minds of our countrymen, abused by the wretched calumnies of a wicked Administration who, in order to perpetuate the slavery of the English, have made it their business to stigmatise the glorious exertions of the French.
>
> We begin with an open and unequivocal declaration of the principles which animate our conduct, and precise definition of the object we mean to pursue, that no individual in any country may mistake our motives or be ignorant in what manner to address us. We declare that an equal Government, unmixed with any kind of exclusive privileges, conducted by the whole body of the people or by their agents, chosen at frequent periods and subject to their recall, is the only Government proper for man; that the British and Irish nations do not enjoy such a Government; that they cannot obtain it until a National Convention be chosen and assembled to lay its foundations on the basis of the Rights of Man; that to effect this great and indispensable object we will use all the means which reason, argument, and the communication of information can supply; that we will endeavour to remove all national prejudices which it has been the interest of tyrants to excite in order to separate and enslave the great family of Man; that we invite individuals and societies of every name and description in the above nations and elsewhere to a manly and unreserved correspondence with our society; and we pledge ourselves to them and to the universe that no composition or sacrifice extorted from the fears of expiring Oppression shall seduce or deter us from persevering with firmness and constancy in the discharge of the important duty we have undertaken.
>
> Here follow the signatures.

No *signed* copy survives, but the signers must have included Paine, Barlow, . . . Wordsworth? The language is impersonal, but all must have agreed to the sober emphasis on enlightenment. The alternative between a government conducted by the people or by their representatives indicates the gap in theory that divided the British and Irish in Paris, the gap in strategy being imposed by the fact, one would suppose, that the Irish already had their insurrectionary

42. British Library: Political Broadsides 648 C 26 (50).

battalion in Dublin, while it would require invading battalions from France to liberate London.[43]

Struggling among Themselves

Having met, with increasing seriousness, after the White's Hotel banquet of November, the British Club gave formal notice in the *Moniteur* of 7 January of its formation and its intention to meet twice a week, as apparently it had been doing.[44] We learn a good deal about these meetings from the fairly detailed, if often judgmental, reports of the spy, Captain Monro.

On 17 December Monro reported that "Mr. Frost has left his house [White's] and seldom makes his appearance. He is, however, one of the society"; also that "the party of conspirators" have definitely "formed themselves into a society." The poet Merry had presided at a meeting the day before—Monro forwarded a copy of Merry's speech to the British Foreign Office—and a Dr. Edwards had arrived to join Maxwell. But Paine was staying in the provinces, "ill or pretending to be so," and Stone had returned to England.[45]

Joining Maxwell may have meant joining him in the French army, or perhaps simply joining his English faction in the society, i.e., those focusing on England. On the 27th (on the other hand) Monro reported that "many of the party had become friends of royalty"—wanting a role kept for a king in the English system if not the French? Or simply opposing the execution of Louis (their more probable position)? But there were still many "who would stand at nothing to ruin their country"—i.e., still wanted a British revolution.[46] On the last day of the year Monro described the remnant as "beneath the notice of any one, struggling for consequence among themselves, jealous of one another, differing in opinion, and even insignificant in a body."

Alger summarizes further reports thus:

With few exceptions they were "heartily tired of politics and addresses [Oswald might have been of this opinion]. Tom Paine's fate [he was tried in London in absentia on 18 December and declared an outlaw] and the unanimity of the English [against France] has staggered the boldest of them, and they are now dwindling into nothing." On 11th January 1793 another address was advocated by Paine and Merry, but was

43. On 4 December Paine wrote to Lebrun enclosing a Dublin newspaper of the United Irishmen, asking him to name a day to dine. Lebrun wanted first to be sure of the state of Ireland; without money we can't do much there, "Pitt is so adroit" (Woodward, "Projets," 2).

44. "On the fifth of the month, the foreigners, for the most part English, Scottish, and Irish, residing in Paris, presented themselves to the secretariat of the Municipality and declared, as required by law, that they will meet together every Sunday and Tuesday, in the name of *Société des amis des Droits de l'Homme*, at the English Hotel of White, No. 7, passage of Petits-Peres" (*Moniteur*, 7 January 1793, 1, col. 4).

45. Alger, *Paris in 1789–94*, 330.

46. Ibid., 330; Alger, "English Eyewitnesses," 164–65.

so warmly opposed by Frost and Macdonald (Macdonnel) that "the dispute nearly ended in blows. I cannot tell how it ended, as things are kept very secret."

Henry Redhead Yorke tells us the particulars. The address invited the Convention to liberate enslaved England. He opposed it, and "we carried it"—that is to say, the address was rejected—"by a majority of one." It was, however, again brought forward, whereupon Yorke and Johnson drew up a remonstrance and seceded. This second address was presented to the Convention on 22nd January [the day after Louis's execution], but I have not found it in the National Archives.[47]

Alger proceeds to make a tally of the club membership at this time:

Thomas Muir, the Scotch advocate afterwards transported to Botany Bay [for his part in organizing a "National Convention" in Scotland in December], arrived in Paris on the 20th January 1793, and no doubt joined the club. . . . Sampson Perry, militia surgeon and journalist, who, to avoid a press prosecution, fled to Paris in December 1792, must also have belonged to the club. Paine, invited to the Hotel de Ville to dine with Petion, Dumouriez, Santerre, Condorcet, Brissot, Danton, Vergniaud, Sieyes, and others took Perry with him. Perry also made acquaintance, at the receptions of Madame Lavit, with Cloots, Couthon, Herault, David, and Laignelot, a Paris deputy. This last ultimately procured his release. Perry, at the instance of Herault, sent a female relative and her friend to England, with letters to Sheridan and other Opposition leaders, in the view of initiating an agitation for peace.[48]

Staggered at some of the news from England they may have been, but still not lacking initiative. We shall find them continuing in the spring.

47. *Paris in 1789–94*, 330–31.
48. Ibid., 361–62, here and below.

FOURTH INTERCHAPTER
THE BLADE DROPS

1793

1 January, Paris. On New Year's Day, Kersaint predicts a combined Fitzger-aldian and Oswaldian future in a speech in the Convention which mounts to these "vérités": on the one hand "the anxieties of prime minister Pitt, absolute master of England these eight years, whose downfall is equally threatened by the storms of revolution or those of war" and on the other "the Irish who seem to lift their faces toward us and to say: 'Come, show yourselves, and we are free.'" "An awareness of these verities . . . is diffused through a multitude of good spirits in England: the government must dread the explosion, and the events of war must hasten it.—It is on the ruins of the Tower of London that you must sign, with the undeceived English people, the treaty which will govern the destinies of the nations and found the liberty of the world."[1]

*

Chronique du mois, January, page 80:

To the Friends of Truth.

Sampson Perry, author of a republican journal in England, *The Argus of the People* (*La Sentinelle du Peuple*) who has defended with energy the rights of man, the French Revolution, Horne-Tooke, and his friend Thomas Paine, has escaped only by flight from the hangman. Perry and another English writer, Merry, famous for a the-atrical work, some republican poetry, and some philosophical writings which we shall come to know, have come to find true friends at the home of the Directors of the press of the Cercle Social, who are to publish in France the persecuted journal, *The Argus of the People*. The English society of the Rights of Man, and Thomas Paine and others will contribute to it with zeal. Friends of freedom, you owe them help, alliance, and fraternity.—Here is the letter of Sampson Perry, to his persecuted friends in London.

1. *Moniteur*, 3 January 1793. Marsh (*History of the Politicks*, 1 : 343n) gives a freer translation, more Oswaldian than mine: "The ships of our fisherman are always prepared to transport a hun-dred thousand Frenchmen, for it is by such an expedition that we shall end our quarrel, on the ruins of the Tower of London."

[The letter is given in English.]

It must however give some satisfaction to the advocates for European Freedom, and to the friends of the human race in general, should they find that *their* Argus is not banished from the world, but that it has been only transplanted from the region of tyranny, injustice and oppression to this happy soil of Liberty and Equality.

—*Argus of the People.*[2]

*

21 January. At dawn the drums of the National Guard began beating the assembly all over Paris. Each section had received orders to supply one battalion to line the route the King's carriage was to take. Henri Sanson—the son [of the executioner]—was among those detailed from his section. He put on his uniform and picked up his gun. . . . In the street, Henri parted from his father and uncles and went towards St. Laurent's, the assembly-point for his battalion. By a coincidence, this unit was to stand guard round the scaffold. Henri was pleased . . . .

—Christophe, *The Executioners*[3]

*

21 January. As I think that every detail will give you pleasure, I add this bit of paper to tell you that our battalion left its barracks to go and encircle the Place de Louis XV and, as soon as the execution was done, a dance of at least a hundred persons, men and women, formed a rondeau, danced with joy, while chanting the song of the Marseillaise, at full throat, and crying: "Voilà la tête du tyran à bas!" Later one noticed that several people, below the scaffold, washed their hands in the spilt blood. This was a way of alluding to what his wife had said after the Revolution, that she would like to wash her hands in the blood of the French. Well, on the contrary, the French have washed their hands in the blood of her husband.

—Unnamed correspondent to unnamed friend.[4]

*

Oswald . . . at the head of his infernal pikemen formed the guard which closely surrounded the scaffold on which the late King of France was guillotined. Immediately after the head of the unfortunate monarch fell into the basket, he and his whole troop struck up a hymn he had composed for the occasion, and danced and sung, like so many Savages, round and round the scaffold!

—*The Secret History of the Green-Room*, 1795.

*

Dr. Maxwell was among the troops that escorted Louis to the scaffold.[5] At least one other member of the British Club was on hand, John Sheares, who

---

2. Possibly Perry's *Argus* thus resumed publication in Paris, but I cannot find further evidence. (The French title identifies it with an earlier Cercle Social newspaper.) The "Directors of the Press" announce, among other things, an edition of *The Poems* of N. Bonneville, in the press.

3. Pp. 118–19; no source given.

4. Lenotre and Castelot, *Iconographie*, 2:302, my translation. Source vague: "published recently [?] in the *Révue retrospective*," a journal published over many decades, with varying title.

5. Maxwell's biographer is impressed by the importance of his assignment to escort the king (to

Fig. 31. The execution of Louis XVI. The tale of Oswald's battalion of men and women dancing around the guillotine is confirmed by this contemporary sketch (in Daubon, 373; SB). Most depictions fill the scene with upright military men, packed much too tight for dancing.

dipped his handkerchief in the blood. And the commandant of the whole operation was General Santerre, Oswald's chief in the Vendée. Carlyle imagines the executioners as "desperate lest themselves be murdered (for Santerre and his Armed Ranks will strike, if they do not)."[6] He notes that pikes were dipped in Louis's blood, but no confirmation of the Oswald story appeared before the recently discovered letter quoted above. The tune may well have been the Marseillaise; it is also possible that Oswald wrote words for the occasion. Since he had been teaching military evolutions to men and women, both sexes must have participated in this dance.[7] Soon it would be time to march to the frontiers, wherever the enemy appeared in strength; better yet, to a Channel port such as Brest, to begin the rescue of Dublin—or London.

the carriage supplied by Clavière) and by Maxwell's ability to give a "minute account of the execution" to the visiting German radical, Konrad E. Oelsner (whose work belatedly appeared in 1911) but cannot accept the report that his hero "lowered himself to the level of dipping his handkerchief in the king's blood" as, surely, only "the delirious French did" (Thornton, *Maxwell to Burns*, 98–99). Monro reported that Maxwell, "a man of violent principles," was still negotiating with the war minister for the command of a company in the French service.

6. *FR*, 559; Alger, *Paris in 1789–94*, 346, mentions Sheares.

7. By 5 February the news reached William Rowbottom, the Oldham diarist, who wrote: "It is

*

21 January. Hassenfratz, head clerk in the war office,[8] tells the Convention that they are "all at us now. We have not a moment to lose concerning Holland, and our fleet are able to beat the English; so if we take the offensive, we should soon be in England. Spain too is not as difficult as you think."

Hassenfratz, like Oswald two weeks later, talks about sixty thousand fighters—but in his plan these are only to defend the borders from Prussian and Austrian invasion, leaving four hundred thousand, after the liberation of Holland, to conquer Britain.

*

30 January, London. R. Watson, D.D., lord bishop of Llandaff, publishes *A Sermon Preached . . . April 1785. With an Appendix*, in which (in the appendix) he expresses indignation at the execution of Louis and fervent praise of the British Constitution.

William Wordsworth sets about writing "A Letter to the Bishop of Llandaff on the extraordinary avowal of his Political Principles," signs it "by a Republican" (unnamed)—but will never bring himself to risk publication—nor to destroy it.

Our republican begins by deploring the moral collapse of the bishop as a statesman. "Every one, who enters upon public life," has to cross the bridge of "Reputation," which "may not improperly be termed the moral life of man." Watson has seemed to be walking on that bridge "unseduced and undismayed," but now "it is feared you have at last fallen, through one of the numerous trapdoors, into the tide of contempt to be swept down to the ocean of oblivion." The republican poet is indignant not only that the once-liberal bishop is, in effect, joining the hue and cry for war, but also that he pretends to have so little comprehension of the nature of republican revolution. And he contrasts his views with those of the bishop of Blois, Grégoire, an elected bishop in 1791, who was attending meetings of the Jacobin Club of Blois when Wordsworth was living there in 1792:[9]

---

true as it is extraordinary that the French armys [*sic*] have a great deal of women in [them] who act both as officers and privates and at the late battle of Hochheim two women in officers uniform were taken one had received 3 wounds and the other that evening was delivered of a fine boy" (Emsley, *British Society and the French Wars, 1793–1815*, 26).

8. One of the people Watt looked up for Priestley. I condense his remarks from a full page in Aulard, ed., *Recueil des Documents . . . des Jacobins*, 4:695.

9. For the text of Wordsworth's "Letter" and its manuscript revisions, and for a thorough commentary, see his *Prose Works*, 1:19–66. Editors Owen and Smyser demonstrate clearly that there are no solid grounds for the still-prevalent idea that Wordsworth put off writing his indignant response until the summer. After "a careful study of the topical allusions in the 'Letter' itself" they conclude "that it was most probably composed in February or March, for *all* the allusions are to events antecedent to the execution of Louis, or to the 'present convulsions' (54) immediately attendant upon that event" (1:20).

Fig. 32. Henri Grégoire (1750–1831), the bishop Wordsworth held up to Watson of Llandaff as a model revolutionary. A constitutional bishop in Blois, where Wordsworth met him, he fought in the National Assembly, alongside Robespierre, against anti-democratic proposals; survived the Terror; fought for religious freedom under the Directory; opposed the Concordat of 1801, becoming a simple priest; opposed the Empire, though Napoleon made him a count; elected in 1819 to the Chamber of Deputies, he was refused his seat, as a radical; he died in poverty, his funeral occasioning a liberal demonstration. Portrait by Raffet in Lamartine, *Histoire des Girondins*, 4:97 (SB). For a portrait with well-brushed hair, see Hunt, *Politics, Culture, and Class in the French Revolution*, plate 11.

If you had attended to the history of the French revolution as minutely as its importance demands, so far from stopping to bewail [the king's] death, you would rather have regretted that the blind fondness of his people had placed a human being in that monstrous situation which rendered him unaccountable before a human tribunal. A bishop [Wordsworth's footnote: M. Grégoire], a man of philosophy and humanity as distinguished as your Lordship, declared at the opening of the national convention, and twenty-five millions of men were convinced of the truth of the assertion, that there was not a citizen on the tenth of august who, if he could have dragged before the eyes of Louis the corse of one of his murdered brothers, might not have exclaimed to him, *Tyran, voilà ton ouvrage.*[10]

There are those of us, Wordsworth continues, who feel a legitimate sorrow that circumstances "rendered it necessary or advisable to veil for a moment the statutes of the laws" to remove the tyrant. But "Any other sorrow for the death of Louis is irrational and weak. In France royalty is no more; the person of the last anointed is no more also, and I flatter myself I am not alone, even in this *kingdom*, when I wish that it may please the almighty neither by the hands of his priests nor his nobles (I allude to a striking passage of Racine) to raise his posterity to the rank of his ancestors and reillume the torch of extinguished David."

Wordsworth also has a response to Watson's hostility to democracy, his approving of "peasants and mechanics when they intrude not themselves into" government. A popular government, says Wordsworth, does not need the "disciplined treachery and hoary machiavelism" that pass for "talents and experience."

If your lordship has travelled in the democratic cantons of Switzerland [Wordsworth had, in 1790] you must have seen the herdsman with the staff in one hand and the book in the other. In the constituent assembly of France was found a peasant whose sagacity was as distinguished as his integrity, whose blunt honesty overawed and baffled the refinements of hypocritical patriots. The people of Paris followed him with acclamations, and the name of Père Gérard will long be mentioned with admiration and respect through the eighty-three departments.

It would be far short of extravagant to conjecture that Wordsworth was familiar with the Collot-Oswald *Almanach of Father Gerard.*

*

31 January, Paris. David Williams is invited to a council at Lebrun's house, where Kersaint and Brissot read reports on the attitude of England. "As the council professed a strong desire to avoid war, Williams objected to several passages" (probably including the appeal to the English people against their gov-

10. The italics are mine: compare the chanting of Oswald's battalion at the guillotine mentioned above. The lowercase spelling of *august* is Wordsworth's—perhaps to uncrown Augustus, the tyrant whose month it pretends to be. Compare the lowercase *almighty* in the next passage.

ernment).[11] "On accompanying Williams to his hotel that evening, Brissot assured him that these passages would be corrected. On the next day, however, Williams was present when Brissot read his famous report to the Convention. All the passages which he had objected to were retained, and the Convention in a fury declared war on Britain and Holland. In addition an address to the English people was to be drawn up" by Barère, Condorcet, Paine, and d'Eglantine. (Condorcet would have the French nation condemn the September massacres; so d'Eglantine refused to sign.) "Yet Brissot was thrown into consternation by the course of events, and at a dinner of the ministers that evening he told Williams, 'It is done. The committee would have it; if we had hesitated the Mountain would have taken the business out of our hands.' Williams adds, 'The measure was the more embarrassing to the Girondists because it was taken at a moment when they were using their utmost efforts to preserve peace with England!'"[12] But Brissot was evidently also aware of the invasion plan Oswald would disclose on 7 February. (See below.)

*

1 February, London. Stanhope issues a protest against war with France, giving a numbered list of reasons. First, "Because war is a state so unnatural, so barbarous in itself, so calamitous in its effects, so immoral when unnecessary, and so atrocious when unjust, that every friend of humanity should endeavour to avoid it; and the establishment of a pacific system ought to be the first policy of a wise and enlightened nation." Second, "Because peace is always for the interest of the common people in all countries. And Great Britain and France, from their peculiar situation, have an evident interest to remain at peace with each other . . . ." And seventh, "Because these misfortunes ought the more to be deprecated, as it surely appears that it would still be most easy to avoid them, if our ministers were to pursue a mild, just and pacific system . . . ."[13]

*

1 February, Paris. Barbaroux of Marseilles explains his vote in the Convention: "I have voted for war against the Cabinet of Saint James, because I hope to see the English people spring up at last out of the stupor in which they have sunk from long habituation to their constitutional slavery, and themselves to avenge us against such a Court . . . ."[14]

---

11. Kersaint, on the diplomatic committee of the Convention, had proposed a committee of general defense; on 4 January, Kersaint (later Pétion) presided, with Brissot, who made a committee report to the Convention 12 January. It contained a violent attack on the British government and an appeal to the English people; yet Williams was expected to be the message-bearer to Grenville to negotiate peace (Williams, "Missions," 656).

12. Williams, "Missions," 657–58, quoting David Williams, who refers to efforts to deal with Grenville, his own mission, Clavière's letter, etc.

13. *Parl Hist*, 30:336–37.

14. *Moniteur*, 3 February 1793.

*

In the February *Chronique du mois* (68–89) Bonneville offers "A word about England," incorporating Oswald's call for the invasion of London into his usual Druidic rhapsodic prose, too involuted to be quoted (or translated) in full. Here are excerpts and digest. (Lord Grey had defied the suggestion of the British court to lament the execution of Louis.)

> How England has fallen! In the House of Commons only one man, Grey, appears not wearing mourning, not wearing on his back mourning for a tyrant so unanimously condemned for his black ingratitudes and his atrocious perfidies that in all the Republic not one petition was presented in his defense. . . .
>
> One strong voice is raised against this war which George the Third, it cries, wishes to declare against the liberty of the human race. . . . On January 30 in all England they preached slavery and tyranny. Poor old England. But this shameful success is only for a time; the good spirits of England see the noose which the Court in despair is slipping around them.
>
> The Court is compelled to resort to impressment; it is frightened at the collapse of credit and by well founded alarms as to the dispositions of Turkey against Russia and Austria.
>
> A simple indicator of public spirit: the English newspapers are saying clearly to the sailors:
>
> *One knows the hour of your embarkation!*
> *But the return?*
>
> An appeal to the [French] nation to descend upon England will turn against the [British] instigators of the war their own efforts to paint the French in hideous colors. The fear which they have inspired will double our advantage.
>
> We heard, in 1786, one of their convulsive prognosticators complain to his listeners of the desertion of his altar. "When the arm of the Lord," he told them, "shall be stretched over England, you will flock together and stumble, confounded and prostrate!"

This sounds like Dr. Strap in Oswald's *Comic Frogs* of 1786. Did Bonneville and Oswald listen to the same convulsive sermons together? But we may wonder what the prognosticator of 1786 meant by "the arm of the Lord" spreading consternation in England. Would it be some French ships sighted in the harbors of Plymouth or Portsmouth?

*

2–4 February. "Observations of an Englishman meditating upon the War against King George III and the British Government." *Révolutions de Paris*.[15]

15. One can see how, in the context of a mounting diplomatic confrontation in which either nation might have made the first declaration of war, the French decision to do so expresses the need to feel in control of developments: not to be an aggressor but to initiate the liberation of those enslaved neighbors. Prudhomme, the editor of the *Révolutions* (Carlyle's "dull-blustering Printer

1st. Establish in Paris a revolutionary committee composed of natives of the three realms, England, Scotland and Ireland; they must be firm and clear-headed patriots deeply familiar with both languages.

2nd. The object of this committee will be to describe to their compatriots the progress (*la marche*) of the French Revolution and its principal events, to disabuse them of the atrocious calumnies spread in their country . . . and to accelerate by the power of reason the collapse of the . . . tyranny which oppresses the British Isles.

This Committee will communicate directly with the Committees of Diplomacy and of War. . . . [It] will have its agents and its presses on the seacoast nearest Britain . . . .

The committee will busy itself supplying "simple and energetic writings" to distribute in all ships "whether of war or commerce."

Attend principally to the destruction of their commerce; for losses will awake the nation.

Forbid and impede British manufactures as much as possible. The stagnation which this will produce in the principal cities and workshops will hasten the fall of George and his horde; and the interruption of the treaty of commerce [Pitt's masterstroke] is all in favor of France, which only imports from Britain some manufactured articles which our own shops could furnish [here speaks a Frenchman—or an "honorary" one] or knick-knacks of steel, &c, which we could and ought to do without, in exchange for which we send them our best regional produce, our best wines, our oils, our brandy, fruits, etc. For I think it will be less troublesome to a French republican to do without steel buttons and a flannel vest from Manchester than to an English lord to do without the wine of Burgundy, of Bordeaux; for the English people, French brandy is a prime necessity. The result will be that our exchange rate will rise as we have less to pay and more to receive with England. (This is just said by the way.)

Avoid general engagements and great combats by sea, in order to give the British time to awake from their stupid and ferocious idolatry . . . . Already the Bank of England sees itself forced to buy gold at a ten percent penalty to redeem its notes . . . which people dare not refuse, for fear of seeing their house burned by agents of the court; but no one wants to hold onto them; it is said they burn holes in the pocket, a bit like our assignats.

Give the full amount of [maritime] prizes captured to the captors . . . . Refuse to accept ransom for ships or merchandise taken as prize from the English.

And then a proposal, similar to Oswald's:

Announce, for the first of July, the arrival of 60,000 French, to aid their brothers the British to reconquer liberty and to give themselves a constitution founded on the rights of man. . . .

[A]s soon as we shall have fraternized with that generous people, the colossus of the coalition will collapse. Once Holland, Prussia, Spain, Portugal, and several secondary German powers attached to the coalition are neutralized—even England, France will breathe again, and the universal republic will make rapid progress.

---

and Able Editor" [*FR*, 649]) would publish (or had already published) the French version of Oswald's *Government of the People*. And just possibly these "Observations" were based on an interview with Oswald. Since they do not sound like his exact views, however, they were more likely those of some other member of the British Club.

Fig. 33. General Antoine Joseph Santerre (1752–1809). Known only as Brewer Santerre until articulate at the storming of the Bastille; three years later, led the welcoming of the Marseillese ("with an open purse, with a loud voice . . . almost no head" [Carlyle, 451]); notorious for advising Parisians to escape hunger by cooking their dogs; general of the troops on duty during the guillotining of the King; failed with all the generals—and other ranks—in the Vendee. Portrait by Raffet in Lamartine, *Histoire des Girondins*, 3 : 33. (SB)

This pseudo-Englishman continues, with suggestions about frightening the English by making feints and brief raids upon the coasts: "they suck in fear of the French with their mother's milk"—and about letting the British disembark on French soil without opposition: "our national guards are there to receive them."

> If the executive council chooses to adopt these ideas and put them into execution, I believe the war by sea will not last three months. . . .
>
> But the great revolutionary measure which will decide, not only the war with the King of England but the war of freedom against despotism, is to declare that the French Republic does not recognize royalty, and consequently she will treat neither of peace nor of alliance except with free peoples . . . .

As a sample of "writings" to win nations to the cause, this is scarcely impressive—but it shows how simple the approaching conflict seemed to some publicists and editors.[16]

*

14 February. G. G. & J. Robinson publish William Godwin's *Enquiry concerning Political Justice, and its influence on General Virtue and Happiness*, 2 volumes, recognized at once as "a great leviathan" amidst a "shoal of minor" treatises. Godwin gave sheets in advance to the French ambassador, with a dedicatory letter to the National Convention. Now he sends a copy of the book with John Fenwick on his way to Paris, to be given to Gen. Francisco Miranda.[17]

16. Comic relief follows in Prudhomme's pages, in a satiric article ridiculing General Santerre, ex-brewer (and Oswald's commander), who has proposed to save food by killing all the dogs and cats in Paris. (Attention, Robert Darnton.) That Oswald's battalion should come under the command of the humorless Santerre was one of the grimmer ironies of Oswald's career. Carlyle enjoyed the laugh at Santerre's "inventive stupidity, imbedded in health, courage and good nature" (*FR*, 535). The Grub-Street author in Oswald may possibly have thought up this running ridicule; yet as it settles into vituperative criticism of the revolutionary committees, it departs from anything recognizably Oswaldian.

17. Marshall, *Godwin*, 118.

9.
THE EXIGENCIES OF WAR

Oswald's Last Discourse

Three days after the guillotining of Louis the Last, the French representative in London, Chauvelin, was given his passport. On 1 February the National Convention voted for war, not against any nations, but against George the Third and against William of Orange, the stadtholder of the Dutch United Provinces (Batavia).

The Jacobin Club that day was busy mourning the death of Lepeletier, a club member who had been stabbed by a former Royal Guardsman for having voted death to the king. (His portrait would grace the April issue of the *Chronique du mois*.) And then attention was directed toward the long-promised Batavian revolution. A member who had just visited La Hague assured the society "that the first clang of our arms will cause thousands of patriots to rise in Holland." And Collot d'Herbois delivered "a great discourse" on the subject, only sketchily recorded:

> He affirmed that it was right to declare war on the Stadtholder alone and not on Holland, to avoid nationalizing the war. It is important above all to treat Amsterdam with caution. Sardinia, which has already lost the Savoy, will be easily subdued. Spain is an adversary to be scorned. Collot d'Herbois concluded thus:
> Britain has a rather more formidable appearance; but she will embrace Austria and Prussia in vain: our victorious armies will bring everywhere terror or death. It is in Madrid, it is in London, under the windows of George, that our troops are going to plant the tree of Liberty. George, perhaps after a bit, will depart from his palace as Louis Capet has departed from the Tuileries: he will leave it to enter the Tower of London, where he will go on the same promenade as Louis Capet. Then the two peoples will embrace. (Applause.) [1]

On Monday, 4 February, Oswald spoke in similar vein, but the minutes are very sketchy, or sketchily summarized by Aulard. Dorfeuille "reads a lecture

---

1. Aulard, ed., *Recueil des Documents . . . des Jacobins*, 5:15. 1 February 1793.

about or to the soldiers," and reference is made to the new minister of war, Beurnonville, who has just been elected by an overwhelming majority in the Convention and has said he would not have accepted if he had not received the strong support of the Mountain.[2]

Someone suggests dealing with monopolists by placing a guillotine near the granaries. (Applause.) And the meeting is over at half past ten. We know that Oswald spoke that day, but not from the documents in Aulard. On 6 February a deputation of Batavian patriots, "adopted children of the French Republic," visited Paris and read to the Convention and the Jacobins their own address and a month-old memorandum they had sent to Lebrun. When both gatherings moved to publish and distribute these, Ducange, the Batavian chairman, undertook to prepare all for the press, with his own preface dated the 7th. He included the "Discours d'Oswald" of the 4th, with the Jacobin Correspondence Committee authorization of that date. This compilation made a tidy sixteen-page pamphlet, but it may be that Robespierre, who had moved publication of the Batavian items on the 6th, was unaware of the inclusion of the Oswald speech. Aulard was not aware of it. It never came back from the printer (see above, p. 5).

Determined to put the British revolution at the top of the agenda, Oswald tells of earlier efforts that were aborted by the influence of Brissot, who can now be easily blamed for everything that goes wrong with the war. This speech is vintage Oswald—plausible, even persuasive from his angle of perception of the potential flammability of the British peoples. It is addressed, in its printed form, to the widest variety of citizens of France, now that there is no king.

I translate it in full, adding italics for emphasis.

Discourse of Oswald, Anglo-Franc

Republicans,

I am going to talk with you for a few moments on an affair of importance, that is, the means of making war on the despot of England. But before talking about the proper steps to follow in that war, it is necessary to determine the prevailing spirit of the English people and the circumstances in which the court of London now finds itself.

The English journals (all hired, as are the journals of Paris) tell you that the British people detest the French revolution; that they regard with horror the act of justice performed on the guilty head of Louis the Last, and in short that they are determined to avenge his death.

This strange tale is repeated, with much exaggeration, by the *Patriote françois*, the *Courier des departements*,[3] and their confreres.

I hardly know, I assure you, which is most to be admired, the impudence of those who give out this tale, or the monstrous credulity of those who believe it. What! a

---

2. The Mountain (*la Montagne*): the revolutionary party of Danton and Robespierre in the National Assembly at this time (ibid., 5 : 19). Out of 600 votes, Beurnonville received 356; Duchatelet, 216; Beauharnois, 14; Servan, 8; Dumouriez, Lacure, and Wimpfen, 1 each; thirty-four others, including Kersaint, General Miranda, Minister Pache, and Roland, none.

3. The newspapers, respectively, of Brissot and Gorsas.

nation change its character at one stroke! What! the English people, imbued from infancy with an indomitable hatred of the *grand monarque*, by what magic charm has it suddenly become the cherisher of the despot and avenger of his death! In all the previous wars between France and England, it was always the hatred of despotism that stirred the English sans-culottes. The grand monarch is preparing chains for you, the people were told; the despot of France is launching *flat boats* against you; he is gathering, to invade you, his hordes of slaves; and, all at once, the English people would rush to their ships and pour out their blood with a generosity truly sans-culottes, to avenge the assaults upon what they thought to be their liberty, even though they were, alas! for the most part, but the blind instruments to serve the ambition of an avid minister, or the contemptible traffic of some vile monopolists.

But, today, all of a sudden the scene has changed; and instead of a people sworn enemy to tyrants, the English are represented to us as ready to pour their blood out on the cadaver of Louis Capet, like the wretched Roman gladiators who fought over the honor of immolating themselves upon the tomb of their masters. The English sans-culottes, we are told, burn to do battle, not against the grand monarch for having attacked their liberty, but against the French sans-culottes, their brothers, for having toppled his throne and cut off his guilty head! *Anyone who can digest such an absurdity is capable of believing that the Thames is flowing back to its source, and that the dome of Saint Paul's is balancing itself in the air, like the tomb of Mahomet.*

But still, if the court of London has reached the point, as they tell you, of having the people share their regal furors, why are they fortifying the tower of London? Why are they reenforcing the guard at the bank? Is it that they fear that the emissaries of the Jacobin Club will come, during the night, to surprise them with a sudden blow? Such an enterprise would be too absurd, especially if the people are on the side of the court. Do they fear, then, some faction in the House of Lords? All the nobles are prostrating themselves at the feet of the monarch. Do they fear the House of Commons? All the honorable members dedicate themselves to the system of abuse which will fatten them: in short, the nobles, the wealthy, the priests, the monopolists are all on the side of the court. What then is the object of their fears? The answer is easy: it is the people, it is the sans-culottes who, far from sharing the regal rages of the court, only await the favorable moment to shake off the fetters which bind them.

But not only the English people detest the war which the court of London has created; even the aristocrats dread it and abhor it. To be convinced of that one need only read the English journals, and above all the *Morning-Chronicle*, which, even while Brissotish[4] against the latest epoch of the French revolution, nevertheless never ceases to protest, forcefully, the war which it regards as a certain way of inoculating the English people with the fury of the French regicides.[5]

Why then, I am asked, do the Paris journals which are on good terms with England tell us that the English nation are conspiring unanimously with the court of London against the French people? I shall explain to you their motives. Intriguers, as you know, want at any price to make use of Louis Capet, because in the game of in-

---

4. Now the newspaper of James Perry; *Brissotant* is a term of insult, not Oswald's coinage; see note 11 below.
5. The implication is that those who wish an English revolution should not flinch from taking the path of war.

trigue a king is a card that can always bring one a great profit. With the use of a king one makes and unmakes ministers, and generals; by the use of a king, also, one may turn to whichever side one chooses and always profit from the transaction. In order that it not be said I calumniate these gentlemen, I shall quote you the naive confession of the amiable Gorsas; here it is:

"When the execution of Louis would only cause the death of one more man, was that not sufficient motive to keep him hostage? What would the tyrants of Europe do, if unhappily they accomplished the end of their schemes? At what price would we obtain peace? On what condition? Alas! on the condition of receiving the laws of tyranny, without even having the choice of tyrant?"[6]—*Courier des departements*, Saturday, February 2. [A fresh clipping.]

So you see that, if it is no longer possible to compromise our principles, if it is no longer possible to bargain with the despots of Prussia, Austria, and London, it is not the fault of Gorsas and his honest colleagues.

But to return to my point, these gentlemen had thought to save Louis Capet by spreading fear with their tall tales of preparations for war by the coalition powers to avenge the death of the tyrant. England above all must have played a great role in the royal conspiracy. The intriguers had also another aim in displaying with ostentation the hostile preparations of the court of London: they hoped, by the threat of a bloody war with England, to force the National Assembly to accept, as an alternative, an alliance with the British government.[7] This infamous conspiracy . . . would rivet forever the chains of the English nation and arrest at the same time, among the people of France, the progress of public spirit, trapped between Brissot on one side, and Fox on the other. Fox, celebrated juggler in the House of Commons, hoped thus to topple the minister Pitt, and to share among the horde of gamblers which surround him and the literary scoundrels of his suite[8] the spoils of the people and the blood squeezed from their misery. *I uncovered this intrigue four months ago, to several deputies of the National Assembly: one undertook to denounce it in the convention and to put in motion other measures which would already, perhaps, have set in motion the revolution of England.* I had the pain of seeing this deputy fall into the traces of the Brissot faction; and not only did he fail to denounce the matter in question, but he even opposed with all his force those who did denounce it.

Here Oswald is clearly alluding to efforts made, after his denunciation of Thellusson in the Jacobin Club in September, to get the same issues raised in the National Convention—of which he was still not a member because no action had been taken on the proposal of French citizenship for the group in which his name had been included. The measures to "set in motion the revolution of England" would have begun with the recall of all French agents, calculated to precipitate war with Britain. But since nothing was done in the Convention, it is impossible to discover which of his Jacobin supporters had been

6. Gorsas seems to have meant, though his language is ambiguous, that if the people should lose the struggle, they would be better off having kept Louis hostage, so they could negotiate for him as ruler rather than the Emperor.

7. That scheme of allying the royal families of Hanover and d'Orleans, which Pétion's London visit was alleged to involve.

8. One so well known to Oswald of the *British Mercury*.

converted to inaction. One of the Batavian patriots now being applauded claims also that his attempt to enlist the Convention in a liberating invasion of the Netherlands in October had been squelched in the same way.[9]

Oswald too is now deploring the time and momentum lost in October. His speech proceeds:

> The revolution nevertheless does advance, with a force whose momentum nothing can stop. The head of Louis Capet will not return to his shoulders, and the war (despite all the sordid lies of the intriguers) will break all the wheels of their treacherous schemes. The death of Capet has consternated the English aristocrats: one lord, who calls himself Landsdown, has complained bitterly in Parliament that the English minister had not distributed enough silver to save the king; with several thousands more, he said, properly put to use, the unhappy monarch might have been saved.[10] You see then how it concerns the safety of the Republic to destroy a corrupting and nearby court, which sends thousands to bribe your legislators and your ministers.
>
> .It appears nevertheless that, despite the ruin of their schemes, the English intriguers are quite pleased with the service rendered by their craft brothers in France. The talents of Brissot have been much vaunted in the House of Commons: the Lords also, in the upper chamber, are ecstatic about the talents of Brissot. Brissot, for his part, praises to the heavens the talents and eloquence of the English lords; and *this sweet reciprocation of adulation between the English milords and le milord Brissot, perfumes all the journals and will even spread incense in the pages of history.*[11]

9. The Batavian is Mokketros, who insists he still follows "the impulses of a burning patriotism" and is now welcomed and reassured by the Convention. You see in me, he reminds them, "that Dutch refugee who, on last October 28, made a motion to declare war against the tyrant of the Batavians." (I find nothing in the record.) "If you had then followed my advice, which was that of the majority of the Convention, the tree of liberty would have been planted in all the United Provinces . . . ." But he explains that, despite the majority sentiment, some members had cast a sufficient cloud of suspicion over his motives to have the proposal buried in committee. Any delay now will increase the danger of a union of British and Dutch maritime power: "*marchons!*" (*Arch Parl*, 58:181).

10. On 1 February the Marquis of Lansdowne, in a context which Oswald chooses to ignore, made the point that the death of Louis "might, in some degree, be ascribed to the pride and obstinacy of his majesty's ministers in refusing to open a negociation with the French republic," since a majority of the National Convention (five hundred out of seven hundred) "might have been obtained at less expense than it would cost to carry on the present war for a single day." There is perhaps more ridicule than cynicism in Lansdowne's remark, since he was arguing that the British ought to be welcoming, not attempting to destroy, the new French regime, and that so-called "French principles" had been, after all, an export from constitutional Britain to France; that the French would be fighting out of genuine enthusiasm now, while British soldiers would have to be hired to fight a nation adopting their own principles: "He did not know whether one Englishman could beat ten Frenchmen, but he was sure, that one enthusiast could beat ten mercenaries . . ." (*Parl Hist*, 30:329).

11. In the same debate (ibid., 327, 334) Lord Lauderdale, speaking as "one of the people," protested the stirring up of warlike prejudice against France. He owned that "the acts of the Convention, for the last three months, have been monstrous and absurd," but saw for all that "an uniform desire of maintaining peace and friendship with England. He read some passages relative to this subject, from a report made by Brissot" (the one brought by David Williams, I think); "and speaking of Brissot himself, added, that he was proud to rank him in the list of his friends. His virtues and talents merited the acknowledgment." A few minutes later Lord Loughborough, speaking for the ministry and for war, alluded to Lauderdale's friendship with Brissot as "a matter of taste," he

Now just how do we make war against the despot of London? It has been proposed to you to make war against him in America, in India, in Ireland, in Scotland. Yet, there is no common sense in all that: *the despot who must be felled is not in Scotland, nor in Ireland, nor in America, nor in India; to strike him you have only to reach out your arm a little; he is, so to speak, four paces from you; he is in London.* It is in London you must attack him; it is in London, amid an immense population, oppressed, miserable, agitated, that it will be quite easy to topple the tyrant. I propose to you, to effect this happy revolution, the following measures:

1st. To constitute your executive council of true sans-culottes, men of character, and above all to rid it of all the friends of the milords;

2nd. To send an invitation to all the British officers and sailors, and to offer a suitable bounty to all among them who wish to enlist in the cause of liberty and equality;

3rd. To ripen and organize, as soon as possible, an insurrection at London, an easy thing, as I have already said, for a minister truly revolutionary;

4th. To accompany this insurrection with *a friendly descent of sixty thousand sans-culottes who will march straight to London, to aid their brothers the sans-culottes of England,* to achieve the revolution of Great Britain.

By these means, the British revolution will be accomplished in three months at the outside: George the sanguinary will soon suffer the fate of Louis the traitor, and soon the stout arm of the revolution will drag to the inevitable *lanterne* the devourers of men, the oppressors of the people. France and England shall then form a single republic [N.B.], and the Anglo-French people (*le peuple Anglo-franc*)[12] will lose all corporate spirit and all local prejudice in the sublime title of Free, Fraternal People (PEUPLE LIBRE-FRÈRE).

The line drawn between fighting only in self-defense and offering assistance to other peoples seems to have disappeared, as well as the propriety of waiting until "Manchester" asks for assistance. Since France and England are to form a single republic, the problem of conquest vanishes. The difference, however, between six hundred Marseillaise being invited to rescue Paris and sixty thousand French sans-culottes being sent by a "truly revolutionary" minister in

---

himself possessing "none of the modern innovating taste . . . for revolutions, massacre, war, confusion, and the murder of kings." Oswald was all too prophetic about the fame of Brissot. Although in his day his name became a slang term for dishonesty—*brissoter* as an equivalent for *escroquer,* to steal, was current by 1791 (Ellery, *Brissot de Warville,* 218)—and although the details of his life, first brought out clearly in Eloise Ellery's biography in 1915, reveal his character as irresponsibly "political" in the bad sense, both ingenuous and disingenuous as a promoter of large schemes or in evading responsibility for their failure; also in his making and responding to accusations—nevertheless biographers (of Wordsworth, for example) in the nineteenth century often made use of association with Brissot as a purifying rite in their heroes' lives. (Wordsworth was mistakenly said to have lived in Brissot's house when in Paris: see below, p. 289, n. 3.) Brissot, for the strongest example, pressed avidly for war—military adventurism on a large scale—and then accused others of anarchy for failing to supply the men and ships he had assumed. On his fatal failure to perceive the need for unity in wartime, see Ellery, 303. But for the story of Brissot's *embastillement* and, to get out of prison, turning spy, we have had to wait for Robert Darnton's chapter "A Spy in Grub Street" in his *The Literary Underground of the Old Regime* (1982), a complex story: "It corrupted him, and in the corrupting it confirmed his hatred of the Old Regime." The fictional self of his memoirs was a reality accepted by associates such as Oswald, until closer acquaintance.

12. In Bonnevillean deconstruction this also means "the Free British."

Paris to storm the Tower and the Bank in London betrays a recognition of differences in revolutionary potential. The miscalculations behind this "plan" are staggering—but less so if compared to those of Brissot or Pitt or, later, the Directory that would send Napoleon to Egypt, or still later the temptations that would send him to Moscow . . . or those in our day that would initiate a Manhattan Project to build atomic weapons.

From Oswald's personal stance and timing it would be easy (but erroneous) to assume that his ideas or at least those of his small faction in the British Club and/or in the Jacobin Club lay quite outside the conventional, let alone the governmental, thinking of the time. No more than Theodore Wolfe Tone was Oswald thinking in a vacuum. Tone, who had helped found the United Irish Society in 1791 and organize the Catholic convention in 1792, would in the next two years assist Fitzgerald in efforts to obtain French military support for an Irish revolution. Both Tone and Oswald were attempting to put on the Paris agenda the invasion plans of successive French governments dating from 1770 (and already then an ancient concept).

During the Great War for Empire, both French and British governments had made preparations for seizing the other's home ground while fleets were far from home. In 1771 British forces had been in readiness for invading France via Dieppe, if Spain had not yielded, on the verge of war over the Falkland Islands. A French memorandum of December 1776, developing the prospect of Britain's military commitment to war in America, and worked out in formal detail in 1778, proposed the collaboration of Spanish and French forces, to hold Dublin, Ostend, Plymouth, Portsmouth—and land sixty thousand soldiers on English soil, three days' march from London. What we thought to be Oswald's figure of sixty thousand is a fixed total in further "secret" plans of 1779, 1780, and 1781–1782, in which, also, Brest is the favored port for embarkation.[13]

Mutual Fears Increase

Despite Captain Monro's impression—and Alger's—the British Club did not fall apart in the winter. Stone may have receded and Frost departed, but a serious committee of action continued almost up to the time Oswald was sent with his battalion to the Vendee at the end of March.

The chance survival of Oswald's *Discourse* keeps us from assuming that after his appointment as battalion commander in October he spent all his time instructing Parisian men and women in marching and pike-wielding on days when the Champ-de-Mars was empty of demonstrations, teaching them how to

13. The "secret" documents of invasion plans, from 1770 to 1782, are quoted in Coquelle, "Les projets de Déscente en Angleterre," 134–56; see also Woodward, "Projets."

discomfit the enemy with Highland shrieks and bursts of Ossianic and Bonnevillean chanting, or dancing the revolutionary Carmagnole.[14] He may not
have spoken up in the Jacobin Club for many months, but from the revela-
tions in his February speech we know that he had been arm-twisting and agi-
tating behind scenes for, in effect, an official order to march his troops up the
Thames—that Oswald was, in short, a would-be Wolfe Tone for England.

Another activist, who would emerge as an intimate of Tone's when an expedition to Ireland was being prepared in 1795, was Nicholas Madgett, a friend of
Stone's and one of the original fifty signing the White's Hotel address. He was
now, at 26, a translator for the Committee of Public Safety, and its security consciousness gave him ideas. On 13 March 1793, Madgett wrote to Lebrun complaining about British espionage (citing the rather outdated matter of Captain
Monro's sending those fifty names, and the fourteen toasts, to London) and
suggesting that a security committee be formed in Paris to weed out spies. He
proposed a committee of "British citizens of tested civism, to purge the city as
well as possible of all Pitt's spies," adding that he had already proposed to the
minister of the navy the establishing of English or Irish commissaries in all
French ports to rescue imprisoned seamen.[15] (Stone, on his attempted return to
England, had been held up with forty fellow travelers for inadequate passports;
there were difficulties about open and declared war.)

Madgett's list of trustworthy patriots for this screening committee, on 22
March 1793, included William Choppin, James Gamble, William Jackson,
Robert Merry, Harold Mowatt, John Oswald, Robert Rayment ("Raymond"),
Bernard MacSheehy ("Sheehy, medicin"), and Robert Smith, of the November
list, plus J. J. Arthur (who would later do some accusing in the Jacobin Club),
Sampson Perry, Barlow, Anderson, Richards, Thomson, Edwards (perhaps Ed-
ward Fitzgerald), and Fleming.[16] Stone, though in Paris, is not included, prob-
ably having expressed a wish for invisibility.

French plans for the revolutionary invasion of Dublin and London were still
on the agenda, if on a back burner. On 18 December a French agent had re-

14. The Carmagnole, a song and round dance, also the revolutionary costume (*carmignole*, altered to *Carmagnole* after liberation of a town by that name in Piedmont in 1792): wide black
trousers, a red cap, a tricolored girdle. Oswald's battalion would have danced in them.

15. Woodward, *Un adherente Anglaise*, 100–101.

16. Ibid., 102n. I have filled out names when abbreviated and given John Oswald his first name,
to reduce the uncertainty to a footnote. Alger confused the two Oswalds; so did Woodward, in
1930, but he got them right in 1931. Col. Eleazer Oswald was not in Paris during the formation
nor the latter days of the British Club. He was given a command in the French army in September
1792, with the assistance of Miranda, apparently, and Servan and Lebrun (*Archivo del Miranda*,
7:443–44), but then he went on an intelligence mission to London (see above) and Dublin. Back
in Paris for a while, he left by 20 February 1793 (see below). Anderson was possibly the J. Anderson who was secretary of Division 19 of the LCS in 1795; see Thale, *Selections from the Papers of
the LCS*, 278. Arthur was J. J. Arthur, born "John James" (in Paris) but using only his initials,
probably "out of admiration of Rousseau" (Alger, *Englishmen*, 192ff.). Though born in France he
counted as an English member of the Jacobin Club—and of the British Club.

ported from Ireland that if war with Britain became inevitable, the Irish could be counted on for their zeal and their willingness as sailors and corsairs.

But another plan, long brewing, General Miranda's project to revolutionize Spanish America, now filled the discussions. Less than a week after the British Club meeting of 20 November, the French minister Gaspard Monge suggested to the minister of war that Miranda ought to replace General Thowenot in a projected expedition to the French West Indies, and he asked Dumouriez to appoint Miranda governor of the French portion of Santo Domingo.[17] Then suddenly, on the 28th, Brissot reported to Dumouriez that he had just had a stroke of genius ("un trait de Lumière m'a frappé"). How would France be able to crush England? By sending Miranda to the West Indies, which would "strike Spain with terror and . . . confound Pitt with his poor, dilatory politics; but Spain is impotent, and England will not budge." [18]

Miranda, far from enthusiastic, suggested that Brissot should look through the proposals Miranda had made to Pitt in 1790, which were now in his friend Pétion's hands.[19] At any rate he was presently busy driving back the armies of counterrevolution in the Netherlands.[20] I suspect that Miranda muttered to friends about the timing of Brissot's bright idea, because on 20 December a close acquaintance and business associate of his, Thomas Christie of London, now visiting Paine in Paris, wrote to Miranda lamenting the current "feebleness and even *defaut de lumières* in the Convention" and concurring with their mutual friend Pétion, who had declared in a recent pamphlet that all the present leaders of the Revolution "were retrograding in some respects: *Des hommes médiocres—sans lumières et qui n'ont pas aucune talent que celle de parler. . . .*"[21] Christie's dinner companions, Mlle Théroigne and John Oswald, agreed. (See Third Interchapter, above.)

On 29 December the French general Fix Dumuy proposed returning to the more direct project of the invasion of Britain and urged the importance of a surprise attack, giving the traditional sixty thousand as the number needed. "If the French under kings conceived the idea, the free French must dare to carry it out." [22]

The time never seemed ripe, however, and the strength of the insurrectionary spirit in Britain never seemed certain. Lebrun ridiculed the banal idea of sending three Irish to sound out sentiment, or a select number of the British Club to spread the spirit of liberty. Three young Irishmen were, in fact, sent to London

---

17. Robertson, *Life of Miranda*, 1:127.
18. Ibid., 1:128, and *Archivo del Miranda*, 13:25–27.
19. Robertson, *Life of Miranda*, 1:130.
20. Miranda had illuminating ideas of his own; after the capitulation of Antwerp to the French on 29 November 1792, he directed his soldiers entering the fortress to replace the emblems of despotism with emblems of liberty—i.e., the names of luminaries: Dumouriez, Pétion, Helvétius, and Rousseau (ibid., 131, quoting the *Moniteur*, 3 December 1792).
21. *Archivo del Miranda*, 13:38.
22. Woodward, "Projets," 1.

and, by March, exposed. But Lebrun did promise to finance the forty thousand volunteers who would initiate the Dublin insurrection, and gave a letter to Paine which was to be sent on to Fitzgerald and Hamilton Rowan, via Col. Eleazer Oswald.

Eleazer Oswald had been in Ireland, on a special passport arranged by Brissot, but when he now tried to use it to go there again, he was stopped by the British consul in Calais, and when he pursued the matter with the aid of the United States ambassador, Pinckney, he was informed that "the pass of Mr Oswald is refused on account of his having served in the French Army." [23] (See above.)

After further inquiry, Pinckney reported that "the Refusal did not appear to be at all grounded on your being mistaken for Colonel Oswald, who commands a Battalion of Pike men in Paris, nor solely on your having served in the French Army." What Pinckney was told by the British agent, but did not pass on, was that there were "abundant reasons for refusing to permit Colonel Oswald to come into this Country." [24] Eleazer Oswald's tribulations were not over, though his ingenuity triumphed over everything but the calendar. Taking a steamer to Christiana and another to Scotland, he arrived in Dublin in May and was back in Paris on 8 June. The official message: "Ireland was not ready to revolt." Perhaps the unofficial or secret understanding remained that if and when it was, French aid would be welcome.

Meanwhile John Oswald's idea of a direct invasion of England was still under discussion by the surviving British Club and by the French government (i.e., by Lebrun's department), to whom Yorke says Oswald submitted his proposals in February. Stone wrote from Paris to his brother in London on 18 March: "At home a descent will be made upon England, with a force that will be almost irresistible, but in what manner I have not yet learnt: I was applied to by General Dillon on the subject [we may recall that Dillon was a special guest at the White's Hotel party in November], but I declined any interference. You must be careful not to mention these circumstances, especially as coming from me." [25]

Stone was greatly impressed by the spirit of the faubourgs of Paris, which had already "enrolled 40,000" volunteers though their quota was only 12,800, and happy that they were not all sans-culottes, "not the lowest of the people." (Besides the descent on England, a "great force will be sent to the Cape of Good Hope, which will proceed to the East Indies.") Yet Stone was still attempting to negotiate a cease-fire; the week before, he wrote of corresponding with Wilberforce, who "has shown my letters to his majesty's ministers" and was "glad to hear that something like pacific dispositions" existed among the British: "there would be little difficulty here, if any fair and proper terms could

23. Dumont, *Souvenirs sur Mirabeau*, 442–43; Woodward, "Projets," 5–6.
24. Woodward, "Projets," 6.
25. *State Trials*, 25 : 1300; Woodward, *Un adherente Anglaise*, 104n, cites partially.

be offered. You see the territory of France is increasing every day . . . and the more it increases, the greater will be the difficulty to come to an accommodation."[26]

The Irish project did not die but, as we all know, eventuated in 1797 in the multimedia "Year of the French." It would take us too far from John Oswald to pursue even the brief subsequent involvements of Stone and the Sheares and other members of the British Club. But we can understand now what Oswald and Redhead Yorke were quarreling about in their last encounter. Alger is right to place that moment in the spring of 1793. Both Yorke[27] and Johnson, he says, "deprecated a French invasion of England, and when they consequently seceded from the club"—disagreeing with Paine, Merry, and Oswald, as we have seen—"Oswald, in a rage, told Yorke he was not fit to live in civilised society."[28]

When, at last, the Committee of Public Safety did decree an invasion of England, though no longer expecting to be met with open arms, the number of armed men stipulated was one hundred thousand.[29]

The idea was still alive but untried long after the British Club itself had melted away. Stone, writing to Tooke from Paris on 15 January 1794, and trusting only hand delivery, recalled the spring of 1793 as a time when "the little commission which you gave me" was hindered by "the untowardness of events." Stone pretends to be alluding to the market for millinery items[30] for "the ladies," but the language (as Lionel Woodward has pointed out) is transparent. Stone had not found "anyone to whom I could properly intrust" that commission, "the fashion being a little changed"; but this coming March will be different, "since the fashion is so much improved, and I have taken all the precautions." The bearer of the letter will clarify "the history of this country," i.e., France at war. Tooke is

26. Paris, 7 March 1793. Several British manufacturers who had been persecuted as dissenters after the attack on Priestley in July 1791 thought of moving their businesses to France. This was a major interest for Stone, and in January 1793 he communicated the idea to the French Executive Council and wrote to Priestley (and Wilberforce, whom he had dismissed with such contempt in 1792). His letters, intercepted, got to the British government, and in March the attorney general proposed a traitorous correspondence bill which, debated in Parliament and the press, seemed meant to frighten people from writing letters but actually was designed to prevent the sale of any kind of articles that might be used by the French army, and the purchase of French lands or fund. It became law in April (Werkmeister, *Newspaper History*, 248–66; Woodward, "Projets," 3–4).

27. Yorke, described as a Creole, was probably born in the West Indies. Before the Revolution he had written a pro-slavery pamphlet, which he took with him to Paris "in order to write a refutation of it." On departing for England he left the still unrefuted pamphlet with "R" (evidently Rayment) and later was told "that Rayment went to the General Security Committee and denounced him as an English spy," using the pamphlet as evidence (Alger, *Paris in 1789–94*, 349).

28. Ibid., 360–61.

29. Albert Goodwin's chapter "English Radicalism in the Wake of the French Revolution and the Loyalist Reaction, 1792–3" (*The Friends of Liberty*, 208–67) has a thickly documented analysis of the false deductions made in both France and England as to the readiness of England for rebellion (esp. 257ff.)—weakened somewhat by his own deduction that "the English reform movement" was strictly "non-revolutionary" in character (248), in effect that no ideological blood ever ran down palace walls.

30. My guess is that "military items" was the intended allusion.

bound to have made "a thousand errors on the subject of your politics [British? French?], as I, though on the spot, have done; but I think I now see land." [31]

An earlier paragraph in the letter makes clear enough what Stone was hoping for from that landing: "I look forward with transport and joy to the moment when the doctrines you have preached shall receive their due accomplishments, when the various parties of ministerialists and oppositionists, dissenters and churchmen, nobles, priests, and kings, shall sink into one undistinguished mass of ruins, and nothing shall be seen or acknowledged but the people, the sacred voice of the people."

This language and these ideas reveal John Oswald's and Nicolas Bonneville's early and continued interest in the spirit of Horne Tooke. [32]

Farewell to Paris

Yorke's famous anecdote about Oswald—that he recommended putting all the "suspects" to death, causing Paine to protest such bloody talk from a vegetarian—does not indicate what category of suspects they had been talking about. The incident must have occurred just before the resignation of Yorke and Johnston in the middle of March 1793, seemingly in a context of revolutionaries calculating the risks of sending massive armies of citizens out of France and leaving the cities and countryside open to royalist insurrection. Concern about the home front mounted after the war declarations of February. As the

31. Woodward, *Un adherente Anglaise*, 105–6; see also 104.

32. Alger (*Paris in 1789–94*, 362–63) summarizes what the future held for members of the British Club he can identify:

Six had violent deaths. Jackson took poison to avoid the gallows; Fitzgerald was killed in resisting arrest; the two Sheareses were executed; Oswald fell in battle, probably through treachery; Newton perished on the scaffold. A seventh, Ward, may perhaps be added. Thirteen suffered imprisonment in Paris—Colclough, MacDermott, MacSheehy, Madgett, Masquerier, Mowatt, Murray, Paine, Potier, Quatermain, Rayment, Smyth, Stone, and Wardell, not to speak of Perry, who had experience both of French and English prisons, while two others, Frost and Yorke, underwent incarceration in England. And Thomas Muir may probably be added, for he was in Paris in April 1793. If we had the full roll of members, we should probably find additional victims, if not of the guillotine, of the dungeon. The Reign of Terror, even to those who escaped its rigours, must have been a cruel disillusion, and those who lived to witness the despotism of Napoleon must have bewailed their shattered hopes. "Do you call this a republic?" exclaimed Paine to Yorke when they met again in Paris in 1802; "why, they are worse off than the slaves of Constantinople."

And this seems an appropriate place to note the survival of Nicolas Bonneville. In the year VI (1797) he published several numbers of a journal whose title combined those of his first two periodicals: *Le Vieux Tribun du people et sa Bouche de Fer*. Later he revived the *Bien-Informé*, with his friend Mercier. But this was not an era of freedom of the press. For allowing himself in this latter journal to compare Bonaparte to Cromwell he was clapped into jail for many years, dying, somewhat insane, in 1838, in a miserable boutique in the Latin quarter of Paris (I paraphrase a paragraph in Hatin, *Histoire politique et litteraire de la Presse en France*, 6:404–5).

armed ranks left for the frontiers, what could be done to secure the nation against counterrevolution? What was to be done about the already identified royalist suspects?

In the Jacobin Club on 27 March, to take a random illustration of the mounting clamor, a letter is read by Desfieux announcing that forty thousand National Guards are proceeding to disarm suspects in Marseilles. Robespierre chimes in with the declaration that "we must occupy ourselves exclusively with the measure of the most importance, which consists of purging Paris of intriguers." A deputation from the Tuileries section reads an address to the effect that "a revolutionary Tribunal was created fifteen days ago, and not one head of a conspirator has yet fallen under the sword of the law. We call your severe attention to the treason of the generals."[33] The day before, 26 March, General Santerre's forces, including Oswald's battalion, had marched out of Paris with orders to go to Brest, a potential embarkation point for international adventure. In the event, their revised destination was the Vendee—an ironic inversion of the anticipated goal. Their new mission was the elimination of armed royalists, suspects, intriguers, village people voting with their bodies against the oppressions of Paris.

This mission, in which Oswald lost his life, must have pressed sorely upon the polarities of his own humanitarian righteousness, his belief in direct democracy and an armed populace. Here in the valley of the Loire were people rising to free themselves, but perceived as dupes of intrigue. With reversed perceptual categories, the volunteer brigades of citizen General Santerre might have embraced as brothers the volunteer brigades of royalist General Stofflet. As for "military evolutions," the tactics of the Vendeans, mostly sans-culottes who left workshops and farms each day to fight till milking time, were much like those of the American rebels. Like the drilled British troops in America, Santerre's drilled Parisians marched in columns (whether or not some battalions changed marching angle by use of Oswald's newfangled egalitarian rhombs) and fired or stabbed on command.

What the planners—intriguers or pure revolutionaries—and the citizen soldiers faced in all directions were not sister nations rising for the fraternal embrace. And we can see a grimly prophetic symbolism in the changing face of *La Chronique du mois* in 1793, the *Cahiers* of our Quatorze. With the falling of the head of King Louis, all the fourteen names fall out of the masthead. Beginning with the February issue, these are the *Cahiers des Amis de la Vérité*, nameless scribes. Beginning in April, all articles are signed simply "par un ami de la Vérité." In July, the penultimate number, these anonymous contributors cry out to posterity for understanding: "Posterity will say, 'That's what a Republic is; at Rome it was a people-king, at Paris a people-tiger! And both peoples perished.

---

33. Aulard, ed., *Recueil des Documents . . . des Jacobins*, 5 : 108ff.

No Republic.'—No, No, the friend of truth who survives us won't permit these blasphemies . . ." (no. 17, July, 80). Not many of the Friends of Verity did survive; Oswald himself survived the magazine by little more than a month.[34]

What had happened in the Vendee, indeed in many parts of the western regions of France? The many histories conflict in emphasis. I have selected what seem pertinent bits of information and interpretation from several of these but will draw upon a concise chapter by Jacques Godechot[35] for a swift overview.

At various stages of the Revolution there were local and regional conflicts or resistance to the often ineffectual reachings out of edicts and officials from Paris. "The replacement of refractory priests by priests who accept the constitution, depicted as bad priests, began to provoke a certain amount of agitation; arrests of refractory priests aggravated matters. . . . We cannot entirely discard the thesis of the republican historians, according to which the insurrection originated in conspiracies organized either by refractory priests or the nobility." An important conspiracy was organized by the Marquis de La Rouairie, who had led a famous partisan unit in the War of American Independence; he returned a lover of liberty without the intelligence or social rank of Lafayette and, soon embittered by lack of recognition, began early in 1790 to organize a counterrevolutionary movement defending local traditions against, for example, the system of elections imposed by Paris. He wanted a monarchy, "tempered" by the old constitution of France (compare the historicism of John Cartwright or even John Oswald), and he advocated bands of partisan fighters like those he had commanded in America. His Breton Association soon had branches in all the western provinces, with committees in each city that had had a bishopric before the Revolution. The troops were formed by former salt smugglers, unemployed now the salt tax had been abolished, by émigré Bretons living in England, Jersey, and Germany, by persons who had lost their posts in consequence of the reforms, and by some members of the general staff of the National Guard. The large towns were rather unresponsive, but not the smaller. In the summer of 1792, the partisans planned to launch their insurrection at the very moment the Austrian and Prussian armies would be approaching Paris. The victory of the revolutionary armies completely upset their plans. (The revolutionary authorities knew of the conspiracy but dared not proceed against it until the overthrow of the throne. After 10 August, Danton hurried the investigation; La Rouairie escaped but fell ill and died in a château in January.)

34. By December the editor of *Révolutions de Paris* (10–18 frimaire, 1/An II) commenting on the new symbolic portraits of "the People" as a Colossus, a Hercules, clubbing a king, suggested that if Homer could call kings "people-eaters," the Franch sans-culottes were now ferocious enough to be called "king-eaters," letting readers assume that anybody now going to the guillotine must have sought to be a king (see Hunt, "Hercules and the Radical Image in the French Revolution," 107–8 and fig. 4).

35. *La Contre-révolution*, 207–24; I digest the account.

The news of La Rouairie's death prevented the leader in the Vendee, M.-J.-L. d'Elbée, from holding down the insurrection till more auspicious times. And at the end of February 1793, the National Convention provoked its internal enemies by decreeing the levy, en masse, of an army of three hundred thousand men to fight its external enemies. (From Oswald's standpoint and Fitzgerald's, the assumption that exporting tens of thousands of freedom fighters would end war forever had been turned on its head like a reversed hourglass.) The volunteers raised in 1791 and 1792 by the Constituent and Legislative Assemblies had rallied to the colors with a genuine spontaneity, but in 1793 the volunteer spirit of the French was exhausted, except in Paris and a few other localities.[36] The Convention felt forced to decree that, in default of sufficient volunteering, municipalities must conscript soldiers by some means—even by lot-drawing, though that was the traditional resort of the old regime, which peasants and villagers had always tried to evade.

The decree which ordered the levy of three hundred thousand was made known in Angers on 2 March and published in the various communes of the western regions on 10 March. On 11 March the insurrection broke out on the entire left bank of the Loire, to the cries "No drawing lots! Down with the militia!" On the 11th, 12th, and 13th everything seemed to blow up at once.[37] At St. Florent, Chanzeaux, Machecoul, and Challans, armed troops appeared to the ringing of the tocsin, shouting war and vengeance. The rebellion soon found leaders, and rapidly swept the region.

It would be an exaggeration to say the rebels stormed and took towns in the first days of the rebellion. Unresisted, they swarmed over them. By the fifth day, they had moved into St. Florent, Tiffauges, Beaupreau, Montaigu, Mortagne, Chemille, Cholet, Challans, La Roche-sur-Yon, Clisson, La Roche-Bernard, Vihiers—almost every important town in the region. By that time the rebel mass had not only a name (the Catholic, or Catholic and Royal, Army) but also a body of recognized leaders—Bonchamp, d'Elbée, Stofflet, and many others.[38]

There were three stages in the great war of 1793: first rebel expansion (until the end of June); next check and attrition (until mid-October); and finally flight (until the year's end). The dividing points are the defeats of the Vendeans at Nantes (29 June) and at Cholet (17 October).

Rebel expansion was in fact fairly well contained after the first few weeks of the revolt. From then on, it was basically a tale of capture, relinquishment, and recapture of cities along the borders of the Vendee, culminating in the taking of Saumur (9 June) and of Angers (12 June). The Vendeans did not occupy these cities; they took them, sacked them, organized shadowy provisional governments, then decamped. During all this period the Republican government was

36. Unless J. H. Stone's report of the exceeding of the Paris quota is not to be trusted.
37. Here I draw somewhat on Tilly, *The Vendee*, 4–5, and then return to Godechot, *La Contre-révolution*.
38. D'Elbée was a nobleman, Stofflet a peasant.

changing plans, placing and replacing generals, shouting treason, sending in-
vestigatory missions, generally failing to meet the rebellion firmly and directly.

During the period of check and attrition, after the failure of the Vendean attempt to take Nantes, the Republicans became more decisive and more successful. (This was when Oswald's battalion, under the sometimes remote command of Santerre and Rossignol and Ronsin, entered the fray, most of the time
pitching its tents outside Saumur.)

On the title page of *Le Gouvernement du Peuple* the author is identified as
Jean Oswald, Anglo-Franc, Commandant du Premier Batallion de Piquiers,
presumably the designation he was given on 1 October 1792, but we know almost nothing about his battalion until 26 March 1793, when it paraded
through the hall of the National Convention on its way to the front. Sampson
Perry's recollection of that occasion sounds accurate. The troops may not have
realized they were going to the Vendee and not all the way to Brest, but the
politicians knew:

> As he was an English subject, it was not thought proper to send him to the fron-
> tiers after the war broke out with this country. The regiment addressed the conven-
> tion to allow them to change their pikes for firelocks, and march against the rebels in
> the Vendee. The request was complied with, and colonel Oswald, with his corps, filed
> through the convention with a knapsack on his back, the same as a private soldier.
> This conformance to the principle of equality by the commander of a regiment, who
> was besides an accomplished scholar, produced an uncommon sensation, and excited
> a burst of acclamation in the members of that senate.

The report in the *Moniteur* is more precise, in using the term *battalion*, not
regiment, but is empty of details: [39]

> The battalion barracked in Paris, in the rue de Babylone, who are marching against
> the revolted ones, obtain permission to file before the assembly, and to take the oath
> of liberty and equality.
> *The President [Jean Debry] to the volunteers:* Go forth to combat the leagued fa-
> naticism and aristocracy; do not allow the brigands to destroy the unity and indi-
> visibility of the Republic, which we have sworn to maintain. Go forth, brave soldiers,
> you are French; your enemies are no longer such, you will conquer.

The sketchy proceedings of the Convention for this day do not mention the
Rue du Babylone and represent the military or revolutionary committee of the
Panthéon section as the sponsoring body. A section spokesman, citizen Julien,
implies that all the companies are from the same neighborhood and proud of
its special dedication to heroes of the nation: "Citizen Legislators, this section,
depository of the ashes of great men, this section, just, severe, intrepid, never a
transgressor of rights, deputizes us to address you and offers to you, by the
organ of my voice, some citizen defenders. These brave soldiers bear themselves

39. *Moniteur*, 15:796.

with a spirit natural to every republican defending the Republic. Posterity, citizens, will judge your conduct toward them."

The first sentence of President Debry's reply suits the occasion: "Citizens, liberty and equality cleave to each other (*s'embrassent*)." But instead of the *Moniteur*'s report of remarks clearly applicable to the Vendee, the Convention secretary who wrote the minutes apparently filled in at this point with the routine phrases that applied to troops marching to the frontiers: "Neglect nothing on which the country's safety depends. The Convention will never forget anything which may be alleged of the wrongs of our brothers who are on the frontiers: the National Convention is to receive your oath."

A reply is made not by Julien but by one of the soldiers, who seems to think that formal assurances are still needed to keep all the companies together in Oswald's battalion:

> I am charged, in the name of my brothers in arms, to request of you a favor: we have formed ourselves into companies; we have chosen ourselves chiefs, men of virtue and experience; we ask your permission to march thus formed, not to separate us ever from this symbol. (*He displays the flag.*) And that you be so good as to give an order to the minister that we are all to join the same battalion, united in the same company [*sic*].

The president agrees, accepts the volunteers' oath to exterminate all tyrants, etc., and "the company defiles into the hall to the sound of the trumpet and the noise of the drum."

And here our story would end, except that one of the great historians of the Vendee, Charles-Louis Chassin, having finished his ten-volume work, decided to compile, with Louis Hennet, a book of documents of *Les Volontaires Nationaux pendant la Révolution* (Paris, 1902). And these two scholars discovered that, while most battalions' histories could be presented in a few pages of lists and tables, the 1st Battalion of Pikemen, named later the 14th Battalion of the Republic, required many tables and lists—and was the only unit among all the volunteer corps for which an almost complete minute book of officers' meetings survived (*Registre Journal des délibérations prises par le conseil d'administration*) as well as a daily record made by a survivor of the battalion who was interviewed in 1824. We can therefore follow the daily business of the piquiers—but not before they left Paris.

Triumph of the Press

During that last month in Paris we can be sure that John Oswald, alias Sylvester Otway, and for a long time simply Ignotus, managed somehow to celebrate—drinking wine in more than one circle, I should think—the personal and political triumph of his great confidence in the printing press represented by the publication in both French and English, early in the year, of his *Sketch* (French *Plan*) for a true commonwealth for the people, followed by a sensational review—not in the journals, so far as I can tell, but in the British House of Commons in early March. Sad for his friends that the title page should prove, so soon, his epitaph:

The Government of the People;
or,
A Sketch of a Constitution for the *Universal Common-wealth.*
By John Oswald, Anglo-Franc.[40]
Commandant of the First Battalion of Pikes, in the service of the Republic of France,
Author of

The Review of the Constitution of Great Britain.

The Cry of Nature; or, An Appeal to Mercy and Justice in Behalf of the Persecuted Animals.

Poems, by Sylvester Otway.

La Tactique du Peuple; ou, Nouveau Principe pour les Evolutions Militaires; par lequel le Peuple peut Facilement Combattre par lui-même et pour lui-même, sans les secours dangerous des Troupe Règles.

Edmund Burke may have ignored Cooper's recommendation that he read Oswald's *Review of the Constitution of Great Britain*, but somehow *The Government of the People* with its more alarming title reached him quickly. In the Commons debate on Sheridan's motion of 4 March 1793, "relative to [i.e., to expose the false allegations of] the Existence of Seditious Practices," Burke, when he stood up to define and attack the dangerous spirit now pervading France and threatening Britain, "remarked on some publication by a Mr. Oswald, now in Paris, who expressed his hopes that all government by representation would soon be at an end, and that France would be freed from the iron yoke of property."[41]

(Oswald, of course, was not limiting his perspective to one country. His concluding paragraph addresses to all mankind a hope that "the collective wisdom of man will break, at last, the iron yoke of property.")

"This was now in agitation all over France," Burke went on. "The old proprietors were pretty well got rid of by murder or confiscation. Those who had shared in the plunder were endeavouring to make a stand, but they would soon be overpowered. The sovereignty of the people was the most false, wicked, and mischievous doctrine that ever could be preached to them."

40. French title: *Le Gouvernement du Peuple, ou Plan de constitution pour la République Universelle*, Traduit de l'Anglais, de Jean Oswald. (Evidently translated *by* someone else for him—Bonneville, perhaps?) English version "Printed at the English Press"; the French version by the press of Prudhomme's *Révolutions de Paris*.

41. *Parl Hist*, 30:554, 4 March 1793 (often mistakenly cited as 28 February, from an error in the running heads).

It would particularly have delighted Oswald, reading this as he may well have done in the newspapers before he left Paris, to discover that the first man on his feet when Burke sat down was his old duelling companion Colonel Macleod, who said: ". . . the right hon. gentleman had ventured to renew one of the most unconstitutional propositions he had ever laid down, namely, that the living mass of humanity did not enter into the constitution." After his allusion to the Oswald pamphlet, Burke had talked on at "considerable length" (according to the reporter), but the central theme of his attack upon popular government had lodged and coiled in the outraged conscience of Norman Macleod for the spring of that instant response.[42]

I think of Oswald, before he marched off to war, as thus making his final contribution to the debate he had conducted in the Jacobin Club, giving both nations his *Plan* (in the French title), in other words his "Social Contract," his "Political Justice," the democratic Constitution which his "speculations" in the *Herald* and *Mercury* had promised—his last fling before he turned full attention to a not very philosophical war; something like Tom Paine's "parting shot" at Dover suggesting a new government for Britain. And he defines himself with that telescopic pun, "Anglo-Franc," available to the sympathetic: British-French/*franc-franque*/candor about Freedom.

Oswald may never have heard—but would have been immensely intrigued if he had—that five days after this Burke-Macleod exchange in the debate on Sheridan's motion, the occasion of that debate was celebrated at a dinner (9 March) of Friends of the Liberty of the Press, at the Crown and Anchor Tavern, with Colonel Macleod one of the three toasts. Another was Major Maitland, who had spoken against Burke's alarm about daggers as weapons for assassination, explaining that the daggers ordered by Dr. Maxwell for the French army were intended "as a weapon for horsemen, armed with rifles."[43]

Sheridan himself presided and spoke at the banquet; the toasts associated "Freedom of the Press" with "The Rights of the People" and "Parliamentary Reform."[44] The *Gazetteer* of 11 March reported the remarks of Sheridan, Erskine, Grey, and Horne Tooke. On the toast to "Lord Lauderdale, Col. Macleod, and the Friends of Reform in Scotland," it observed only that "These

42. Ibid., 30:556.
43. This was no doubt a bit disingenuous. It was at least widely believed that daggers [*dards*] had a military function similar to that of the pike. Maxwell was apparently convinced of that, having found that guns would cost too much, and "after listening to Americans in Paris boasting of just what damage could be inflicted by a long knife in the hands of an expert. . . . Combatants at Cullodin having proved the bayonet to be the queen of weapons and the American woodsman having demonstrated the deadliness of the sheath knife, others had been quick to learn. The Home Office was hearing almost daily reports such as the passing from Harwich to London of large posses of Frenchmen 'armed with daggers' or of 'Twenty five Marseillois sent over to this Country armed with daggers for the purpose of assassinating and cutting off any obnoxious characters'" (Thornton, *Maxwell to Burns*, 67).
44. Werkmeister, *Newspaper History*, 234–37.

three Gentlemen returned their thanks in elegant and apposite speeches."[45] The reported remarks attributed despotic or antireform intentions to governmental alarm about the "pretended insurrections" in England (thus Sheridan: "The *spectre* of insurrection was nothing more than a *Fury* begot by *Falsity* out of *Fright*.—It was intended by those who had pledged themselves to support the coalesced Despots, to deter men who were united to promote a Reform").[46]

If we continue for a further moment the highly probable conjecture that John Oswald in Paris found occasion to look at the London newspapers of February and March 1793, we can find in them many things that would have struck him sharply. One was the name of that infamous multinational pirate Peter Isaac Thellusson heading a list of six who called a public meeting 2 March "for the purpose of encouraging the capture of French armed Ships or Vessels, cruising against the British Commerce."[47] Another, the name of Mrs. Crouch, featured in the season's "GRAND SELECTION" at Covent Garden during Lent, singing (most prominently) "Captivity, a serious air," of which the *Gazetteer* of 22 February gives a full text of twenty-four lines. "Captivity" is "supposed to be sung by the unfortunate Marie Antoinette, Queen of France, during her confinement in the Tower of the Temple."

But Oswald would have been cheered to read that the old organizer Horne Tooke was still doing his "cordial" best to keep the Westminster reformers together, Whigs and Radicals, at least in the public eye. When Sheridan, Grey, and Maitland opposed Tooke's resolution condemning an encroachment on the liberty of "the subjects of Britain and Ireland" by the Irish House of Lords, as "of too much importance to be passed at the present moment," Tooke merrily said "that he should have proposed it before dinner; but that he was apprehensive the gentlemen were *too hungry* to *hear reason*. He then, in a handsome manner, agreed to the adjournment."[48]

45. Macleod, as M.P. for Inverness-shire, would continue an outspoken friend of reform. Coleridge, in his political magazine, *The Watchman*, of 9 March 1796 (no. 2, pp. 77–81), both quoted and editorialized upon Macleod's vigorous opposition to the British use of "One hundred Blood Hounds and 20 Spanish Chasseurs" to hunt down rebellious Maroons in Jamaica. "The conduct of the French (General Macleod observed) had never reached such enormity. I have seen war in all its Shapes and Horrors, but I never saw such barbarity as this." If the report proved true, Macleod pledged himself to bring Lord Balcarres, governor of Jamaica, "to the Bar of the House of Peers to answer for so horrible a measure."

46. London *Gazetteer*, 27 February and 2 March 1793.

47. For privateering, that is, officially sanctioned piracy. Armed vessels owned and officered by private persons were given "letters of marque" by the government, for aiding the war effort by taking the enemy's merchant ships as "prizes." For a close investigation of the official and unofficial complications of such speculative activities, see Betty Rizzo's report on "John Sherratt, Negociator."

48. *Gazetteer*, 11 March 1793. It would also have pleased Oswald to read that James Ridgway could still be found among the friends of freedom. An announcement of a second meeting of the Friends of the Freedom of the Press (17 March) advises that signatures to the *Declaration* of their last meeting, printed copies of which may be had of J. Ridgway, can be received up to four o'clock "This Day." It would hardly have surprised Oswald to see that the Tory publisher, John Debrett, was on the privateering committee.

Death in the Vendee

Since November 1792, Oswald's battalion had been stationed in an ancient barracks in the Rue de Babylone, near the parade grounds of the Champ-de-Mars; previous to that it had been in the Lourcine barracks (in the Gobelins section not far from the Panthéon) where seven companies had been brought together to form the battalion.

The place of origin of only one of the seven is known, a company first raised in the section *du Panthéon français* in the region of the Cercle Social and its booksellers. More than one of Oswald's ultimate "companies" may have originated in this section; its *comité revolutionnaire* seems a likely focal point of his early agitational efforts and drilling of men and women. It was the most populous section of the city and famous for its revolutionary demonstrations,[49] as when it refused to let the mayor of Paris be chosen except by direct popular vote.[50]

We may suppose Oswald to have been living, for a year or more, in or near the barracks of his battalion, with his two drummer boys, and infant son and daughter, and his wife, or wives.[51] His "troops" were ordinary citizens armed with pikes, replacing drilled National Guards who had parted for the frontier. Former members of elite corps such as the grenadiers, wanting to abolish distinctions, would rip off their epaulettes, trample their cloth hats under foot, and clap red bonnets on their heads. Other relics of a bygone era would have been eradicated, in Oswald's circle, long before the National Convention decree of 28 November that "every arm or battalion of national volunteers" must "efface or cover, by 15th January next, with stuffs of three colors, all emblems of the so-called royalty which are still found in flags, standards, and voitures of the armies of the Republic. Costs will be charged to the treasury of the army."[52]

49. The section had originally been named after the church of Sainte-Geneviève, but its name changed when the church was dedicated as a Pantheon of the Great Men of the Nation, upon the death of Mirabeau in 1791.

50. On 27 June 1793, the sans-culottes of the Pantheon section would declare that even worse than the evil caused by rebel arms in the Vendee was the lack of open political education (Soboul, *Parisian Sans-culottes*, 92).

51. Perhaps the actuality was quite unconventional. Perhaps it was not only Oswald's ideas that "were calculated to scandalize his contemporaries." Perhaps, leaving Bathsheba and the children in Kent, he acquired another wife in Paris, mother of the "infant son and daughter" whom Sampson Perry found with him in 1793. We do know that the two future drummer boys were with him in Paris well before he had a battalion, however. If two wives survived him (living amicably together in Paris, according to Redhead Yorke, visiting them in 1802), Yorke's report of two children would not include the former drummers, one by then dead, the other in his twenties. The infants of 1793 would fit the tale. (Here Wordsworth's version is of no help; he could no more have given children to the villain in his play than could Shakespeare to Lady Macbeth.)

52. *Moniteur*, 29 November 1792, 1414.

1. From Paris to Thouars

When the First Battalion of Pike-bearers marched off to the Vendee, we know they left their pikes behind, from the recovered tables of supplies, with carefully tallied records of arms of various kinds. Oswald's advocacy of the pike was not doctrinaire, we see.[53] And not counting the tables, the printed transcript of the Officer's Journal, with careful indication of which documents are in Oswald's hand, for instance, fills 94 printed pages. Here, first, is the route list made by volunteer Jean-Jacques Herbillon, who retired in 1824 as a captain:

Noms des villes, bourgs, villages, camp, bivouacs où j'ai tenu garnison, logé, cantonné, campé, bivouaqué où combattu depuis que je suis militaire.

26 mars 1793	Arpajon	Depart de Paris.
	Étampes.	
	Angerville.	
	Artenay.	
ler avril-[4 mai]	Orléans.	
	Beaugency.	
	Blois.	
	Amboise.	
	Tours.	
	Azay-le-Brulé.	
[15–21 mai]	Chinon	Affaire avec un bataillon du Calvados.
	Saumur.	
	Saint-Mathurin.	
	Angers.	
6 juin-[30 mai-9 juin] ..	Ingrande[54]	Combat sur la Loire.
13 juin	Le Louroux-Béconnais. Retraite sur Tours.	
	Le Lion-d'Angers.	

53. The first requisition in the register concerning arms is that made in Paris 15 March 1793, for 542 guns and 206 sabers. In a stock-taking list of January 1794 (in a plan to build up the battalion to the official strength of 1,067 effectives) there "exist" 423 guns and 11 sabers, and the guns *needed* are counted as 617 (which would make a total of 1,083—to help with some whose guns are under repair), the sabers needed, 196, to make a total of 207 (sabers for officers mainly). The initially formed battalion, of 8 companies, in which all the nonofficers are called "piquiers"—subsequently "volontaires"—would add up to only 620 including staff. Add a company of grenadiers, who marched with them, and the figure comes close to 700; I take the early orders (including those for shoes and other clothing) to indicate a total of between 600 and 700. And presumably in March there were already 100 or so guns in hand. But I don't understand the steady number of sabers, 206/7 (for officers only); it should go up more than that for the later 1,067 total (see Chassin and Hennet, *Les Volontaires Nationaux*, 347–48, 362). The 1794 list includes a company of 8 musicians. Originally each company has 48 *piquiers* and 12 *chasseurs*, which totals 60; the 1794 lists have 60 in the grenadier company but 100 or more in the other companies. The difference between grenadiers and light infantrymen (in the British army and presumably the French, originally) is defined in *The Gentleman's Compleat Military Dictionary* of 1759 thus: "the grenadiers are generally the tallest and briskest fellows, and always the first upon attack"; the light infantry are also picked men, "of more active build, lightly armed, and ready for the service as flankers."

54. "Le bataillon accompagnait un convoi d'Angers à Ingrande: il devait se randre ensuite à Tours."

> Château-Gontier.
> Laval.
> La Chartreuse.
> Le Mans.
> Château-du-Loir.
> Tours.

26-[29] juin	Camp De La Membrolle.
1er juillet	Langeais.
	La Chapelle-Blanche .... Chaleur extraordinaire.
	Saumur.
	Camp de la Gueule-du-Loup.
	Saint-Mathurin. Bivouc.
	Bivouac de ...
	Camp d'Angers.
8 juillet 1793	Bivouac de Brissac .... Extrême chaleur, 38°4'.[55]
14–15 juillet	Fline. Bivouac de Martigné-Briand ... Bataille. Victoire.
16 juillet	Bivouac de Martigné .. Combat. Caissons à Montilliers.
17 juillet	Bivouac de .... Bataille.
	Bivouac de Vihiers.
18 juillet	Bivouac de Coron ...... Bataille. Blessé, fait prisonnier.

Here Herbillon, wounded and made prisoner, was not returned to the battalion until November. But battalion records indicate:

4–21 aout	Chinon.
23 aout	Thouars.
12–13 septembre	? Fierce fighting at Pont-de-Cé; attack hurled back by Parisian commander Bourgeois, the 12th.
14 septembre	Thouars .... Oswald and three others slain.

The rest is not needed. The biographers sometimes report Oswald as slain at Ponts-de-Cé (variously spelled, perhaps a loose indication of the general region).

It may be noted here that 16 March was the day of receipt of an order from Santerre to go to Brest; that is the day the piquiers took the name of 14th Battalion of the Republic.

Until mid-July the camping route indicates a tedious getting acquainted with the villages and local patriots, and some minor skirmishes in very hot weather. Later there would be a long wait for a coordinated plan of battle. On the surface the journal of executive meetings turns out to be a record of supplies and arrangements, vital to those concerned but dreary reading. Looking through it, we see the conflicting battle plans slowly maturing; then we look for Oswald's final battlefield.

55. Over 100° Fahrenheit.

2. *Registre Journal*

The first recorded meetings of an already elected administrative council, at Paris on 1 and 9 March, concern the payment and distribution of money for "shoes and gaiters," agreed upon after "mature deliberation." On the 15th we learn the name of the general of the brigade,[56] Citizen Fief, from an authorization for receiving 542 complete muskets (*fusils*) and 200 sabers. In Oswald's hand, the editors tell us, is an unsigned receipt for them to be delivered to Citizen Vignot, second in command. On the 20th a notice signed "Oswald, chef de bataillon, Risse, Lafond, Billion," expresses astonishment that Vignot has spent money without previous deliberation by the council. On the 30th they are in Orleans, meeting in the home of Citizen Crignon-Sircon, village sugar-baker, where Commandant Oswald is lodged. On 9 April they calculate their daily costs, and the council demands of the legislative commissioners enough cash to distribute the daily twenty-five sous needed to avoid a deficit. Again a very solemn document, signed by Oswald and a quarter-master, an adjutant-major, and a captain. What they discovered was that the twenty-five-sous payments received while in Paris had dropped to fifteen sous in the field. (Armies are expected to forage for enemy supplies.) On the 19th an authorization comes from the Convention delegates on mission in Orleans, Julien de Toulouse, Prieur, and Bourbotte.[57]

May is very quiet. The skirmish at Chinon doesn't require mention in the journal. On the 30th, at Ingrande, a permanent camp for several weeks, eight officers sign an agreement (not Oswald, whose approval apparently goes without saying) to support a group of citizen musicians and their organization, by levying a sum on officers, according to their pay. The music master, who will take charge of the musicians, is authorized to wear the ribbons of sergeant major, under orders of the staff-major. On the 31st, Oswald again not present (unfortunately), the staff officers with Vignot presiding vote to exclude from the battalion all the women, married or unmarried, in particular "la citoyenne Chevallier, femme d'un volontaire de la 4e compagnie." "We've noticed that such women are the mothers of all the vices; we must cut while the sap is rising. Done at Ingrande, 31 May."

On the next day, 1 June, the detachment which Vignot commands is assembled at Risse's quarters, by Oswald's orders, to make the following declaration: "The volunteers of said detachment, in the presence of Oswald, commander in chief, after swearing to speak the truth, have declared it for a fact that they have never seen, during fire, commander Vignot at their head." (Here, in Oswald's hand but erased, evidently as too strong for those compelled to sign: "[they] disapprove entirely of his receiving any honors.") "And that he is

56. Of perhaps four battalions.
57. Chassin and Hannet, *Les Volontaires Nationaux*, 373–75; subsequent entries will be easily located by the dates given.

never found on the field of battle when there is action against the rebels." Further, the volunteers of said detachment, being asked whether, on consulting their consciences, they think that Citizen Vignot comports himself as a brave man or a lazy, effeminate one (*en lache*), they would reply unanimously that he behaves like a person "lache et sans valeur." "The following volunteers have signed." All this, we are told, is in Oswald's hand; there are thirty signatures, including an adjutant, a captain, and two corporals. The commandant has really cracked the whip. (Note: the document up to the erasure is in a secretary's hand; Oswald took over at that point and penned the rest and no doubt watched over the signing.)

Vignot was granted eight days to produce character witnesses, and on 7 June the council is offered six depositions (only four by soldiers who can sign their names) to the effect that Vignot has been seen present under fire. Hard facts seem absent. Sargent Damiron has seen Vignot go out when there was a small alert and not return. Baptiste Chartron, who signs with a cross, has always heard good things of Vignot. Corporal Clement, however, has seen him at the head of the troops up there with the general, and has always heard people feel honored to be in his detachment. Cannoneer Fragnière, after seeing the accused speak to the general, saw him in action at the head of a troop. Two others make similar affidavits.

Eleven officers then sign a statement that they have heard the depositions, are aware of the contradictions and, since "among us there can only exist men free and of great courage," expect Citizen Vignot hereafter to double his "*exactitude*."

On the same date fifteen officers (including most of the eleven) by unanimous vote order that Citizen Morlet (who had been demoted) be restored to his post and made lieutenant the moment the battalion takes up arms. Also this day, by law and the general's orders, four laundresses are authorized to be lodged and paid as volunteers, and two subtlers (*cantinières*) shall have lodging only.

Ingrande, 9 June. (After four days of battle, a soul-searching document, probably imposed by Oswald's earnest rhetoric.)

> The citizens composing the officers corps . . . having met at the residence of adjutant-major Risse of said battalion, after having discussed the affairs of the battalion, after having seen with the greatest sadness that despite all our efforts to attain discipline, insubordination is destroying all hope for that unity from which should flow the force and glory of all battalions of the Republic; hence, all seen and all considered, the interests of the Republic weighed in the balance of justice, we the undersigned officers have decided, by oath made among us, that, if we are not able to achieve at once and this very day the discipline which we desire for the good of the Republic, we demand and are certain the general himself will grant our demand, a resigning of our commissions, a resignation in which we promise to leave this moment to go and combat the enemies of the Republic and of Liberty *as soldiers*; and we add our promise to obey the superiors whom we find.

This manifestly Oswaldian document sounds like an unintended testimony to the veracity of the legend that he was slain in battle by his own men—for the collapse of discipline is attested, whether in the recent "combat sur le Loire" (see the route list) or in a future backlash from the signatories—or rather perhaps the non-signatories, for in the journal a table of captains, lieutenants, and sublieutenants is made out, to be signed, but remains blank.[58]

On 15 July, after a considerable battle for two days at Fline, the council meets at the quarters of General Joly, brigade chief camping at Martigne. Officers present, including Oswald and Risse, decide not to grant the request of Citizen Potot, captain of the 4th Company, to be reinstated in the functions from which he had been suspended in January by a council of discipline held at Tours.[59] He had been accused of taking by force and keeping for several days a horse belonging to the collier at Ingrande. Said Potot is one of the worst offenders among officers guilty of retaining horses they have commandeered, retaining six at the least, which has given a very bad name to the battalion and occasioned great scandal among the troops.

While meeting with General Joly, on the same day, the council reopens the case of Citizen Vignot, still suspended. General Joly wants a certified report to be delivered to General Menou. "Said Vignot having, fortuitously, been killed in combat at Martigne-Briand [this day or the day before] the procedure terminates."

Some of the council's minutes and other papers were lost in the battle of 18 July. The surviving journal resumes in August. On the 1st, Oswald calls a meeting to vote for a new administrative council; Captain Joly of the grenadiers is named president by an absolute majority. Meetings twice a week are now necessary, because of much business and several errors in the accounts. Acquier overstayed a dated pass and his ranking is given to another. Risse doesn't get the promotion to captain he was promised; he must await the next vacancy. Many bookkeeping squabbles occur.

On 14 September Oswald is slain at Thouars. If we read on in the *Registre*, we shall see such a waning of revolutionary *lumières* as to make us regard his death as a merciful release from what could have been increasing frustration. For his passing happened to coincide with a rapid and radical "change of heart" in the Republic. In Paris the Convention, by November, "cast a disillusioned eye upon its former, almost lyrical expression of natural rights which had included equal status for women."[60]

58. Would this be a copy? But most documents in the journal are signed in situ. And why make a table? I suspect that Oswald walked out to leave the officers to consult their consciences—and that they did.

59. What was any part of this battalion doing in Tours in January? A transcription or scribal error for June, probably.

60. I quote Themistocles Rodis ("Marriage, Divorce, and the Status of Women During the Terror," 47), who cites the debate of 17 November: "One of the first to express this change in attitude was Chaumette, procurator of the Paris Commune. Amid a chorus of approving voices, he first

The officers of Oswald's battalion by secret ballot on 25 September elect a new commandant, Captain Joly. In October and early December the battalion is engaged in battles which, with deaths and desertions, reduce it from its original 1000 men to 280.[61] At a meeting at Ponts-de-Cé on 22 December, Joly insists on enforcing the exclusion of women from the battalion (according to a council decree of last 30 May, which Oswald had managed to ignore) because the presence of women can be a nuisance or even pernicious, from the talk they spread among the troops and their quarrels among themselves. The officers' council orders that the wives of Captain Leblanc and Lieutenant Balmette of the grenadiers and of Citizen Ranche, captain of the 4th Company, shall be required to retire within 24 hours from the Ponts-de-Cé, as useless. A week later Citizen Chamousset, who has delivered this message, reports disrespectful words used by Balmette against him and the council. But since Balmette promises to send his wife away within the day, the council is indulgent: to punish his insolence Balmette is sent to prison for four days, with a warning to be more circumspect in future.

On 18 January a new member of the council, Morisset, accuses Billon, Chausson, and Joly of having served in the King's Guard and cites a law requiring expulsion of such persons. Joly presents a service certificate proving that when there *was* a King's Guard he was in the 103rd Regiment of infantry, which he left to enter the gendarmery. Chausson and Billon swear they were never in anything but regular army corps. Joly is suspended 14 May, acquitted the following November, restored as chief on 19 December 1794.

On 24 May 1794, in a distribution of fresh clothing, "each of the two Oswald brothers" is assigned "1 *habit* and 1 *veste*."[62] On 1 November 1794, Oswald's name comes up in a discussion of the special organization of the pike corps, with a double complement of officers. His appointments have been criticized by officers who did not understand this special arrangement. It explains certain apparent discrepancies in the account.

---

scolded a deputation of women for bursting unheralded into the Convention . . . and then moved for confirmation of his conviction that 'the woman's place [is] in the home and only the man's in politics.' Not only was his motion unanimously accepted, but it was also decided to prohibit the deputation from speaking."

61. Chassin and Hennet, *Les Volontaires Nationaux*, 355–58, reconstruction of the unit, then stationed at Ponts-de-Cé; implications of disorder.

62. "Oswald (Jean), *volontarie, de Londres*" is listed in the 1st subdivision of the 2d Company in January 1794 (ibid., 365); "Oswald (Guillaume), *volontaire, de Londres*" (371) in the 4th subdivision of the 8th Company. The first name is not given in the listing of "Oswald, *tambour, mort à Crémone*, 5 Novembre, 1796" (463). Whoever started the rumor that the two sons were slain with their father was replaying the Laocoön legend. In *Cumbrian Discovery*, 127, Molly Lefebure gives an instance of the same legend in an account in Leland's *Itinerary* of 1710 of the storming of a fortress. King David II of Scotland slew the warrior defending it, we are told, after strangling his two sons "before their father's face." Lefebure has since discovered that those two sons, of Sir Walter Salebey, actually survived intact.

3. Ignorance and Treachery—and a New Writing Project

Skirmishes which people like Vignot seem to have avoided, but in which Oswald died, are seldom reported in detail. The few even recorded name only the generals. In short, we cannot "follow our hero's battle career"; it would be illusory and distracting to supply a map and a tale of actions. Battalions are not separately mentioned, nor even brigades compounded of battalions. The generals were indeed busy, some having just been transformed from city politicians into militarists overnight; the battles that mattered to them were those going on in the Convention and the Jacobin Club.

Once the troops of the Republic had got familiar with the territory, rumors of military magic on its way kept them idly waiting. Occasionally a battalion or a regiment would be dismissed for the day, to pillage.[63] In late June the magic finally arrived—in the form of twenty thousand elite (i.e., seasoned) troops from the garrisons of Valenciennes and Mainz (Mayence), where they had been under seige by the Austrians and, upon surrender, freed to return to France but never to return to the war. (Putting down rebels was not interpreted by the French commanders as coming under that ban.) The Royalists in the Vendee, however, viewed these troops as oath-breakers to be slain without quarter. For the generals of the Republic the only question was, "What army was to absorb this precious contingent and assure itself of the collaboration of such an offensive instrument?" Its "models of military fame" included "a Haxo, a Beaupuy, a Kleber."[64]

Meanwhile, the generals and the politicians on mission, from the Jacobin Club and the Convention, entangled themselves in quarrels over strategy and tactics. A plan was put forward by Canclaux to attack the rebels via the town of Nantes, with small detachments from many directions; he set about organizing a camp nearby for the purpose. A plan urged by Rossignol involved a massive attack via Angers and Saumur and encirclement. "The Nantes plan drew more approval, doubtless because Canclaux was more experienced than Rossignol and because the ex-marquis was better liked than the old silversmith."[65] The vain politician Philippeaux, deceived by the burghers of Nantes who knew him well, judged it irresistible. He went to the army of Mayence while it was still at Tours and persuaded his political colleagues to agree with him—Merlin and Rewbell, both quite ignorant of the Vendee. Most of the generals, however, preferred the Rossignol plan, as did Choudieu, who had been on mission since March.

Intrigues in Paris and Saumur led to a council of generals and politicos at Saumur. Three generals and seven politicos were for the plan of Canclaux;

63. See *Nouvelle Revue Retrospective* 103 (1903): 59.
64. Mallery, *Les Cinq Vendées*, 63.
65. Dubreuil, *Histoire des insurrections de l'Ouest*, 1 : 226ff.

seven generals and three politicos were for that of Rossignol; Rewbell, presiding, swung the vote in favor of Canclaux and Philippeaux. Politically, the moderates (*les honteux*: shamefaced) won out. Historians can only agree that neither plan was likely to prevent the shambles that followed.

By this time the Vendean rebels—the blues—had organized the cadres of their army, with d'Elbée as general in chief, proclaiming that anyone refusing to take up arms against the National Convention would be treated as its accomplice. Plans were made to upset the plan adopted by the Republicans at Saumur, and attacks were launched on 5 September, by Charett on the vanguard of Canclaux and by d'Elbée on the camp of Lecomte, and by Joly. Lecomte was driven into swift retreat, and the Vendeans, exceeding the orders of their own council of war, massacred all the Republican prisoners. As for the *levée en masse* (universal conscription) which Paris had to believe successful even in rebel country, the convention was told it had produced an incredible four hundred thousand new recruits in twenty-four hours. A sober figure would have been nearer fifteen thousand, still enough to dilute and confuse the volunteer regiments, if not the seasoned veterans of Mayence.[66]

One paragraph in the extensive account I have been drawing upon will take us rapidly to Thouars on the day of Oswald's death:

> On September 6, the brigade of the avant garde seized d'Erigné, which was retaken at once by Rochejacquelein[67] and d'Autichamp, only to be lost again. These affairs and some others of slight importance . . . delayed for several days the general offensive which resumed towards the 16th of September.[68] The two divisions of the army of Saumur were commanded by Santerre and Duhoux. As for other affairs . . . there were those of Martigne-Briant and of Thouars where the Vendeans were as clearly defeated as at Erigné and at Doué. In the latter encounter, La Rochejacquelein was wounded in the hand and Stofflet in the thigh. At Thouars, Lescure, who had begun the attack, was routed by general Rey who with regular troops arrived in time to rescue the "*levée en masse*."

No one tells us where the 14th Battalion meshed in, whether among the "regular troops" or as a body that had absorbed a portion of the *levée*. Oswald at least escaped the indignity of the defeat that ensued:

> Proud of these successes, Santerre advanced on the 18th as far as Coron, in the direction of Cholet. He commanded about 16,000 men, of whom 6,000 were regulars.[69] But he had imprudently drawn out his column over more than three leagues and allowed the artillery to get caught up among infantry. [Cholet is about 20 miles from Thouars.] Hence a first attack . . . had been checked. The Vendean chiefs . . . issued such vigorous calls for peasants that d'Elbée soon had at his disposal a suffi-

66. Doubtless Stone's figures for the great rise in enlistments in Paris (cited above) were similarly inflated.
67. A name to remember: see below.
68. Here Dubreuil is quoting Mallery, *Les Cinq Vendées*, 64.
69. On the 16th Santerre had dictated a boasting letter which the *Moniteur* printed on the

ciently strong army. He had it take up positions on the surrounding heights, from which it could direct unobstructed fire upon the republicans clumsily engaged "in deep roads and coverts, where they could not manoeuver". . . . So the victory was soon decided, the army of Santerre was completely beaten, and in the retreat, the wretched peasants of the levées en masse . . . seized with fright, whelmed with fatigue, let themselves be killed without defending themselves. The Vendeans, weary of the carnage, let some of the men go, bestowing life upon them. The army of Santerre was fully dispersed in this day's battle and it fled this time all the way back to Saumur. The insurgents captured a dozen cannons.

Enough. During these skirmishes and battles, the representatives sitting with pen and ink in the camps or villages could regale Convention and Club with dispatches such as the one by National Commissioner Momoro, with greetings from "our brave general in chief Rossignol" in Saumur, 13 August, telling of a lieutenant guillotined for having fled from the enemy while his company stood firm. (Vignot had been a lucky one; no talk of guillotines in Oswald's council.) And of how sixteen of our hussars came upon forty enemy cavalry at Thouars, leading six carts of grain: the hussars shot three, dangerously wounded several, and captured the carts and grain for our patriots. "Not one of our sixteen received the slightest scratch."

But no one reported to Jacobins or Convention the action at Thouars in which Oswald's battalion fought. I can find only this brief summary in a history published in 1840:[70]

> The blues had established a fortified camp on the rocks of Erigné. On September 8, Bonchamp and La Rochejacquelein carried this post with the bayonet, leaving the Ponts-de-Cé undefended. During the combat Henri received a bullet in his hand . . . but he fought on. Stofflet replaced him in command of his corps. On the 14th the latter marches against the republicans entrenched at Doué. Santerre has a much larger army and excellent generals. He does not fly. A charge of horse and a coordinated movement by general Turreau turn the right of the Vendeans. Stofflet is wounded in the thigh; but his wound does not prevent him from withdrawing his badly cornered troops, who had not yet got into serious peril.
>
> The same day, Lescure leaves his camp at Saint-Sauveur. He tries with two thousand men to attack the blues assembled at Thouars under the command of Burac. They were a fraction of those *levées en masse* who were supposed to inundate the Vendee.
>
> He is about to scatter them, when general Rey arrives with his division and forces Lescure to rally his troops who are already chasing the fleeing blues. It was after this affair that one discovered on the battlefield the cadaver of a woman with weapons still in her hand. The *Moniteur* and other journals announced that this was madame

---

24th: "Citizens, our day offers nothing remarkable except that the enemy flies before us, and that our army, which was only 6,000 men on leaving Doué, has increased now to 40,000 men, with whom we are making small patrols of 12,000 . . . ."

70. Cretineau-Joly, *Histoire de la Vendée Militaire*, 1:222–23.

Lescure, others said that this woman was the Jeanne-d'Arc of the Vendee, the miraculous Virgin who made the peasants fanatic.

Madame Lescure lived to write about this Amazon whose body was found where we were looking for Oswald's:

The news-sheets made a great story out of this. Some said it was I and others that it was Jeanne de Lescure, the sister of the brigand-chief. It was thought that she was regarded in the Vendee as a saint, like Joan of Arc. This last guess was just as inaccurate as the others.[71] All the generals had issued strict orders forbidding women to join the forces, threatening to expel with ignominy the first woman found in the ranks, and during the short period of recruitment not even *vivandières* were enlisted. A short while before the action at Thouars, a soldier had come up to me at la Boulaye, saying he wanted to confide in me. It was a woman, who wanted to change her woollen vest for one of Siamese cloth such as they served out to the poorest soldiers. Fearing to be recognized she had applied to me, begging me to say nothing to M. de Lescure. I found out that her name was Jeanne Robin from Courlay. I wrote to the vicar of the parish about her. He replied that she was a very good girl but that he had never been able to dissuade her from going to the war. She had been to communion before leaving for the front. On the day before the battle of Thouars, she went to find M. de Lescure and said to him: "General, I'm a girl. Mme de Lescure knows this. She also knows that there is nothing against me. Tomorrow there'll be a battle. Tell them to give me a pair of shoes. After you have seen me fight, I am sure you won't send me away." And in fact she fought without ceasing in sight of M. de Lescure, calling to him, "General, you won't get ahead of me; I shall always be nearer the 'Blues' than you." She was wounded in the hand, but that seemed only to raise her spirits. She showed him her hand and said, "That's nothing at all." At last she was killed in the hand-to-hand fighting into which she had dashed like a fury.[72]

71. The idea that there was a Virgin of the Vendee is a Republican invention, says Dubreuil (*Histoire des insurrections*, 224– 25); the miracle was the women's courage. According to the *Memoires* of the daughter of commander Rochejacquelein, however, although "there cannot have been, altogether, more than ten women in disguise who were bearing arms," there were several "in other divisions." She saw "two sisters of fourteen and fifteen years, who were most courageous. In the army of M. de Bonchamp, a girl had made herself a cavalier to avenge the death of her father; she accomplished prodigies of valor in all the wars of the Vendee, under the name of l'Angevin: she is the only country woman who did combat who is still alive. I saw also one day arrive at Chollet a young woman, large and quite beautiful, who carried two pistolets in her belt and a sabre: she was accompanied by two other women armed with pikes; she was brought to my father as a spy and on interrogation replied that she was of the parish of Everybody (*Tout-le-Monde*), and that there women form the guard when the men go into the army. She received much praise; her slightly martial air rendered her still more charming" (*Mémoires de Madame la Marquise de la Rochejacquelein* [1918], 217–18). And need we dismiss as mere "popular credulity" (as Emsley does, *English Society and the French Wars*, 26) the diary entry of 3 February 1793 by William Rowbottom about "two women in officer's uniform" captured at the battle of Hochheim? One "had received three wounds and the other that evening was delivered of a fine boy." Such warriors did make good theater, of course. Collot, in the Jacobin Club on 3 March 1793, presented a "heroine, dressed as a man, who took part in the last campaign with her husband and asks to return to the war" (Aulard, ed., *Recueil des Documents . . . des Jacobins*, 5:62).

72. George Pernoud and Sabine Flaissier, eds., *Mémoires of Madame la Rochejacquelein*, trans. Richard Graves, 302–3.

On the 14th, sitting in his tent at Saumur, General Rossignol made this report to the Convention; the fifteen thousand men having got multiplied by ten:

> The tocsin sounds everywhere, the inhabitants of the fields have taken up arms, 150 thousand men armed with fusils, pikes, haches, faulx, have joined themselves to us, both at Augers and Thouars, Doué and Saumur; the great blows are about to be given. . . . Today, the 14th, the rebels have begun their attacks at Doué, at Thouars and at Hervan; we do not yet have the details of this latter place. But we have completely beaten the enemy at Doué and at Thouars. We hear that in the affair of Thouars, where general Ray commanded, 15 men were wounded, 6 killed. We have taken from the enemy two cannon, three munitions wagons, the fore-wheels of a piece which we threw into the water, unable to save it but that we may fish it out. We don't yet know the number of enemy dead at Doué.
>
> The rebels attacked the army at 11 a.m. at all points; they had two eight-pounders and six four-pounders. Our left was for an instant forced. General Santerre, who commanded the avant-garde, sent the 5th battalion of the formation of Orleans who restored battle contact there. In the center, the flying artillery, consisting of a 12 pound cannon and a howitzer (*obusier*), repulsed the brigands. One of our howitzers set fire to one of their munitions wagons. We captured one of their 8 pound guns and a howitzer which, after having been reversed, had fallen into their hands. Their forces were bearing close upon our left, already fatigued; but the dragoons of the 16th regiment, the hussars of the 7th and 8th fell upon the enemy cavalry and managed to disperse the rebels; all the soldiers and contingents bore themselves like heroes. We have slain a great company of enemies; we are beating them back on all fronts. The roads of Vihiers and Brissac are strewn with their dead; we hope to be at Mortagne within two days; the gendarmerie have consistently sustained their reputation for bravery. Among the brave soldiers who have distinguished themselves Mouran, commandant of the battalion of l'Unité [a Paris section] wounded in a recent affair by a ball which pierced his buttocks, has done wonders at the head of his battalion; citizen Gereau, sub-commander of the second, having been pierced by a ball in the shoulder, continued to command immediately after the dressing of his wound, and followed the rebels to the bottom of Concurson. The soldiers of the army of the coasts of La Rochelle followed the example of the army of Mayence, the same ardor animating them, the same success crowned their efforts.

Signed: ROSSIGNOL.[73]

I surmise that Gereau was Michel Gareaux, of Paris, a sergeant of the first subdivision of the company of grenadiers in Oswald's battalion. If Oswald had survived his wounds, he might have appeared in this account; or in the public prints, if he had died in combat with Jeanne Robin. Indeed, if slain drummerboys had fallen beside him, that too would have thrilled the Convention. I mean to say, the battlefield was scrutinized closely enough, after all, to make the silence about Oswald suggest that the legend of the boys' death was a later

73. *Moniteur*, 16 September 1792.

invention. The legend of his dying in conflict with his own men has plausibility, but I think the verdict has to be: nothing proven.[74]

The spirit of Oswald lived on for a while, ironically, in Collot, who seemed to be with characteristic ambivalence under his influence. In the Convention on 18 September Collot speaks for a proposal he is making to extend the definition of "suspects" to include merchants of provisions who price food exorbitantly (we must fetch down the mercantile aristocracy) and disseminators of false news, good or bad, that harms our armies; and (a Collot accommodation as good as Danton's) that all suspects be, not slain, but locked up until the war's end.

"Armons nos soldats de piques!" is Collot's cry on the 20th. And indeed at this time "the pike again seemed to be the only answer to the problem of combating tyranny," observes Soboul. "On 14 August, the Convention listened to an address praising its many attributes—'the most feared of all weapons . . . this terrible and invincible arm.'"[75] But the solutions I think Oswald would have liked best are those proposed by Chaumette ("Hyper-Jacobin" to Carlyle) in the Jacobin Club, 23 August:

> Two things combine to destroy the morale of the republicans: ignorance and treachery. It is not enough to arrest suspects, and the *levée en masse* is full of difficulties. We should request the Convention (1) to decree deportation for all aristocrats and suspects; (2) to raise *an army* [instead of that mass levy] choosing the best 24 men of each canton, armed, which would mean 200,000 armed Jacobins; (3) that the Jacobins get busy on a new writing project, similar to the *Almanach of Father Gerard*, to make the people see the excellence of the popular constitution it defines. This is a great way to combat ignorance.

It is so ordered; Chaumette is to undertake the writing. (Collot is not mentioned.)[76]

Another member of the Quatorze, more legal-minded and now a judge, has a symbolic idea. "On the proposal of Garan-Coulon, the Assembly decrees that the cap of liberty be substituted for the *fleur-de-lys* painted on all the mileposts which line the roads of France."[77]

---

74. But Alger's conjecture (*Englishmen*, 77–78), repeated by Veitch (*The Genesis of Parliamentary Reform*, 222), that Maxwell, since he disappeared from Paris, may have died with Oswald in battle, has no foundation. Dr. Maxwell lived to serve as companion to Robert Burns in his dying years, 1795–1796, Burns calling him "my most intimate friend," who comforted him medically but also shared a "mutual belief in the French Revolution" (Thornton, *Maxwell to Burns*, 175). He died in 1834.

75. *The Parisian Sans-culottes*, 226.

76. Aulard, ed., *Recueil des Documents . . . des Jacobins*, 5:370.

77. *Moniteur*, 20 September 1793.

10.
LAST WORDS

―――――◆――――――――――――――――――――――――――――――

"This remote prospect it is alone that cheers my heart"

Originally I meant to end this book with a summary and an assessment of Oswald's character and ideas. All his "biographers" have some of their information wrong, and some have tilted their evaluations. While attempting to sift out the facts and probabilities from the accumulating scraps of biography and hearsay, and to place them in the varying contexts of his unusual career, I have come, and the reader I hope with me, to be more familiar with him and yet more curious about him. My search has produced many questions about his life—how many children did he leave behind, and how many wives; how did his battalion feel toward him; who were his real friends, and how did they get along with him in private? But an evaluation of his personality and his philosophy must await a closer study of his works in their Enlightenment context than I have given them. All I can hope to do here is to bring him and his works to the attention of modern readers.

Accurate identification of context, however, can supply credibility as the story fills out. Taken in isolation, or in the supplied context of the later Terror, Yorke's Oswald drawing his sword to end a conversation can seem terrible. In April 1793 the Jacobin Duperret, who drew his sword during a dispute in the Convention, "an honest man, good father, good friend," and then felt he had been possessed by "a kind of sacred madness," was behaving the same way in the same alarm-filled period. To remind us of that time, briefly, we need only Carlyle's chapter headings for March and April: "Growing Shrill," "Fatherland in Danger," and "In Death-Grips." Fitting the act to the dreadful context increases our comprehension and sympathy.

Regarding his resemblance to the Oswald of Wordsworth's *Borderers*, manifest in the broad outlines of his military career and in his attempt to combine revolutionary action with vegetarian beliefs, I have come to realize that beneath the surface resemblances—which Wordsworth could have derived from gossip or from the biographies in reviews—these two Oswalds were very different persons. For his drama, in 1797, Wordsworth needed a pair of contrasting revolutionaries and drew somewhat upon the career of John Oswald for his "Robespierre" type of villain. Actually he first named him "Danby," then "Rivers," and only forty-five years later "Oswald."[1]

The character analysis of this villain, which Wordsworth offered in 1797 and repeated briefly in 1842, depicts him as "a young Man of great intellectual powers, yet without any solid principles of genuine benevolence," who, as a revolutionary warrior, is "betrayed into a great crime" and then deliberately betrays another revolutionary warrior, "an amiable young man" like Wordsworth, into a form of parricide resembling regicide. John Oswald could be shaped into such a villain only by removing his brain and grafting the central mutinous action of Fletcher Christian of the good ship *Bounty* (very familiar to Wordsworth) in the place of Oswald's duel with Macleod. In short, Wordsworth's purpose was to write a drama in the vein of Schiller's *Die Räuber* and not to evaluate John Oswald. He remembered the name, indeed; he even used it for one of his military heroes during the later Napoleonic era.[2] He knew a good deal about Oswald but never wrote directly about him.

I believe that the study of John Oswald and the investigation of the revolutionary enthusiasm that was in the air and the projects that were in debate during Wordsworth's Paris weeks (plans to take what Wordsworth called "philosophical war" to Dublin or to London, or to join some unit of the French army) may help recover the perceptions and intentions of Wordsworth at that time. For example, consider his leaving Annette and unborn Caroline at the end of 1792; and his returning to Paris in October 1793 (if true)—can he have been one of the spies of the British Club sent to London to sound out the insurrectionary potential? But the further development of such inquiries is work for a different study.[3]

1. For Wordsworth's manuscript notes of 1797 and 1842, see *The Borderers*, ed. Osborn, 62–68, 813–15.

2. Like many authors, Wordsworth seldom invented names. When in *The Excursion* (7.757–816) he wrote about the Grasmere Volunteers, which he had joined for a day in 1803, he named their commander "Oswald," lamenting his early death and defining him as a hero in whom "a scholar's genius shone," a valiant instructor in "the rudiments of war," "like a chief / And yet a modest comrade," and—shades of John Oswald's vegetarianism—a youth who opposed the shooting of wild animals for food, despite his "steady aim" with quoit or football. Years later, in 1841, Wordsworth gave the name "Oswald" to the villainous Rivers in *The Borderers*; and he said that the actual Grasmere commander he had in mind in *The Excursion* was a "gallant young man" named George Dawson, whose father had led him to take "delight in scholarship" (*Poetical Works*, ed. De Selincourt and Darbishire, 467).

3. It is much harder to find solid information about Wordsworth's movements and associations in France than about Oswald's (see Reed, *Wordsworth: The Chronology of the Early Years*, passim). The legend that he had resided in the same building as Brissot when in Paris, for example, seemed fully confirmed by the deductions of J. R. MacGillivray in a note in *TLS*, 29 January 1931; yet it was later found that Wordsworth had directly denied this legend when it was called to his attention (see Moorman, *Wordsworth: A Biography; The Early Years*, 202n). It seems more certain that, as Moorman observes, Wordsworth did a great deal of reading in the months away from

Regarding William Thomson's notion, "which he laboured to prove by a long deduction of circumstance, that Bonaparte was in reality John Oswald, the son of the jeweler in Edinburgh," I am not sure even that we have it right. The fullest report of Thomson's idea comes from Maj.-Gen. David Stewart and reeks with disapproval, which may not have been Thomson's in spirit. "He alleged," says Stewart, "that Oswald . . . was a violent Republican, as was once the supposed Bonaparte—that he changed his religion, and became Mahomedan—that though he talked much about liberty, it was only liberty to act as he chose, as he was cruel, tyrannical, and imperious in his practice—that he was a man of great courage and fearless enterprise—that he was fond of Ossian, had his poems always in his mouth, and spoke in heroic language; all which was seen in the character and conduct of Bonaparte; therefore Oswald and Bonaparte must have been the same."[4]

For one thing, Oswald may have been imperious in his officers' council, but he was not a Napoleon, keeping to his tent, instilling fear. I do not know just where Oswald was during the attack on the Tuileries in August 1792, but he would not have been looking on, as Napoleon was, with detachment and scorn of the mob. I know what Sampson Perry meant in describing him as "the meekest man living," and I can feel grief for him, but not the "vain and unthinking grief" which Wordsworth caught himself feeling for Napoleon. I am not even sure whether there was some glitter in Oswald's eye, as in the Ancient Mariner's, that turned people away just when they were about to make him a citizen of France or to continue a serious argument, or whether it was just bad luck that no one followed up the announced intention about the citizenship—and that his February speech got printed but not put into the proceedings. I have no reason to doubt Perry's statement that an obituary account was given to the Convention expressing "the gallant and exemplary conduct and courage of this officer, even when the name of an Englishman was in no repute in Paris,"[5] although no such account has been found. The Thouars battle was by report effectively conducted even if not strategically important. And considering how haphazard was the reporting of remarks in the Jacobin Club and the Convention, we are fortunate to have as much on record as we do.

The repute of British citizens was indeed low that September. On 1 August the Convention had passed a decree, effective in October, sending the traditional enemies of France to prison who "had been imprudent enough to remain in France after the declaration of war against Britain"—to quote the Scottish *Lives* version, which records a legend that Oswald himself, as a Jacobin, was exempt from such treatment and "was particularly blamed" for this decree.

Paris; all I can say is that *if* he read Oswald's political works then, his response must have been very different from Burke's—or from Redhead Yorke's.

4. David Stewart, *Sketches of the Highland Regiments*, vol. 2, note 5.

5. *Argus*, 26 December 1795.

(He had left Paris long since, of course.) On the other hand, the legend adds that "he warned his countrymen of the measure, and impressed on many of them the danger they incurred by remaining in the country." The point being that he was more than a bit mad—a vegetarian wild for blood, yet still human: "In this at least there was no want of national or friendly feeling." [6]

Oswald had left the capital long before any such decree, yet in that March of alarm and disarray, especially within the revolutionary movement, he may well have foreseen the coming anti-British sentiment and hence both approved of the security measures suggested for the remnant of the British Club and advised uncommitted British citizens to leave.

Oswald as Hero of Anglo-French Collaboration

At this point I should like to quote the highly retrospective evaluation of Oswald by Eugene Varé published in Paris in 1858 as the first of an intended series of sixteen-page studies of English poets, the memorial purpose of which was to "introduce the French to all the English poets, not only Shakespeare, Byron, and Scott," at a moment in history when Oswald's ideal of Anglo-French collaboration had come to fruition. In the recent Crimean War, Varé's countrymen had fought "side by side" with the British and would appreciate as triply suitable the "great surprise" of beginning with the almost-unknown John Oswald: British, and a poet, and a soldier, "one of the great precursors of the Anglo-French alliance." [7]

Varé's main source was the anonymous life of Oswald in the 1821 *Lives of the Scottish Poets*. He does not quite say as much, but he is severe upon "the Scottish biographer, who is far from sharing the ideas of its hero" and has made "so severe a critique of him." We can agree with this French admirer that "A bit less declamation and a bit more chronology and history would have better suited our purposes." He hopes, nevertheless, to be able to make Oswald remembered and, "if not loved, at least lamented and respected." Agreeing with the biographer that Oswald's ideas and doctrines "went much further than the common run," he insists that they must be taken seriously. "There has never been a more intrepid Pythagorean. . . . Though unable to explain why man is armed with canine teeth, he abstained no less religiously from all kinds of meat . . . ." Unaware of the guillotine symbolism of wearing one's hair "à la Titus," Varé deduces that Oswald attached importance to the "little matters"

---

6. Eugene Varé, in *Etudes sur les Poëtes Anglais: John Oswald* (see below), embroiders on both sides of this tale, having Oswald vote for the decree yet intervene "courageously in favor of . . . his countrymen who, not personally associating with the revolutionary movement, had imprudently lingered in France."

7. This first fascicle was the last; the series did not go on. But Varé's correction of the bias in the *Lives* did influence the later essay of Lichtenberg.

of dress and so struggles to justify such "oddity" in the mind of a potentially "great spirit."

He does appreciate how such a spirit must have welcomed the French Revolution and even put aside his natural hostility to bloodshed in accepting the reality that "for the health of the state, one may well sacrifice several thousand men." Sad that Oswald was assigned to "one of the revolutionary legions commanded by career officers." Yet even had he not died in battle, a man with "such excess in his ideas, above all on the part of a foreigner," would have "paid for the 'Universal Republic'" as Kock and Clootz did, or have "accompanied Danton to the scaffold." Thermidor he could not have survived. At the end, Varé apologizes for having said "very little about the poet" but observes that, "very happily for mankind, one may be a friend of progress without also being a great poet," since, candidly, "despite the somewhat circumstantial praise given him by Robert Burns, Oswald is no more than a pleasant versifier."

But Oswald was "a brave soldier, whom one must never reproach for an excess of fervor in the cause of democracy and some aberrations of spirit which belonged more to the evil of the times than to the character of the man. Oswald was good, loving, moderate even in his excess. . . . He did not hesitate to sacrifice himself in order to give good soldiers to his new country," nor to speak up in the Jacobin Club "courageously in favor of his countrymen." [8]

On Liberty and Law—and Love

And now let us all read the luminous words of:

The Government of The People, &c.
By John Oswald, Anglo-Franc.
Printed at the English Press. [9]

. . . Now, it is upon the rights of man, or, in other words, on the nature of man alone, that a just government can be founded. The whole art of government, there-

8. Varé has the occasions of his speaking up confused, as in his source, but the idea fits the actual spirit of Oswald's defense of "Manchester" and his insistence on international fraternal communication.

9. The telescopic pun *Anglo-franc* (not Anglo-Jacobin) implies to the sympathetic: British-French/*franc-franque*/candor about Freedom. Earlier I suggested that the imprint on Oswald's *Review of the Constitution,* "Paris, printed at the English Press by Gillet, 1792," meant a book printed in London for sale in Paris. The *Government* imprint, however, has no printer's name but a Paris address, "No 1412, rue Notre Dame des Champs." Possibly both books were printed in Paris, first using Gillet's name, though he remained in London; later using Stone's. Stern ("The English Press in Paris," 316), identifying the "first book" of Stone's "English Press" as Barlow's *Vision* (July 1793), deduces that the press was located in Rue de Vaugirard, Barlow's own address (later, at least). A clue suggesting "British Club" efforts to establish a press in Paris in autumn 1792 (when British spies were reporting the plans of Oswald and Stone and others to disseminate democracy from Paris) is a spy's report of October 1792 that Eleazar Oswald was in London purchasing "new types" for shipment somewhere (PRO TS 11 965/3510, A 2; noted by Nicholas Roe). Ultimately

fore, is reduced to this, to ascertain and to execute the Will of the People: and a Constitution should mean neither more nor less than a political machine, by which the will of the nation shall at all times be ascertained and executed. . . . A nation that does not assemble, cannot even be considered as existing in a state of society.[10] . . . A nation that does not deliberate, cannot will; for . . . no proposition can be clearly understood that is not previously discussed. Let us suppose, for instance, that the French Nation had been assembled two or three years ago, to decide, without deliberation, Whether the King should have the *suspensive veto*? It is extremely probable, that the great majority of the people, puzzled by the barbarous obscurity of the phrase, and imagining that the *suspensive veto* meant only some insignificant bauble, like the crown, or the scepter, or some such glittering trinket of royalty; it is extremely probable, I say, that they would, without hesitation, have granted this privilege to the king. Had they, on the contrary, examined the proposition, most certainly they would never have committed to the hands of an individual, often an idiot or a madman, and from the vice of his education almost always a fool, the power of controlling the will and counteracting the wisdom of the nation. . . .

But the people, say the politicians, cannot deliberate except by their Representatives. Now, if the nation can deliberate by proxy, they may also assemble by proxy, and decide by proxy, and thus the whole Sovereignty of the People will dwindle down to

"*Vox et preterea nihil*," [11]

a vote to choose their masters; and the government will resemble that shadowy semblance of things, in which poets pourtray [*sic*] the nether world,

"Where unsubstantial shadows mock the sight." [12]

I confess I have never been able to consider this representative system, without wondering at the easy credulity with which the human mind swallows the most palpable absurdities. Were a man seriously to propose, that the nation should piss by proxy, he would doubtless be regarded as a madman; and yet, to *think by proxy*, is a proposition which we hear not only without astonishment, but even with approbation. We cannot exercise for each other the meanest functions of animal existence; and can we then perform for each other the highest functions of intellectual life? But the fact is, that although we cannot think for each other any more than we can love for each other, or eat and drink for each other, yet, by the habit of delegating to others the task of thinking for us, we insensibly unlearn to think altogether; and this answers wonderfully well the charitable purpose of those Gentlemen who are willing to save us the trouble of thinking for ourselves. . . .

One Man imposed upon his moon-struck audience, with a Mission from the God-

Stone became the chief printer in Paris, printing the government tax papers (Alger, *Englishmen*, 68).

10. This is the phrase used to dismiss Yorke—or did Yorke concoct the details of his "recollected" conversation from this pamphlet? It obviously fascinated him.

11. "A voice and beyond that nothing": proverbial Latin phrase, sometimes applied to the nightingale.

12. Not traced, but perhaps (suggests Rick Boland) an Oswaldian echo of Shakespeare's sonnet 61, line 4: "While shadows like to thee do mock my sight?" (perhaps both based in Petrarch).

dess of the Night; another, in virtue of representing the Sun, dazzled into political blindness the weak eyes of his countrymen; Moses, as the representative of a mixed monster Half-God Half-Devil, led through the desert the slaves of the Egyptians; and, in virtue of representing a poor crack-brained Fisherman of Jerusalem, who lived a many hundred years ago, the proud Pontif of modern Rome sends to hell the souls of the deceased, or transmits them as it pleases his Holiness to heaven.

But the most plausible of all frauds, and withal the most successful, was the pretence of representing the People. The General of a standing army became King or Chief of the Nation; . . . the King . . . the National Assemblies . . . the Military . . . in short, such was the kind solicitude of those several classes of men to save the people free from all the cares of acting or thinking, that at last they made it high treason for the People to act, think, or wield a weapon for themselves. The People were even forbid to assemble, *for any rational purpose*, under the penalty of being shot at.

The system of representation recalls to my mind a certain class of Indian Physicians, who cured all diseases with a dance: if the sick man could not dance for himself, the Physician danced for him; and this, it was said, operated *virtually* the same effect. Representation is at all times ready to dance for the people, her poor patient who cannot dance for himself, and all she requires in return is—that he should pay the piper.

In fine, the representation supplanted the reality . . . the column of government was reversed, and the political man was made to walk upon his head. This anarchy . . . was called order, and the first efforts of man to regain his natural position, were treated as . . . if heaven and earth were going to mingle together, and that chaos were again about to swallow up the world. An eloquent madman[13] wrote an exhortation to the Princes of Europe to suffocate . . . the monstrous birth of Liberty; and contributed . . . to encourage that conspiracy of kings which has hastened, perhaps, by half a century, the overthrow of royalty in Europe. . . . The political mountebanks among the English, who have long managed, certainly with great dexterity, the magic lanthorn of representation, invented a jargon peculiar to themselves. They talked of the balance of the three powers, the great advantage resulting from the reciprocal check of kings, lords, and commons, and so nicely on a thousand rope-dancing difficulties of political refinement did they poise the great interests of the nation, that the wonder-struck spectator was every moment in fear lest the tottering fabric of the state should tumble upon the stage, and break in pieces like a glass bottle. . . . The jugglers of the Constituent Assembly borrowed the jargon of their elder brethren of England.[14] They declared, that the government of France was representative, that is to say, that the government should not in reality belong to the people, but only in representation or shew; in short, it was to be a sham-government of the people. . . . they were ready to say to the nation, "you shall be king;" but they were willing also to add, in the words of the drunken sailor in The Tempest, "and I shall be vice-roy over you."

It is however extremely probable, that when the revolution ceases to reel . . . this language of intoxication will no longer be tolerated in the deputies of the nation: I

13. Burke, of course.

14. Oswald's footnote: "Fox, Pitt, and other mountebanks of the English Parliament, had a much greater share in the *confection* of the deceased Constitution, than is generally imagined. They, it was, in a great measure, that prompted the jargon of Barnave, and instructed the serpent subtleties of La Fayette and d'André." (Not given in the French edition.)

will venture to predict, that if the second Constituent Assembly [i.e., the Convention] should form a constitution, founded on what is called, the principles of representation, that it will not last so long as the first. In a short time . . . the people will be satisfied with nothing short of a real and actual exercise of the Sovereignty . . . . Let us suppose, for instance, that the National Assembly [15] should propose for deliberation, Whether the land should be cultivated in common, or divided equally between the individuals of the nation? the neighbourhoods would instantly take into deliberation the question agitated by the National Assembly, and the whole understanding of the nation, would, at the same moment, be exercised upon the same point. [Six pages are given to specifics of assembling and administration.]

With regard to the . . . objection . . . that public affairs would so occupy the attention of the Nation, that people would have no time to attend to their private concerns; I have remarked that this objection is commonly found in the mouths of men, who yet think it no waste of time that the people should dance attendance at the heels of the Priest for six months in the year. They think it perfectly fit, that the people should pass their time in the performance of barbarous ceremonies, too ridiculous for the practice of a dancing dog . . . .

But . . . what is, or ought to be, the great end of government but to unite men in bands of brotherhood? [16] And how is that to be effected, except by assembling often to deliberate in common? The best government, therefore, will be that which renders the actions of men as public as possible; and it is by this means only, that we can establish the reign of WILL, LIBERTY, LAW, LOVE which in the primitive wisdom of language, proceed from the same root, and signify the same thing. [17] Let us hope, that in the future progress of the Revolution, the collective wisdom of man will break at last, the iron yoke of property, [18] and restore to our Children the felicities of the Golden Age; the common inheritance of the earth; the unbounded community of enjoyment.— This remote prospect [and here suddenly he looks up with sad if glittering eye] it is alone that cheers my heart, in the midst of the corruption of society; this it is alone that pours into my bosom the balsam of consolation, amid the soul corroding cares that consume my existence.

FINIS.

15. Above, Oswald calls the National Convention "the Second Constituent Assembly," because that's what it ought to be; here he is not talking, anachronistically, about the National Convention or earlier National Assembly, but about the ideal system built up from Primary Assemblies.

16. Not "douces etreintes" here but "liens de la fraternité."

17. In his first page (not quoted here) Oswald asserts the derivation of "Will, Liberty, and Law" from the same root. He now adds "Love," the introduction of which is as crucial for the Revolution as the introduction of Luvah among Blake's Four Zoas. (Oswald's root source is the name "Apollo.") But he decomposes it thus: Law = los, *leg = to bring together, collect; love, i.3 = *leubh, to be fond of; will = *wel, to wish, to choose.

18. This is the phrase that staggered Burke.

Appendix A

Royal Proclamation of 1 June 1787

[Seal.] By the King. A PROCLAMATION For the Encouragement of Piety and Virtue, and for the preventing and punishing of Vice, Profaneness, and Immorality. George R.

Whereas We cannot but observe, with inexpressible Concern, the rapid Progress of Impiety and Licentiousness, and that Deluge of Profaneness, Immorality, and every Kind of Vice, which, to the Scandal of Our Holy Religion and to the evil Example of Our loving Subjects, hath broken in upon this Nation:

We therefore esteeming it Our indispensable Duty to exert the Authority committed to Us for the Suppression of these spreading Evils, fearing lest that they should provoke God's Wrath and Indignation against Us, and humbly acknowledging that We cannot expect the Blessing and Goodness of Almighty God (by whom Kings reign, and on which We entirely rely) to make Our Reign happy and prosperous to Ourself and Our People without a religious Observance of God's Holy Law:

To the Intent that Religion, Piety and Good Manners, may (according to Our most hearty Desire) flourish and increase under Our Administration and Government, have thought fit by the Advice of Our Privy Council to issue this Our Royal Proclamation, and do hereby declare Our Royal Purpose and Resolution to discountenance and punish all manner of Vice, Profaneness, and Immorality, in all Persons of whatever Degree or Quality, within this Our Realm, and particularly in such as are employed near Our Royal Person; and that for the Encouragement of Religion and Morality, We will, upon all Occasions, distinguish Persons of Piety and Virtue, by Marks of Our Royal Favour.

And We do expect and require, that all Persons of Honour, or in Place of Authority, will give good Example by their own Piety and Virtue, and to their utmost contribute to the discountenancing Persons of dissolute and debauched Lives, that they being reduced by that Means to Shame and Contempt for their loose and evil Actions and Behaviour, may be thereby also enforced the sooner to reform their ill Habits and Practices, and that the visible Displeasure of good Men towards them, may (as far as it is possible) supply what the Laws (probably) cannot altogether prevent:

And We do hereby strictly enjoin and prohibit all Our loving Subjects, of what Degree or Quality soever, from playing on the Lord's Day, at Dice, Cards, or any other Game whatsoever, either in publick or private Houses, or other Place or Places whatsoever:

And we do hereby require and commend them, and every of them, decently and reverently to attend the Worship of God on the Lord's Day, on Pain of Our highest Displeasure, and of being proceeded against with the utmost Rigour that may be by Law.

And, for the more effective reforming all such Persons, who, by reason of their dissolute Lives and Conversation, are a Scandal to Our Kingdom, Our further Pleasure is, and We do hereby strictly charge and command all Our Judges, Mayors, Sheriffs, Justices of the Peace, and all other Our Officers and Ministers, both Ecclesiastical and Civil, and all other Our Subjects, to be very vigilant and strict in the Discovery and the effective prosecution and Punishment of all Persons, who shall be guilty of excessive Drinking, Blasphemy, Profane Swearing and Cursing, Lewdness, Profanation of the Lord's Day, or other dissolute, immoral, or disorderly Practices; and that they take care also effectively to suppress all publick Gaming Houses and other loose and disorderly Houses; and also all unlicensed Publick Shews, Interludes, and Places of Entertainment, using the utmost Caution in licensing the same;

Also to suppress all loose and licentious Prints, Books and Publications, dispensing Poison to the Minds of the Young and Unwary, and to punish the Publishers and Venders thereof; and to put in Execution the Statute made in the Twenty-ninth Year of the Reign of the late King *Charles* the Second, intitled, *An Act for the better Observation of the Lord's Day, commonly called* Sunday; and also an Act of Parliament made in the Ninth Year of the Reign of the late King *William* the Third, intitled, *An Act for the more effectual suppressing of Blasphemy and Profaneness*; and also an Act passed in the Twenty-first Year of Our Reign, intitled, *An Act for preventing certain Abuses and Profanations on the Lord's Day*, called Sunday; and all other Laws now in Force for the punishing and suppressing any of the Vices aforesaid; and also to suppress and prevent all Gaming whatsoever, in Publick or Private Houses, on the Lord's Day; and likewise, that they take effective Care to prevent all Persons keeping Taverns, Chocolate Houses, Coffee Houses, or other Publick Houses whatsoever, from selling Wine, Chocolate, Coffee, Ale, Beer or other Liquors, or receiving or permitting Guests to be or remain in such their Houses in the Time of Divine Service on the Lord's Day, as they will answer it to Almighty God, and upon Pain of Our highest Displeasure.

And for the more effective Proceeding herein, We do hereby direct and command all Our Judges of Assize and Justices of the Peace, to give strict Charge at their respective Assizes and Sessions, for the due Prosecution and Punishment of all Persons that shall presume to offend in any of the Crimes aforesaid; and also of all Persons that contrary to their Duty, shall be remiss or negligent in putting the said Laws in Execution; and that they do, at their respective Assizes and Quarter Sessions of the Peace, cause this Our Royal Proclamation to be publickly read in Open Court immediately before the charge is given.

And We do hereby further Charge and command every Minister in his respective Parish Church or Chapel to read or cause to be read this Our Proclamation at least Four Times in every Year, immediately after Divine Service, and to incite and stir up their respective Auditors to the Practice of Piety and Virtue, and the avoiding all Immorality and Profaneness,

And, to the End that all Vice and Debauchery may be prevented, and Religion and Virtue practiced by all Officers, Private Soldiers, Mariners, and others who are employed in Our Service by Sea and Land,

We do hereby strictly charge and command all Our Commanders and Officers whatsoever, that they do take care to avoid all Profaneness, Debauchery, and other Immoralities, and that by their own good and virtuous Lives and Conversation, they do set good Examples to all such as are under their Care and Authority, and likewise take care of and inspect the Behaviour of all such as are under them, and punish all those who shall be guilty of any of the offences aforesaid, as they will be answerable for the ill consequences of their Neglect herein.

Given at Our Court at *St. James's*, the First Day of *June* One thousand seven hundred and eighty-seven, in the Twenty-seventh Year of Our Reign. God save *the King*.

LONDON: Printed by CHARLES EYRE and ANDREW STRAHAN, Printers to the King's most Excellent Majesty. 1787.

APPENDIX B

PROSPECTUS OF AN English Newspaper, PRINTED AT PARIS.

On Monday the 3rd of May, 1790, will be published, (to be continued every Monday and Thursday) an ENGLISH NEWSPAPER, ENTITLED, *The Universal Patriot.*

TO THE PUBLIC.

A celebrated French writer asserts that no language ever surpassed in point of energy, the English, or breathed in accents more emphatic the sentiments of Freedom. To the cultivation of the English language in this country may in a great measure be attributed the late glorious Revolution. By the study of English Authors, by conversing with Englishmen, by discoursing on English affairs have the French imbibed those principles of Liberty, which directing to worthy ends their native activity of mind, have enabled them to plan and animated them to carry into effect a system of Government freer and more liberal than that which long has been the object of their envy and admiration. The Revolution in France, in turn, it is hoped, will rouze from a state of political delusion the supine Englishmen of the present day and the French Nation will have the glory of giving a LESSON OF LIBERTY to the people whose disciples they have been.

To accelerate to the utmost in their power *a consummation so much wanted and so devoutly wished for*, a set of Gentlemen, Britons, by birth, but by sentiment and principle, Universal Patriots, have engaged to furnish their countrymen with an accurate and candid account of the progress of legislation in the National Assembly, as well as of French Affairs in general; transactions which through the venal channel of English Newspapers, the Aristocracy of both countries have been at infinite pains to disguise, to ridicule and traduce.

The Debates in the British Parliament and the political events of England, will also be narrated in the UNIVERSAL PATRIOT, from the best information and with a veracity not the less accurate for that the Editor will not have before his eyes the terror of the Pillory, nor the dread of those vexatious prosecutions for libels, engines which the British Ministry have ever ready in their hands to crush whoever shall be hardy enough to expose to light the *pious mysteries* of a Government corrupt and systematically hostile to the cause of Freedom.

To applaud and cherish in every corner of the Globe the infant efforts of that noble cause shall be the peculiar care of the UNIVERSAL PATRIOT.

In IRELAND the sons of Freedom, will be encouraged in their exertions to shake off a yoke to which they have too long and too patiently submitted.

The SCOTCH will be exhorted to persevere with firmness in their REFORM and to recover those rights which betrayed, at the union, by a venal and pusilanimous Nobility have been ever since the trafic of Pedlars, and the sport of Ministerial Slaves.—In short through the medium of the UNIVERSAL PATRIOT, the human race in general will be taught to consider as their only enemies those who invade the rights of MAN, and who withold from their *fellow men* the first, the greatest, the most invaluable of blessings, FREEDOM!—FREEDOM! without which Man is scarcely superior to the Brute and which even Brutes prefer to every bait of pleasure and every blandishment of sense!

Such are the grand objects of the UNIVERSAL PATRIOT.—It's slighter regards will run over the *quicquid agunt homines*, the pursuits, the Arts, the amusements, the follies, the whole multifarious farago of human life.

The UNIVERSAL PATRIOT will be printed on a sheet in folio, in four pages containing three columns each.—Price to subscribers will be at Paris 42 liv. per annum, *two louis* for the Provinces of FRANCE, and two guineas for LONDON, and so in proportion for a lesser time.

Subscriptions for the UNIVERSAL PATRIOT are received by M. Oswald, at l'Hôtel d'Angleterre, No. 243, rue Montmartre; by M. Barrois, Junior, Bookseller, Quai des Augustins, No. 18. by M. Léjay fils, Bookseller, rue d l'Echelle; by M. Mess, at Meuricés Hôtel, at Calais; by M. Etherington, Harford Place, Drury Lane; and by M. Chuber, opposite Greniers Hôtel, Jermyn-Street, LONDON.

APPENDIX C

Circular of the Society of Jacobins of Paris to the Patriotic Societies of England, Scotland, and Ireland.

[3 October 1792; my translation from the French (Aulard, ed., *Recueil des Documents . . . des Jacobins*, 4:345–49), somewhat abridged. No English text located. Drafted by Oswald, presumably.]

Englishmen, our friends and our brothers!

An ineluctable denouement has just raised France to the height of the most august destiny. Despotism is forever crushed; the French people have regained all their rights; we are at last free, we no longer have a king.

The circumstances which produced this great revolution have been atrociously misconstrued; the lying reports of the newspapers hired by your government have been misleading you. We scorn the tyrants but we cherish the peoples; we esteem above all our brothers of England, we owe them the truth. . . . May our example inspire in the generous hearts of the proud British the hope for a liberty disencumbered of the vices of courts. . . .

You know, brothers and friends, by what rapid efforts the French people arose from the stupor of a tyranny maintained by bayonets for fourteen centuries. Nearly succumbing under the weight of their chains, they grew indignant and broke them. Yet, by a fatal blindness, the first use they made of their freedom was to entrust it to their most mortal enemy. . . . The traitor Louis the Last, loaded with the favors of a nation which he had outraged, turned against her all the means she had entrusted to him for glory and for her defense.

Did the National Assembly make a law solicited by the wishes and needs of all France? Armed with his *veto*, he prevented its happy effect. Were there men covered with public shame? He called them to important posts. An enormous civil list had been granted him, in a moment of delirium, to sustain the supposed splendor of the throne. He used it to sow in the 83 departments the seeds of corruption. . . . Abroad, his agents had no other mission than to raise up enemies for us, and at home his satellites and vile trusties expressed an open loathing of all good citizens, conducting a silent war against them. . . . Pressed by the spectacle of his crimes, perhaps by his remorse, or warned by some passing glances of indignation from a people not entirely shorn of dignity, this perfidious king . . . withdrew into his palace, raised barriers and grills between the people and himself, had moats dug, called around his person all that France contained of the most vile, and embodied them as the garrison of his castle, preparing it for a state of war in the middle of Paris. From out this den of crime he hurled proclamations calumniating the better citizens and insulting even the moderation of the people.

As these evils were put in readiness to fall upon our heads, the enemy awaited only the final signal from the Tuileries to advance. His march was sure: a faithless minister had prepared it, the generals of his choosing were to direct it. . . . Even after the day of August 10, the commanders were so cowardly as to surrender our positions. . . . A moment more and liberty would have been destroyed for ever. Yet at sight of danger so imminent, numerous defenders rushed to all parts of the empire. Uniting with the Marseillaise, with the brave citizens of the faubergs and the city, they swore together to exterminate the tyrants and to save France.

Cries of *Vengeance! Liberty! Hate the king!* succeeded to the bitter silence of grief and the sentiments of a homicidal forbearance. As soon as the tocsin sounded, the people arose, and the castle of the Tuileries was invested as the last retrenchment of despotism. Louis the Last, accompanied by the execrable Austrian, had just passed in review his conspirators and encouraged them to carnage. "One faction," he told them, "wishes to overthrow the constitution and end the days of your king. Immolate that mob. . . ." That is what the audacious one called the French people.

After this monster had received the horrible assurance that Frenchmen were ready to imbrue their hands with the blood of Frenchmen, too cowardly to share the dangers of his accomplices he fled, unknown to them, to the National Assembly where, hopeful of success, he began in his heart to designate his victims even among those to whom, he hoped, he would owe the saving of his vile existence.

Meanwhile our brave assailants announce that they have come to purge the palace of its crimes, to rid it of the authors of the evils of France, gathered around the king, and to deliver the king (this prince) over to himself, or even to the people, if he is still worthy of that. The proud bearing of free men terrified the slavish garrison of the castle, who fled or hid and left to the Swiss the job of carrying out the atrocious plan they had conceived, of cutting people's throats, lacking even the courage of assassins.

The crimes meditated by kings have a peculiarly atrocious character. The conduct of the Swiss on this occasion was a fresh example of this sad truth. The fédérés presented themselves at the doors of the Tuileries; they addressed words of peace and amity to the soldiers of the Swiss regiment of the royal guard; those responded with signs of fraternity and called our unfortunate brothers, while offering guns to those among them who had only pikes. Seduced by these treacherous demonstrations, they entered the castle courts without defiance, not perceiving the frightful trap which awaited them, as a discharge of musket fire, coming from the interior, assailed them at all points. This dastardly betrayal raised indignation to a peak; our intrepid citizens listened only to their courage; a hundred mouths of fire are leveled at the palace; each cannon blow destroys a prejudice, and the throne of a tyrant crumbles under the confident blows of the avenging thunder of the people.

A new day dawns for the French; all that recalls the idea of royal tyranny is proscribed; . . . and the National Convention, in decreeing the abolition of royalty, has simply expressed the mandate which the deputies brought with them from all parts of France to the post to which their fellow citizens had elected them.

Before they came together, liberty was menaced by further conspiracies. You cannot fail to have been told, brothers and friends, that streams of blood ran on September 2; but you may well have been kept from learning that no sooner had Louis the Last been flung into the prison where his betrayals landed him than the hordes of the tyrants, immobile till then, were rushed with great speed to our frontiers. You will have been told, no doubt, that fifteen thousand citizens departed to meet them, and that, Paris finding itself stripped of so large a part of its forces, the jailed conspirators formed the project of breaking out of the prisons and butchering the wives and mothers left defenseless. You have been told that this infernal plot, uncovered, was followed, in the first moment of profound indignation, by the terrible vengeance of the people.

But at last the scene has changed. Ah! brothers and friends, if only you could witness the virtues which the hatred of kings and the birth of the Republic have caused to bloom amongst us. At the first call of the country, freed of the tyrant who dishonored it, thousands of soldiers presented themselves for her defense.

France offers the spectacle of a camp of Spartans ready to die at Thermopylae, or perhaps to triumph in the fields of Marathon. The Romans crushed, without walls and without soldiers, the league of Porsenna, and we, who reckon as many warriors as citizens, we have already taught our enemies that it is not so easy to approach the walls of Rome.

English, friends and brothers, oh! you who have been the first to shake off the prejudice of national hatreds, atrocious error which the tyrants have too well known how to spread to enchain the peoples, rejoice with us: your brothers of France are free and republican; you will not know how to be indifferent to such a great event, which advances by several centuries the universal liberty.

A very warm sentiment has prompted us to show you the tableau of our country's condition: the sentiment is amity. Do not fear that any apprehension, that any meanness of spirit has soiled our motives; they are pure as republican virtue, that virtue which inspires as much horror for kings as love for all the peoples.

Appendix D

Address of the British Club, dated November 24 [1792]

(A digest)
Address of the English, Scotch, and Irish resident
and domiciled in Paris.

Citizen Legislators.—The British and Irish citizens now in Paris, animated by the sentiment of liberty which your principles have imparted to the French republic, assembled on Sunday 18th November, to celebrate the brilliant successes of your arms . . . offer . . . their congratulations. . . . Hitherto wars have been undertaken only to satiate the vilest passions; they have consequently been conducted only by the most iniquitous methods. You have taken up arms solely to make reason and truth triumph. It doubtless appertained to the French nation to enfranchise Europe, and we rejoice to see it fulfilling its great destinies. Let us hope that the victorious troops of liberty will lay down their arms only when there are no more tyrants or slaves. . . .

Our good wishes . . . render us impatient to see the happy moment of this great change, in the hope that it will no sooner arrive than we shall see the formation of a close union between the French republic and the English, Scotch, and Irish nations. . . . We are not the only men animated by these sentiments. We doubt not that they would be also manifested by the great majority of our countrymen if public opinion were consulted, as it ought to be, in a national convention. . . .

Appendix E

Signers of the Address of the British Club, dated 24 November, read to the Convention on 28 November 1792.

[Arranged in alphabetical order for convenience. I have added, within brackets, names of persons who did not sign but are known to have been present at White's Hotel on 18 November or who later joined the club. Italics indicate persons referred to in the present study.]

Thomas Armfield
[*Joel Barlow*]
Matthew Bellews
John Bradley
B. Bulmer
William Choppin
Caesar Colclough
Jeremie Curtayn
William Duckett
Edward Ferris
Edward Fitzgerald
John Frost
James Gamble
T. J. Gastineau
David Gibson
Joseph Green
N. Hickson
William Francis Jackson
Richard Joyce
Pearce Lower
Thomas MacDermott
J. E. MacDonnell
Bernard MacSheehy
N. Madgett
Thomas Marshall
L. Masquerier
William Maxwell
Robert Merry
Harold Mowatt
[*Thomas Muir*]

B. Murray
William Newton
J. O'Neill
Robert May O'Reilly
[*Eleazar Oswald*]
John Oswald
[*Thomas Paine*]
[*Captain Sampson Perry*]
Thomas Potier
J. Usher Quartermain
Robert Rayment
William Ricketts
Rose
Stephen Sayre
Henry Sheares
John Sheares
J. Skill
[*Charlotte Smith*]
R. Smyth
J. H. Stone
J. Tickell
Francis A. Tweddell
John Walker, sen.
William Wardell
William Watts
Joseph Webb
[*Helen Maria Williams*]
[Captain Wilson, of Manchester]
[*William Wordsworth*: in spirit]
[*Henry Redhead Yorke*]

N.B.: Stone signed again as president, O'Reilly as secretary; Frost missed the meeting but reached Paris by 22 November, in time to sign.

Wm Francis Jackson

Robert Merry

Wr Mary O'Reilly

J. E. Macdonnell

Wm Watts

Thos Marshall.

John Oswald.

Jno Walker Sen.

Thos Potiers

L e Marqueriea,

Ric myt

N. Hitkson

J. J. Gastineau

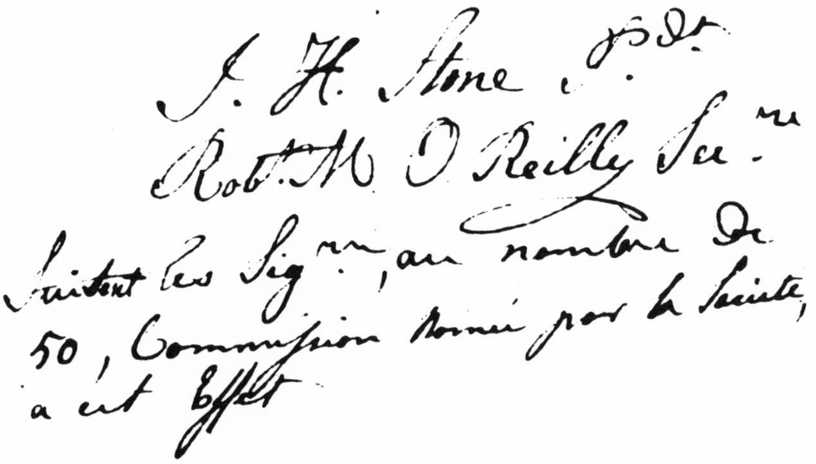

Fig. 34. Oswald's signature, among others, on the British Club declaration of 18 November 1792. (Archives Nationales, ANC²⁴¹278)

APPENDIX F

Other Oswalds

There were several Oswalds in the British diplomatic service in the 1780s and 1790s, and there are several references to Col. Eleazar Oswald, some of which can be confusing; but these have all been sorted out and need not be itemized.

Various Oswalds in literature have been called to my attention, some of them probably or possibly based on John Oswald, some on the diplomatic Oswalds.

One of the literary Oswalds, noted by Burton Pollin, is the subject of a sentimental elegy, "Oswald, A Poem," in Charles Lloyd's *Poems on Various Subjects* (Carlisle, 1795), which as Pollin observes has a few "outcroppings of Wordsworth's favorite words and phrases," mostly about painting nature "in Truth's bright hues." But the poem is an eventless recapitulation of the feckless career, from love and hope to despair and suicide, of a youth whose breast was warmed by "love of Nature," but was as responsive to her "forms of Terrour" as to scenes that gave "the peaceful thought." His reading included too many Gothic tales. His friend and his love betrayed him; his "heaven-taught intellectual powers" were weakened "by woes." And he was so acutely aware of "The dark abuses of the social plan! / (Social misnam'd—unsocial, selfish, base!)," and so sensitive to bloody Tyranny, galling Slavery, and "the shrieks of War's disgust," that, seeing that Error and Luxury and Woe would prevail, he fell, stabbing his "virtuous heart" and letting Vice triumph. The poet, however, hopes that "another Oswald" may arise, when Truth and Liberty and the Rule of Reason join to make Benevolence prevail. I offer no comment.

Wordsworth would have known of Lloyd's poem; may have derived a nuance. A later literary Oswald, in Walter Scott's Gothic drama *The Doom of Devorgoil* (1818; published 1830), seems to be no relative of Wordsworth's or Lloyd's, let alone John Oswald. He is a Scottish baron, poverty stricken, who dwells in a collapsing and haunted castle. The plot concerns his daughter Flora and his ward Katleen (*sic*) and a match that will keep the castle from utter collapse and open its hidden treasure chamber.

I have not seen *Oswald; a Metrical Tale: Illustrative of a Poetical Character* (in four cantos, Edinburgh, 1817); it was in Wordsworth's own library (sale catalogue 4981).

The Oswald in Madame de Staël's *Corinne* is modeled on a young Portuguese diplomat, with whom she corresponded in 1805–1815.

BIBLIOGRAPHY

A. Oswald's Writings (in chronological order)

Note: A collection of Oswald's complete works (if all can be recovered) is in preparation. Information about library holdings of any on this list—especially the lacking portion of *Le Tactique du Peuple* or even possibly those May issues of *The Universal Patriot*—will be greatly appreciated.

1. Humberstone Obituary. *New Annual Register for 1784*. (Repr. *London Chronicle*, 10–12 November 1785.) (Conjectural attribution.)
2. Collaborative role in articles signed "Ignotus" (or later so designated) in *The Political Herald and Review*, 18 nos., July 1785-January 1787. (Conjectural attributions.)
3. Letter "To the Printer of the London Chronicle," signed "H.K." 6 April, in *London Chronicle*, 20–22 April 1786.
4. *Ranae Comicae Evangelizantes: or, The Comic Frogs turned Methodist*. London: printed for E. Macklew, No. 9, Haymarket, 1786. Price One Shilling. Pp. 48, sigs. A-F.
5. *The Alarming Progress of French Politics*. London, 1787. (Not located.)
6. *The British Mercury*. No. 1—12 May 1787; no. 2—26 May 1787; no. 3—9 June 1787; no. 4—23 June 1787. London: printed for J. Ridgway; and sold by all the booksellers in town and country. (Plates dated 1787.) (Not located.)
7. *Euphrosyne, an Ode to Beauty: addressed to Mrs. Crouch*. By Sylvester Otway. London: Faulder, &c. 1788. One shilling. Quarto. (Rev. in *Monthly Review* 29 [Oct. 1788]: 369 ["Monthly Catalogue, Dramatic"].) (Reprinted in *Poems*, 1789.) (Not located.)
8. *The British Mercury*. A new edition, to which is now added, The PRIESTS of APOLLO . . . Embellished with Three Caricature Prints, exhibiting, *The Brain-Sucker*, the *British Lion*, and *Moses erecting the Brazen Serpent in the Desart*. A New Edition. London: Printed for J. Ridgway, No. 1, York-street, St. James's-Square, and L. Macdonald, No. 454, opposite Villers-street, Strand. 1788.
9. *Poems*; to which is added, *The Humours* of John Bull, An Operatical Farce, in two acts. By Silvester Otway. London: Printed by Macrae, for J. Murray, No. 32, Fleet-street. 1789. Pp. 137. (An earlier variant of "Louisa" is printed in *Lives of the Scottish Poets*, 179, probably from a newspaper. *Lives* also gives [179–80] "The Virgin's Dream," of five quatrains; source not given.)
10. *Prospectus of an English Newspaper, Printed at Paris* entitled *The Universal Patriot*. (To begin 3 May 1790.) (Broadside, signed "M. Oswald, at l'Hôtel d'Angleterre, No. 243, rue Montmartre . . . .") (No copies of the newspaper located. Prospectus in Daniel Lyson's Collectanea, British Library, shelf no. 1881.6.6 [reported by Jim Dybikowski].)

11. *The Universal Patriot* (announced in no. 10). (No copies located, but in no. 18 said to have contained "outlines" of no. 18, apparently thus counting as its "first edition.")

12. Poems and an essay in *The World* of London, 8, 12, 30 July; 10 August; 19 October; 7 December 1790, signed variously "Oswald," "Otway," and "Sylvester Otway." (See note 20 to Chapter 5 above.)

13. *The Triumph of Freedom! An Ode*, to commemorate the anniversary of THE FRENCH REVOLUTION. By JOHN OSWALD .... Paris. Printed for the Author. (Accepted by the National Assembly, 4 September 1790.) (Reprinted in some editions of *The Almanach of Goodman Gerard*, French and English.)

14. *The Cry of Nature; or an appeal to Mercy and to Justice, on behalf of the Persecuted Animals.* By John Oswald, member of the Club des Jacobines .... London: Printed for J. Johnson, No. 72, St. Paul's Church-yard, 1791. (Notes: 83–156.)

15. *Review of the Constitution of Great Britain.* By John Oswald, Paris, 1791. (Not located. But "second edition" cited in title page of *Almanach*—see next entry—and listed in 1791 *Annual Review* as among works "Published in the first six months of 1791.")

16. *The Spirit of the French Constitution: The Almanach of Goodman Gerard.* For the year 1792. Being the third year of the aera of Liberty; A work crowned by the Society of the Friends of the Constitution, held at the Jacobins', Paris; by J. M. COLLOT-D'HERBOIS, Member of the Society. Translated, at the request of the Author, By JOHN OSWALD, Member of the Society, and Author of a *Review of the Constitution of Great Britain.* Sold by Ridgway Bookseller London and At the Printing office of the Social Circle, Paris, 1791. (First phrase of title not in French editions.)

17. *La Tactique du Peuple*, ou Nouveau principe pour les évolutions militaires .... Par John Oswald, Anglois, membre de la société des Amis de la Constitution séante aux Jacobins. Première Partie. À Paris, Chez Gueffier, Imprimeur-Libraire, quai des Augustins, No. 17. (No date; but by March 1792. Only first part located.)

18. Placard recommending pikes. (Paris, March 1792; not located except in *Journal général* transcript, 6 March.)

19. *Review of the Constitution of Great-Britain.* Third Edition, with considerable additions. By John Oswald. "Thou art weighed in the balance, and art found wanting." Paris, printed at the English press by Gillet, 1792. (That is, printed in London, shipped to Paris in sheets.) Advertised in *Chronique du mois*, September 1792, 23, as for sale in "Paris, au Cercle Social, rue du Théatre-François, No. 4." (Imprint trimmed away during the binding of the British Library copy; visible in Bibliothèque Nationale copy.) (Gillet's press was still in London in 1793 and 1794.)

20. *Examen de la Constitution de la Grande-Bretagne.* (Presumably this was a French translation of item 19, but possibly allusions seen may be mere translations of the title.)

21. *The Government of the People; or, A Sketch of a Constitution for the Universal Common-Wealth.* By John Oswald, Anglo-Franc .... Paris: Printed at the English Press, No. 1412, rue Notre Dame des Champs. First Year of the French Republic. (21 September 1792 to 20 September 1793; quoted by Burke in February 1793.)

22. *Le Gouvernement du Peuple, ou Plan de Constitution Pour la République Universelle*, Traduit de L'Anglais, de Jean Oswald, Anglo-Franc, Commandant du Premier

Batallion de Piquiers . . . . A Paris, de l'Imprimerie des Révolutions de Paris. 1793.
23. *Discours d'Oswald, Anglo-Franc.* Pp. 10–15 in *Pieces Remises au Comité de Correspondance, par le Citoyen DuCange, Patriote Batave.* Pp. 16. (Oswald's *Discours* is immediately followed by the designation "Extrait du procès-verbal," and the statement that the society, in its session of 4 February 1793, ordered the printing of these pieces, to be sent to the affiliated societies. Eight signatures follow, and the imprint: "De l'Imprimerie de L. Potier de Lille, rue Favart, N° 5." But the first page states that these are "for the committee of correspondence . . . according to its order of 6 February 1793." Only Oswald's piece was a discourse in the society; the other pieces are documents read and speeches delivered to the National Convention on the 6th.)

B. Reviews and Notices

(Items in this category are arranged chronologically. Items 2, 7, and 16 through 27 contain some sort of biographical comment on Oswald.)

1. Review of *Euphrosyne* in *The Monthly Review* 79 (October 1788): 169. (One ironic paragraph.)
2. Notice of "Oswald" in Marshall, *Catalogue of Five Hundred Celebrated Authors of Great Britain, Now Living.* London, 1788. (Author's full name not known.) (Reprinted without change in 1819, making Oswald seem still living.)
3. Review of *Poems* in *The Monthly Review* 81 (October 1789): 367–68. (Reviewer identified in editor Griffith's copy as "O," probably Thomas Ogle, probably a medical man, notes Betty Rizzo.)
4. Review of *Poems* in *The Gentleman's Magazine* 59 (November 1789): 2:1020. (Partly cribbed from *The Monthly Review*.)
5. Review of *Poems* in *Biographical and Imperial Magazine* 2 (1789): 371–73.
6. Review of *Poems* in *The General Magazine and Impartial Review* 4 (January 1790): 67–68. (With Oswald's "Edwin's Ghost" heading the "Selected Poetry" on p. 80, without identification.)
7. Review of *Poems*, followed by "Anecdotes of the Author," in *The European Magazine* 17 (March 1790): 198–99.
8. Review of *Poems* in *The Analytical Review* 6 (March 1790): 325–26.
9. Listing of *Review of the Constitution* in *The Analytical Review* 10 (August 1791): 535.
10. Review of *The Cry of Nature* in *The Monthly Review* 7, n.s. (January 1792): 34–36. (By "N" according to Griffith's marked copy; not identified.)
11. Review of *The Cry of Nature* in *The Scots Magazine* 54 (January 1792): 21–22, signed "M" (i.e., borrowed from *The Monthly Review*).
12. Review of *The Cry of Nature* in *The Analytical Review* 12 (appendix, April 1792): 535–36.
13. Review of *The Cry of Nature* in *The English Review* 19 (May 1792): 385.
14. Notice of *Review of the Constitution* in *The English Review* 20 (October 1792): 310. (Returns upon Oswald the idea he had borrowed from Tooke, to observe

that the whole of this work "may justly be considered as a libel on the British constitution.")

15. Review of *The Cry of Nature* in *The General Magazine and Impartial Review* 6 (end of 1792): 22–23.

16. Biographical note in Joseph Haslewood, *The Secret History of the Green-Room*, "new edition, 1795," attached to the chapter on Mrs. Crouch. London for J. Owen, No. 118, Piccadilly.

17. "Anecdote of Lieutenant Colonel John Oswald, who commanded a Regiment in the French Service." In *The Argus or General Observer*, ed. Sampson Perry, pp. 172–73. London, 1796; under date of 26 December 1795.

18. Item 16 (above) partially reprinted, with acknowledgment, in Joseph Ritson, *An Essay on Abstinence from Animal Food, as a Moral Duty*. London: R. Phillips, 1802.

19. Paragraph in a review of Ritson (item 18) in *The British Critic* 22 (November 1803): 438–39. ("During the whole reign of terror in France," Oswald "was the active agent . . . of that diabolical crew.")

20. Yorke, Henry Redhead. *Letters from France, in 1802*, pp. 160–63. London: Printed for H. D. Symonds by Bye and Law, 1804.

21. "John Oswald—Sylvester Otway." In *Lives of the Scottish Poets*, by The Society of Ancient Scots, 2:172–80. London, 1821. (Attributed to Joseph Clinton Robertson in the catalogue of the University of St. Andrews Library.)

22. Stewart, David. *Sketches of the Character, Manners, and Present State of the Highlanders of Scotland, with details of the Military Service of the Highland Regiments*, vol. 2, note 5. 3d ed. Edinburgh: Constable, 1825.

23. Arnault, A. V., et al. *Biographie Nouvelle Des Contemporains ou Dictionnaire historique et raisonné*. Paris, 1827. (Very brief and faulty note on "Oswal [Jean].")

24. Varé, E. *Etudes sur les Poëtes Anglais: John Oswald*. Paris: J. Claye, Rue Saint-Renoit, 1859. 16 pp.

25. Anderson, William. "John Oswald." In *The Scottish Nation*, 2:268–69. Edinburgh and London: A. Fullarton, 1863.

26. Henderson, T. F. Listing in *Dictionary of National Biography*. London, 1890.

27. Lichtenberger, André. "John Oswald Ecossais, Jacobin et Socialiste." *Révolution Française* 32 (1897): 481–95. (The only extensive study. Reprinted in A. Lichtenberger, *Le Socialisme Utopique* [Geneva, 1978], 220–44.)

28. Stewart, Captain John, compl. *The Royal Highland Regiment, the Black Watch . . . .* Edinburgh: T. & A. Constable, 1913.

C. Publications of the Cercle Social

Furet, François, ed. *Nicolas de Bonneville and the Cercle Social: 1787–1800*. New York: Clearwater Publishing, 1980. (Forty-seven titles on 201 microfiches, including *La Bouche de fer*, *La Chronique du mois*, and the works of Bonneville and others.)

D. Collections of Debates and Trials

1. *Arch Parl*: Mavidal, J., et E. Laurent, comps. *Archives Parlementaires*, première série, 1787–1799. 82 vols. Paris, 1868–1892.
2. Aulard: Aulard, F. A., ed. *Recueil des Documents pour l'histoire du Club des Jacobins de Paris*. 6 vols. Paris, 1889–1897.
3. *Hist Parl*: Buchez, P. J. B., et P. C. Roux-Lavergne. *Histoire Parlementaire de la Révolution Française: ou Journal des Assemblées Nationales depuis 1789 jusqu'en 1814*. Paris, 1833ff. 43 vols. (Carlyle's main source.)
4. *Journal des Débats de la Société des Amis de la Constitution séante aux Jacobins à Paris*. Nos. 1–556 (June 1791-December 1793). (Published almost daily; as was the *Journal des Débats* of the Assembly and, later, Convention, not to be confused; not cited here.) (Main source for Aulard, but often more complete.)
5. *Parl Hist: The Parliamentary History of England*, ed. William Cobbett, 1st ser., vols. 27–35. London: Longman and Co., 1813–1819.
6. *State Trials: A Complete Collection of State Trials*, ed. T. B. Howell and T. J. Howell, vol. 25. London: R. Bagshaw: Longman & Co., 1818.
7. *Suite de Procès-Verbal de l'Assemblée Nationale*. Paris, 1790.

E. Manuscripts

1. Archives Nationales, Paris. $F^7 4774^{60}$: Cited by Goodwin (*The Friends of Liberty*, 21) as "J. Oswald"; extensive search yields nothing related to Oswald. There is an "R. Oswald" file, of no relevance. $F^7 4774^{70}$: Pétion's correspondence with English radicals.
2. Archives of the Royal Literary Fund, Case File no. 15.
3. Church of Jesus Christ of Latter-Day Saints. CFI File. Microfilm index of vital statistics.
4. National Library of Wales.
5. Public Record Office (PRO), London. TS 11/962/3508. SCI meeting of 9 March 1792. TS 11/965/3510 A 2. 22 October 1792.

F. Periodicals

1. *Analytical Review*. See B.8, 9, 12.
2. *Annual Register*.
3. *Annual Review*. See A.15.
4. *The Argus or General Observer*. See B.17.
5. *Biographical and Imperial Magazine*. See B.5.
6. *Bouche de fer*. See list C. (Abbrev. *Bdf*.)
7. *British Critic*. See B.19.
8. *British Mercury*. See list A. (Abbrev. *B Merc*.)
9. *Chronique du mois*. See list C. (Abbrev. *Cdm*.)
10. *Courier de l'Egalité*. Ed. J. R. Hérbert, montagnard.

11. *Courier des 83 départements*. Ed. Gorsas.
12. *English Review*. See B.13, 14.
13. *European Magazine*. See B.7.
14. *Gazetteer and Daily Advertiser*, London.
15. *General Magazine and Impartial Review*. See B.6, 15.
16. *The Gentleman's Magazine*. See list B.
17. *Journal de Paris*.
18. *Journal général de France*, Paris. See A.18.
19. *London Chronicle*. See A.3.
20. *London Critic*. See A.3.
21. *Manchester Herald*.
22. *Le Moniteur universal*, Paris.
23. *Monthly Review*. See A.7 and B.1, 3, 4, 10.
24. *New Annual Register*. See A.1.
25. *Le Patriote françois*, Paris. Brissot's daily.
26. *The Political Herald and Review*, London. See A.2.
27. *Les Revolutions de France et de Brabant*, Paris. Desmoulins's daily.
28. *Les Revolutions de Paris*, Paris. B. Ed. Prudhomme.
29. *The Scots Magazine*. See B.11.
30. *Tribun du peuple*. See list C.
31. *The Universal Patriot*, London and Paris. Only Prospectus survives.
32. *The World*. See A.12.

G. Books and Articles Cited

(Not a catalogue of works consulted nor a comprehensive bibliography of areas studied.)

Abbot, John S. C. *The French Revolution of 1789 Viewed in the Light of Republican Institutions*. New York, 1859; 2d ed., 1887.
Albrecht, Wilber T. "The English Review." In *British Literary Magazines*, ed. Alvin Sullivan, pp. 102–6. (Listed below.)
Aldridge, A. Owen. *Thomas Paine's American Ideology*. Newark: University of Delaware Press, 1984.
Alger, John Goldworth. *Englishmen in the French Revolution*. London: Sampson Low & Co., 1889. (Cited as *Englishmen*.)
———. "English Eyewitnesses of the French Revolution." *Edinburgh Review* 168 (1888): 137–70. (Preceded by "English Actors in the French Revolution," 166 [1887]: 445–64.)
———. *Glimpses of the French Revolution: Myths, Ideals, and Realities*. London and New York: Sampson Low & Co., 1894.
———. *Napoleon's British Visitors and Captives 1801–1815*. Westminster and New York: A. Constable & Co., 1904.
———. *Paris in 1789–94: Farewell Letters of Victims of the Guillotine*. New York and London: George Allen, 1902.
Almanach du Père Gérard, by Collot d'Herbois; English translation by Oswald: see list A.

Anderson, William. "John Oswald." In *The Scottish Nation*, 3:268–69. Edinburgh and London: Fullarton & Co., 1863.

Andrews, Alexander. *The History of British Journalism*. 2 vols. London: Richard Bentley, 1859.

Aspinall, Arthur, ed. *The Correspondence of George Prince of Wales 1770–1812*. 8 vols. Oxford and London: Oxford University Press, 1971.

———. *The Later Correspondence of George III*. 5 vols. Cambridge: Cambridge University Press, 1970.

Aubusson, Pierre Armand. *Profession de foi politique d'un bon françois*. Paris, 1789; new ed., 1792.

Aulard, F. Alphonse. *The French Revolution: A Political History, 1789–1794*. Trans. Bernard Miall. 4 vols. London, Leipsic, New York: T. Fischer, 1910.

———, ed. *La Societé des Jacobins: Recueil des Documents pour l'histoire du Club des Jacobins de Paris*. 6 vols. Paris, 1889–1897. (See list D.)

Bailyn, Berndt. *The Ideological Origins of the American Revolution*. Cambridge: Harvard University Press, 1967.

Baker, Keith Michael. "Enlightenment and Revolution in France: Old Problems, Renewed Approaches." *Journal of Modern History* 53 (1981): 281–303.

———. "A Script for a French Revolution: The Political Consciousness of the Abbé Mably." *Eighteenth Century Studies* 14 (1981): 235–63.

Barbaroux, C. J. M. *Mémoires (inédits . . . avec des eclaircissemens historiques par MM. Berville et Barriére)*. Paris: Baudouin frères, 1822.

Barker, John. *The British in Boston*. Cambridge: Harvard University Press, 1925.

Beer, Max. *A History of British Socialism*. 2 vols. London: G. Bell & Sons, 1919.

Billington, James H. *Fire in the Minds of Men: Origins of the Revolutionary Faith*. New York: Basic Books, 1980.

Biographical Dictionary of Actors, Actresses, Musicians, Dancers, Managers, and Other Stage Personel in London, 1660–1800. Vol. 4. (Cited as *BDAA*.)

Biographical Dictionary of Modern British Radicals. Vol. 1, 1979. New York: Humanities Press. (Cited as *BDMBR*.)

Bisset, Robert. *A History of the Reign of George III. to the Termination of the Late War* (i.e., in 1801). 2 vols. New ed., Albany, N.Y.: B. D. Packard, 1816. (1st ed. London: T. N. Longman & O. Rees, 1803.)

Bonneville, Nicolas de. (See list C.)

Bourdin, Isabelle. *Les Sociétés Populaires á Paris pendant la Révolution*. Paris: Universite de Paris, 1937.

Bourne, Henry E. "Improvising a Government in Paris in July 1789." *American Historical Review* 10 (1904–1905): 280–308.

Brissot de Warville. *Á ses commettans sur la situation de la Convention nationale, sur l'influence des anarchists et les maux qu'elle a Causés . . . .* Paris [1793].

———. *Á tous les Republicains de France, sur la Société des Jacobins de Paris*. Paris, 1792.

Bronson, Bertrand. "Walking Stewart." In his *Facets of the Enlightenment: Studies in English Literature and Its Contexts*, pp. 266–97. Berkeley: University of California Press, 1968; 1978.

Brooke, John. *King George III*. New York: McGraw-Hill, 1972.

Brown, Philip A. *The French Revolution in English History*. Ed. J. L. Hammond. London: C. Lockwood & Son, 1918; 1923.

Browning, O., ed. *The Dispatches of Earl Gower, English Ambassador at Paris, from June 1790 to Aug. 1792*. 2 vols. Cambridge: The Camden Society, 1885.

Bulletin of The New York Public Library. (Cited as *BNYPL*.)

Bulletin of Research in the Humanities. (Cited as *BRH*.) (Continuing *BNYPL*.)

Burke, Edmund. *Reflections on the Revolution in France, and on the Proceedings in Certain Societies in London Relative to that Event*. London: J. Dodsley, 1790 (1 November).

Bussière, Georges, and Emile Legouis. *Le Général Michel Beaupuy (1755–1796)*. Paris: Périgueux, 1891.

Cannon, Richard, comp. *Historical Record of the . . . Royal Highlanders . . . .* London: Parker et al., 1851.

———. *Historical Record of the Royal Irish Regiment of Foot*. London, 1848.

Carlyle, Thomas. *The French Revolution: a History*. 1837; New York: Modern Library, 1934. (Drawn upon when firmly documented.)

Castelot, André, et G. Lenotre. *Les Grandes Heures de la Révolution française*. Paris, 1968.

Censer, Jack Richard. *Prelude to Power: The Parisian Radical Press, 1789–1791*. Baltimore: Johns Hopkins University Press, 1976.

Cercle Social. Documents: see list C.

Chassin, Charles-Louis, et L. Hennet. *Les Volontaires nationaux pendant la Révolution*. 3 vols. Paris, 1899–1906.

Christie, Thomas. *Letters on the Revolution of France . . . Part 1*. London: J. Johnson, 1791.

Christophe, Robert. *The Executioners: A History of the Sanson Family, Public Executioners in France from 1688 to 1847*. Trans. Len Ortzen. London: Arthur Barker Ltd., 1962.

The Chronicle of the Royal Highland Regiment, the Black Watch. Edinburgh: David L. Wilson-Farquharson, 1913.

Clarke, Michael, and Nicholas Penny, eds. *The Arrogant Connoisseur: Richard Payne Knight 1751–1824*. Manchester: Manchester University Press, 1982.

Clubbe, John. "Carlyle as Epic Historian." In *Victorian Literature and Society: Essays Presented to Richard D. Altick*, ed. James R. Kinkaid and Albert J. Kuhn, pp. 119–45. Columbus: Ohio State University Press, 1984.

Cobban, Alfred, and Robert A. Smith, eds. *The Correspondence of Edmund Burke*. Vol. 6. Cambridge: Cambridge University Press; Chicago: University of Chicago Press, 1967.

Cockburn, (Henry) Lord. *Examination of the Trials for Sedition . . . in Scotland*. Edinburgh: David Douglas, 1888.

Coleridge, Samuel Taylor. *The Watchman*, ed. Lewis Patton. (Bollingen Series 75.) Princeton University Press, 1970.

Collot d'Herbois. *Almanach*. (See list A.)

Colman, George. *The Iron Chest*. London: Cadell & Davies, 1794.

Conway, Moncure Daniel. *The Life of Thomas Paine*. 2 vols. New York and London: G. P. Putnam's Sons, 1892.

Cooper, Thomas. *A Reply to Mr. Burke's Invective against Mr. Cooper, and Mr. Watt, in the House of Commons, on the 30th of April, 1792.* Manchester: Falkner and Co., 1792. Pp. 84.

Coquelle, P. "Les projets de Déscente en Angleterre." *Revue d'histoire diplomatique* 16 (1902): 134–57.

The Correspondence of the Revolution Society in London With the National Assembly and With Various Societies in France. London, 1792. (SUNY, Stony Brook Library. Spec. DC 158.5 H8.)

Crétineau-Joly. *Histoire de la Vendée Militaire.* 4 vols. Paris, 1840–1842.

Darnton, Robert. *The Literary Underground of the Old Regime.* Cambridge: Harvard University Press, 1982.

———. *Mesmerism and the End of the Enlightenment in France.* Cambridge: Harvard University Press, 1968.

Davies, K. G., ed. *Documents of the American Revolution 1770–1783.* Dublin: Irish University Press, n.d.

de la Rochejacquelein, Marquise. *Mémoires de Madame la Marquise de la Rochejacquelein écrits par elle même.* 4ᵉ edition. Paris: L. G. Michaud, 1819.

Delsaux, Hélène. *Condorcet Journaliste (1790–1794).* Paris: Librarie ancienne Honoré Champion, 1931.

Déprez, Eugène. *Les Volontaires Nationaux (1791–1793).* Geneva: Slatkine Reprints, 1977.

Des Granges, Charles Marc. *Le Romantisme et la critique; la presse littéraire sous la réstoration, 1815–1830.* Paris: Société de Mercure de France, 1907.

Dictionary of National Biography. (Cited as *DNB.*)

Dictionnaire de Biographie Française. (Cited as *DBF.*) Paris: Latouzet et Ané, 1933.

Dotson, Craig W. *The Paris Jacobin Club and the French Revolution.* Diss., Queens University, Kingston, Ontario, 1974.

Dubreuil, Léon. *Histoire des insurrections de l'Ouest.* 2 vols. Paris, 1929–1930.

Dumont, Étienne. *Souvenirs sur Mirabeau et sur les deux premières Assemblies Legislatives.* Paris, 1832.

Dusaulx, Jean. "L'Oeuvre des Sept Jours . . . ." In *Mémoires de documents divers sur la Bastille et de fragments concernant la captivité du baron de Trenck,* ed. Simon N. H. Linguet, pp. 137–76. Paris, 1866.

Dutt, R. Palme. *The Problem of India.* New York: International Publishers, 1943.

Eden, William, Baron Auckland. *The Journal and Correspondence of William, Lord Auckland.* Ed. G. Hogge. 4 vols. London, 1860–1862.

Ehrman, John. *The Younger Pitt.* New York: Dutton, 1969.

Ellery, Eloise. *Brissot de Warville: A Study in the History of the French Revolution.* Boston and New York: Houghton Mifflin, 1915. (Full bibliography.)

Elliott, Marianne. *Partners in Revolution: The United Irishmen and France.* New Haven: Yale University Press, 1982.

Ellis, Lucy, and Joseph Turquan. *La Belle Pamela (Lady Edward Fitzgerald).* London: Herbert Jenkins, 1924.

Emsley, Clive. *British Society and the French Wars, 1793–1815.* Totowa, N.J.: Rowman & Littlefield, 1979.

Erdman, David V. "Blake and the Night Sky: Art against Armies." *BRH* 85 (1981): 296–304.

———. "The Dawn of Universal Patriotism: William Wordsworth Among the British in Revolutionary France." (In Johnston and Ruoff: see below.)

———. "Citizen Stanhope and the French Revolution." *The Wordsworth Circle* 15 (1984): 8–17.

———. "Coleridge in Lilliput: The Quality of Parliamentary Reporting in 1800." *Speech Monographs* 27 (1960): 33–62.

———. "Grub Street behind the skirts of Margaret Nicholson." *Factotum* 12 (1981): 25–27.

———. "Oswald, Gillray, and Royal Proclamations." *Factotum* 16 (1983): 26–27.

———. "The Otway Connection." In *Coleridge's Imagination: Essays in Memory of Pete Laver*, ed. Richard Gravil et al., pp. 143–60. Cambridge, London, and New York: Cambridge University Press, 1986.

———. "Wordsworth as Heartsworth: or, Was Regicide the Prophetic Ground of Those 'Moral Questions'?" In *The Evidence of the Imagination*, ed. Donald H. Reiman et al., pp. 12–41. New York: New York University Press, 1978.

Fitzmaurice, Lord Edmond. *Life of William, Earl of Shelburne, afterwards First Marquess of Lansdowne.* 3 vols. London: Macmillan & Co., 1875–1876.

Fortescue, John W. *A History of the British Army.* 13 vols. London and New York: Macmillan, 1899–1930.

Fuller, Major General J. F. C. *The Conduct of War, 1789–1961.* London: Eyre & Spottiswoode, 1961.

Furet, François. *Interpreting the French Revolution.* Trans. Elborg Forster. Cambridge: Cambridge University Press, 1981.

Garrigues, Georges. *Les Districts des journaux et des journalistes de la Révolution française (1789–1796).* 2 vols. Paris, 1845–1846.

The Gentleman's Compleat Military Dictionary. London, 1759.

Ginter, Donald E., ed. *Whig Organization in the General Election of 1790: Selections from the Blair Adam Papers.* Berkeley: University of California Press, 1967.

Godechot, Jacques. *La Contre-révolution: Doctrine et Action, 1789–1804.* Paris, 1961.

Gooch, G. P., and Ghita Stanhope. *The Life of Charles, Third Earl Stanhope.* London: Longmans, 1914.

Goodwin, Albert. *The Friends of Liberty: The English Democratic Movement in the Age of the French Revolution.* Cambridge: Harvard University Press, 1979.

Gower, Lord Granville Leveson. *Private Correspondence 1781 to 1821*, ed. Castalia Countess Granville. 2 vols. New York: E. P. Dutton & Co., 1916.

Graham, Henry Grey. *Scottish Men of Letters of the Eighteenth Century.* London: Adam & Charles Black, 1908.

Green-Room. (See list B.)

Gronbeck, Bruce. "Ridgway" entry in *BDMBR*.

Haig, Robert L. *The Gazetteer 1735–97: A Study in the Eighteenth-Century English Newspaper.* Carbondale: Southern Illinois University Press, 1960.

Hamel, Frank [pseudonym of Miss Fanny Hamel, proprietrix of Grafton's Book Shop in London]. *A Woman of the Revolution: Théroigne de Méricourt.* London and New York: Stanley Paul & Co., 1911.

Hampson, Norman. *Danton*. London: Duckworth, 1978.

Hamy, M. E.-T. "Note sur Diverses Gravures de Bonneville Représentant des Nègres (1794–1803)." *Anthropologie* 10 (1899): 42–46.

Hargreaves, Reginald. *The Bloodybacks: The British Servicemen in North America and the Caribbean 1655–1783*. New York: Walker, 1968.

Harivel, Philippe. *See* Le Harivel, Philippe.

Harris, Robert D. *Necker: Reform Statesman of the Ancient Regime*. Berkeley: University of California Press, 1980.

Haslewood, Joseph. *The Secret History of the Green-Room*. New ed., London, 1795.

Hatin, Eugène. *Histoire politique et litteraire de La Presse en France, avec une introduction historique sur les Origines du Journal et la Bibliographie générale des journaux depuis leur origine*. Paris, 1860.

Hayley, William. *Memoirs of the Life and Writings*. Ed. J. Johnson. 2 vols. London: H. Coburn & Co., 1823.

Henderson, Ernest F. *Symbol and Satire in the French Revolution*. New York and London: G. P. Putnam's Sons, 1912.

The History of the Robinhood Society. London: James Fletcher and Co., 1764.

Humberstone obituary. (See list A.)

Hunt, Lynn. "Hercules and the Radical Image in the French Revolution." *Representations* 2 (1983): 95–117.

———. *Politics, Culture, and Class in the French Revolution*. Berkeley: University of California Press, 1984.

Ioannisian, A. *Komunisticheskie idei v gody velikoi frantzuzskoi revoliutsii*. Moscow, 1966. (Draws on Volgin, q.v.)

Jarrett, Derek. *The Begetters of Revolution: England's Involvement with France, 1759–1789*. Totowa, N.J.: Rowman & Littlefield, 1973.

Johnston, Kenneth R., and Gene W. Ruoff, eds. *William Wordsworth and the Age of Romanticism*. New Brunswick, N.J.: Rutgers University Press, 1987.

Kates, Gary. "The Cercle Social: French Intellectuals in the French Revolution." Ph.D. diss., University of Chicago, 1978.

———. *The Cercle Social, the Girondins, and the French Revolution*. Princeton: Princeton University Press, 1985.

Kelly, Michael. *Reminiscences*. 2d ed. London: Henry Coburn, 1826.

Kennedy, Michael L. *The Jacobin Clubs in the French Revolution: The First Years*. Princeton: Princeton University Press, 1982.

Kent, C. B. Roylance. *The English Radicals, an Historical Sketch*. London: Longman & Co., 1899.

Knight, Richard Payne. *A Discourse on the Worship of Priapus*. London, 1786; new ed.: Chiswick Press, 1864.

La Gorce, Pierre de. *Histoire Religieuse de la Revolution Française*. 3 vols. Paris: Librarie Plou, 1912.

Lamartine, Alphonse. *Histoire des Girondins*. Paris: Furne, 1847.

Laprade, William T. *England and the French Revolution*. Baltimore: Johns Hopkins University Press, 1909.

Lefebure, Molly. *Cumbrian Discovery*. London: Gollanz, 1977.

Lefebvre, Georges. *The Coming of the French Revolution, 1789*. Trans. R. R. Palmer. New York: Vintage Books, 1947.

Le Harivel, Philippe. *Nicolas de Bonneville: Pre-Romantique et Revolutionnaire 1760–1828.* Oxford and London: Oxford University Press, 1923. (Reviewed by André Monglond; see below.)

Lenotre, G., et A. Castelot. *Iconographie: Les documents qui forment l'iconographie de La Mort du Roi.* Vol. 2: *Les grand heurs de la Revolution française.* Paris, 1963.

Lescure, M. F. A. de. *Correspondance Sécrète inédite, sur Louis XVI, Marie-Antoinette, la cour et la ville de 1777 à 1792.* Vol. 2. Paris: H. Plon, 1866.

Levron, Jacques. *La Revolution française.* Paris: Arthaud, 1966.

Levy, Darline Gay, et al. *Women in Revolutionary Paris 1789–1795.* Urbana: University of Illinois Press, 1979.

Lichtenberger, Andre. "John Oswald . . . ." (See list B.)

———. *Le Socialisme et la Revolution française.* Paris: Falcon, 1899.

———. *Le Socialisme utopique.* Paris: Falcon, 1898.

Litchfield, R. B. *Tom Wedgwood, the First Photographer.* London: Duckworth & Co., 1903.

Lives of the Scottish Poets. (See list B.)

McDowell, R. B. *Ireland in the Age of Imperialism and Revolution.* Oxford and London: Oxford University Press, 1979.

Madelin, Louis. *Danton.* Trans. Lady Mary Loyd. London: Wm. Heineman, 1921.

Magnus, Sir Philip Montefiore. *Edmund Burke, a Life.* London: J. Murray, 1939.

Malleray, Henri de. *Les Cinq Vendées.* Paris: Angers, 1924.

Malone, Dumas, Ph.D. *The Public Life of Thomas Cooper 1783–1839.* New Haven: Yale University Press, 1926.

Marken, Jack W. "William Godwin and the *Political Herald and Review*." BNYPL 65 (1961): 517–33.

Marsh, Herbert (successively Bishop of Llandaff and of Peterborough). *History of the Politicks of Great Britain and France from the time of the Conference at Pillnitz, to the Declaration of War against Great Britain.* 2 vols. London, 1800.

Marshall, Peter H. *William Godwin.* New Haven: Yale University Press, 1984.

Marx, Karl, and Friedrich Engels. *Die Heilige Familie: Gegen Bruno Bauer und Konsorten.* St. Petersburg, 1906.

Mathiez, Albert. *Autour de Danton.* Paris: Payot, 1926.

May, Gita. *Madame Roland and the Age of Revolution.* New York: Columbia University Press, 1970.

Methley, Violet. *Camille Desmoulins: A Biography.* London: Martin Secker, 1914.

Mill, James. *The History of British India.* 3 vols. London, 1817. Ed. of 1820 reprinted in New Delhi, 1972, with introduction and index.

Minto, Nina, Countess of, ed. *Life and Letters of Sir Gilbert Elliot, First Earl of Minto.* 3 vols. London, 1874.

Miranda, Francisco de. *Archivo del General Miranda.* 28 vols. Caracas: Academia Nacional de la Historia, 1932.

Monglond, André. "Nicolas de Bonneville a Propos du Livre de M. Philippe le Harivel." *Review d'Histoire Littéraire de la France,* 33 (1926): 408–14. (See above, Le Harivel.)

Moor, Lt. Edward. Review of Knight's *Discourse* in *British Critic,* October 1794.

Moore, Thomas. *The Life and Death of Lord Edward Fitzgerald.* New York, 1855.

Moorman, Mary. *William Wordsworth: A Biography; The Early Years.* Oxford and London: Oxford University Press, 1957.

Morris, Gouvernour. *A Diary of the French Revolution.* Ed. Beatrix Cary Davenport. Boston and London: G. G. Harrap & Co., 1939.

Morton, A. L. *The Everlasting Gospel: A Study in the Sources of William Blake.* London: Lawrence & Wishart, 1958.

Muirhead, James Patrick. *The Life of James Watt, with Selections from his Correspondence.* 1858. 2d ed., rev. London: Murray, 1859.

Ogilvie, William. *An Essay on the Right of Property in Land.* London: J. Walter, 1782.

Pallain, George, ed. *La Mission de Talleyrand à Londres, en 1792.* Paris, 1889.

Palmer, R. R. *The Age of the Democratic Revolution: A Political History of Europe and America, 1760–1800.* Vol. 1: *The Struggle*; vol. 2: *The Challenge.* Princeton: Princeton University Press, 1959–1964.

————. *Twelve Who Ruled: The Year of the Terror in the French Revolution.* Princeton: Princeton University Press, 1941.

Pariset, E. "La Société des amis de la Revolution de Londres." *Révolution française* 29 (1895): 297–325.

Patrick, Alison. *The Men of the First French Republic: Political Alignments in the National Convention of 1782.* Baltimore: Johns Hopkins University Press, 1972.

Pernoud, George, and Sabine Flaissier. *Mémoires of Madame la Rochejacquelein.* Trans. Richard Graves. London: Secker and Warburg, 1961.

Poisson, Charles. *Les Fournisseurs aux Armées sous la Révolution Française: Le Directoire des Achats (1792–1793) J. Bidermann, Cousin, Marx-Berr.* Paris: Librairie Historique A. Margraff, 1932.

Pollin, Burton R. "Permutation of Names in *The Borderers,* or Hints of Godwin, Charles Lloyd, and a Real Renegade." *The Wordsworth Circle* 4 (1973): 31–35.

Pollock, John. *Wilberforce.* London: Constable, 1977.

Priestley, Joseph. *Theological and Miscellaneous Works,* ed. John Towill Rutt. 25 vols. London, 1817–1832.

Reed, Mark L. *Wordsworth: The Chronology of the Early Years.* Cambridge: Harvard University Press, 1967.

Reinhard, Marcel. *Chûte de la royauté.* Paris, 1969.

————. "Le Voyage de Pétion à Londres: 24 Octobre–11 Novembre 1791." *Revue d'Histoire Diplomatique* 84 (1970): 5–64.

Rizzo, Betty. "John Sherratt, Negociator." *Bulletin of Research in the Humanities* 86: 372–429.

Roberts, J. M. *The French Revolution.* Oxford and London: Oxford University Press, 1978.

Robertson, William Spence. *The Life of Miranda.* 2 vols. Chapel Hill: University of North Carolina Press, 1929.

Robinson, Eric. "An English Jacobin: James Watt, Junior." *Cambridge Historical Journal* 11 (1953–1955): 349–55.

Roland, Madame. *An Appeal to Impartial Posterity. . . . In Four Parts.* 1st American ed., corrected. New York: A. Van Hook, 1798.

Romilly, Sir Samuel. *Memoirs.* 3 vols. London: J. Murray, 1840.

Rose, R. B. *Gracchus Babeuf: The First Revolutionary Communist.* Stanford: Stanford University Press, 1978.

————. *The Making of the Sans-culottes: Democratic Ideas and Institutions in Paris, 1789–92.* Manchester: Manchester University Press, 1983.

————. "The Paris Districts and Direct Democracy, 1789–1790." *Bulletin of the John Rylands Library* 61 (1979): 422–43.

————. "Socialism and the French Revolution: The Cercle Social and the Enragées." *Bulletin of the John Rylands Library* 41 (1958): 139–66.

Rothenberg, Gunther E. *The Art of Warfare in the Age of Napoleon.* Bloomington: Indiana University Press, 1978.

Russell, John Russell, 1st earl, ed. *Memorials and Correspondence of Charles James Fox.* 4 vols. London: R. Bentley, 1853–1857.

Saxe, Maurice, Marshall of France. *Reveries, or, Memoirs Concerning the Art of War.* Trans. Sir William Fawcett. Edinburgh: Sands, Donaldson Murray, and Cochran for Alexander Donaldson, 1759.

Schneider, Ben Ross, Jr. *Wordsworth's Cambridge Education.* Cambridge: Cambridge University Press, 1957.

Servan de Gerbey, Joseph. *Discours sur le progrès des connoissance Humanes en général, De la Morale, et De la Législation en particulier, Lu dans un Assemblée publique de l'Académie de Lyon.* 1781.

Shaw, Thomas. *Travels, or Observations relating to Several Parts of Barbary and the Levant.* Oxford: Printed at the Theatre, 1738; London, 1772.

Soboul, Albert. *The Parisian Sans-culottes and the French Revolution 1793–4.* Oxford and London: Oxford University Press, 1964.

Stanhope, Charles. *A Letter from Earl Stanhope . . . 24 February 1790.* London: Printed by G. Stafford, for P. Elmsley, March 1790. (A reply to Burke's speech on the army estimates.)

State Trials. (See list D.)

Stern, Madeleine B. "The English Press in Paris and Its Successors, 1793–1852." *Papers of the Bibliographical Society of America* 74 (1980): 307–59.

Stewart, John, The Traveller. *Travels over the Most interesting Parts of the Globe, to discover the Source of Moral Motion.* London: J. Ridgway, 1790.

Sullivan, Alvin, ed. *British Literary Magazines: The Augustan Age and the Age of Johnson, 1689–1788.* Westport, Conn.: Greenwood Press, 1983.

Sydenham, M. J. *The Girondins.* London: Athlone Press, 1961.

Ternaux, Louis Mortimer. *Histoire de la Terreur 1792–1794.* 2 vols. Paris: M. Lévy, 1870.

Thale, Mary, ed. *Selections from the Papers of the London Corresponding Society 1792–1799.* Cambridge: Cambridge University Press, 1983.

Thelwall, Mrs. Cecil Boyle. *The Life of John Thelwall by his Widow.* 2 vols. London: Macrone, 1837.

Thiers, Adolphe. *History of the French Revolution.* Trans. Thomas W. Redhead. London and Edinburgh, 1863.

Thompson, E. P. *The Making of the English Working Class.* New York: Pantheon, 1964.

Thompson, J. B., ed. *English Witnesses of the French Revolution.* Oxford: Blackwell, 1938.

Thornton, Robert Donald. *William Maxwell to Robert Burns.* Edinburgh: John Donald Publishers, 1979.

Tilly, Charles. *The Vendee*. Cambridge: Harvard University Press, 1964.

Todd, F. M. "Wordsworth, Helen Maria Williams, and France." *Modern Language Review* 43 (1948): 456–64.

Veitch, George Stead. *The Genesis of Parliamentary Reform*. London: Constable & Co., 1913.

Volgin, V. P. "Djon Osval'd i 'Sotsial'nyi kruzhok'" ("John Oswald and the 'Social Circle'"). *Novaia i noveishaia istoriia* (1962), no. 3.

Walling, William A. "Wordsworth's *The Borderers*: A Critical and Historical Study." Ph.D. diss. New York University, 1966.

Walter, Gerard. *Histoire des Jacobins*. Paris: A. Somogy, 1946.

Werkmeister, Lucyle. *The London Daily Press, 1772–1792*. Lincoln: University of Nebraska Press, 1963. (Cited as *Daily Press*.)

———. *A Newspaper History of England, 1792–1793*. Lincoln: University of Nebraska Press, 1967. (Cited as *Newspaper History*.)

———. "Some Account of Robert Burns and the London Newspapers, with special reference to the Spurious *Star* (1789)." *BNYPL* 65 (1961): 483–504.

Westminster Forum. *A Short History of the Westminster Forum*. 2 vols. London: T. Cadell, 1781.

White, Arthur S. *A Bibliography of Regimental Histories of the British Army*. London, 1965.

Wickwire, Franklin, and Mary Wickwire. *Cornwallis: The Imperial Years*. Chapel Hill: University of North Carolina Press, 1980.

Williams, David. "The Missions of David Williams and James Tilly Matthew to England, 1793." *English Historical Review* 53 (1938): 651–58.

Williams, Gwyn A. *Artisans and Sans-culottes: Popular Movements in France and Britain during the French Revolution*. London and New York: W. W. Norton, 1968.

Woodress, James. *A Yankee's Odyssey, The Life of Joel Barlow*. Philadelphia and New York: Lippincott, 1958.

Woodward, Lionel D. *Un adherente Anglaise de la Révolution Française: Hélène-Maria Williams et ses amis*. Paris: H. Champion, 1930. Rpt., Geneva, 1977.

———. "Les Projets de Déscente en Irlande sous la Convention, et les Refugiés irlandais et anglais en France: D'Après des documents inédits." *Annales Historiques de la Révolution français* 8 (1931): 1–30. (Cited as "Projets.")

Wordsworth, William. *The Borderers*, ed. Robert Osborn. Ithaca, N.Y.: Cornell University Press, 1982.

———. *The Poetical Works*. Ed. Ernest de Selincourt and Helen Darbishire. Oxford: Oxford University Press, 1949.

———. *The Prelude or Growth of a Poet's Mind*. (Text of 1805.) Ed. Ernest de Selincourt. Oxford and London: Oxford University Press, 1933.

———. *The Prose Works*, ed. W. J. B. Owen and Jane Worthington Smyser. 3 vols. Oxford and London: Oxford University Press, 1974.

Worrall, David. "Blake and the Night Sky. I. The 'Immortal Tent.'" *Bulletin of Research in the Humanities* 84 (1981): 273–95.

Yorke, Henry Redhead. *Letters from France, in 1802*. London: Printed for H. D. Symonds by Bye and Law, 1804. (See list B.)

———. *A Letter to the Reformers . . . .* Dorchester: T. Lockett; London: H. D. Symonds, 1798.

———. *On the Means of Saving Our Country* . . . . Dorchester: T. Lockett; Exeter: McKenzie and Son, 1797.

———. *These Are The Times that try Men's Souls! A Letter to John Frost. A Prisoner in Newgate.* London, James Ridgway, York-street . . . 14th July, First Year of Imprisonment in Newgate. (Dated, p. 79: "Derby, July 1, 1793.")

Young, Arthur. *Autobiography*, ed. M. Betham-Edwards. London: Smith, Elder & Co., 1898.

INDEX